BRING THE NOISE

SIMON REYNOLDS

BRING THE NOISE
20 Years of Writing About Hip
Rock and Hip Hop

Soft Skull Press
an imprint of
COUNTERPOINT BERKELEY

First published in the U.K. in 2009 by Faber and Faber Limited
First American edition, 2011

Library of Congress Cataloging-in-Publication Data

Reynolds, Simon.
  Bring the noise : 20 years of writing about hip rock and hip hop / Simon
Reynolds.
      p. cm.
  Includes bibliographical references and index.
  ISBN 978-1-59376-401-2
  1. Rock musicians—Interviews. 2. Rock music—History and criticism. I.
Title.
  ML385.R49 2010
  781.66—dc22
                                        2010013032

Cover design by Jason Snyder
Interior design by Faber and Faber Limited
Printed in the United States of America

Soft Skull Press
An Imprint of Counterpoint LLC
1919 Fifth Street
Berkeley, CA 94710

www.softskull.com
www.counterpointpress.com

Distributed by Publishers Group West

10 9 8 7 6 5 4 3 2 1

To my girls, Joy and Tasmin

CONTENTS

For deleted scenes, out-takes, news and other related material, visit the
Bring the Noise blog at http://bringthenoisesimonreynolds.blogspot.com/

INTRODUCTION

Trying to pull together a 'representative' collection out of twenty years' writing and several million words was a huge challenge. So I did something else. *Bring the Noise* doesn't corral all of my favourite pieces of writing, or cover all my favourite artists; many personal touchstones, among them Aphex Twin, Royal Trux, Saint Etienne, World of Twist, Position Normal and A.R. Kane slipped the net. Instead I've woven a kind of history of the last twenty years in popular music. *Bring the Noise* picks up where *Rip it Up and Start Again* left off, which happened to be more or less when I started writing for a living (the last months of 1985). Sifting through two decades of interviews, reviews, features and essays, I've traced a thread involving the interplay between white music and black music – specifically, the alternately fraught and fertile relationship between 'hip' rock and hip hop. *Bring the Noise* presents the competing claims of black street music and the white underground to be both the cutting edge of innovation and a voice of resistance. And it tracks the way that periods of cross-town traffic and musical miscegenation have alternated with periods where rock and rap have seemingly chosen to go separate ways.

Many of those who came of age in the period covered by *Bring the Noise* have felt an equally powerful attraction to alternative rock and to hip hop. That's how I felt in 1986 as a music journalist just embarking on my career: unable and unwilling to choose between The Smiths and Public Enemy, Husker Du and LL Cool J. You don't *have* to choose, of course, and it's striking how so many people have grown up with a sense of double allegiance (even triple, with the arrival of rave and the nineties electronic dance culture) as the natural state of things. But it's equally remarkable how many people *did* pick sides (and still do). Some white fans invested all their belief and passion in hip hop, seeing it as the vanguard, the sole bastion of culturally dissident energy – and as a result have had to grapple with all the complex issues related to being a white acolyte of a music still largely made by and for black kids. Others, whether through simple sonic inclination or a sub-conscious desire to avoid the contradictions of being a 'wigga', stuck with indie-rock, regarding its distorted guitars and alternately angst-racked and ironic lyrics as the true expression of the modern bohemian impulse.

From its title on down, *Bring the Noise* is unabashedly rockist, enthralled by notions of subversion and 'underground', dissent and disruption. But isn't it blindingly obvious that rap is riddled right through to its hard-as-hell core with the same values? Without ideals of authenticity, 'realness', integrity, street credibility, the genre would barely exist; likewise, metaphors of music as war/crusade/cause/move-ment pretty much underwrite the entire hip hop project. Yet *Bring the Noise* is also a book about *pop*, in a particular sense – true, the artists covered don't often sound 'poppy', but their music is both popular and, more often than not, populist. The focus is on bands that mattered to me but also meant something to multitudes of people out there in 'the real world', and who moreover *wanted* to have that kind of mass impact, who felt the pull of ambition and the drive of will-to-power. Nothing against esoteric and hermetic sounds (our home is crammed to the rafters with that kind of thing), but the music that consistently excites me most as a writer as well as a listener is the stuff that reverberates beyond the purely sonic.

Bring the Noise is about pop in a very particular sense – music that's entered the pop arena from 'outside'. I'm hooked on that moment of splintery impact when something *un*pop ram-raids its way into the charts. It could be that the kind of formative experiences that were common to my generation – being ambushed by an unfamiliar sound via *Top of the Pops* (now deceased, of course) or Radio 1 – are becoming scarcer in our data-saturated environment of pop ubiquity and hyper-knowingness. Still, for me these have always been the most exciting moments, those breakthroughs when the underground goes overground . . . The Smiths on *Top of the Pops* doing 'This Charming Man', the surprise of hearing a Fall song on daytime radio, Nirvana's 'Smells Like Teen Spirit' going into monster-heavy rotation on MTV or, most recently More Fire Crew bringing grime into ten million living rooms with the rowdy jabber and battering beats of their Top 10 hit 'Oi!' . . .

This obsession with the aesthetic ambush is why *Bring the Noise* actually has nothing to do with the 'noise' genre: all those overlapping sub-styles of squall and atonal abstraction that come out of industrial music, free jazz, musique concrete and sound art. The concept of 'noise' has made a big comeback in recent years, and the abstract

xi

sound dronologists and improv guys are fine by me, actually. No, the irritating end of it is all those artists aiming for ye olde 'shock effect', their pure noise laden with content of tediously 'transgressive' nature (all the old clichéd faves of vileness and violation: serial murder, neo-Nazis, yawn, zzzzzz . . .). The blindingly obvious fact is that no one shockable is within earshot; there's no real disruption or challenge in these scenes, because they're screeching to the converted. 'Noise' is all about context, so when I say the groups in this book 'bring the noise' I'm talking more about a noise-*effect* – music that disturbs the peace of pop, shakes its status quo – than about distortion or atonality.

The noise-effect often occurs in the absence of 'noise' in the ears-are-wounds sense: the 'cultural noise' of Morrissey's fey flamboyance and gauche misery; the idiot-shaman Shaun Ryder's drug-damaged drivel; Snoop Dogg's serpentine nonchalance and murderous panache. That said, a lot of the music in *Bring the Noise* is fairly noisy in the commonly understood sense of the word: Husker Du's blasting blizzards of open-tuned guitar; the bass-booming, metal-riffing, scratched-to-fuck rap of the mid-eighties; nineties hardcore techno with its blaring mid-frequencies and hard-angled stabs; Nirvana's loud–quiet dynamics and grungy guitar tone; the alien vocal grain and rude slanguage of dancehall MCs; the disjointed, clunky beats and gruff bombast of crunk and grime. All were typically greeted upon their arrival with protests of 'that's not music, that's noise!'. These popular but unpop sounds have echoed the trajectory of twentieth-century avant-garde classical music, which advanced through incorporating non-musical sounds, aestheticizing mistakes, deploying randomness, and asserting the percussive and textural over the melodic and harmonic. Whenever I hear complaints that a new sound is 'soulless', 'unemotional', 'dark, empty, inhuman' or 'just not music', my ears prick up. These spasms of disgust and horror, and the pining for a lost warmth or funk that generally accompany them, are often early signals that the New Thing has emerged.

As much as this serial reinvention of 'noise' resembles the avant-garde, it's also totally *rock* in spirit. The original rock 'n' roll, it's worth remembering, was an invader, bruising its way into the mid-fifties charts of sickly sedative pop. 'That's not music, that's noise' was how many greeted rock 'n' roll, aghast at its loudness and vulgarity, its raw-throated screaming and hysterical delirium of non-sense (Little Richard's 'Awopbopaloobop'), and above all the stridently percussive insistence of a sound that to many seemed to be 'all beat' and no melody. 'Jungle music', they called it, recoiling in loathing and fear; as it happens, my absolute favourite music of the nineties named itself 'jungle' and initially provoked similar revulsion from the guardians of taste and musicality.

All this is why *Bring the Noise* struck me as the right title. It also appealed because of Public Enemy's pivotal role during the early part of the book's time span. And the group's producers, Hank Shocklee and the Bomb Squad, were nothing if not inspired noise-makers, looping and superimposing samples of squealing jazz trumpets and shrieking soul singers on tracks like 'Rebel Without a Pause' and 'Bring the Noise', to create nagging riffs as urgent and provoking as the group's lyrical content. As Shocklee put it: 'We don't like musicians. We don't respect musicians . . . We have a better sense of music, a better concept of music, of where it's going, of what it can do.' As attitudes go, that's pretty punk rock.

Following the dance between white and black music over two decades, *Bring the Noise* addresses the ways in which these encounters, especially the white-on-black transactions, have served as the motor of change in pop history. Time and again, whites have embraced black music but 'got it wrong' when they moved beyond simple emulation and tried to come up with their own take; more often than not, such 'bastardizations' have been more exciting than when whites success-fully imitated the black source with timidly conscientious fidelity. 'Getting it wrong' doesn't just apply to musical creativity, though, but to the roles of listener and critic too. No one can think seriously about pop music without contemplating the issue of race; equally, it's impos-sible to think for long about those issues without getting tied up in knots. So a good chunk of this book could be seen as the collation of my mis-understandings and mis-recognitions of black music. Across twenty years of thinking about things in the heat of the journalistic moment, you'll find flip-flops, contradictions, blind-spots and deaf-spots galore . . . but also, I hope, a steady progress towards that unreachable horizon, enlightenment.

'Getting it wrong' is an inherent aspect of all cross-cultural traffic. Even in a one-on-one conversation, no one can grasp the full content of another's utterance, register or absorb all of its submerged resonances. So how much more is this so when entire cultures tune in to each other's transmissions? Then again, if pure signal and zero distortion was possible, there'd be no friction and no sparks; confusion is the *prima materia*, the alchemical mulch, for creativity and change. So bring the noise.

AUTHOR'S NOTE

Most of the pieces selected here are reprinted exactly as they appeared originally. In a handful of cases, though, some extreme infelicities have been rectified, and generally, errors on my part and screw-ups created by others during the copy-inputting process have been changed to how they were intended to appear. The exceptions to the above are the pieces identified as 'director's cuts': these are the articles as originally submitted by me, before being cut down, resequenced and adapted to the magazine in question's house style during the editing process. It's not that these changes weren't appropriate, or indeed often an improvement, but in certain cases I have opted to revert to a style closer to my own 'voice' and versions that are longer than what actually ran in print.

WHAT'S MISSING?

The State of Pop in 1985

Something's wrong. Everyone knows this, acknowledges it, but it's still hard to point out, precisely, what's supposed to have slipped into abeyance, eluded us in pop. It isn't faith in music as threat – even the purveyors of overtly oppositional rock no longer believe in rock's missionary power. Nor can we constitute the problem as one of poverty of ideas and change in music – there are still records to buy, 'progress' is pretty much at a constant, at least as strong as it's ever been.

John Peel caught the shape of the lack well when he said: 'I don't even like the records I like.' Direction and meaning seem to have seeped away. What's gone into a coma is not so much music as writing about music. The last great rhetorical efflorescence was the 'new pop explosion' – which now seems a purely arbitrary binding of disparate initiatives, heroes and charlatans. People seem to have lost the will to construct chimeras like New Pop that get people excited. Groups and writers just seem to be *plugging away*. Writing, in music papers and fanzines alike, is almost all at the level of relentless specificity – this record, that gig – rather than what it all amounts to. The flood of re-issues has abetted this eclecticism, and obscured the issue of current poverty. Fanzines, far from being an alternative, are worst offenders, terminally biographical – at any moment you can take your pick of twelve or twenty interviews with the Membranes or Billy Bragg. Paradoxically, it is precisely the fecundity of activity, documentation, debate, even – to an extent – of quality, that prevents a unity of alienation occurring; if a period of enforced silence, dearth, boredom, prevailed – then maybe something as sensational as punk would emerge. As it is, a pernicious adequacy keeps us muddling on . . . just

I

vaguely aware that all the motion and meaning may be going nowhere and meaning . . . *less*.

Independent music is torn between a kind of constructive abstention (let pop die on its dancing feet) and seeing the problem as simply one of access – give 'real music' airplay. Few indie groups manage to turn their backs completely on pop – most of their energy going into self-conscious distancing from chart sound.

Our listening is bound up in oppositions – our very hearing, understanding, of these groups is tied to *what they're not* – not 'bland', 'soft', 'inane' – but 'raw', 'hard', 'powerful', thus 'real' and 'honest'. These terms aren't eternal musical values but a way of positioning the record and the listener vis-à-vis one another – we read the record to see where it fits in 'the struggle'. These groups – Membranes, Jesus and Mary Chain, Yeah Yeah Yeah Noh, New Model Army, Red Lorry Yellow Lorry – see themselves as a continuous flow of resistance – Big Flame talk of 'ugly noise undercurrents . . . a facelift . . . a new way of cleaning your teeth' – and that's it: music as a harsh scouring force, a purging agent (of 'luxury', hi-tech sound), a war of attrition. As Jesus and Mary Chain put it: 'smashing the state of pop'. The trouble is nearly all these groups have nothing more to say to us but a self-righteous declaration of non-complicity in the state of pop. They are bound to (the) opposition, fail to make their own significance. Their alternative textures – abrasiveness, uncooked production – are familiar, merge into a grey wall, skirt around the listener's consciousness. It's a different sort of BLANDNESS – for me there's more disruption in a single trail of Morrissey's falsetto. These hallmarks of indie sound, all copied from a few really innovative groups (Siouxsie, Fall, Joy Division, Birthday Party), are like the key elements of progressive rock (musicianship, solos, sheer length of tracks, FM-radio mixing), just ciphers to indicate allegiance, superiority/opposition to teenybop glam. We are *confirmed* by them. Where's the 'danger'?

Indie music, perhaps unconsciously, is in opposition to two other chart trends. It is almost entirely in revolt against the all-pervasive influence of black music. Funk and soul have followed a similar trajectory of influence in the eighties as R&B did in the sixties – first taken up by innovators as radical (PiL/Talking Heads/Gang of Four/Heaven 17/Scritti/ABC) – then working its way down to become the base matter of all pop. Wham!, Thompson Twins, Spandau, Annie Lennox, Phil Collins – the same vocal inflections, mannerisms and beat. (When whites took up and vulgarized R&B, blacks left it en masse – perhaps the appropriation of soul will drive blacks to something new.) Indie groups – and this applies to US hardcore and country-punk too – have reacted by returning to anything white – Iggy, Jim Morrison, Cave, Mark E. Smith, Beefheart, Lou Reed, country, folk. They are equally in revolt against mongrelization in pop. In the early eighties the idea of the melting pot of musics seemed progressive – 1981 was the year of the cocktail. Again, innovators – ZE, Was (Not Was), Scritti, McLaren – broke ground, but later groups reaped mass success – Culture Club and Style Council, whose names embody the notion of a rainbow coalition of races, genres and eras. It's interesting to note how Was (Not Was)'s LPs, which seemed radical at the time, made a fusion of hard rock and soul close to what is merely staple stuff in the charts now – Prince, Go West, Power Station, Duran: rock disco, black HM. The indies have set themselves against this pluralism – once called 'breaking down barriers' but really, as Paul Oldfield put it, crossover-as-maximum-market-penetration – against the dominant textures of luxuriant sound, the impatience and greed that leads the likes of Paul Young and Eurythmics to clot their records with pilfered source musics. The search is for some kind of purity – either in noise/dirt or in roots/folk. Polyglot equates with cosmopolitan, mass-produced, commodity. Purism, again, codes authenticity.

The Americans have their own resistance to the homogenized charts and it's received a lot of attention over here – the phrase trad rock slipping, somewhat defensively, into reviews, allusions to a sort of movement. It's true that in the American context even the slightest gesture towards realism is tantamount to radicalism – most US pop taking its textures, as Chris Scott has observed, from the high life, or fantasies of success and glory, vinyl soft porn or 'guys movie' action and adventure. But it's sad that virtually all the new groups have turned to the past for inspiration. The collective sensibility reminds me of the Populists, the nineteenth-century American political movement that nearly halted industrialism – the same nostalgia for a simpler world, rural values (community *and* self-reliance), the same anti-urbanism. There's a similar *patriotism* too – whose nearest equivalent in Britain is Oi! – the idea that true nationhood resides, not in the plutocrats, but in the People, the underdogs. (This patriotism resurges in a musical anti-Anglophilia – all that new pap shit of ours that chokes their charts – it was our groups who first taught the US record biz the potential of white soul crossover.) Springsteen, Fogerty, Los Lobos, Jason and the Scorchers, Long Ryders, et al. . . . . these are honest, likeable fellows, and some of their records are fun enough. But after *Sulk* and *Heaven Up Here* – *futuristic* music – it all seems . . . well, a bit of a comedown. What can we learn from them? Husker Du are the only group making sense of America today – their mangled psych-metal-punk is new music, its dynamic the lived contradiction between American 'reoccurring dreams' of space and freedom and purpose, and the claustrophobia and anomie of urban life. Other exceptions – the Replacements let rip the cry 'Unsatisfied' with such vigour as to leave behind their historical traces; R.E.M. and Meat Puppets – timeless psychedelia, the beauty of bewilderment and awe.

Another movement has set itself against pop, but aims to supplant it, to infiltrate. They too constitute the problem as a lack of authenticity – but locate the absence very specifically: what's missing isn't just passion or soulfulness but the soul of the sixties and early seventies. Their 'realism' is filtered through a discourse derived from gospel, the Old Testament. But the born-again soul groups have co-opted black music to a rock idea of the function of pop: propaganda and threat. In its insistence on the Message and on street cred, the new soul is very much cramped and shadowed by New Wave (with its emphasis on lyrical relevance). Most of these soul-sters were mods or ska-ites, and before that, punks. Ska was an attempt to keep the momentum of punk going – shuffling the music a bit, aligning it with the racial issues of the late seventies. Equally the New Soul just carries on the side of punk that was least stimulating (slogans, youth rhetoric, documentary reportage) rather than the more artistically interesting element (punk's theatre of rage, disgust and nihilism). The New Soul simply slots into the British youth market's built-in demand for Protest and is no real departure. The shift to a commercial dance sound is justified by the idea of 'offensive optimism' and the soulboy notion that working-class kids have always preferred black dance music.

What strikes about the soul of the Style Council, Kane Gang, Faith Brothers, Redskins, Fine Young Cannibals, is how male, how rockified, it is. Weller's voice is the eternal personification of white guilt. No black artist would be so dour about it. Dexy's Midnight Runners are a useful paradigm – soul for them was a form of exertion – performance what Barney Hoskyns called (in reference to the Jam, though) a 'gymnasium of exhortation'. Dexy's songs were a series of manifestos and clarion calls for a new, pure music – always *about* to be born. Dexy's used to work out together, they abstained from alcohol and drugs. Developing your body and your soul – exercise/suffering, both a weird machismo. (*Jamming* on Big Sound Authority – 'wait till you see this man sweat' – sweat as honesty, commitment.) Kevin Rowland's first band – a punk band – were called the Killjoys. That sums it up. None of the 'young soul rebel' groups have yet provided a moment of bliss – and as I've outlined, I think the reasons are structural and historical rather than artistic.

Is the problem with pop a lack of honesty or soul anyway? In a literal sense, most modern pop is soul-derived. The usual complaint is that it is synthetic, fake. But the charts have never been so clogged with passion and sincerity – the truth is that Howard Jones and Paul Young *are* baring their souls – it's just that their souls are mediocre. The experiences they present are such a flattened-out approximation of real life, so drained of real life's singularity, as to be less than real, like a statistician's case study. There are no stories in Howard Jones's songs, no snatches of plausible dialogue, no authentic tones or concrete detail – but neither is there the cliché's perfection or epic nonsense you get with myth-making pop, the high unreality of sixties melodrama. Just lowest common denominator humanist platitudes. The true horror of Howard is not that he is bland synthpop but that people clutch at him as a bastion of Meaning against Wham! and Duran – his is proper music, it means something, he *means* it. Of course he is just one of a host of ADULT pop stars – Eurythmics, Sade, Paul Young, Nik Kershaw, Alison Moyet – whose sin is decorum. They have learned from punk, they will never repeat the glaring abuses of an earlier rock aristocracy, perhaps never be usurped. These new artists – New Pop's legacy, its attenuated remnant, the cleanliness and ambition without the artfulness and androgyny – have integrity, they want to *communicate* as well as be stars. Unlike earlier pop stars, they have been careful not to be ripped off – *they* handle the business side, share production, invest their earnings. They aren't puppets. Their anti-drugs stance is less a strikingly austere rejection of trad rock 'n' roll degeneracy than the obverse of their solid business sense. THESE ARTISTS ARE COMPLETELY IN CONTROL. The shallow spread of this 'quality' music, its relentless taste and intelligence, makes me yearn for a bright blue flash of brilliance . . . or some terrible breach, errors of vulgarity, epic foolish gestures (all praise to Frankie). Genius or stupidity – anything immoderate. The new breed make me nostalgic for duplicity and excess, admire the few stars who appear to be deranged, sick fucks like Prince or Michael Jackson. Michael singing about fish or socks is more exciting than Annie Lennox's Greatest Passion.

Call for escape routes? One is to supersede rock entirely, at least as it is constituted as *youth* culture, to aspire to the status of art. So, Nick Cave. The alienation articulated in Cave's work is so abstract yet vivid, so extended, that it can in no way be localized within the subcultural frame . . . His approach is literary – unlike the majority of groups interested in 'horror' or 'sleaze', he doesn't rely on simple effects of depiction (which often have an anti-pop motive) but works at language, makes a poetry of the unthinkable. Primary emotions are taken, but dramatized within a fantastical narrative edifice. Of course, this is to turn one's back on pop successfully (Cave looks set to become the post-punk Leonard Cohen, or Jim-Morrison-had-he-lived, struggling for recognition as a poet, selling records to a fixed cult).

The other approach is to invade the pop citadel, subvert pop by a *greater* glamour, expose its pallor, make it look cheap. So, The Smiths. Not as a solution, something to imitate – but a proof that sensation can still exist within the pop arena. The Smiths lie at the confluence of all the felt needs – for something new but still accessible, for dissent *and* poetry, for passion *and* thought. And their music . . . a sound impossible to identify either as 'soft' or 'hard' . . . seemingly implacable in its crystalline drive, yet incredibly fragile . . . a gentle flurry of chords like razor blades in your heart. For me The Smiths reinstate both the strangeness of pop, its otherworldly elegance, *and* its connection with reality.

Recent critical attempts to resuscitate The Smiths stress the humour, Marr's musicianship . . . but the point of The Smiths is precisely their unseemly misery. They catapult into the charts – whose dominant textures today are of Success, Potency, acceptance of normal aspirations – a spectacle of dissatisfaction and doubt. For many The Smiths are the only group making a connection between pop and (their) reality – the experience of adolescents, the unemployed, the fucked-up, are written out of pop's script. Today pop, as never since before rock 'n' roll, consists of the celebration of ADULT life – money, status, travel, chic lifestyles. The charts reek of self-management, upward mobility, satisfaction – and so The Smiths speak of obsession and devotion, advocate dissipation, resist brutalization and the sense-dulling forces of materialism, fashion, cheap thrills. Their enemies are those who laugh at the idea of sensitivity, who abet what comes with the new conservatism – an entrenchment of normal sex roles and sexuality.

Morrissey on *Top of the Pops* is deeply embarrassing. Only Ian McCulloch has visited an equivalent outrage – both bared their nipples, acted drunk or spastic, swooned. Were 'prats'. Which means only that they've tried to puncture for a few minutes the glacial cool of pop, make a sort of divine grace out of awkwardness, get through. The performance side of The Smiths is crucial. The standard scripted pop moves let us know where we are – in the presence of 'charisma', 'sexiness', 'stardom'. It is the 'naturalness' and inevitability of these gestures, this unreflecting, incommunicative showbiz language, that Morrissey tries to disrupt – an eloquent incoherence. He's pop's own Micalef. The 'opposition' of The Smiths is vested not in slogans or preaching, but in the body of their sound and the body of their singer.

Perhaps their ideas are spent, but they've left a swathe of sombre glamour across eighties pop. They've about twenty great songs, and strange – although they're described as dour or (snigger) angst-ridden – they are more exultant and alive than almost anything I've heard.

The pop globe is straddled by soulboy music – the music of the upwardly aspiring working class, the club soundtrack to having a good time after a hard week's work. Julie Burchill and Robert Elms have celebrated the concomitant death of the idea of music as art/transgression: Julie, 'Sade embodies exactly how a sane, healthy adult should view music – as an aural after-dinner mint'; Robert declaring that working-class youth – who, as *everybody* knows, are what pop is all about – prefer clothes to music, have always preferred black dance music and find the downward aspirations of middle-class bohemianism/dirty rock rebellion inexplicable and pathetic. The opposition 'music as entertainment versus music as art' has been a constant from early on in pop's history and is largely class-based. Psychedelia/progressive rock/punk/alternative music – this has largely been the music of art schools, students and sixth-formers – people with more leisure, who use music to define their personalities, discuss it in terms of artists, oeuvre, or society. Black pop, on the other hand, has little idea of 'progress': change comes about not through debate, revolutions in rhetoric or criticism, borrowing from high art or literature; black pop's history is that of changes in production, of what's technically possible – not changing ideas about what music's for, what it means.

To put myself behind the idea of pop as art is accordingly to risk being put down as middle class, somehow not part of pop, because nothing to do with the 'instinctual' street; even to risk accusations of racism (as Green has made of The Smiths). Still I'm suspicious of people like Burchill and Elms's insistence on a purely functional attitude to music – they seem to have an inordinate joy in diminishment, reducing the capacity of things for meaning (always in opposition to the *inflation* of meaning by pretentious people like myself). And I'm repelled by the textures of modern pop – pseudo-sophistication, *classy* sounds, nouveau riche chic, hygiene, polish – how they tie in with the new conservatism, how they made perfectly straight demands from life, and from sexuality and gender. The soul boom has led to an over-investment in passion, and devaluation of lyrical intelligence. That black music can be the vehicle for the extreme and the excessive is undeniable – unfortunately something structural about its *usage* means that its orbit is more often the banal and prosaic. That's why it's necessary to herald a new white bohemianism.

Monitor issue 3, July 1985

Monitor was a 'pop journal' based In Oxford and started by me and some friends in 1984 shortly after we'd graduated. It really wasn't your typical fanzine: glossy and well-designed, it initially featured no interviews or reviews, just thinkpieces. (The review policy changed *real* quick when free records started arriving through the mail, but we stuck to 'no Interviews' until almost the end, the exception being a Sonic Youth profile nearly entirely devoid of quotes.) Many of the essays were diatribes about the State of Pop – hence 'What's Missing?', a document of the glum disorientation felt by those of us who'd been carried along by the future-rush of post-punk and New Pop to find ourselves, by 1984, struggling to grub up some enthusiasm about thin fare such as The Triffids. The piece lays out many of the core ideas I would explore and oppositions over which I'd flip-flop wildly during my first few years at *Melody Maker* (and ever after, arguably). The final allusion to 'a new white bohemianism' echoes an earlier *Monitor* article called 'Radical Dance Fictions: Funk's Fictional Threat'. A critique of post-punk's privileging of black music and the equation of 'roots/rhythm/radicalism', the essay concluded: 'What seems more productive now is a rereading of white rock heritage – groups who commit violence to the texts of such as the Doors, Byrds, Velvets, Birthday Party, garage punk and psychedelia . . . It's music that chafes at the tenet that black music alone has a hold on desire or rhythm; music ignorant of questions of responsibility, social conscience and the imperative of "upfulness" (a very narrow understanding of what black music "is all about" anyway), made by groups who see themselves as artists rather than propagandists, who deal in poetry rather than reportage.' Which ties back to the most jarring thing, for me, about 'What's Missing?' (apart from the excessive use of italics, which I've actually toned down here), the reference to 'lyrical intelligence'. Soon, I would take the opposite tack, championing sonics over text, fascination over meaning.

THE REDSKINS

Central Polytechnic, London

The only soul we got tonight was the pre-gig tape, sublime seventies slices of Billy Paul, Fontella Bass, Womack . . . Personally, I was grateful – I find vaguely repellent the idea of The Redskins unlocking the secrets of this magical music, harnessing its redemptive and transfiguring power, only to *use* it as vehicle for protest. So ulterior. No, this is a ROCK band – but one that seems to constrain its punk energy by grappling with an idiom that doesn't come naturally. A load of 'yeahs', grunts and Kev Rowlandisms do not a Soul Preacher make.

The Redskins' great mistake is their limited interpretation of soul – they see it as an *upful* spirit (what about the blues?), then reduce this essence further to a specifically political positivism. A Redskins show consists of constant affirmation, which rapidly becomes wearing. For some reason, hope, pride, strength and unity are incredibly dreary subject matter for pop. Redskins songs endlessly chivvy along doubters and flaggers – who are hard to find in the fervent crowd anyway.

The Redskins don't reach me because Chris Dean isn't a poet, he can't make the mechanisms of power breathe, he can't engage any emotions apart from determination. He's a journalist, telling us mostly what we know already, and telling it baldly. I like the paradoxes of 'Burn it Down', but little else. This benefit for anti-apartheid raised money and a feeling of solidarity, and I wouldn't trespass on those feelings. But I like my pleasures to be a little less self-confirming.

A guest speaker highlighted this inadvertently – attacking apartheid articulately, he went on to remind us to fight racism in Britain too. There was an irony in the almost complete absence of black faces in the audience. The Redskins say they want to have nothing to do with the middle-class institution of youth culture, they want to appeal across the barriers of generation, race and class. They've fastened on to soul and funk as a universal pop music. But the group only has significance in a rock context. Their audience is mostly under twenty-five, white and male; not even rock mainstream to judge by the array of hip haircuts at the gig. The Redskins, whether they like it or not, are *serving* a market. As with all the new soul groups, under the soul finery you will find the dowdy spirit of New Wave, of social realism. The Redskins are the Clash of the new soul and what we really need is its Sex Pistols. A group that can work from soul's *unrealism*, its dangerous ecstasy, to make unreasonable demands.

A group that actually provokes its audience, rather than caters to them.

Melody Maker, December 1985

The Redskins' version of black music eliminated the 'blues' aspect (low-down, dejected) in favour of the upright, move-on-up side. When they launched a crusade against 'miserabilism' (introspective rock groups like The Smiths, the Cure, Echo & the Bunnymen, etc.) their slogan was 'Reds Against the Blues': sadness and depression was equated with political defeatism and capitulation to the Tories, unemployment and oppression deemed more fitting subjects for pop than love, loss and the more existential forms of alienation. Rejecting mope rock ('Is this the blues I'm singing?' pondered Ian McCulloch on 'Rescue'), the Redskins and their fellow travellers (the Style Council, Faith Brothers, the Christians) proposed a strategy of 'offensive optimism': a mod-descended notion of 'pride and dignity' as a weapon, of Style and Youth as a victory in itself. Hence the sleevenote to the Style Council's 'Shout it to the Top':

Say
Yes! to the thrill of the romp
Yes! to the Bengali Workers Association
Yes! to a nuclear free world
Yes! to all involved in animal rights
Yes! to fanzines
Yes! to belief

This sort of resistance-through-affirmation talk used to drive me up the wall at the time, but to put it in its context: this was circa the miners' strike, the NUM being the last barrier to unrestrained Thatcherism. So the Redskins' blustery exhortations to 'keep on keepin' on' had a resonance that someone like myself, on the dole by choice, never fully felt. Nowadays, I feel a sneaking affection for figures like Chris Dean with their motormouth conviction. Scarred by the first Clash album, by those classic Jam singles, his kind could never shake off the huge political expectations invested in music during punk.

ZAPP

Hammersmith Odeon, London

Zapp live were perhaps the most extreme spectacle I have ever witnessed, with both band and audience abandoning inhibitions more extensively than at any rock gig I've attended, for all rock's Dionysiac rhetoric. And yet the SHOW! was clearly rehearsed with military precision, as it was performed exact in every deranged detail the very next night.

What's fascinating is how this kind of excess has an everyday currency. Soul takes straight values, traditional gender protocol, and inflates them to epic, surreal dimensions – as in the Battle of the Sexes duet between Shirley Murdoch and Roger Troutman tonight. The SHOW! is all monstrously exaggerated sexuality, seriously saucy – full of ludicrous arse-shaking, mimed cunnilingus, Roger stripping to his briefs . . .

Roger is an incredible SHOW! person – one minute goose-stepping across the stage plucking blues guitar, the next reappearing on top of a stack of amps, then dragging a luckeee ladeee out of the audience for a cartoon clinch, or impersonating Presley, or venturing way out into the crowd on a bodyguard's back while playing a harmonica. Every so often he asks, rhetorically, 'London, Englaaaaand! Can I do anything I wanna do? Can I go crazeee?'

The music's fab, a fat, freaky, juddering funkquake. Zapp's unique ingredient is those dexterously vocoderized vocals, that extra ultra-tremulousness that simulates a meta-ecstasy, a bliss beyond imagination, let alone realization. This is the dangerous utopianism of soul.

Best night out for years.

Melody Maker, July 1986

Hard to imagine *any* band I'd want to see live on two successive nights, so I must have been really BLOWN AWAY. Apart from a slightly enervated Bobby Womack a few years earlier, I imagine this was my first full-on exposure to the black performance ethos (a commitment to entertainment and razzle-dazzle approximately 100 times more intense than your average indie-Britband). A couple of years later I got to interview Troutman and he was as ridiculously 'on' in front of my tape recorder as onstage. Zapp recordings from this period ('Computer Love' and 'It Doesn't Really Matter' were small hits) were fine but the Dayton, Ohio group's defining masterwork remains 1980's 'More Bounce to the Ounce', a colossus of post-Funkadelic weirdgroove; the longer version gets otherworldly two-thirds of the way through, Roger's multi-tracked, electronically processed (not vocoder but voice box à la Pete Frampton) vocal spiralling off towards the peaks of the mystic East, a superfly cartoon of Tim Buckley's *Starsailor*. It was nice to see Troutman enjoy a mini-comeback in 1996 (guesting on Tupac and Dr Dre's 'California Love') and ghastly to hear of him being murdered by his own brother a few years later.

YOUNGER THAN YESTERDAY

Indie-pop's Cult of Innocence

Pop has never been *this* divided.

Over 'here' is the world of the 'alternative' – indies, inkies and fanzines, stubbornly and vainly insisting that ours is 'the real pop', that the glossy substance that's somehow hijacked the Chart is an impostor. Over there, the music that most people in the world take as pop. In between, a chasm of mutual ignorance and suspicion.

It's a breach between white and black definitions. 'Serious rock' has never been so white, mainstream pop so black, so exclusively based in R&B, soul and disco. What's noticeable is that the attributes for which the indie scene despises chartpop are, in black pop terms, its best qualities – for sickly/sentimental/saccharine read *soulful*, for hygiene and polish read *a classy sound*, for slickness read *elegance*. What the music press ritually attacks in chartpop is what, for most people, black or white, is most POP! about pop – glamour, opulent production, showiness.

Green once described the music of indie groups like The Smiths as 'racist', and, in a sense, he's right – there's a hopeless lack of exchange or communication between hip white rock and black pop. Each finds the other preposterous and perplexing. Blacks can't understand how anyone would want to look, or sound, scruffy, make a racket you can't even dance to. And flip through the collection of your average Cure fan and you'll find precious few Janet or Michael Jackson records (the only 'disco' record will be 'Blue Monday').

I don't believe Morrissey is *that* extreme when he declares hatred for funk, or pronounces that 'reggae is vile'. The irony is that these indie hipsters tend to be more politically aware than most, more keen to align themselves with anti-racism, yet are totally estranged from black culture.

13

Examine indie-pop closely and you'll see that, at every step, it defines itself as pop's opposite. For instance, chartpop is still based around the primacy of the dance beat, but what's striking about recent indie-pop is its undanceability, how it's long since abandoned R&B roots for albino sources like The Velvets, Television, sixties psychedelia, rockabilly, folk.

In fact, 'serious rock', from the hippies through to now, is a HEAD culture, oriented towards contemplation and bodily passivity. Records are treated as artistic or social statements, there's an emphasis on lyrics and artistic intention, and the primal scene of consumption is the bedroom.

Mainstream pop is a BODY culture, oriented around dance and spectacle rather than 'meaning'. Of course, people will dance to indie-pop, even when it's as fiercely anti-dance as Jesus and Mary Chain's 'Never Understand', but, strictly, indie-pop really demands physical responses that contravene the norms of dance-as-sexual-flaunting, that involve a sacrifice of cool. Jangly-pop ought to be danced with Morrisseyesque feyness, above-it-all gestures that echo the 'free dancing' of the counter-culture, while the Beefheartian thrash of bands like Stump and A Witness incites a bacchanalian delirium. Increasingly, what's even more appropriate is *immobility* before a bombardment of noise: the music of Husker Du, Jesus and Mary Chain, Sonic Youth, incites you to flip your wig, or be frozen in noise, blissed out.

Current indie music contains an implicit drive to rise above, to forget, the body that's in marked contrast to chartpop's hysterical investment in the body. You can see the head/body opposition at work in differing approaches to the love song. Chartpop foregrounds sexual passion, specific body need. The guarantor of true love is physical ecstasy, sexual *success*. The soul voice is ubiquitous – in its hoarse, husky grain and its traces of R&B earthiness you can practically hear arousal and dilation of blood.

Indie-pop tends to present love in almost quaint terms of devotion and idealization, barely alluding to sex. Love is vested in difficulty as much as success. There are far more unrequited love songs. The actual experience of being-in-love is presented differently, not as racked passion, but as an almost out-of-body experience, a dreaminess or entrancement, a rapture not of the senses but of perception and intellect. Which is why indie groups tend to choose a vocal style that denotes 'purity' – the little girl voice of The Shop Assistants, the folk idiom used by Morrissey or James, or other voices of male vulnerability (Pete Shelley's campness, Edwyn Collins's preciousness, sixties voices like Syd Barrett, Roger McGuinn, Arthur Lee, Lou Reed).

Indie-pop's focus is more on the words than on the singer's manner-isms. Because love is consummated/constituted not in the flesh and its throes, but in intense exchanges of language – the unique *details* of courtship, confidences, the scene. But this is a time when chartpop grows ever more 'adult' in its treatment of relationship – either more and more explicit and suggestive, or mature and 'progressive' (Julie Burchill has noted how black pop is increasingly Me Generation/*Cosmo*-speak in tone).

Indie-pop treats love as romance rather than sex. Against the health and efficiency of chart love, we have the stricken awe of The Bodines' 'Therese' – 'it scares the health out of me!'. Once rock drew its power from flaunting the body, revealing the 'raw truth' of desire. The direct-ness, dirt and carnal insistence of rhythm-and-blues was a dangerous energy. What's interesting is the process by which we've reached the point where 'purity' and 'pure love' seem more radical than sin, more transgressive than libertinism or 'setting your body free'.

* * *

It's six years since Edwyn Collins declared 'worldliness must keep apart from me', twenty years since The Byrds sang 'I was so much older then / I'm younger than that now' – now these dreams are coming to a new fruition. An idea of innocence and childhood possesses and pervades the indie scene. It's there in the names – Soup Dragons, Woodentops, Five Go Down to the Sea, Flowerpot Men, sweet names like James, June Brides, Mighty Lemon Drops, Talulah Gosh. It's present in the lyrics and cover artwork of groups as varied as The Smiths, Cocteau Twins, Membranes, James, Woodentops ('we should be climbing trees').

It's there in the way fanzines privilege naivety and enthusiasm and mess. Numerous desires crystallize in the fantasy of 'being like a child again' – grief for a lost spontaneity, impulsiveness and unselfconscious-ness; desire to recover the ability to dream, to have a magical, wide-eyed relation to the world; a hope of remaining unsullied. This is a romantic conception of childhood that could *only* be held by literary-minded types (i.e. your typical indie fan/music press reader). Ordinary people would find this idealization and nostalgia for childhood daft. Real kids want to grow up as *fast* as possible, be glamorous like Simon Le Bon or Madonna. Which is why mainstream pop reflects, as never since before rock 'n' roll, adult aspirations, adult sophistication.

Childhood's become important (again) because it provides a range of imagery that's fertile in dissident potential. Rock rebellion was based in the censored 'truth' of adolescent desire, but this form of misbehaviour is not just allowed now, it's *enforced* as a prescribed model. Images of healthy sexuality and youth vitality saturate the media. Hence the recourse to a model of deviancy earlier than the teenager.

The sixties loom large in the indie scheme because they were the last time that ideas of childhood and lost innocence were current. The Yippies, the Situationists and radical psychoanalysis proposed the recovery of play as *the* crucial component of cultural revolution; they used play as a political strategy and as a critique of Western consumer passivity. Elsewhere, the music of Pink Floyd, The Byrds, Love, etc. abounded with imagery of childhood and of gardens (Eden before the Fall), reflecting a belief that growing up is just a process of brutalization and dis-enchantment.

Moreover, latent in our indie scene are ideas that echo the concerns of the sexual/psychoanalytical politics of the sixties. The flirtation with androgyny and camp, the prevalence of love songs with genderless love objects and free of fixed sexual protocol, the defence of sensitivity and 'the wimp', the refusal of performance-oriented sex – all these connect not just with feminism but with radical psychoanalysis's project of a return to the 'polymorphous perversity' of the child (an undirected and limitless sensuality). In The Smiths, for instance, the refusal of maturity is as much a rejection of the strictures of adult sexuality as of work.

I'm not suggesting that a new counterculture is about to spring out of our indie scene, just that some of the desires are the same. No, I'd stress that these radical currents remain sublimated in music – there's been no attempt to connect dream with practice, no attempts at cultural improvisation to transform everyday life.

Style is where the sixties and childhood collide. Indie types often seem to be endeavouring to look like an ordinary person of the sixties or fifties. There's a taste for pre-permissive clothes – cardigans, frocks, overcoats, those short jackets and anoraks, caps and headscarves, quaint jewellery, short back-and-sides that must seem peculiar to those who once *had* to look like that and now relish the right to long hair and perms.

Mixed in with these archaic elements are childish things – duffel coats, birthday-boy shirts, outsize sweaters, bows and ribbons and ponytails, beardlessness. Fresh faces and bare ears. Stray punky elements persist, plus psychedelic items, but the effect of these garish primary colours and patterns is just as infantile, because childhood is the only time bright colours are appropriate. In trying to dress unlike adult women are supposed to dress to look sexy, girls like Fuzzbox have slipped into a style rich in connotations of paedophilia. And so many of these boys and girls *look* anorexic.

The indie style is an elaborate, stylized way of indicating authenticity. The sixties and childishness both represent a simpler, happier, more genuine time. The sixties are seen as *rock*'s childhood, a moment of innocence before bloated middle age, before pop was overdetermined by criticism. A time when the idea of youth was young.

And the sixties also stand for a time when the working class were 'real' – poor but happy, oppressed but united. The American indie scene adopts a similar stylized authenticity (based in country and psychedelia) against a similar enemy – MTV's co-opting of rock as just one component in the leisure apparatus.

This consumer paradise is the future. And so independent music is forced to set its back to the future, enter a wilful, defiant exile. The Smiths are famed for their Luddite tendencies, but this spirit pervades the scene – the fanzines that sing the delights of mono record players and flexis (against the CD), the hostility to video, the revival of the DIY ethos. To oppose the passivity our entertainment culture induces requires making a virtue of lo-tech and lo-fi. Otherwise the modern premium on perfection dispossesses us of our right to make things, to make a culture.

The indie scene is struggling to protect 'innocence' in the face of a sophisticated culture. That's why indie music is based on almost totally white sources. The DIY ethos has no resonance in black music, which does set a premium on sophistication and professionalism (lest Frank Owen box my ears, I'd better say that hip hop is an exception here).

Rebel rock could once base itself in the delinquent 'animalism' of R&B, but now that sexual energy is just part of the entertainment mainstream, just healthy vitality. The conflict presented in The Stones' 'Satisfaction' between desire and materialism doesn't apply any more. Increasingly, being a success in life requires development of your body's capacity for health and pleasure – from aerobics to health food to competitive sex.

Our alternative scene contains two approaches to resistance. Some try to make sex dangerous again, linking it with sickness and debauchery and violence (the brutalists and immaculate consumptives and dark noise types). More radical is what I've described above – a forgetting of the body, a rediscovery of romance and of the psychedelic properties of noise. Husker Du and Jesus and Mary Chain are the sublime union of both – chaste rapture *and* celestial noise.

A new kind of youth culture taking shape, based in romanticism and asceticism? Make no mistake, 'How Soon is Now', 'Still Ill', 'You've

Got Everything Now', these were the lost 'Satisfaction' and 'My Generation' of our time. Lost because the independent scene is just an island, an asylum, that no one wants to know.

To most people in the world, pop means Madonna, and Queen, and Dire Straits, all those worn, staid forms of 'breaking free'. I'm talking of a bohemianism that's cleansed of the self-destruction and fast living of earlier forms of rebellion. A quiet withdrawal, a defection as much from (the old) youth culture as from straight society. For pop itself is now a process of normalization, of training desire. Faced with a leisure paradise that promises satisfaction, what's radical is not just to make more demands, but to insist that satisfaction itself is an illusion. Faced with the infinite accommodation of consumer capitalism, the radical response is to abstain, to cling stubbornly to the will to misfit.

* * *

You will have gathered that this isn't a critique, more of a soft celebration. I recognize the scene's introversion, its impotence, its subtle racism; I enjoy black music from hip hop to new jazz, but always it's to *this* music that I return. Music that's saddened by dreams, torn between fatalism and the imprecise desire for something more. 'There are brighter sides to life and I should know because I've seen them / But not often.'

This music inhabits neither a subculture nor the mainstream, though it may stray to puzzle the outside world, infiltrated by Echo, U2 and others. It lives in the interstices of *possibility*, those gaps in the social fabric where people can convince themselves, for a while, they've not grown up, not given in. Sixth-formers, students, art schools, the new 'dole cultures', the alternative career structures – wherever it's possible to subsist outside the pressures of adjustment and adaptation, the pressure to *make your mind up*. A rootless communality, without geography, that's articulated through the media. That's why The Smiths and James have more in common with Husker Du and Meat Puppets than their own neighbours. Because the same predicament has brought them into being, demanded their beauty.

These are the people who only know what they do not want.

Something *is* happening. *Obviously* there's no threat to the outside world, but *within* the helplessly contracting, hopelessly isolated orbit of the 'alternative' scene, there are new shapes emerging. Here's a little contribution to counter the unstimulating commentary of those who insist it's just a matter of renewed 'vitality', an 'upsurge' of vibrant 'energy'. Scared shitless of making premature exhortations, they say there's no movement, just some new bands. Against this dour deflation, here's an *inflation* of meaning. I say, *jump* to conclusions!

Melody Maker, 28 June 1986

The piece that made my name. Bizarrely, there was even a letter about it in *NME*'s readers' letters page, complaining that the paper never did that kind of piece any more. The only problem was that as much as I liked what the subculture stood for, I was ambivalent about the shambling bands' scrawny music. So 'Younger than Yesterday' was a manifesto for something I didn't fully stand behind; a manifesto, also, that none of the bands rushed forward to embrace. Indeed when I did a follow-up piece focused on the movement's fashion element, some scenesters described it as the death-knell for 'cutie' (a word briefly in vogue to describe the ultra-naif tendency of bands such as Talulah Gosh, who did songs like 'The Day I Lost My Pastels Badge' and featured my *Monitor* comrade Chris Scott on bass). The look was 'anoraksia nervosa': the shamblers always seemed to be small and thin, and they wore sixties-style children's anoraks and similar non-adult garments. The look was suggestive of 'clothes your mum buys for you', the innocence of a time before the child takes on interest in style, self-expression, youth culture, competitive cool. Early in 1987 I vented my disappointment with the music in a piece called 'Regressive Rock', castigating a new breed of indie runts who'd frozen pop history at 1966 and 1978 (just before the leaps into psychedelia and post-punk), the sonic analogue of anorexia's arrested development.

Yet 'cutie' – or as it's now more commonly known *C86*, after the *NME* cassette compilation of the key bands on the scene – has proved surprisingly enduring. Birthed by shambling diehards like the Sarah label, there's an international network of 'twee-pop' that encompasses the likes of Belle & Sebastian; Riot Grrrl and its UK counterpart (the 'Huggy Nation' bands clustered around Huggy Bear) was the politicized, overtly feminist offshoot; Kurt Cobain was a huge fan of the Pastels, the Vaselines, et al.; Manic Street Preachers revered two shambling bands that had an unusual political consciousness, Big Flame and McCarthy, and the latter group evolved into the great Stereolab; Saint Etienne and Primal Scream, meanwhile, fused *C86* with house music. The legacy is larger than I would ever have imagined at the time.

NASTY BOYS: RAP

What is hip hop's uneasy fascination? Where's the pleasure in having some stranger berate you about how they're the best, the ultimate, how they're gonna devastate you?

I don't think there *should* be an easy relationship between hip hop and rock criticism. I think hip hop means trouble, and it should trouble the orthodoxies into which critics try to slot pop music. Hip hop is identified with a 'truth' of the street, and this truth is assumed to be in some way proto-socialist, or at least humanist/humanitarian. But what if 'the street' contains desires that us liberal hipsters can't really countenance?

Hip hop's pleasure lies in nakedness. The music is stripped, fleshless, free of frills or plumage, streamlined for efficiency. But in terms of motivation, too, there's a minimalism or nakedness. Hip hop reflects straight values and aspirations, but as in a kind of distorting mirror, one that strips away the veils of protocol and ideology, the cant about freedom and enterprise and choice. Hip hop reveals the *impolite* reality of capitalism – dog eat dog struggle. The competitiveness between MCs and bands is a metaphor for the struggle of all against all; there's an absence of solidarity, of a collective vision. The ghetto is like this: black violence against blacks is always rising.

Similarly there's a naked obsession with the trappings of status. Songs like 12:41's 'Success is the Word' show a naive fascination with 'sophistication', with the trinkets and surfaces of high life – cars, furs, jets, diamonds, champagne. Pop is about *fantasies*. Criticism that identifies black music with 'authenticity' misses the point that the authentic desires of most blacks are to be inauthentic – to be anywhere but the street. When funkateer Prince Charles's 'Cash Money' was being hailed by all the white crits as a raw protest song, it was real funny when he appeared on Janice Long and said it was about how he wanted to make loads of money. Such confusions arise because rock fantasies are about returning to this mythical 'street', this lost 'real'. But blacks find rock culture's downward aspirations ludicrous: they can't renounce the privileges of affluence that most of them never had.

A hip hop track, then, doesn't contain a 'real person' but a persona constructed out of the interaction between the rapper's desire to be not himself, and the range of imagery/models available in mass culture/the media that allow him to be something else. As Frank Owen writes, 'hip hop exists between street and screen'. Writing about hip hop nonetheless still harps on this wearisome authenticity shtick – think of David Toop's placing of rap in a lineage stretching through the R&B shouters, the plantation work chants, way back to Africa, think of the knee-jerk cant about 'pride' and 'dignity'.

Let's examine this 'pride' closely. Apart from the valorous exception of records like the Roxanne series, this is *male* pride. Black machismo has always been a defiance in the face of a racist society that *unmans*, by denying blacks access to status. But the cry 'I'm a Man' has always been problematic – there's an overcompensation that results in aggression, a demand for victims and victory to shore up the ego – the endless vistas of 'sucker MCs'. Masculinity is hardness, entails a brutalization of the self, of others. Manliness can only be defined in opposition to womanliness. Hip hop is riddled with misogyny – from the rappers who boast of being heartbreakers or of their sexual appetite/prowess, to songs like Mantronix's 'Ladies', with its strict notions of femininity (to reassure men uncertain of their masculinity). Women exist only as facets of the rappers' status, to be scored. The hip hop ego always tries to impress, too hard.

And hip hop music is a metaphor for violence – that punishing beat, the abrasive attack of scratching is a kind of killing machine. The language used to valorize the music – 'rock', 'wreck', 'damage' – is violent too.

Hip hop is a hyperbolic reflection, virtually a caricature, of the system – capitalism/patriarchy. Inevitably those who are excluded from full status in society only want that status, and its material trappings, more severely. It's noticeable that the traditional escape routes of the working class (black or white) – sport, crime, pop – are ultra-macho and mega-acquisitive. Yet rock criticism still struggles to recruit the 'pride' of hip hop/black pop into a left-wing political scheme that's wholly inappropriate. Remember the fuss over dreary records like Afrika Bambaataa/James Brown's 'Unity', over 'Renegades of Funk' and 'The Message' and all those records about 'cash' and 'dollar bill y'all'? But hip hop's 'protest' songs strike me as primarily documentary, offering no solutions, no utopianism, no criticism, even. They say: this is how it is, this is how tuff you gotta be. The spate of records like 'Survival' make me think of Christopher Lasch's analysis of the survivalist mentality in *The Minimalist Self*: the solitary ego, beset on all sides but fighting on, streamlined for survival through the excision of all affective/cooperative bonds. Bodybuilding/breakdancing is a metaphor for survivalism – this asexual, desensualized dance is a display of prowess, an armouring of the body in readiness for trouble.

This analysis ignores for the moment the humour – musical and lyrical – of hip hop, along with the sheer avant-garde exhilaration of the sound, but I do think that a big part of the *pleasure* of hip hop is that it's *appalling*. There's something recalcitrant and unsound that can't be ironed out, that won't fit into a *City Limits* worldview. And yet these records coerce. Why? Maybe it's useful to compare hip hop with other forms of male teenage vileness that I disapprove of but can't resist. Hardcore/psychobilly/sixties garage punk/heavy metal all work on the same premises of (stylized) machismo/misogyny as hip hop, and there are musical affinities – jerky, unsupple rhythms, an aura of violence, noise. Heavy metal's swords 'n' sorcery obsession parallels electro's sci fi/video game phase – both providing a range of masculine warrior archetypes. Both heavy metal and hip hop spend a lot of time self-reflexively boasting how hard they're gonna rock you.

Hip hop can present an epic solipsism, an arbitrary and aggressive will, comparable with that which animates 'Anarchy in the UK' or an Iggy and The Stooges song. Hip hop, like punk, nihilistically inverts values – 'bad', 'wicked', 'ill', 'treacherous' are all good terms – but this is also an exposure of what it really takes to get on in free market society. Value and meaning have absconded, the only authority is the self, there are 'so many ways to get what you want' . . .

This megalomania is a monomania. Rappers really have nothing to say, they just want to prove themselves, show they exist. There's no meaning, just assertion, a scream in the face of eternity. Hip hop intimidates because its motor is fear – the fear of anonymity and failure. There's something tragic about the rapper, about his victories in a vacuum. What happens to these self-proclaimed stars when their glory disperses? A rapper's ego punctured must be a pitiful thing.

Above all, hip hop is about the intoxication of violence – those clenched voices are a constant reminder of the possibility of force. Hip hop allows us the dizzying pleasure of enjoying both triumph and submission simultaneously – we can identify with the persona of the song at the same time as we're being threatened, put down, dominated by the singer. Hip hop connects with those same areas of (male?) power psychology that respond to the myth-resonant confrontations of boxing or other sports.

The message turns out to be something we white liberals shouldn't want to hear, but precisely because the music's NASTY, packed with ugly contradictions, it retains the power to agitate and transfix where the ideologically sound, neatly aligned music of groups like Fine Young Cannibals and The Redskins doesn't.

Melody Maker, 19 July 1986

Hard to believe, but in 1985 rap was widely perceived (in UK hipsterland anyway) as not so much a passing as a *passed* fad. The black music bigged-up in *The Face* or *NME* end-of-year critics' polls were styles like go-go, African music, contemporary soul, 'jazz-dance'. I too started 1986 completely bored by rap. What flipped my head around was Mantronix (and Mantronik's production of T. La Rock), the hard-riffing Def Jam sound of LL Cool J and Beastie Boys, and Schoolly D's debut. Hip hop became hugely hip again, but the appreciation it received gave me a weird sense of disconnect: critics seemed to gloss over, or mis-recognize, the most compelling element in the music, its rage and (Sid) viciousness. Hence this polemic, arguing that if rap was 'black punk' it wasn't in the worthy Clash/Jam 'social comment' sense but punk as a theatre of tyranny and domination, appetite-for-destruction and wanton will-to-power. Actually, subsequently, most rap turned out to be more like the black heavy metal: fantasies of alpha male triumph, of warrior male gore and glory. Which makes sense: as much as it's a black thing, rap is also a *teenage boy* thing, all hormones and hostility.

Plenty of wild sociocultural generalizations here (bear in mind I'd only just turned twenty-three) but the one bit that really makes me wince is the line about rappers having 'nothing to say': back then the genre *was* 99 per cent boasts and threats, but 'content' soon arrived with Public Enemy, Rakim, et al. Still, I reckon the piece does capture an abiding essence to rap that would only get stronger with the emergence of gangsta. (The reference to 'anonymity and failure', incidentally, is a second-hand lift from Robert Warshow's famous essay about the mobster movie, 'The Gangster as Tragic Hero'.) It also expresses my enduring bemusement about rap as a form of 'entertainment', how we pay good money to experience what in real life we'd run a mile from: bug-eyed sociopaths threatening cruel-and-unusual deaths, nouveau riche bores droning on about their wealth and possessions.

BEAT HAPPENING

Beat Happening (K Records/Rough Trade)

Beat Happening are Calvin and Heather and Brett and they're from Olympia, Washington, on the north-west coast of the USA. Perhaps this is the *Next Big Thing*, perhaps there are hundreds of West Coast shambling bands out there. But I like the idea of them being some kind of freak happening. To me they seem to come from another planet.

'Shambling' is a useful means of entry to what Beat Happening are all about. Like many of our indie bands, Beat Happening use incompetence as a springboard to glory. They don't have a proper drum set, often appear to be hitting *things* that come to hand, and so have the shuffling, faltering beat of Jesus and Mary Chain or Shop Assistants. And the way they've been recorded captures the sounds of the music being *made* – the creak of the strings and plectrum, the rustle of percussion. Voices are creased, sometimes they fail. My friend Chris says this sort of thing is important because when you can *hear* the group struggling with instruments they've yet to master, when you can hear the *concentration*, you know they care. Fluency means less feeling, because it's the result of rehearsal.

And like many of our indie groups, Beat Happening are obsessed with innocence. They appear to be slightly older (one's at college, another works) than the experiences they write about – first love, picnics on the beach, swimming in the lake, 'we don't care / if there's sand in our hair' – they're looking back to the purity of that joy and pain. Quite instinctively they've decorated the record with 'cutie' graphics – a crayon-scrawl logo just like our own Pastels, a chalk doodle of a cat in a spaceship.

Their music reinvents sixties garage punk, not so much the proficiently raucous rhythm-and-blues on compilations like *Pebbles* and

Mindrockers, as the more eerily inept stuff on *What a Way to Die* and *Back From the Grave,* groups like The Hombres, We The People, the Outsiders. Choosing to model themselves on these lost tearaways constitutes a discreet dissidence against the pop mainstream.

On the sleeve insert they talk of an indie 'cassette revolution' that's 'exploding the teenage underground into passionate revolt against the corporate ogre'. On their anthem 'Bad Seeds' they exhort 'a new generation / form a teenage nation / this time let's do it right . . . They make a lot of rules / They tell a lot of lies / but if we don't wanna / We won't behave.' There's a delicate poise between pastiche and underlying seriousness here, that's delicious, almost camp.

Their magic comes out of the friction between the limits of their ability and the scope of their ambition. Perhaps it's only because they can't make chord changes very fast yet, but their use of minimalism and repetition suggests that this music is the missing link between Question Mark and the Mysterians and The Fall, between Primal Scream and Suicide.

'Bad Seeds' out-zombies Lux Interior. 'I Spy' is a join-the-dots Link Wray stomp that extends itself with the diagrammatic exactness of a Kraftwerk. 'I Love You' is like the Velvets fronted by Alan Vega – 'I woke up / I had a tear in my eye'. But best of all are the songs where they've purged garage punk of its misogynist insolence and reanimated it with a proto-feminist tenderness. 'Run Down the Stairs', 'What's Important' and 'Fourteen' are psychedelic lullabies midway between We The People's 'Eyes the Color of Love' and The Woodentops.

Maybe Beat Happening will get skilled, lose that special tension that arises when urgency is confined within close musical quarters. Right now, they're the most enchanting, unearthly thing to come out of America since the Meat Puppets. Our own shamblers have yet to produce anything this strange, this moving.

Melody Maker, November 1986

K Records had actually been founded way back in 1982 and circa this Beat Happening debut Calvin Johnson was already a little too old at twenty-four to be play-acting the teenager! His fantasy about 'the teenage underground nation' versus 'corporate rock' would reach fruition through K's influence on both grunge and Riot Grrrl. Johnson organized the International Pop Underground Convention, a six-day indie-pop festival that took place in Olympia in August 1991 (just before 'Smells Like Teen Spirit' broke) and proved to be a key moment in the emergence of Riot Grrrl. Kurt Cobain esteemed K as a beacon of purity in a corrupt world and he proudly wore the label's logo – a small K inside a shield – on his forearm, a tattoo he did himself using a sewing needle and ink. Nirvana's breakthrough smash got its title from graffiti that Bikini Kill's Kathleen Hanna sprayed on Cobain's apartment wall, 'Kurt smells like Teen Spirit': not a reference to some elan vital of renegade youth, but to the fact that Cobain was dating Bikini drummer Tobi Vail, who used a deodorant called Teen Spirit. Before teaming up with Hanna, Vail had played in a K Records band called The Go Team – a duo with Calvin Johnson.

While we're talking 'incestuous', 'my friend Chris' = Chris Scott, who'd penned a pair of brilliant pieces for *Monitor* on the aesthetic, and *ethic*, of incompetence in indie-pop. The first celebrated fanzines' refusal of professionalism – a riposte to a piece I'd done critiquing zine culture – while the second, 'Concrete Pop', analysed how the shambling sound of the Pastels, Shop Assistants, and Woodentops jolted both players and listeners out of rehearsed-to-living-death, going-through-the-motions music.

BACKS TO THE FUTURE

The Folk and Country Resurgence in Alternative Rock

Groups who use accordions and fiddles *taken seriously*? Nick Cave covers of Johnny Cash and Glen Campbell songs? The Grateful Dead, Creedence Clearwater, Fairport Convention as *reference points*? Bob Dylan and George Jones now cooler than Bobby Womack and Mantronix?!

There's been a weird turnabout in hip orientation this last year or so – a switch from black music to folk and country as influences. Five years ago funk was universally taken as *the* appropriate base for adventurous/intelligent/subversive activity in pop – by groups as diverse as Heaven 17, Scritti Politti, Talking Heads, ABC, Cabaret Voltaire, Style Council . . . All the rhetoric about Sex, Sweat and Blood and Dance Don't Riot seems incredibly dated now, but at the time there was a vague idea that sex, desire, glamour could be dangerous, a threat. Another guiding idea of the early eighties was of a radical eclecticism – the melting pot of music, a rainbow coalition of races and eras, postures and images. But, inevitably, these ideas moved rapidly from the left field to the centre stage of pop. The moment people like Phil Collins got hip to modern black production techniques it was no longer possible to maintain the fiction of funk's intrinsic radicalism; the moment lesser spirits like Eurythmics picked up on postmodern pick 'n' mix, it became impossible to believe there was anything clever about eclecticism.

Now that their ideas have become domesticated in the mainstream, the indie scene has abandoned them and staged a retreat – a flight from production, from technology (the synthesizer, sampling, the studio-as-instrument), from chartpop's hypersexuality, from musical cross-breeding. A return to PURITY. What's been revived is the (moral)

27

conviction that what you put on a record must be reproducible on stage. This new purism embraces anything 'authentic' – folk, Cajun, country, soca, African. Anything either old or Third World. There's a hankering for a lost pop innocence, a return to the sound of a time when the idea of youth was still young. A lean, underproduced sound.

Now that the charts are choked with white imitations of black music, the indie scene embraces anything white. A discreet, but implicit, racism has been reinstalled, a revival of the mid-seventies progressive rock snobbery about 'that disco shit'. Five years ago it would have been inconceivable that a song like 'Panic' by The Smiths, with its notorious 'hang the DJ / burn down the blessed disco' chorus, could have struck a chord.

So why are so many politically right-on hipster types drawn to the music of the most redneck, reactionary and backward parts of America? Why do you find *City Limits* readers dancing perfect jigs and waltzes at Tex-Mex festivals on Clapham Common?

American roots music is being used by groups in this country (and in America) as a critique of contemporary rootlessness – the way MTV/stadium rock/the disco are superseding the conviviality of live performance in pub or bar. What's happening in the USA anticipates what's happening throughout the West – the erosion of local communities and geographical identities, and the atomization of society into a mass of detached consumers, who are plugged into the media's pleasure circuits. American folk musics are being used against the spread of the new American yuppie culture worldwide.

There's a haunted awareness on the indie scene that progress is 'freeing' us into a world without the anchorage of faith or narrative, 'freeing' us of the norms and values that tie, but also console. The cowboy's drift and the ghost town have become potent metaphors for our present. Five years ago troubled spirits would have used funk's tension to express their paranoia and disorientation, but now they're drawn to the desolation, despondency and fatigue of folk and country.

The Smiths sing 'It's over and it hardly began'. The June Brides moan that 'there's no place like home' to be found anywhere. The Mekons say 'we're falling like leaves from the trees'. Nick Cave resuscitates an ancient C&W song called 'Muddy Water' as a contemporary metaphor – it's the tale of a family whose farm is flooded again and again and who lose the will to carry on: 'We won't be back to start all over . . . it's hard to say just what I'm losing.'

You can find a similar feeling that possibility has subsided into entropy in a host of groups – The Pogues, Costello, the Band of Holy Joy, Lloyd Cole, James, Husker Du, Throwing Muses, and many more.

All are influenced by folk and country. These bands make up a lost generation, the dying embers of punk – people who are still teased by the memory of what it was once like to have a hope of change. There's a parallel with the way the folk-rock and country-rock movements of the early seventies stemmed from the disillusion of the burnt-out counterculture.

But folk and country offer indie groups more than a fantasy of community – both present a vision of love as absolute, either totally redemptive or totally devastating. In this era of yuppie narcissism and self-sufficiency, chartpop's representation of love is increasingly secular and 'progressive' ('On My Own' and 'Ain't Nothin' Goin' on But the Rent' are benchmarks of the new pragmatism). So those who still believe in the romance of broken hearts, ruined lives, obsession and devotion are drawn to the religious imagery of country, its tales of betrayal, guilt and revenge. So someone like Nick Cave moves from art-terrorism to interpreting Gene Pitney's 'Something's Gotten Hold of My Heart' because the song's melodrama accords with his own vision of love as possession and affliction. And he can profess admiration for country and western's hall of fame of self-destructive stars – singers like Gram Parsons, Hank Williams, Johnny Cash, George Jones, Jerry Lee Lewis, Presley – who lived on the edge, and sometimes fell off it.

The return to tradition is a revolt against technology, against yuppie self-management, against health and efficiency, against 'progress'. It's the first wave of dissent in rock that hasn't made the 'New' its rallying cry, the first anti-modernist revolt. Backs to the future, certainly, but then these people would also say: back to the things that really count. I wonder.

iD, winter 1986

Given the resurgence of interest in folk these last several years (the Folk Britannia festival/documentary series, the glut of compilations of vintage 'wyrd folk', and the network of contemporary troubadours and minstrels known as 'freak folk'), it's disconcerting to recall that there'd been this earlier revival of interest. Today, it's specifically UK folk of the most esoteric sort (Vashti Bunyan, Comus, Forest) but in the mid-eighties, the emphasis was on American roots music (I recall the Mekons saying that while they loved the Band they'd never had any time for Fairport Convention or anything chunky-sweatered and real ale-y). Nor was there anything mushroom-munching trippy or mystical about the eighties rediscovery of folk and country: the music was very much about former punks dealing with their sense of disillusion and their political demoralization following Thatcher and Reagan's re-election, drowning their sorrows with alcohol (very much the drug of choice). Folk-punk was pioneered by

The Pogues (led by a drunkard vet of 1977) and The Men They Couldn't Hang (Clash-obsessed jigsters who saw themselves continuing a centuries-old tradition of UK folk songs railing against the ruling class). But it was those other punk survivors the Mekons who were the true poets of the new despondency, albums like *Fear and Whiskey* and *The Edge of the World*, and songs like 'Hard to be Human Again' and 'Darkness and Doubt' capturing the bereft and adrift feel of the time.

HIP HOP AND HOUSE SINGLES REVIEWS

Dead Weird

Salt-N-Pepa – 'Beauty and the Beat' (Next Plateau import)

Hip hop's internal economics (the impulse towards heavier beats, towards more daring, alarming juxtapositions) are pushing the music beyond any dance utility, into the realm of the psychedelic. The beauty of 'Beauty and the Beat' is the way female DJ Spinderella cuts sections out of organic, groovy black pop – a trail of blues guitar, a rumble of go-go, a snatch of seventies soul clavinet, some call and response – and reassembles them in a harsh, *inorganic* way. This is surgery of the order of Frankenstein, a dance monster constructed out of ill-fitting, inconsistent limbs. Wholly disparate ambiences are forced into friction. There's nothing stable in this music: rhythms shift, are subject to lapses, sudden subsidence. There's a constant danger of tissues rejecting one another. This pop barely hangs together as a body, and the only reliable human thread is the supercilious female rapping. Salt-N-Pepa are all over the place, and out of it.

Lame Ducks

Raze – 'Let the Music Move U' (Grove Street)
Private Possession – 'This Time' (Fourth & Broadway)

House music has turned out to be something of a lame duck, a nonstarter, if not quite a flop in the same league as go-go. (Shouldn't gloat really.) In truth I don't think there's much to the music anyway. Where hip hop actively *destroys* sense and identity, wrenches up roots, House music strikes me as sleekly, *meekly* anonymous, a faceless and placeless efficiency, without attitude or charisma. Everything is mixed in smoothly, layers are built up and faded out gently, there are no fissures or chasms or wounds as in hip hop, no violence. In a club, House tracks can course through the body like electricity, sheer fluid elation. The hi-hat bashes your brain to pulp by sheer metronomic attrition. It's a music of tiny details and shifts, minuscule fascination – the *consistency* of a bass motif can be what hooks you: compact, nagging, the sound of a bowel tremor. But even the best records sound weak outside a club. And House really *does* all sound the same – a mixture of 'Walking On Sunshine', Hi-NRG, D-Train, Man Parrish. Raze's new single is much like their previous semi-hit 'Jack the Groove'. Private Possession sound like a spindly D-Train, all kick and no bottom. Death to disco!

Hot To Trot

C-Bank – 'No Matter How I Try' (Next Plateau import)

C-Bank have been making great records for years, like the staggering 'One More Shot'. The kind of record that New Order are always trying to make, but minus the bedsit anguish that enables New Order to sell New York dance production to their vast student miserygut constituency. C-Bank are a perfect example of the anonymous pleasure of disco, of how disco works through bits, rather than through a coherent narrative, as in rock. Ignore the thin, replaceable vocal – the heart of this 'song' (where the emotion resides) is in a strange call-and-response between a shudder of clotted synth (reminiscent of Liaisons Dangereuses) *over there* and, in the other corner of the mix, a tiny trickle of piano, a tear tinkling out of an eye. Seismic rumbles of bass impart a sense of impending calamity, huge phalanxes of synth rear up, there's this super *quacking* noise, lots of kick in the drum programmes . . . all in all, this record is inhuman, inane, but a monumental piece of dance architecture.

Melody Maker, 10 January 1987

Rip it Up

The best rock record this week is by a hip hop group, **Ultramagnetic MC's**. 'Travelling at the Speed of Thought' (Next Plateau, import) starts with a beat that is pure Rolling Stones circa 'Jumpin' Jack Flash', a beat so supple and exuberant you want to leap around and holler and break things. And the masterstroke – a sublimely teasing edit from the chorus of 'Louie Louie', the anthem of a thousand garage bands as covered by the Kingsmen, Motorhead, and Black Flag! I could weep for joy. The sixties punk tearaway reincarnated in the eighties B-boy motormouth! What a vindication of the 'black rock'/hip hop wig-out fantasy! What a fabulous record!

Another interesting hip hop trend: **DJ Jazzy Jeff and the Fresh Prince** mercilessly shred and scatter some sultry, mellow jazz on 'A Touch of Jazz' (Jive, import). Moods are shattered and subjugated to the beat. The potential here is limitless; I'd love to see what someone like Herbie Luv Bug could make of Weather Report's dense polyrhythmic jungle, or the new jazz savagery of Art Ensemble of Chicago or Sun Ra . . .

The dominant trend in hip hop still seems to be scratching and sampling old school R&B grooves, although there are signs that this is running out of steam. **The Microphone Prince**'s 'Who's the Captain' (Music of Life) is based around a ghostly refrain constructed from a trail of doo-wop. **The Classical Two**'s 'New Generation' (Rooftop) consists of some git-on-UP's strewn rather unimaginatively over a Clintonesque pulse. Rather more interesting is the new **Eric B And Rakim** single. 'I Know You Got Soul' (Fourth & Broadway, import) isn't in the same league as the unearthly 'Eric B. Is President', but Eric B. is still evidently some kind of Hendrix of scratch. Here a collection of chants, pants, groans and grunts, an outpouring of deep soul testify-ing, is crucified, turned into nonsense. What was once whole and human is turned into a series of inhuman *effects*; soul is smashed, not commemorated, by the fad for old school grooves. The nihilism of twelve-inch culture is killing soul!

Start Again

The traffic between hip hop and rock only seems to work well in one direction, as yet. Both **Zodiac Mindwarp and the Love Reaction**'s 'Prime Mover' (Mercury) and **Gaye Bykers On Acid**'s 'Karma Nosedive' (In Tape) are unfruitful attempts by others at a hip hop/rock dialogue. Gaye Bykers' is the bloodier and more raucous of the two, but ultimately both records are useless because they have no grasp of the low end of the sonic spectrum that's crucial to hip (and rock for that matter). For all their priapic bluster, these records lack bollocks. Get a Roland 808 if you want to kick ass like The Beasties, boys. The fundament-als of bass-biology interface is something that **Sugar Ray Dinke** understands: 'Cabrini Green' (Rhythm King) has this graunchy, bowel-quaking riff, which I'm sure has been pilfered from some forbidden recess in rock history . . .

Two great dance records. Go-go may be dead, but it has maintained a kind of zombie existence in hip hop, where thankfully it is held down in a subservient position, its percussive girth *used* to bolster hip hop's megalomaniac schemes. **True Mathematics'** 'After Dark' (Champion) employs diced chunks of 'Still Smokin'', severed from the rather affable ambience of the Troublefunk original, and relocated to an ominous nocturnal inner city scenario, in which the chant 'the beat is bad' acquires a whole new resonance. And **Jesse Rae's** 'Houdini' (WEA): Zapp's Roger Troutman crams every second of his production with as much squirming ecstasy as it can hold, but there's this ludicrous (and very nasal) Scottish voice, and I'm very sorry, but I just keep thinking of sporrans and haggis. Actually this is a very strange and very funky record and, towards the end Jesse spirals off into some delirious scat as though Fulton Mackay was metamorphosing into Prince in front of your naked and astonished eyes.

Three Wise Men's 'Refresh Yourself' (Rhythm King) brings out a whole side to hip hop that 'soul-cialists' seem ignorant of: the side that believes in private initiative, the Power of Positive Thinking, assertiveness-training, self-definition through competition. The 'politics' of hip hop, such as they are, have far more to do with the right-wing fantasy of the self-sufficient individual (who exists 'outside' politics) than with any left-wing vision of collectivism. Three Wise Men inform us, chidingly, that it is up to us to change our circumstances, us and no one else. Thankfully we can ignore their tedious exhortations and enjoy the hyperactive dub and metal mixes on the B-side . . .

Melody Maker, 2 May 1987

C-Bank belonged to a post-disco meets post-electro genre called Freestyle that was hugely popular with Hispanic kids in New York. Most famously DJ-ed at the Funhouse by Jellybean Benitez, Freestyle influenced Madonna's early pre-megafame club hits (back when she was Benitez's girlfriend) as well as New Order circa 'Blue Monday' and 'Confusion'. I can't figure out why I slagged off the house records but then *immediately* went on to exalt C-Bank, when both could equally be celebrated as radically impersonal disco-as-new-sonic-architecture. I felt it was only fair to show me making a completely dud prediction. Still, you'll just have to take my word for it: there *was* a moment in early 1987 when house seemed like a fast fading fad. There'd been some huge hits and a lot of hype, and in the North (where they prefer uptempo beats) the Chicago sound's popularity grew steadily. But London clubland dropped house in favour of rare groove (vintage seventies funk). Later in 1987 came a track that totally converted me: Nitro Deluxe 'This Brutal House', its very title seemingly confirming my feelings that most house music was a bit mild. Also known as 'Let's Get Brutal', the tune's fusion of electro bass pressure and house hypnotism made it a touchstone for the early Warp Records scene.

'Hip hop wig out' was a slogan touted by *Melody Maker* comrade Frank Owen and me as part of our polemic with the soul boys of *NME/City Limits/The Face,* fervent adherents of rock-is-dead. We stressed the resemblances – sonic and attitudinal – between rap and rock: the noise, the aggression, the riffs (either sampled guitar licks or scratch as a rhythmic device). Hip hop at that point seemed to be getting so wound up, it was approaching total seizure. Instead of move-your-body party music, it offered punishingly slow monsterbeats that B-boys nodded their heads to, arms folded across the chest. The touchstone tracks for me were Schoolly D's 'P.S.K. (What Does it Mean)' with its vast, cavernous beat too slow and spaced-out for dancing, and Skinny Boys' 'Rip the Cut', its abrasive drone-riff sounding like someone puking down a deep well. Crushing your consciousness like a scrap-metal compressor, these heavy, headbanger tracks seemed to have more in common with Black Sabbath or Big Black than with R&B. 'Twelve-inch culture kills soul' refers to the avant-ugliness of this phase of rap, as well as the scratchadelic eeriness of tracks like 'Eric B. Is President'. But this pet slogan of ours was disproved not just by how quickly rap moved to a new warm 'n' groovy phase based around sampling funk breakbeats and jazz licks, but by the sheer soul of Rakim's voice, a suave version of James Brown's superbadness. Hip hop's relationship to R&B is obviously not patricidal but a complex blend of respect, irreverence and pragmatism (recycling vintage licks being cheaper than hiring musicians). The sampled musicians achieve immortality, albeit anonymous, through being subsumed within the 'changing same' of the black musical continuum. Indeed Rakim's lyrics to 'I Know You Got Soul' would themselves be 'honoured' through endless sampling ('pump up the volume') or versioning-with-a-twist ('my style, identical to none', 'been a long time, I shouldn't have left you / without a dope rhyme to step to', 'it's not where you're from, it's where you're at', etc.).

HUSKER DU

Warehouse: Songs and Stories (WEA)

This is rock. Not rock 'n' roll, not swingin', groovy, lean and compact. Not even raunch. This is ROCK – powerchords that would crack apart the sky. Husker Du don't belong with the new authentics, bar bands sweating out a closeknit clinch with their fans. Unlike Springsteen (who by sheer presence can shrink stadia back to the dimensions of the primal R&B joint), there's no intimacy, no sweat, nothing *earthy*. Husker Du are making a monument, a mountain, a glacier, out of rock again, rather than burrowing along at grass roots.

Oblivion. 'Nothing changes fast enough / Your hurry worry days / It makes you want to give it up / And drift into a haze' – 'These Important Years'. Rock noise is the uptight white adolescent's release, emptying the mind, then filling it with nothing but its own dancing frenzy. Noise as metaphor for inner turmoil *and* its transfiguration. Over five LPs (and this is their *second* double) Husker Du have turned over and over the details of drift and bewilderment, yet *still* manage to wrest an improbable grandeur from the small squalor of everyday inertia. Fuck the chirpy, *unforgivable* 'Road to Nowhere' – this is the true, hurting sound of the spirit chafing against the rut of existence, chafing at the intractable. The 'violence' of this music is an attempt to flay past numbness, through dulled senses, to reawaken feeling.

'Think with your hips' has been the message of rock 'n' roll, of pop. But this rock says: rise above, kiss the sky. Like U2/R.E.M./J&MC, this music is psychedelia without drugs, a rock that has left behind loins, juice, even heat, and found a new, frosty kind of intensity. A celestial impulse.

This is a new sound. Heavy metal is bastardized R&B, R&B sexuality coarsened and stiffened and blunt. But Husker Du 'bastardize' or metallize folk. They strip folk of roots and soil, blast it to the heavens. Imagine the Jimi Hendrix Experience playing The Byrds' *Younger than Yesterday*.

Better than ever. Voices midway between scar and balm, savaging as they soothe. Harmonies that swell, soar, then bleed into the horizon. Divine lullabies like 'Up in the Air', cracked apart by blocks of noise. 'No Reservation', 'She's a Woman', 'You Can Live at Home', 'Friend', 'You're a Soldier', 'Ice Cold Ice' . . . classic pop structures, almost borne under by the foaming weight of noise brought to bear.

My fantasy. A million heads wigging out, blissed out, in rock noise. A soulboy's bad dream. Style, rhetoric, tasselled loafers, import twelve-inches, blown, scattered to the winds. A million heads, lost in music, in worship. The return of ROCK.

Melody Maker, July 1987

To put this in context: the UK pop mainstream was swamped by black and white versions of soul/funk/R&B, and rock felt like the underdog. Believe it or not, you seldom heard the sound of an electric guitar in the pop charts. The exceptions were either plangent jangle (U2/R.E.M./The Smiths), lite-metal (although a harder strain did start to come through with Guns N' Roses and Anthrax) and Goth-turned-rocky (The Cult, the Mission). But the really exciting rock of the day seemed totally blocked from the mainstream. Major labels gamely signed up the cream of alternative rock – Husker Du, Dinosaur Jr, Replacements, Meat Puppets – but with little prospect of access to MTV or the radio. The fantasy at the end of the review is an expression of frustration, desperate because it seemed desperately unlikely it could ever come to pass. It remained an impossible dream right up to the moment 'Smells Like Teen Spirit' went into heavy rotation on MTV.

MANTRONIX

Forget 'The Song'

Mantronik does not write Good Songs. He is not an author, but an engineer, an architect. His music is not the expression of his soul, but a product of his expertise. What Mantronik does is construct a *terrain*, a dance-space in which we can move, float free. Unlike the Rock Song, there's no atmosphere, no nuances, no resonance, here: instead, simply a shifting of forces, torques, pressures, gradients. Mantronik's work (and it is work) is neither expressionist nor impressionist – it's cubist, a matter of geometry, space, speed, primary colours (not the infinite shades and subtle tones of meaning). Populist avant-gardism.

The song is the primary object of Rock Criticism – the work of art as a coherent, whole expression of a whole human being's vision. Most rock criticism is poor Lit Crit, forever trying to pin down pop to What's Being Said (whether that's nuggets of 'human truth' or blasts of 'social commitment'), forever failing to engage with the materiality of music. A Mantronix track isn't a song, a finished work, but a process, a space capable of endless extension and adaption; a collection of resources to be rearranged and restructured. Hence the six different mixes of 'Who is It?'; hence the closing 'Edit' on the last LP *Music Madness*, in which the whole album is compressed into a volatile six-minute reprise; hence the 'Primal Scream Dub' of 'Scream', the fantabulous new single, virtually an entirely new piece of music altogether . . .

Forget the Human

Pop is drowning itself (and in the process drowning us) with 'humanity' – from the sickening, hyperbolic 'care' of 'Let it Be' and 'We Are the World' to the firm, all *too* firm flesh throbbing in 'I Want Your Sex'. Swamped by this benign, beige environment, this all-pervading *warmth*, it's scarcely possible to feel the shiver down the spine, the sharp shudder of ecstasy: modern pop just massages you all over, comforts and reassures. Practically every waking minute of our lives we're condemned to be human, to care for people, to be polite, to be socially concerned. Shouldn't our leisure (at the very least; for a start) be a place we can escape our humanity? A place to *chill*?

Mantronix make perhaps the most nihilistic music on the planet today; only house could claim to be more blank. Unlike rock nihilism, this is nihilistic without any drama, without an iconic figure like Michael Gira or Steve Albini – the creator simply, silently, absconds; creates an environment in which nothing of himself resides.

Unlike the first LP, which shared with hip hop a boastful, 'deffer than the rest' rapping style, on *Music Madness* the megalomania is vested in the whole expanse of sound, the inhuman perfection of the dance environment, rather than a charismatic protagonist. Poor MC Tee! This last token of the human seems to be fading fast. It's as though someone has taken an eraser and all but rubbed him out of the picture: a little lost voice wandering in a vast, intimidating Futurist adventure playground. And the words uttered, in that fey, fragile voice are little more than psychedelic gibberish, a vestigial anchor for us to centre our attention, otherwise dispersed and fractured across the jags and fissures of the mix. Mantronik is candid about the relative importance of text and material: 'the words don't mean shit, there's no lyrical structure, but the music *pumps*!'

You're horrified, but after all, isn't pop all about the desire to tran-scend or step sideways from the cage of one's humanity? To be more, less or other than simply, naturally human: to become angel, demon, ghost, animal (butterfly or invertebrate). Mantronik's desire is to be superhuman; he envies the prowess, the infallibility of the machine. He loves all the sci-fi films (the techno-heroic strand in science fiction that buffs call 'hard sci-fi', rather than New Wave s.f.'s odysseys into 'inner space'). There are links between Electro's space age imagery and the sword 'n' sorcery/superhero comic book elements in heavy metal, speed metal ... similar male fantasies of omnipotence and invulnerability.

For Mantronik, sampling is his 'special power', the key to demi-godhead. 'You can take a sound, any sound, and you can tamper with it. Add other sounds to it. Look at its wave formations on a screen, and change the patterns around. And you don't have to take sounds off records, you can get them from the environment, from hitting things against the wall, anything. And with my set-up, I can record music right up to the point of doing vocals, in my bedroom. *Then* I go into a studio. With samplers, I never read the instructions. I like to learn from my mistakes and incorporate blunders.'

Forget Soul

For Mantronik, the history of Black Dance Music doesn't begin with James Brown, Sly Stone, George Clinton, even Van McCoy or Chic; it begins with Kraftwerk and flowers with Trevor Horn's Art of Noise. It was the krafty krauts' glistening plastic vistas and stainless girders, plus Art of Noise's fleshless, faceless, sense-less and soul-less techno-symphonic sky's-the-limit mastery that first made him want to make dance music. Indeed, Mantronik seems to take Trevor Horn as a kind of guardian spirit or touchstone, talking of how he's 'now working on stuff that would blow Trevor's mind. I'm working on things Trevor wouldn't even *understand*.'

Mantronik's attitude to the past is strictly utilitarian, postmodern pagan; there's no veneration, no allegiance to outmoded beats. His reprocessing of the past is in accordance with functionalist criteria, not nostalgia. 'All those old seventies percussion lines were recorded real rough, real shitty, using dirt cheap reverbs. There's a certain old, gritty sound you just can't achieve in a modern studio. What I do is take that old sound and bring it back, into the future.'

There's nothing in the way of the rockthink cult of the origin, of roots here, but rather an insatiable pursuit of the *fresh*, the ultra-modern. 'The old music bores me.' Styles and beats have a rapid turnover, are produced in factory conditions. Mantronix are simply the latest stage in a long history of black music; the largely unwritten history of corporate design, brand names, backroom technicians, rather than sacred cow artists or communities struggling to be heard.

What troubles critics about Mantronix, about house, is that they're *illegible*. You can't read anything into them. There's no text, just texture, and those who endeavour to wrap meanings around the music are always shown up, the failed despots of discourse. The sheer opaque, *arbitrary* force of the music slips the net of meaning, again and again.

Instead, for those who *listen*, there's the fascination of details, a seduction in the endless intermittence of dub. 'The new stuff? A whole mix of things. Not play-it-safe. Kind of teasing, flirtatious. I'm not gonna give it to the listener all at once. It's like if you're going out with a girl, and she gives it you straightaway, you lose interest.' Mantronix never lose you, even as you lose yourself.

Melody Maker, 1 August 1987

'Good songs' was a bugbear of mine in those days. Not good songs per se (I like a shapely melody, who doesn't?), but the critical fixation on the Song as the be-all and end-all of music. Apart from the fact that there's hardly a shortage of well-crafted, heart-felt tunes in the world, what irked me was this way of treating music as surrogate literature (the song as short story or mini-screenplay), in the process totally ignoring sound-in-itself: the insistence of riffs, the sensuousness of timbre, the sorcery of production, the marvel of groove, the mystery of melodic beauty itself. So this piece is a sort of manifesto-in-advance for electronic dance music (compare with the later piece 'Historia Electronica': a sort of manifesto-after-the-fact for rave). Having said that, it's quite hard to put back on the head that thought 'human' was a bad thing for music to be. The polemic against Soul reprises the savage critique of the 'total-itarianism of passion' written with David Stubbs (another *Monitor* alumnus) earlier in 1987 and titled 'All Souled Out'. As for 'cubist' – well, I rather think I must have been thinking of Mondrian, whose style is strictly speaking Neoplasticism.

THE SMITHS

A Eulogy

Infatuation is the true pop response, not considered and evaluative: we all see that, even celebrate it. Why then do we have such trouble with what follows on from infatuation – partisanship, irrational, abiding faith? I'll come clean: for me, The Smiths can do no wrong. Donning my critic's cap, I can see they have regularly produced weak work. But this is what a love affair is *like* – a long waiting out for a repeat of that initial, *initiating* rapture. And The Smiths have regularly delivered that hit, restored to me that first rush.

For all the attempts of critics (especially on this paper) to acknowledge and celebrate the erotic relationship between star and consumer, *fanaticism*, the *un*critical, is the one thing rock criticism can't cope with. But maybe the Letters Page sluggards we regularly castigate for their disproportionate and blind loyalty to New Order or whoever, maybe *they*'re closer to the truth of pop than we'll ever be.

Anyway, on with the serious business, the responsible criticism. Just remember that behind and beyond the lattice of argument course the juices of adoration: pop's primal gush.

Why were The Smiths 'important'? Because of their misery. Never forget it. Around *Meat is Murder* the critics suddenly discovered Morrissey's humour – George Formby was trundled out as a reference point. If you ask me, The Smiths could have afforded to be more *humourless*. The Smiths' finest moments – 'Hand in Glove', 'How Soon is Now?', 'Still Ill', 'I Know It's Over' – were moments of reproachful, avenging misery, naked desperation, unbearable reverence – free of the 'saving grace' of quips and camp self-consciousness. If there was laughter it was black, scornful, scathing. If The Smiths had only produced sunny, cuddly stuff like 'Heaven Knows', 'Ask', 'Vicar in a Tutu', they would have merely presaged the perky negligibility of The Housemartins, the sound that grins itself to death. The Smiths were heroic party-poopers at the *Top of the Pops* office do, glowering at the forced jollity; they were like those gauche youths who turn up to house parties only to cling to the dark corners in chaste disdain, driven by the naive, vaguely inhuman conviction that all merriment is a lie.

The extent to which they were funny actually diminished their impact: it made Morrissey loveable, but it made the music easier to live with, deprived it of edge. Compare The Smiths with Throwing Muses. Both Morrissey and Kristin Hersh work with and within the flux of adolescence – the vacillation between agoraphobia and claustrophobia, possibility and constraint, the feeling that one's body, and the cultural meanings attributed to it, are a cage.

Morrissey crystallizes that flux, turns it into couplets, quips, aphorisms, insights, a wisdom we can draw comfort from. Hersh reproduces that fraught flux, her voice *is* flux. The Smiths are a synopsis of pain, a resolution – awkwardness and alienation ennobled, given poise. Hersh is the *presence* of pain, of falling apart; her voice, the intolerable stress it inflicts on the words, is the sound of the inconsolable wrestling with the insoluble. The difference is between commentary and embodying, identification and voyeurism. It's the reason why The Smiths are more powerful as a pop institution, and why Throwing Muses are more powerful as art.

And The Smiths were important because of their extremism, their unbalanced view of the world, their partiality. Morrissey is a character in a pop era of nonentities, and characters are always lopsided, contrary, incomplete, the sum of wounds and bigotries. There's no such thing as a fully rounded character. Morrissey is 'half a person', his very being constituted around lack, maladjustment – this is the vantage point from which he launches his impossible demands on life, his denial of the reality principle. Satisfaction and adjustment could never enter The Smiths' picture, for this would breach their identity.

This is why Morrissey can't 'develop' as an artist. How can he grow when his very being is constructed around the petulant refusal – 'I *won't* grow up'? The refusal to be responsible and motivated, to get a job, to take on the brutalization and disenchantment entailed in 'gainful' employment. The refusal to collude in the state of dreamlessness that is adulthood, even to the pyrrhic point of clinging stubbornly to the state of being unsatisfied, forever. Having perfected this petulant stance, all he can do is *reiterate* it – with a self-deprecating acknowledgement of the onset of self-parody, 'Stop Me if You Think You've Heard This One Before'.

Not that Morrissey's misery is something we simply identify with. What The Smiths were about was narcissism, damaged, exploding back with a defiant fantasy of martyrdom. The Smiths seduce us into *aspiring* to the same heroic pitch of failure and exile. The tragedy of The Smiths is that Morrissey could only become the victim of the perfection of his style. Like Jagger, like Rotten, he is condemned to live out its pantomime forever.

* * *

When The Smiths first appeared they seemed to be a reaction against the opulence/corpulence of nouveau riche New Pop. Really, they were a return to a different vision of 'new pop', the Postcard ideal. The Smiths were the second coming of Postcard – the whiter-than-white 'pure pop'; the sexual ambiguity; the Luddite insistence on guitars; Edwyn Collins's avowed rating of romance over sex; the swoon instead of the earthy R&B rasp; the flustered undanceability.

What The Smiths returned to the charts was something that pop had seemingly left behind – adolescence. New Pop had rapidly lost its mischief and settled down into a post-rock, post-teenage maturity, peddling naff fantasies of sophistication to a new generation of monied teenyboppers whose only desire was to grow up as soon as possible. The Smiths, on the other hand, provided fantasies of innocence to those in the process of leaving behind their adolescence. Their constituency was the silent majority of music paper readers that critics love to sneer at; students, ex-students, and those destined to be students (sixth-formers and fifth-formers).

Situated in the space between the constraints of childhood and having a career, these are people who dream for a while of wanting a vague something more from life, yet are saddened by these dreams because they know deep down they'll probably relinquish them, buckle down to a life of mediocrity. When this happens, the records get harder to listen to, the music gets to be like a reproach, stirring up the taunting ghosts of prematurely forgone dreams. Nagging 'but . . . you've got everything now', 'please save your life / because you've only got one' . . . which is why people give up pop music, in the end.

New Pop, far from being a bright new beginning, turned out to be merely the inauguration of global designer-soul, the soundtrack to the new yuppie culture of health and efficiency. In the face of the benign totalitarianism of leisure capitalism and its off-the-peg self-improvement, The Smiths glamorized debility and illness, advocated absenteeism, withdrawal, the failure to meet quotas of enjoyment. The profound embarrassment of Morrissey's dancing turned the lack of oneness with your body into glamour. All the self-squandering and deficiency of lifeskills that animated The Birthday Party and The Fall, The Smiths turned into brilliant, glamorous, consumable pop, two-minute bursts of otherness in the heart of the charts.

They were meant to be The Rolling Stones of their time. If The Stones' appropriation of black R&B sexuality was the supremely relevant response to straitlaced, petit bourgeois English suburbia, then The Smiths' refusal of the travesty of healthy sexuality that black pop degenerated into, was the appropriate response to eighties 'liberated' suburbia. The Smiths deployed the imagery of provincial Northern life, the residues of a lost Englishness, as a weapon against the cheap hedonism of an Americanized southern England. The very parochial stuffiness that The Stones reacted against had somehow become an alluring and reproachful memory.

For The Stones, desire was obviously the enemy of materialism, work and a planned life. But today desire has become incorporated into the domain of *your life's work*. Getting in touch with your body, getting in touch with your soul, has become a humanist work-out. 'Satisfaction' had become *feasible*, something you could plan for. The Smiths, hooked on the glamour of the misfit, could only occupy an IMPOSSIBLE position, attempt to create a rock music where aggression was replaced by vulnerability, hedonism by asceticism.

From the private pain, the furtive 'minor language' of unrequited obsession, that they began with, The Smiths went public, became the rock band, the pollwinners, ombudsmen for wider grievance. Whether speaking out for the silent rock majority against the soulboy mediacrats, or representing The Smiths as media martyrs, Morrissey ascended a paranoiac spiral of statesmanship (paranoia is only inverted narcissism) – check the progression from 'Panic' through *The World Won't Listen* and *Louder Than Bombs*, to *Strangeways, Here We Come*.

Morrissey is a new kind of pop star. Steeped in the history of pop, in writing about pop, himself a fanatic, he has an acute understanding of the mechanics of fan obsession. And like various other bright fellows, he wants to use the mechanism of idolatry to introduce some kind of intelligence and difference into pop.

Unlike most of these bright chappies, Morrissey is a natural. He has *it*. And this is when the most interesting pop occurs – when the enigmatic, illegible, wholly arbitrary forces of fascination (with a singer's face, body, voice) coincide with meaning. Not that Morrissey realizes this. His own version of The Smiths' importance is incorrigibly trad rock – hailing them as the sole vanguard of Meaning and Humanity in the Age of Formica. He'll dismiss Prince because 'he imparts nothing', not realizing that both he and Prince 'say' more in a single trail of falsetto than in their entire lyric sheet; that their difference, their resistance, is embedded in their very mode of utterance. But that's The Smiths for you – a weird mix of the reactionary *and* the progressive. Luddite rockism and polymorphous androgyny. Perhaps the appropriate contradictory response to schizophrenic times, where we're leaving a repressive past for an unknown, unstable future. Who wants to grow up? Who wants to go back?

Melody Maker, 26 September 1987

I'm struck by how, in this requiem for The Smiths, the contributions of the band – let alone songwriting partner Johnny Marr – get nary a mention! Especially remiss when you consider the difficulties the solo Morrissey had in finding side-men to match the musical distinctiveness of The Smiths. Durutti Column's Vini Reilly helped make *Viva Hate* half-great, and there's a fair few flickers through the rest of the solo career. But only *Your Arsenal*'s 'Seasick but Still Docked' and *Vauxhall and I*'s 'I Am Hated For Loving' hold a candle to The Smiths at their peak. The adulation for his two twenty-first-century comebacks to date is wishful thinking, a sentimental (if wholly understandable) pining for Characters of Mozzer's magnitude, for a figure who's simultaneously pure pop and anti-pop: 'one of us', *in there*. In his *Viva Hate* review David Stubbs nailed the point and purpose of Morrissey in his true moment and absolute prime: 'Morrissey is needed, not as an ombudsman, or a figure of the eighties, but as a horrified figure *against* the eighties, who has turned his back on the march of pop time as the last keeper of the sanctuary of self-pity, apartness, exile.'

PUBLIC ENEMY

Get this. Public Enemy are a superlative *rock* band. Everything about them, from their attitude (renegade street cool given extra edge by a fierce dose of radical chic) to their sound (an implacable juggernaut of grunge-metal riffs, white noise, dub-space and galvanized R&B beats) puts them in *our* camp, and dead sets them against the designer soul we all abhor, the smooth, suave, placatory pseudo-sophistication that smothers the entire surface of Planet Pop. However you define 'rock' – as urgency, aggression, vehemence, the will both to face reality and to exceed its limits, or just as big noise – Public Enemy fit the bill.

I'm in the offices of Rush Management, sister company of Def Jam, located in Manhattan's Lower East Side not far from the Bowery (as in 'bum') and CBGBs. Sat opposite is the articulate and emphatic Chuck D, chief firebrand and ranting poet of Public Enemy, 'the Black Panthers of Rap'. And I'm asking Chuck if this monstrous, brutal noise of theirs actually belongs to the category of Black Music any more or does it (as I believe) represent a complete break from black pop tradition?

Chuck doesn't quite agree: 'Hip hop *is* black because it uses elements of soul and R&B – the tension, the friction – that have been lost. Most music made by black people today is caught up in synthesized overproduction, it's trying to cross over, and it sounds GREY.'

As in bleached-out, whitified, Burchill's beigebeat?

'No, just *grey*, period. Rap music has more soul than any of this so-called soul.'

Hmm, can't see it myself, can't really relate hip hop's frigid, heart-less solipsism to soul's limpid, outreaching warmth. I reckon Chuck

47

D's belief in a continuity between R&B and hip hop is a kind of *moral conviction* (Chuck sets great store in blacks having a consciousness of their history). I can't see *any* precedents in black pop for the harsh drone-squall of 'Terminator X Speaks With His Hands', for the piercing blare of unidentifiable sound on the extraordinary 'Rebel Without a Pause', nor for the way these noises are repeated mechanically, inexpressively, without inflection, wholly alienated from the human touch, in an endless cycle of attrition.

Chuck, where soul and funk are about getting loose and grooving, your kind of hardcore hip hop is wound-up, clenched, it's hardly a release, more like further harassment.

'What we like to do is take elements from soul that make you feel good and draw you in, and put those sounds and beats next to noises that are gonna push you away. So the listener is kind of coming and going, walking a line, thinking "Oh lord, turn that off" and, at the same time, not wanting to turn it off.'

This is the opposite of fusion: a kind of suspended animation fission, where inconsistent sounds are frozen in mutual contradiction, within the same soundspace.

'It's a *conscious* process. Records like "Public Enemy No. 1" take a helluva long time to mix, cos it's very easy to turn people off, but not so easy to get a balance between turning people on and harassing them.'

What happens technically?

'The sampled sounds come from anywhere. Take "Rebel Without a Pause". A lot of people said *that* noise came from a James Brown grunt, but what they didn't realize was that it was a *blend* of the grunt and a Miles Davis trumpet, which produced a sound that wavered. And then we took that tone and *stretched* it. The drone on 'Terminator X Speaks' and 'M.P.E.' is a backwards fire truck!'

Amazingly, 'Rebel', the B-side from the last single that has now become a club sensation and a highly sought-after rarity, *isn't* going to be given another push, although it is appearing on the next album. Instead, there's another single off the *Yo! Bum Rush the Show* album-masterpiece: 'Sophisticated' (the 'Bitch' of the original title and 'all the curses' have been excised so's to court radio) backed by a new track, 'Bring the Noise', which is appearing on the soundtrack of the movie of *Less Than Zero*.

'It's a pumpin' track, 109 beats per minute, which is fast for hip hop. It's a gamble.'

Death to Disco

Chuck D adheres to the Def Jam party line: that rap is black rock 'n' roll, that it's based around rock 'n' roll's 4/4 beat rather than disco's pulse beat, that its renegade, vandalistic attitude is the antithesis of disco's aspirations to showbiz acceptance.

'My thing is I don't like House music. I first heard it as a DJ, when I was doing radio shows, and I said then that I thought the beats lacked soul, they didn't *move* you. Certainly you could move to it, by choice, but they don't *move* you like a 4/4 beat does. You can use that disco pulse beat, but you have to have something that's FUNKY in there, a bassline, otherwise you just got all these drum machines playing like a load of metronomes. I think it's EASY to make those kind of records. I like that M.A.R.R.S. record cos it mixes up House with hip hop, but Chicago House, like go-go is . . . overrated, and you can tell because neither House nor go-go has sparked in *other* areas. Whereas hip hop, which has been kept down cos it's the young black man speaking LOUD, has broken out *all* over – in the South, in California, in Britain, Europe, Japan . . .

'And I dislike the scene that's based around House – it's "sophisti-cated!", anti-black, anti-culture, anti-feel, the most ARTIFICIAL shit I ever heard. It represents the Gay scene, it's separating blacks from their past and their culture, it's upwardly mobile. People see the music as a luxury item, a social status thing, something to "elevate me from all that B-boy shit I was into when I was a teenager, something to lift me from my normal surroundings" – and I hate that shit, I HATE it. It's not so much the music as the attitude that goes along with it of "don't speak loud, dance to the music". It's BULLSHIT.'

Trad rock objections to disco, these, but the point is that this magical dissolution of origins, of class, race and sexual differences, is what the dancefloor is all about. House constructs its ideal consumer as a biracial androgyne, lost in a swirl of polymorphous sensuality and fantasy glamour, lost for words and lost to the world. Immediately outside the club, the world and all its differences impinge: people kill each other on the doorsteps of paradise (or even the Paradise Garage).

'Hip hop and rock have ATTITUDE – the idea that if you're upset about something, you express it through your music, if you like some-thing, you express it through the music. This is something that House does not do. It's completely expressionless. And, for a lot of blacks, it's just something to support if you don't want to be into hip hop, for whatever reasons.'

Rebel With a Cause

They try, oh but they do try. Whenever Left-inclined subcultural theorists encounter a black pop culture, they always follow the same syllogistic reasoning. Blacks are an oppressed class. Such-and-such is a music of black origin. Therefore, such-and-such a music must be animated, at however sublimated and submerged a level, by currents of resistance to the way-things-are. Often the desperation to locate such micro-resistance, to uncover a subtext of cultural dissidence, results in bizarre interpretations. So the venerable Dr Paul Gilroy can argue in *City Limits* that Eric B and Rakim's 'Paid in Full' is a 'demystification of their means of production'.

Demystification, eh? The guys are on the make, they want in, they're *counting* their money, and if they're not as cynical as Schoolly D (who won't put out unless he's paid in full, IN ADVANCE), it's still hardly worth *celebrating*. So much for all the cant about hip hop serving a community. The trouble with hip hop is that, no matter how you juggle the subcultural arithmetic, the end product is not going to be a clearly defined 'contribution to the struggle'. The politics of hip hop occupy a different space altogether.

Take Public Enemy. Chuck D's political orientation derives from the inspiration of the Black Panthers, the sixties black activists. 'It's something I'm still learning about, so I don't know how much I can tell you. Right now, we've been meeting up with some former Panthers from the Oakland area, California, where the Black Panthers first started. There were a lot of racial problems in that area, and what the Panthers did was to structure and organize a force that represented order and strength to the community. They started off peacefully, but, as their demands got rejected, they grew more militant. We're meeting up with ex-Panthers and we're trying to spark off a revival.

'Louis Farrakhan [the leader of the Nation of Islam] is interested in our programme to revitalize and re-educate black youth. We want to build self-respect and a sense of community, because blacks are in a sorry state.'

What caused this demoralization and debility?

'There was complacency in the seventies, after the civil rights victories of the sixties. Plus some of our leaders were killed off, others sold out, or fled. There was propaganda by the state to make it seem like things had changed, a policy of tokenism elevating a few blacks to positions of public prominence, on TV shows and stuff, while the rest was held down. Blacks couldn't understand how they'd suddenly got these advantages, and so they forgot, they got lazy, they failed to teach their young what they had been taught in the sixties about our history and culture, about how *tight* we should be. And so there was a loss of *identity* – we began to think we were accepted as Americans, when in fact we STILL face a double standard every minute of our lives.'

Has there been no improvement in attitudes or opportunities whatsoever? I thought the whole Def Jam stable, for instance, came from a middle-class, suburban background . . .

'People go on about this, about us having cars when we were kids, but y'know, a black suburban neighbourhood is still a black neighbourhood. Black America *is* suburban – places like the New York ghetto aren't the norm. What we need is to build a sense of community and a sense of *business*. We're in a capitalist society, we can't overthrow this government, so we must learn to use the system.'

So your vision of how to change things isn't socialist or collectivist . . .?

'Only among ourselves, black people. I have . . . socialistic ideals, but I also have an awareness of what's real and feasible. Obviously, for America to survive, it'll have to become socialistic, ultimately, cos the system's crumbling now. But, in the meantime, we have to stand on our feet, raise ourselves, because nobody else will do it for us.'

The meantime is a *mean* time. Compare seventies 'political' soul with Public Enemy. With 'What's Goin' On', 'Love Train', 'Why Can't We Live Together', 'We Gotta Have Peace', as well as pristine woe you also got a glimpse, in the angelic purity of the harmonies and arrangements, of a utopian vision of how things should be – a rainbow coalition of love and equality. Compare the plaintiveness of 'Backstabbers' with the vengeful 'You're Gonna Get Yours', Public Enemy's metal-motored anthem. With Public Enemy, there's no vision of the perfect world that is the goal of struggle, there is only a faithful sonic analogue for the disharmonious, fraught social environment and a fetishization of the state of being prepared – masked and armoured – to deal with it. Public Enemy are hooked on the glamour of the means of militancy and mobilization, barely aware of the vague halcyon end.

Would Chuck D even like it if there was integration?

'Once again we're talking fantasy, man! Of course I'd like it if everybody white married somebody black, and then the next generation were all black. Then there'd be no double standard, except the kind of sick, fucked-up thing black people have among themselves that makes them judge between different shades of darkness. But this integration is never gonna happen. So people should stick to their own. Without a strong sense of black consciousness, there's no cohesion, and no survival. The Chinese, the Jews, they stick together, deal with each other. Blacks don't.'

Doesn't rap just reflect that lack of community, what with all the rivalry between MCs and between posses, all against all?

'Yeah – but inside each and every rapper there's something that's saying: "I'm yelling out loud for shit that ain't right." Now he don't know what, cos he's uneducated. A rapper speaks out loud, and really he's asking for help. Cos for the last fifteen years no information has been given to him about the system and so he doesn't understand why he acts the way he acts.'

We're back with subcultural theory again – daily life as rife with acts of micro-resistance, pre-conscious skirmishes with bourgeois ideological hegemony, unarticulated rage – if only it could be channelled into revolution! (The Black Panthers tried to do just that, taking the fact of young black male street criminality, and trying to radicalise it.) Or there's the Situationist dream that all you needed to initiate total revolution was a federation of teenage delinquent gangs – the conclusion of 'too much posse'?!

Soul on Ice

Throughout popular culture, being black is being installed as a signifier for being *more human*. From the histrionics of George Michael and Mick Hucknall, to the Kronenbourg ads (a young *City Limits*-reading man who plays saxophone is tutored in reaching into the depths of his Soul by a wizened black master of the instrument called Earl Page – the slogan: 'A Different Kind of Strength'), blackness is being elaborated as a model of oneness with your body, of being in touch with your emotions, of a new, more acceptable kind of masculinity. The cluster of ideas here have quite a genealogy – the depth that comes with a history of Suffering; the idea of the Black as warmer, looser, less hung-up than the white; the offensive notion of 'natcherel riddim'.

While white pop bases itself entirely around the form and ethos of Black Passion, what's fascinating is that black pop has gone in the opposite direction, becoming colder, more inhuman – in the case of hip hop, more wound-up, manacled; in the case of House, dispassionate, inexpressive, plastic. Hip hop is (to abuse Eldridge Cleaver's fine phrase) – SOUL ON ICE – a survivalist retreat from engagement with the outside world or other people, back to the frozen shell of a minimal self. There's a new kind of relation to the body, not the slow suffusion of 'getting in touch', but more domineering a regime, a priming of the machine in readiness for self-defence or massive retaliation.

This is the DISS'TOPIA. An eternal now forever teetering on the brink of extinction, a world without narrative (that's why 'Rebel Without a Pause' is like a locked groove): the hip hop ego traverses a 'treacherous' soundscape, constantly faces sonic ambush or mined terrain, always overcomes, can never rest.

Klaus Thewelweit, in his book, *Male Fantasies*, takes the Freikorps – First World War veterans who formed into right-wing militia in the post-war years in order to suppress proletarian Communist uprisings, and who later became a substantial component of the Nazi street-fighting cadres – and examines their correspondence, diaries, poetry and favoured literature in order to psychoanalyse their attitudes to women and femininity. He notes a startling consistency in the imagery used: women, female sexuality, emotion (the feminine side of men) and popular Communism, are all described in terms of floods, lava, 'streaming', unstaunchable flows of fluid. Thewelweit suggests that masculinity is constructed around a chronic terror of being swept away on a tide of desire, of being swallowed up by oceanic feelings, of the borders of the self being dissolved, and this fear goes back to the original moment of being severed from the mother, the moment at which the male ego was constituted. Men can only consolidate their selves by trampling again and again on femininity, both *inside* and outside themselves.

The relevance of this to hip hop should be fairly obvious. If soul singers like Al Green and Prince melt sexual divisions into a world of fluid, androgynous bliss, then hip hop freezes sexual divisions, hard. In more sense than one, hip hop is not a *fluent* music. As Chuck D says: 'Rap is like psychology – you can see people's insides.' Are they a pretty sight?

Where do women fit into the Public Enemy picture? Do they?

'Of *course*, they have a place. Man is husband and woman is wife. You can only go to that point with me. You can even have black women leaders to a degree. But I think that, where America has elevated a few women in a process of tokenism, in order to keep the black man down, as we pointed out in "Sophisticated Bitch", then I think it's maybe time to go back to some kind of *original structure*.'

This reminds me of an open letter written by a Black Pantheress to a sister who was more feminist and had complained about black men's attitudes to their women: 'Don't cut your black man's balls off, sister. Because the white man has already cut off his balls once, and how's he ever going to be a real man if you don't support him?'.

You seem to be into firm, fixed borderlines – between races, between sexes, between straight and gay.

'Borderlines have to be set, because borderlines are *there*. If ten whites and ten blacks go to an interview, and ten jobs are available, you can bet your life it ain't gonna be five/five, it'll be nine white jobs and one black. So, for us there has to be cohesion. And men should be men and women should be women. And there's no room in the black race for gays, a black gay can't raise a kid, the kid's gonna be confused enough as it is being black. Lines have to be set. There has to be guidance. The shit has to be stable.'

So uncertainty is a privilege, a luxury for white middle-class people (like me).

'Uncertainty is bullshit, as far as black people are concerned.'

Farrakhan's name comes up again. 'You see what someone like Farrakhan has to face is a hostile media who'll take what he says out of context. Like the "Hitler was a great man" comment. What he meant was that he was a mighty and powerful man, not a *good* man. A great organizer of men.'

I don't know, even a disinterested and dispassionate admiration for Hitler's leadership prowess is distasteful and suspect.

'Right now, we need leaders. We're the only people who can raise ourselves. I don't think anything will be achieved in my lifetime, but a start can be made, and maybe by the next century we'll be so strong and independent that only overt aggression will threaten us, a wave of lynching. Right now, they don't need to destroy us, cos we're doing it to ourselves.'

Finally I get to talk to Griff, leader of Security of the First World, Public Enemy's security force and . . . well, it turns out to be rather more complex and peculiar than I'd imagined.

'The name Security of the First World reflects our belief that Africa and Asia are not the Third World and that America is *definitely* not the First World. If you look at history you see that mathematics and science and all kinds of culture began in Africa and Asia. So our job is securing the knowledge of that history. Our job is the Preservation of the Young Black Mind. And that's a big task. We have meetings and discussion groups where we educate ourselves in our history and culture, or we discuss the present conditions of blacks in America and Africa.

'But our main function is to attend concerts of Public Enemy. There we're onstage to project images of strength and order, send signals to our people that these are young black men who are standing up, who ain't gonna back off, that's for sure. We're not trying to control their physical behaviour at the concert, although we can't have any rampaging, we're trying to control their mind, not their physical safety.

54

We want to indicate to them that there is an ability to bind and conform in a chaotic situation. We wear paramilitary uniform, because everybody wears uniform today – Gaddafi, Khomeini. What else do we do? We mingle with the crowd, we talk, we enlist. We've met up with Farrakhan's son. Everybody who joins gets involved in physical training. Martial arts.'

So as to acquire a sense of one's own power?

'Because once you know yourself mentally and physically, you're better able to *deal*.'

One of the things that struck me this trip was the way Americans use the word 'to deal' intransitively – a sure indicator of the survivalist mindset of the whole nation.

'We do drill, it's called the Fruit of Islam. It brings about *harmonious totality* among ourselves. Sixty guys all in one step.'

Getting wasted on drink, drugs or women is right out.

Ahem. What *can* I say? Rectitude in the face of chaos. An admiration for Colonel Gaddafi ('blacks in America didn't know who to side with'). Harmonious *totality*. No faggots. Uniform and drill. It all sounds quite logical and *needed*, the way they tell it. And it's all very dodgy indeed.

If there's one thing more scary than a survivalist, it's a whole bunch of survivalists organized into a regiment. It must be that when a group of young men band together in a tight unit and around a very *channelled* mindset, a particular structure develops, and it's pretty much the same structure, or 'desiring machine' that's behind Communist youth groups, the Freikorps, any army anywhere in the world, and Fascists.

Fortunately, Public Enemy and Security of the First World are sufficiently powerless ('fifty-two and growing') to remain fascinating to us pop swots, rather than disturbing.

'A lot of the critics pick up on the violence element,' says Chuck D. 'But they don't understand that it's an analogy. It's like "my Uzi weighs a ton". No gun weighs that much, it's a metaphor, a strong image, cos you got to grab people, *wake* them up. It's like if I hit you over the head with this stapler, you'd give me 100 per cent attention, maybe even 150 per cent! So what I'm doing is cracking heads, but *verbally*, and with NOISE!'

Let's hope it stays that way.

Melody Maker, 17 October 1987

Gotta give myself a pat on the back here for two things. 1) Making the rock connection, something substantiated a couple of years later when PE teamed up with Anthrax to do a thrash

55

metal remake of 'Bring the Noise'. Later I learned how Hank Shocklee and the Bomb Squad deliberately deployed mid-frequency sounds to give Public Enemy records a sonic attack similar to punk and metal. 2) Okay, maybe the Freikorps allusion was a little over the top (I got some flak for this, 'it's different when an oppressed minority does this kind of thing', etc.). Except maybe not, given the scandal that blew up over Professor Griff's anti-Semitic comments, further exacerbated by Chuck D's lyric in 'Welcome to the Terrordome'. I felt a vindicating rush of retrospective clairvoyance when PE started airing loads of loopy racial theories in their interviews, like the notion that white people liked acid-rock because they were descended from tribes in the Caucasus who lived in caves with lots of echo! I interviewed Chuck D a second time, and unchastened by the controversy, he described PE's new single 'Can't Truss It' in terms of genocide envy. 'There was a Jewish holocaust, but there's a black holocaust that people still choose to ignore . . . it's hard to believe that for two hundred years ships sailed the ocean with a cargo of slaves . . . Jews are screaming over the 1932–1945 period – that's the headline for their story of persecution which stretches back to the Middle Ages. The black holocaust goes back centuries too, but we don't have that headline.' True enough, but not the most diplomatic way of making the point, given the recent brouhaha. Despite considerable reservations, PE remained a favourite noise and a touchstone for their ability to make political-cultural waves. For four albums (two of which, #1 and #3, are solid gold), PE did what no rock band then or since seemingly could: not just comment on, but connect with, real issues and real stakes in the outside world; aggravating the contradictions and making the wounds rawer and harder to ignore.

LL COOL J

This weekend, as I wait for the phone call that will tell me when I'm finally to be admitted into His Presence, I have time – plenty of time – to muse on Who LL Cool J Thinks He Is.

LL Cool J is probably the most magnificent megalomaniac in the hip hop gallery of distended egos. There's rap that's more chilling (Schoolly D), noise that's more brutally avant-garde (Public Enemy, Skinny Boys), but no one's so eloquent about his omnipotence as LL. His raps are the closest hip hop's come to poetry. No one dreams up more humorously preposterous scenarios as flattering backdrops for the display of invincibility. On 'I'm Bad', the cops are in pursuit of a big brother with dimples and a Kangol; at the end, through sirens and the theme from 'Shaft', comes the panic-stricken radio voice of an officer – 'I think I need backup! I think I need backup!' – and suddenly, somehow, LL is in the car with him in possession of the mike. On 'My Rhyme Ain't Done', the Pope gets God to bring Michelangelo back from the dead so's to paint a picture of LL's head, he plays polo with the Queen, journeys to the centre of the earth, goes through the TV screen to chill out with cartoon characters like Spiderman, Snoopy, Tom and Jerry, and Mickey Mouse, visits Wonderland ('all the while my eyes were on Alice's behind'), and travels through time to meet Washington and Sitting Bull. And 'since I'm a good friend of Father Time / I'm not getting older as I say this rhyme'.

I think about LL's comparisons of himself to Napoleon and Hitler, about *strange* lyrics like 'They call me Jaws / My hand is like a shark's fin' and 'I'm an executioner / I should wear a black hood.' I consider that voice – bug-eyed, white-knuckled, Tyson-veined, clenching you up inside taut and murderous, making you want to stomp victims. I think about other journos' tales of his brattish behaviour, of the fact that the evaporation of my weekend is down to LL's last-minute whim-decision on Thursday to go AWOL instead of boarding a plane. I'm even struck by how his face has a vague resemblance to a Nazi helmet – that sleek, matte finish, that dull *glans* sheen. And does he *really* say, in one song, 'I'm the Nietzsche of Rap'?

Slowly, a vision of LL Cool J takes form. There's a truism that under a pop *persona* lies a real *person*, flawed and vulnerable and human. But maybe there is no 'real' LL Cool J, just a shell, an aggregation or accretion of claims and fantasies. Empty vessels make the most sound. Maybe being larger than life is LL's truest being, maybe when he's impossible he's most himself: as he raps it himself, 'even when I'm bragging I'm being sincere'. Maybe that should run, 'only when I'm bragging'?

As it turns out, my vision of Who He Is is somewhat different from LL's. Not that I exactly confront him head-on over the contested nature of his identity, more that a strategy of leading questions (give 'em enough rope) met with doggedly humane, humanist replies. LL *appears* to be distressingly level-headed. Judging by this showing, success has *not* gone to his head – to my ill-concealed chagrin. He's civil, and if not overly friendly, always *gracious*.

Over here, some people are miffed with LL for breaking big with a piece of saccharine soft-centre cornball like 'I Need Love'. Others (Stuart Cosgrove in *City Limits*) have hailed the dawn of 'lovers' rap' – like lovers' rock, a female-oriented offshoot of a militant, masculine music. So was 'I Need Love' a calculated crossover bid?

'Not at all. It's funny you should even ask that. It's just a ballad. I had two ballads on the first album, 'I Can Give You More' and 'I Want You', but they didn't have as much *music*, they was more minimalist. I just made a ballad, and it happened to crossover, but it wasn't *made* to crossover.'

So it's just a different side to LL?

'It's no different side – HA HA HA – I just made a smooth record.'

Does the song come from personal experience?

'It's *true* – when I wrote it that day, I needed love.'

You were thinking regretfully about all the hearts you've broken?

'Yup.'

Have you ever had *your* heart broken?

'No – as you can see from that record.'

What's your idea of the perfect girl?

'I don't believe there's any such thing as a "perfect girl". There's *nice* girls.'

[Pressing on in hope of some rank, unsound remark] – What qualities make up a 'nice girl'?

'What kind of qualities? She can't be greedy. Or too meaty. Nice looking, a *nice* girl – you KNOW what a nice girl is, a nice girl to me is a nice girl to you!'

How do you approach girls that you fancy?

'I don't. I just say "hello". I treat 'em all with respect – doesn't matter if I like 'em or not.' LL gargles some phlegm around the back of his throat. He has a cold.

Do you go in for sweet-talking?

LL and his minions have a good long laugh at my dogged pursuit of this line of enquiry. 'I guess every guy who takes a girl out does a bit of sweet-talking. But I tell the truth, I don't run the same line on all of them, I'm real spontaneous in that area.'

[One last desperate probe] – There *is* quite a difference, a chasm, between the romantic balladry and the bulk of your material, which is extremely aggressive?

'It's just another part of music, man. You can't take it as such a deep thing.'

Evidently LL believes he can bridge the gap: indeed, *Bigger and Deffer* was originally going to be called *A Gangster and a Lover*. Of course, in reality, the tough but tender man, the guy who's a hard-hearted operator in the big bad world and a gentle lover in private, is a myth, he just doesn't exist. I like 'I Need Love' because the female fantasy it appeals to/exploits is as underripe and implausible as the boys' fantasies of breaking hearts and busting balls that LL normally traffics in. When will London's 'post-rock' mediacrassy learn to *face*, let alone celebrate, the ludicrous, the impossible in the black pop they espouse so vigorously?

So now you're starting to be massive both here and in the States . . . presumably you always wanted to be the centre of attention, but does it ever get to be a strain?

'Nothing is perfect, right. But sometimes you enjoy it. Like recently I went to a motor vehicle place cos my temporary licence had expired and, instead of waiting in a long long queue, some of the girl security guards knew who I was and they shuffled me through real quick. I got my licence in half an hour and, if I was ordinary, I would have had to wait for a long, long time. But sometimes, when I want to go to the movies and chill out with a girl, it's hectic. So it goes back and forth.'

You have a lot of girl fans, for a rap artist. Why are you the first rap teen heart-throb?

'I don't like the sex symbol idea, because you can get a scar here and be *over*. But I guess the girls maybe heard the early ballads, saw where I was coming from. I'm on *it* like that, I *like* girls and they like me, it's a chemistry thing. But I didn't start with that in mind, I just wanted to be LL, and then it growed in that direction.'

Do you ever worry about surpassing what you've done? How can a scenario like 'My Rhyme Ain't Done' be topped?

'That was a fantasy thing. It's real visual, if you turn the lights out in your room and just listen to it. That day I was *dusted*, tripping! I don't mean dusted as in taking angel dust, I mean I went off into another land, into myself.'

You don't believe in taking drugs, do you?

'I don't get high. Cos you get bags under your eyes and your career gets shortened.'

Drink?

'Not really. I drink a little Mo-et Chandon,' he says in a sophisticated sing-song, tapping the ice bucket with his foot. 'I'm on a healthy tip, you know. I don't do push-ups everyday, but I don't get high. Clean-cut, do what I got to do, living this life, working hard, trying to make something outta myself.'

There's that picture of you boxing on the back of the album . . .

'I like boxing. I like *fighting*, period.'

Will there ever come a point where you have nothing left to prove?

'I never had nothing to prove,' he says at first, as if mindful that it may be uncool to admit to ever having been less than totally assured. 'Well, with the second album I had to prove the first was no fluke, to those who were saying I couldn't cut it without Rick Rubin. With the third album, I have to prove it again. I'm always gonna stay hungry, always have the eye of the tiger. I'm not gonna put on a pair of sunglasses and move to Cali and be Hollywood Cool J.'

Is LL a character?

'Oh no, I'm *me*, offstage and onstage. This is how I am. Unlike some rappers, I'm me *all* the time.'

So you're super-confident all the time! Isn't that a strain?

'Everybody who wants to be successful has to be confident.'

Were you always this confident, even as a child?

'I don't want you to mix confidence with being arrogant and conceited.' He looks wary. 'You might be on that tip, I don't know. A better way to put it is, "proud of what you achieve", a sense of establishment, of accomplishment.'

But what LL excels at is 'talking on myself' which involves a paradox – rap is about being proud of your pride, striving to be the best at saying you're the best, becoming somebody through an art whose message boils down to the simple assertion 'I *Am* Somebody'. Meaning evaporates, content absconds, there is only assertion, force, presence, an arbitrary authority. For all his verbosity, LL is the logocrat who presides over the death of Meaning: a density of variations on an attenuated, minimal theme, all art and no matter. The message is the mode of utterance (articulating the relationship between rapper and fan as despotic monologue) and that message is simply 'I'm *telling* you.'

'It all goes back to when you start out rapping in the park. You want to make a name for yourself, you want to be better than the guy who went before you. You've got to talk about how bad you are *better* than he talked about how cool he was. That street attitude of wanting to be recognized, that eye of the tiger attitude, carries on to when you start recording.'

Do you ever have any doubts or fears?

'Doubts or fears?' – LL gropes for a platitude – '*Everybody* has doubts and fears. If you don't have them, then you're not human.'

Cravenly, I let slip the chance to cry: yes yes, exactly, that's the issue, that's what I'm trying to establish, just how *human* you are.

'What, do you think I'm Superman, that only Kryptonite can destroy me?'

Well, a lot of the record is about being invincible . . .

This LL only accepts when some of his lyrics are quoted at him. 'But I also talk about positive things, like how people should stay on at college and make something of themselves. I talk about love.'

Can you imagine wanting to be anyone but yourself?

'No, I can honestly say I'm glad I'm me.'

Not even someone in history?

'No, I really want to be me.' Sniggering, he adds, 'You just want to see who I compare myself with. That's how the English press works.'

(Yup, I was hoping for Hitler, Genghis Khan or Pol Pot.)

Amused, LL muses: 'Hmmm, maybe I'd be . . . a good king. That doesn't kill his slaves, y'know what I'm saying. Ha, that ends up getting murdered by someone in the court!'

A benevolent despot – to offset the malicious tyrant of vinyl, the LL who is not particularly distressed by the notion 'when you're rich you got friends / when you're poor, you're alone'.

Do people ever bug you?

'Sometimes. I don't like to call it bugging. Sometimes people ADMIRE you a little too much. Sometimes they let you know how much they like you *too* much.'

What's the next record going to be like?

'Ha – I ain't saying! But it'll be more *threatening*.'

And that's that. LL shakes my hand, a clasp so firm and vigorous I'm almost pulled out of my seat.

The LL Cool J I met was neither the 'real LL', the little boy that perhaps exists miles beneath the armour, nor the *real* LL, the young rap autocrat, but a platitudinous, regular-seeming being that perhaps only exists in interview. Remember, in America, they don't have a music press, pop stars are not expected to open up *or* to discourse on the outside world – just to be 'nice'. Anyway, in print, I'm as despotic as LL is onstage, and I know I'm right. LL is a hip hop Fuehrer. Submit to the sweet kiss of his rap jackboot today.

Melody Maker, 7 November 1987

I still think LL Cool J might be my favourite rapper – MC-ing has gotten way more sophisticated flow-wise since his day, but there's a time-defying perfection to LL's delivery, a stark clarity and punch. Talking of which, 'Mama Said Knock You Out' gets my vote for most powerful rap performance ever. Reviewing the album in question, at a point when LL's profile seemed to be slipping, the track struck me as being like an over-the-hill former champion making a vain bid to retake the world heavyweight title; lines such as 'I'm the man of the hour / Tower of power . . . ' oozed the gripping pathos of a doomed but still deluded dictator like Ceauşescu or Saddam Hussein. But of course that song and its album did put LL back on top. And he's *still* going strong, arguably hip hop's most enduring star, even if nowadays the trademark Kangol hat makes him look a bit like a Flowerpot Man.

DINOSAUR JR

They're not much to look at, Dinosaur. It's hard to connect this shaggy, sheepish trio with the tempest they unleash, live and on vinyl. They are unimpressive, and *unimpressed* – seemingly – by anything and everything, but least of all, by themselves. The rest of us may be enjoying the dawning realization that *You're Living All Over Me* is one of the year's masterpieces, but Dinosaur themselves are groggily unconscious of just how good they are.

It's as though the noise is somehow independent of them, that it's *chosen them*, that they're just motes, broken reeds, in a gust that storms *through* them. When Dinosaur play live, there's a slackness to J Mascis's wrist that seems incommensurate to the shock wave, the ridge of pressure, that buffets you as a result of its languid flick. Mascis holds the guitar almost vertical, pointing skyward; there's a certain angle of holding beyond which the guitar ceases to be a *weapon* (neither phallus nor the cutting edge of 'attitude'), where the fretboard opens up into a firmament, what David Stubbs calls 'the new guitar air'. Dinosaur reach that critical angle, that point where self-projection is surpassed by self-dispersal, where a band is celebrating the noise, rather than using the noise to celebrate themselves. Maybe just *allowing* the noise.

Perhaps it's as well Dinosaur don't have pride. If they started to hold their heads a little higher, walk tall, they might emerge from the spiritual slump, the crumpled fogginess of being that, paradoxically, enables them to speed across the horizon. Confidence rarely makes for great music. And Dinosaur are the sound of galvanized lethargy, vibrant despondency. Grey skies have seldom blazed so bright, surged so furiously.

Everything interesting in rock is happening at the extremes – rectitude *or* lassitude, hypermotivation (Public Enemy, Nitzer Ebb) or complete unmotivation (Dinosaur, Band of Susans), militant or dormant. Rigid backbone or wholly spineless. Raised consciousness or

63

floored semi-consciousness. The fanatic's inhuman clarity of vision, eyes wired and wide, or the mystic and the mixed-up's haze, eyes half-closed. The rant or the murmur. The middleground – capability, emotional competence, commitment, continence, dialogue – is completely uninteresting. Against this world of getting on, getting things done, getting (yourself) together, Dinosaur are radically non-committal, untogether. They're supine, but they fly far higher.

To put it another way, Dinosaur don't *recognize* the indisputable 'relevance' of The Staple Singers' 'Respect Yourself', it's not part of their tradition. Not that they muster themselves for anything as concerted as frittering away their potential, just that they lapse, succumb to a subsidence that perhaps only American middle-class kids are capable of, becoming the conduits for an amorphous vastness of sound.

When I meet J Mascis (the guy who failed to turn up for an interview in New York with me because he lost the piece of paper with the address on) I'm greeted by a dazed, dopey Eeyore grin. There's something boneless about J, something redolent of the halfwit (or perhaps an even smaller fraction of the full complement). He responds to my questions with genial bafflement, a stymied catatonia: he can't figure out why anyone would want to know, but at least finds the rigmarole faintly amusing. Lou Barlow, the bassist, seems to be in pain; Murph, the drummer, unperturbed.

There's some confusion about the name, they've been forced to amend it to Dinosaur Jr. 'We got sued by this group called The Dinosaurs, who are comprised of former members of Jefferson Airplane, Quicksilver Messenger Service and Country Joe and the Fish,' explains J.

The members of Dinosaur started in hardcore bands. What made them begin to widen their frame of sound, stray into wiggy territory?

'They were influences from before then, *before* the third, second and first generations of punk even. It's pretty standard rock chronology – Beatles, Aerosmith, Sabbath, Ramones, Pistols, Eater, UK Subs . . .'

Hold on . . . *Eater*?!?

'That LP's my favourite of all time.'

Are you a . . . cheerful bunch?

J (archly): 'Of *course*!'

Lou: 'No. Definitely not.'

J: 'I think so.'

Lou: 'No.'

The whole aspect is somewhat . . . bleak.

Lou: 'Pretty bleak, yeah.'

J (mock incredulous): 'No! No way!'

Lou: 'Comparatively.'

J: 'We're not *starving.*'

Murph: 'Not physically, but *emotionally.*' (Laughs) 'Emotionally, we're starving. Whatever I deal with is a struggle.'

That's sad.

Murph: 'I try not to think too much.' That's the sound of Dinosaur – the mind being wiped clean, returned to a slate-grey blankness.

What's your attitude to life, J?

J (as though emerging from a deep sleep): 'What? Oh, I don't want to get into this. I don't even wanna think about my philosophy of life.' Minutes seem to elapse. 'Paaaarty all the time.' Unconvincing.

Lou has a strange way with a bass: he seems to be cuffing it, chastising it. 'I used to play hardcore guitar, and you really work your wrists. I used to be able to twice as fast, but my bones have atrophied.'

Live, I felt like I was surfing, or standing on a shingle beach, facing breakers. You feel yourself surging, swaying slightly at the hips. The sound hits you in the face like spray.

Murph: 'Most of the songs, J will say "ride on the cymbals", fill out the sound. Otherwise there's too much emptiness.'

J: 'Smashing on the cymbals swirls everything together.'

The other element of flux that leaves the listener breath-bereft and hurtling are your guitar effects.

J: 'They have names like Electric Mistress, Clone Theory, Big Muff, Cry Baby. They're all real cheesy weirdness effects, old and out of date. They're more severe than the effects you get today.'

This parallels the way groups like Band of Holy Joy and Suicide like to use outmoded, primitive synth technology because you get harsher, more alien, fake tones.

J: 'It's all that sounds *good*. The new stuff, it works on a smaller range, it's designed for *subtleties* rather than . . . *harshities.*'

Murph delivers pizzas. J still goes to college. Lou takes care of old ladies in resting homes and half-way houses. Is Dinosaur the best thing in their lives?

Murph: 'No. probably the worst.'

Lou: 'It's just the *thing*, it's part of our lives.'

What's your favourite activity, then? Or favourite passivity, even?

Murph: 'I used to like skiing in the winter.'

Lou: 'I *used* to like music a lot. Hahahaha!"

Have you not got one, J?

'It sounds too hard . . . to sit down . . . and figure it all . . . out.'

Lou: 'It's kind of cool being in Europe and stuff.'

You don't *sound* as though you think it's cool, I say tetchily.

They rally a bit. 'Oh no, I really *do* think it's cool.'

Murph: 'Oh yeah! [adopts showbiz voice] It's-rilly-great-to-be-here-an-we-lurve-Englaaaaand . . .'

Do the songs have precise meanings, J?

J squirms, shrugs, looks helpless, lets out a low moan.

Do you prefer not to think about these things?

'Not at the moment. Probably never. It doesn't matter.'

Lou: 'Doesn't get you anywhere.'

Murph: 'And maybe you don't *want* to get anywhere.'

Lou: 'It takes too much from yourself to think about it, so to preserve yourself, you stay away from it.'

J: 'Everything's a bunch of mixed-up feelings mashed up together . . .'

And is the net result uplifting or dejected?

J lets out another low whine of reluctance. 'Either . . . Or both. Or neither.'

Is Dinosaur your favourite band?

'Nah.'

'No way.'

'Nope.'

What is?

Murph: 'I like the Good Rats, from Long Island. I still play that record.' Ah, *that* one.

Lou: 'I like the Swans.'

Somehow from the Swans the conversation shifts to animals, and then to pets. Any interest in having one, J?

J (wailing): 'Naaaa . . . they all *die!*'

Not worth getting involved?

Murph: 'We had a cat once and my dad took him sailing and he jumped ashore and we never saw him again.'

J: 'My tur-tle . . . ran away. Very *slowly*, he ran away.'

How did you develop your lonesome, creased, Neil Young voice, in a *hardcore* context?

'I don't know . . . when I started to sing, I guess . . . probably through listening to all this rock damage . . . what can you *say*? How do you *walk*? How do you *shit*? How do you *sing*? It's hard to get a grip on these things.'

What do you think of British bands, their self-consciousness, their grip on what they're about?'

Lou: 'It's kinda cool, you get a whole package. Like the Jesus and Mary Chain, they *created* their whole scene. It's okay. US bands just *do* it, it's more generalized.'

US bands aren't into selling themselves . . .

Murph: 'US bands are into the music, rather than the package. Maybe cos there's so much TV, you've got people selling themselves and projecting themselves so much all the time.'

Do you spend a lot of money on records?

J: 'Not any more.'

Lou: 'Used to spend a LOT of money on records . . . '

J: 'My mom's money. I used to take twenty dollars out of her purse and hide it under a vase or something, and if she hadn't found it after a week it was kinda mine.'

If she hadn't noticed it, she evidently hadn't missed the money and can't really have needed it in the first place! This sluggish casuistry seems to sum up Dinosaur – the band who can't even rise to a fully fledged crime!

One of the best 'tracks' on *You're Living All Over Me* is 'Poledo', an eerily beautiful ectoplasmic tone that could go on in perpetuity, created by Lou out of bits of tape in his bedroom. 'It's *not* a tape loop. I recorded this sound from a piece of classical music on the radio, and made a tape of it lasting fifteen minutes. Then I started to layer stuff over the top at different speeds, little swatches of sound over and over again, and I got all these weird overtones and stuff. I've been doing this kind of thing since I was fourteen.'

Will you do it again on other records?

'Maybe. It just fitted there. I don't know whether it'll occur to me again.'

What kind of things work you up?

J: 'How do you mean?'

Motivate you?

'Huh . . . hmmmm . . . not having to do . . . not being in one place all the time . . . trying to find places that aren't home. I've been there every minute of my life – and it's kinda getting to me. There's not too many rooms in the house.'

Dinosaur are husks, but it's better this way. If they imposed themselves, the music wouldn't be so imposing. If they had more of a grip, we wouldn't get blown away.

Melody Maker, 12 December 1987

I first heard Dinosaur Jr on the Homestead compilation *The Wailing Ultimate*, which seemed more epochal when I reviewed it earlier in 1987 than it does now. I quoted a sleevenote chunk from Great Plains frontman Ron House – 'With the possible exception of The New Seekers, I don't think there's been any band with less soul than Great Plains. Whether you define "soul" as the "certitude of essence", "the way James Brown moves", or "the pride in your own value", we don't have it' – which then and now seems to capture a certain (dis)spirit of American indie-rock: the white middle-class slacker painfully aware of his deficit of 'realness', responding to privilege with a passive-aggressive squandering of opportunities and wasting of potential. My line about Mascis's "boneless" quality was weirdly echoed on Dinosaur Jr's next album *Bug,* with the song 'No Bones'. In another sense, Dinosaur Jr dissolved *rock*'s vertebrae, vaporizing the riff, powerchord and bassline in a blizzard of serrated haze. My Bloody Valentine took this logic of blissed amorphousness to the next level; years later, Kevin Shields would play in the appropriately named J Mascis and the Fog.

I interviewed Dinosaur Jr a couple more times and Mascis got steadily better at dealing with the ordeal of giving press, while I had learned how to take a more oblique approach with their sort of band. The third time was actually enjoyable: Mascis & Murph made a good double act, and it was fun to ask things like 'how bad would things have to get before you took up arms against the state?'. Still, as much as this first encounter (backstage at the Hammersmith Clarendon) was as painful as squeezing a blood sample out of a baby's heel, it feels like the authentic Dinosaur Jr, the true essence of their soul-less soul.

THE RED HOT CHILI PEPPERS

Hammersmith Clarendon, London

So the Clarendon faces closure, and yes it's a sad day for rock, another step in the drawn-out death of the London gig circuit, and where *will* the Buttholes and Bad Brains of this world play – *but*, here, tonight, sauna-sweltering in this rank sty of Grebo flesh, this post-punk meets pre-punk sewer, such a closure can only feel like an elementary and overdue sanitary measure.

This is the Red Hot Chili Peppers' constituency, for sure. The Red Hot Chili Peppers read like a good idea: an alliance of funk and metal, the best of both worlds, a doubling of pleasures (what drug experts call 'potentiation'). But then look what happens when you mix funk and jazz – separately two of the finest things in life. Each undermines the other, mutes and dampens their respective effects.

The problem for the Chili Peppers is that funk and metal are further away than ever, much further than in the age of funkadelia they hark back to. Metal has become monolithic, no longer beastly but cruelly hygienic, the proverbial sonic abattoir. And funk – who plays funk, these days? Modern black dance is assembled in the studio. This Organic Anti-Beatbox inevitably comes over a little dated.

The giveaway is their overbearing penchant for ye olde slap bass. Once, around 1981, the sound of slap bass was for me and all the other white-dopes-on-funk the very definition of ecstasy. Now slap bass strikes me as a lost, Claptonesque craft that should be allowed to slip quietly into disuse. After all, few black musicians play in that style any more.

The Red Hot Chili Peppers come across as a kind of *National Lampoon*'s Gang of Four. Body paint making them like fluorescent salamanders, they have that generic hardcore look, Neanderthal

69

features combined with Bullworker bodies, and they see their lame buffoonery as a major service to us and to the world. Like so many of these 'wackeeee' US bands, they combine sexism with a fervent loathing for racism. (All of them seem to have written at least one song about the genocide of the Red Indians.)

At their best, they're like a lumpen, sub-virtuoso approximation of Hendrix, funk fluency combined with rock's serrated edges. At their worst, they're like late Zappa, or a yob version of Firehose. This 'funk' is too clenched, too trammelled by hardcore dynamics to approach true maggot-brain diuretic gross-out.

There are some fab moments, like the great nervous tic of a chorus in 'Me and My Friends', rising up to buffet you in the face like surf. And the forthcoming LP is extremely fine. Live, though, the Red Hot Chili Peppers are too curvaceous and wriggly to be speed metal, but too hasty and ham-fisted to shimmy and wiggle like funk. They are neither carnal nor apocalyptic, neither swagger nor hurtle. It feels forced, albeit at times almost interestingly *wrong*.

Melody Maker, February 1988

The bit that puzzles: the sudden outburst of enthusiasm for the 'forthcoming LP'. I guess I *was* once a sort-of-fan, having bought *Freaky Styley* out of curiosity, possibly swayed by the double association of George Clinton (who produced it) and Gang of Four's Andy Gill (who produced their debut). By the nineties, however, the Chili Peppers seemed utterly loathsome (I once described Anthony Kiedis's 'soulful' wordless warbling bit midway through 'Under the Bridge' as 'the most unpleasant sounds to emanate from a human throat' during that decade) and they spawned an entire genre of rocked-up funk that was almost entirely devoid of appeal. Flea seems like a nice guy though.

MORRISSEY

I think I've met them all now. For me, there are no more heroes left. And no new ones coming along, by the look of it. It could be that this is a time marked by a dearth of characters, or that the smart people in rock aren't interested in self-projection but in obliterating noise. But really, I think, it's the case that, in this job, you don't have the time to develop obsessions, what with the insane turnover, and all the incentives to pluralism.

The heroes you have kind of linger on from a prior period when only a few records passed through your life, when you had time to get fixated, spend days living inside a record. It's a real effort to click back to that frame of mind, which is bad because fanaticism is the *true* experience of pop – I think of the splendid devotion of all those bright girls who, as soon as they've got hold of the new Cure or New Order or Bunnymen record, immediately set to learning the lyrics by heart then spend days exhaustively interpreting the Tablets From On High, struggling to establish some fit between their experience and what is actually some drunken doggerel cobbled together in a studio off-moment.

Seriously, I approve. I approve the deadly seriousness, the piety, the need for something sacred in your life. However deluded.

It's become a reflex for critics to castigate the readers for being partisan, for being sluggish and singleminded in their choices. We exhort you to disconnect, discard and move on, acquire a certain agility as consumers. But maybe this ideal state of inconstancy we advocate only makes for fitter participants in capitalism. For the one thing that makes rock more than simply an industry, the one thing that transcends the commodity relation, is fidelity, the idea of a relationship. There are voices that you turn to as a friend, and you don't just turn your back on your friends if they go off the rails. You hang around. You give them the time of day. So – in the year in which we've forced the text-centred discipline that is rock writing to incorporate everything it has excluded for so long (the relationship between the star's body and the fan's, the Voice, the materiality of music) – maybe it's time to make criticism grapple with what undoes it, 'the uncritical'.

Happily, my finally getting to meet Morrissey coincides with the release of one of his great records (they seem to alternate quite evenly with duff ones), so there's no awkward rub between loyalty and the critic's 'responsibility'. *Viva Hate* feels implausibly *fresh*: the music's breathing again, free of a certain stuffiness and laboriousness that had set in seemingly irreversibly in The Smiths' twilight period. All due respect to Johnny Marr (though the haircuts never get better . . .) but, like most people 'blessed' with skill, there was a tendency to be used by one's versatility rather than to use it. Songs were getting written to accommodate guitar conceits, pointless feats and smotheringly unnecessary elaboration. With his producer's rather than instrumentalist's sensibility, Stephen Street is inclined to give a song only what it *needs*. And I never much cared for the bumptious, muscular side of The Smiths – 'What Difference Does it Make', 'I Started Something I Couldn't Finish' – anyway, so I welcome the spaciness Vini Reilly brings as new guitarist, whether it's the lurid wig-out of 'Alsatian Cousin' or the dew-and-moonbeam ECM iridescence of 'Late Night, Maudlin Street'.

In American teen slang, Vini is 'a space' – a dreamer, someone not all there. Hailed by Paul Oldfield as 'the missing boy of pop', someone whose resistance takes the form of an absenteeism from life, it strikes me that Reilly's mystical anorexia is unusually suited to Morrissey's neurasthenia, his supine delinquency.

What do you feel about the album? Whenever you have a new record out, you generally opine that it's the best thing you've ever done . . .

'It's quite different for me now – and this might sound absurd – but there really isn't anything to judge it against. Times are very different and my life has moved on, since The Smiths, in very specific ways, and *Viva Hate* is in no way the follow-up to *Strangeways*. So in a sense I do feel that it is the first record.'

Are these changes personal, or artistic . . .?

'Certainly in a personal way, it's entirely changed. All the people that surrounded me twelve months ago have entirely changed, whether it's the group, the people around The Smiths, or Rough Trade.

Practically everybody that surrounds me now wasn't there a year ago. And, yes, I'm very pleased with what I find.'

Stephen Street is one constant, though . . .

'But working with Stephen as a producer is quite different from writing with him, and even his personality has changed dramatically, within this sphere; he's more relaxed, and more exciting.'

What are the respective merits of Marr and Street?

'Johnny was very hard, as a musician: he played in a very interesting, aggressive way. Stephen does not. But the gentle side of Stephen is something I find totally precious.'

And what about Vini – had you followed his career in Durutti Column?

'With a vague interest. Nothing deep. I'd never met him, or saw him play. But I had all his records. When it came to working on the album, it turned out that Stephen had produced Vini's last record. Stephen suggested him, and it was perfect. What I liked was the extremity of his beauty, and the erratic quality. He's also extremely humorous. The whole session was extremely humorous. But Vini's not terribly interested in pop music, whereas Johnny was absolutely steeped in every manifestation of pop.'

Why *Viva Hate*? What's the thinking behind the title?

'Like many other titles, it simply suggested itself and *had to be*. It was absolutely how I felt post-Smiths and the way I continue to feel. That's just the way the world is. I find hate omnipresent, and love very difficult to find. Hate makes the world go round.'

Does that sadden you? Or do you have a need to hate? Is hate one of the things we do to reinforce the sense of our own identity, our separateness?

'I do find people quite hateful, naturally. I think people feel hate very easily, and they need it in their lives, they need to distrust and to criticize.'

Is that bad? Natural?

'Well, it's just there really. But then I always thought the human race was very very overrated – by rock critics generally.'

Why did you ask for His Master's Voice to be reactivated as your label?

'I was presented with a great choice of defunct labels and designs . . . things like Decca. I didn't want to be on EMI, and Parlophone seemed like the obvious mod suggestion, which I didn't really want either. His Master's Voice, I thought, had a certain perverted grandiosity and thus spoke to me very directly. I'm the only artist on it.'

And the last one was Joyce Grenfell, twenty years ago . . .

'Yes. Spot the difference!'

73

That pleases you a great deal?

'Yes. I hope other groups don't sign to the HMV label. People like
. . . The Icicle Works. That would be awful! I have hundreds of HMV
records in my collection. People like Paul Jones and Johnny Leyton.
His most known hits were "Johnny, Remember Me" and "Wild
Winds", which got to Number 1 and Number 2 respectively, but he
had a ragbag of semi-failures like "I'll Cut Your Tail Off", which for
some unknown reason staggered and died in the lower forties.'

Viva Hate, unsurprisingly, returns again and again to the
Englishness that obsesses Morrissey. For instance, the probable next
single 'Everyday is Like Sunday' pores over the drab details of some
benighted seaside resort . . . 'Hide on the promenade / Scratch out a
postcard / How I dearly wish I was not here . . . trudging slowly over
wet sand . . . win yourself a cheap tray . . . share some greased tea with
me' . . . Typically, Morrissey seems to cherish the very constraints and
despondency of a now disappearing England, fetishize the lost limits.

What is this love/hate relationship you have with Englishness?

'There are very few aspects of Englishness I actually hate. I can see
the narrowness, and love to sing about it. But I don't hate Englishness
in any way. All aspects of England, whether it be underclass, or
extreme affluence, I find very interesting and entertaining. And it's still,
I feel, cliché as it may seem, the sanest country in the world.'

But there is the echo of Betjeman-on-Slough in the line 'Come!
come! come – nuclear bomb!' I mean, if it was such a rotten holiday,
why hark back to it?

'That never really occurred to me. The pleasure is getting it out of
your system, saying "never again" instead of "same time next year".
And the British holiday resort is just like a symbol of Britain's *absurdity*
really. The idea of a resort in Britain doesn't seem *natural*.'

On the same subject, there's the line in 'Bengali in Platforms':
'Shelve your Western plans / And understand / That life is hard enough
when you belong here.' Don't you think the song could be taken as
condescending?

'Yeeeees . . . I do think it *could* be taken that way, and another journalist has said that it probably *will*. But it's not being deliberately
provocative. It's just about people who, in order to be embraced or feel
at home, buy the most absurd English clothes.'

'An ankle star that blinds me . . . a lemon sole so very high . . .' –
this is the first of the many seventies references that permeate the
album. Presumably your adolescence always was co-terminous with
the seventies . . . but why have you *now* started to make explicit references to power cuts and suedeheads? Why is it that you and everyone

74

else have embarked on this reassessment of that decade, all at the same juncture?

'It's a great accident. I just felt the need to sing about 1972.'

So what was the zeitgeist, the vibe?

'The seventies were like two decades really, the first half and the second were like two different times. And obviously the middle was dreadful. The first half was curious. Obviously it was still very much linked to the sixties, an extension of them. But [the] glam rock explosion was, for me, fascinating. It had never happened before and that made it so intriguing *and* so despised. And then, in the mid seventies, it became discofied and easy and American. And then, in the late seventies, there was once again that sense of great obstreperousness, which made life so interesting – which it hasn't been since. There was a great deal of talent and imagination and that doesn't happen very often. It was also very privately English, which I thought was very helpful, because, once again, it was a matter of the rest of the world catching up with England, instead of the reverse. And it was a national thing, it brought the provinces alive, and people began to focus on Manchester and other places in a very intense way. Punk was very fair.'

This is the standard view of the seventies, of course, as calcified still further by the *NME*'s feeble gesture of 'reappraisal', and the abiding tenet is that everyone was waiting out the early seventies for something to happen. But I wonder, did people really feel at the time as though they were living through tawdry and impoverished times?

'Not really. I think that was just the tempo of the times. And old photographs are always embarrassing. Perhaps in ten years you'll look back and think the way you look is immensely humiliating.' (Maybe sooner.) 'And I might feel the same way also. But one can't deny that the style of the seventies was the pinnacle of debauched nonsense and human ugliness.'

Again, on 'Late Night, Maudlin Street', you say: 'I never stole a happy hour around here' – but the whole effect of the song, the way your murmured reveries drift in and out of Vini's entranced playing, just makes the whole time and place seem magical, otherworldly, and incredibly precious . . .

'It is a trick of memory, looking back and thinking maybe things weren't that bad, but of course, if you concentrate, you realize they were. But I don't want to sing about football results or importune people to dance. There are too many other people doing that, and I feel sad there aren't people making serious statements. I feel slightly let down. I feel I should look about and see streams of groups being angry and extremely hateful – but it's just not happening at all.'

For me, the song is the centrepiece of the album. But you seem not so much angry, as succumbing to memories, drowning in them, leaving this world behind . . .

'But, I think, *finally* exorcising the ghost of that past and those small times.'

It reminded me of the comparison The Stud Brothers made between you and Sinead O'Connor: the 'rigorous autobiography', the way both of you seem to have stopped living in order to document more completely your adolescence.

'But my life never really started at any stage – which I know you won't believe, but it's true – so it never really got stopped at any point. But obviously the past is what makes any person. It's because of *your* past that you're sitting there now, with your list on your knee. Not because of the future or the present. I can't *help* thinking about the past.'

'Where the world's ugliest boy, became what you see here, I am – the world's ugliest man'. Isn't that a little coy? You must be fairly confident about your looks, by now?

'Well, thank you, but no – if I see a picture of myself in a magazine, I quickly press on and get to the classified ads. And if by some quirk I see myself on television, I instantly change channels.'

The line 'Women only like me for my mind' is clever . . .

'It's the final complaint, I suppose, in the long list of complaints about the past.'

It's still not widely appreciated that men can want to be objects, as much as agents, of desire.

'But I think men are seen like that, actually – now. Men are aware of their sexuality in a way they previously weren't, or weren't supposed to be. I think women have become very open about their needs and desires, and this was entirely due to feminism. By women being open about sex, it made life much easier for men. And this is why feminism helps everybody, to be slightly more relaxed about life.'

There's the line about taking 'strange pills' . . . is suicide something you personally have approached?

'Yes, occasionally. Obviously, I've dwelt on it with magnificent interest.'

And you see it as often a noble decision?

'I do, I *still* do. Obviously, the traditional viewpoint is to scowl, but I don't understand that.'

There are certain situations where I can imagine it's a very strong statement about your power over your own body, and a gesture of throwing off the 'jurisdiction' of the medical and therapeutic 'authorities' . . .

76

'Yes, and it's also a very *hard* thing to do. It takes enormous courage and strength. Sometimes, obviously, I think it very unfortunate that people reach that stage. It would be very ideal if life was repetitiously joyous. But is it?'

Nope.

Mindful of Morrissey's Genet-style, um, interest in ruffians, as evinced by 'Suedehead', I ask: have you always been drawn to people who are tough and streetwise and unlike yourself?

'I'm enormously attracted to people who can look after themselves. I'm obsessed by the physical, in the sense that it almost always *works*. It's a great power to be very physical, to be able to storm through life with swaying shoulders, instead of creeping and just simply relying on your Thesaurus. It doesn't work! I've had so many conversations with people trying to convince them of a particular point, and although I find words central to my life . . .'

You'd like to be capable of violence . . .

'*Nothing* shifts or stirs people like a slight underhand threat. They jump. But most of the friends I have are very verbal and cross-legged individuals and not very demonstrative in any way. So I've never belonged to any physical set. The song "Break Up The Family" is strongly linked with "Suedehead" and "Maudlin Street", that whole period in 1972, when I was twelve, thirteen. "Break Up" is about a string of friends I had who were very intense people and at that age, when your friends talk about the slim separation between life and death – and you set that against the fact that this period of your youth is supposed to be the most playful and reckless – well, if *you* utilised *that* period in a very intense way, well, that feeling never really leaves you.'

Did you all consider the family a bad idea?

'No, we didn't feel that at all. The family in the song is the circle of friends, where it almost seemed, because we were so identical, that for anybody to make any progress in life, we'd have to split up. Because there was *no* strength in our unity. And that's what happened, we did all go our separate ways, and quite naturally came to no good. I saw one of them quite recently, and it was a very head-scratching experience.'

Because he'd turned into the complete opposite of what you all had been?

'No, not at all. Which is the confusion.'

And your gang, were you outcasts, victimised by 'The Ordinary Boys'?

'Yes, but half of it, I have to confess, was the effect of deliberate choosing. We chose to reject the normality of life, and be intense and individual.'

Do you think, in ten or twenty years, your life will still be structured around these playground antagonisms?

'Yes. People don't really change, do they? They don't change. And the playground antagonisms are replaced by other . . . more adult antagonisms.'

Office antagonisms.

'Yes. Canteen antagonisms . . . getting heavily antagonised while you're queuing up to purchase a doughnut. But surely you have a happy question?'

The last track on *Viva Hate* is a rueful little ballad with the self-explanatory title 'Margaret on the Guillotine', which describes 'the wonderful dream' (i.e. the gory and spectacular public execution of our PM) that all 'the kind people' harbour. The chorus, repeated five times, is the plaintive, rhetorical question: 'When will you die?' You realize all of this will cause you no end of trouble?

'Anything that's very clear-cut and very strong causes difficulty, doesn't it? But why should it? I'm not looking for attention. In this case, attention is the last thing I really need. I don't want to be in the *Daily Mirror*. There is something in this above controversy and outrage and all these over-familiar words. It's too easy to be controversial.'

So you mean it? You'd like to see her dead?

'Instantly.'

In a cruel, bloody sort of way?

'Yes.'

Would you carry out the execution?

'I have got the uniform, ready.'

One line in the song seems to me to be very revealing: when you say you want to see her killed 'Because people like you / make me feel so tired . . . so old inside'. If you compare The Smiths with the previous Great White Hopes, the Pivotal Rock Bands of preceding eras, it's clear that the rebellion of The Stones, Who, Pistols, Jam, was based in some kind of activism or at least action, an optimism about the potential of collective or individual agency. But The Smiths' 'rebellion' is more like resistance through withdrawal, through subsiding into enervation. The fantasy in 'Margaret on the Guillotine' is more like wishful thinking than the resolve to do violence, or even personify violence theatrically, onstage. Isn't the effect of 'Margaret' just to encourage wistful resignation?

'Maybe, but I do also firmly believe in action. But also there's a great sense of doorstep rebellion, and stamping of feet. I think, above all, that dealing with people's manipulations *is* very tiring. You grow old very quickly when every day of your life you're trying to win arguments. Politically, I *do* feel exhausted. I do feel there are no more demonstrations, no more petitions to be signed. I think those things and group meetings and crèches, are completely boring and a waste of time. I do feel a sense of apathy.'

I'm interested you talk about 'stamping of feet', because this fantasy of offing Mrs Thatcher, as though this would somehow solve every-thing, as if the 'evil' in this country weren't a tad more structural and entrenched – well, there's something a bit childish and petulant about it.

'Believe me, I'm totally aware of that. But there's also something important about it. The song is silly, it's also very heavy, and it's also very brave. And I sit back and smile. Surely you can see that the very serious elements in it put the kind of straightforward, demonstration, "Maggie Maggie Maggie Out Out Out" protest song, in its place and make it seem trite and a little bit cosy?'

The thing with protest songs is that pop's always been about the immediate, spontaneous, and puerile, it hasn't the patience to slog through subcommittees and lobbying and making orderly demands through proper channels. Pop isn't programmatic, it wants the world and it wants it now, and it's much more satisfying to hear about your enemy being slaughtered. Even if it's just a fantasy . . .

'Is it? You obviously haven't listened. I think it's possible. The times are quite ropey. Things are touch-and-go. You don't believe me?'

But it's like you say, there's this battening down that's seeping throughout society and the result is enervation and retrenchment. You can feel it on every level of life. A 'trivial' example: when you get on a bus. They've got rid of the conductors, to save costs, and you have these pay-as-you-enter buses, and getting on and off takes longer and is more stressful, journeys are longer, and you can see ordinary people get more harassed, bottling it up. But the effect of being shat on is to set people against each other. While the nasty people have banded together, the money people.

'Well, yes, there's a lot of organized suffering in England right now.'

* * *

I feel a fool doing this, it's like defending eyesight or breathing, but the ghosts of The Stud Brothers are leering at me in the corner of my vision, cackling in a saturnine sort of way about 'jessie tendencies', so I feel I must put pen to paper on the subject of POIGNANCY. It seems to me that, in its own gentle way, poignancy is as profound an intimation of the contradictions of being, of the screwiness of this world, as any of the mindfuck experiences or headlong plunges into the horror-of-it-all that we conspiratorially celebrate.

Poignancy (and this is why its domain is the minor key) is the exquisite meshing of two contradictory feelings. It's a piercing beauty, or a sweet ache. Anyone who's ever *treasured* their pain, tried to prolong it, toyed with exacerbating it or been driven to dwell on inside it long after recovery was an option, preferring the company of ghosts to the dreamlessness of everyday society – that person understands poignancy.

But poignancy isn't just retrospective, it's also a mourning of the Moment as it passes, the rapture that's the same as grief, a radiant apprehension of death.

Morrissey has always lived and breathed the poignant, always secretly treasured the gulf between him and the loved one, the difference that makes love possible but makes possession illusory, a delusion, so that, in the end, we are all unrequited lovers. And poignancy is why he obsessively prizes and keeps open ancient wounds. And it seems to me that The Stud Brothers understand poignancy, and the reasons why its proper language is the ease of elegance, perfectly well, actually – it's just that they vest the power of poignancy *entirely* in women, which is all very well, but doesn't exactly go against the schizoid grain of the entirety of Western civilization, and that when the poignant registers in the vocabulary of a pop male, it's a repugnant indication of some appalling limpness of being, whereas with Sinead/All About Eve/Heart it is *alluringly* frail.

I just think, ultimately, that the Lester Bangs aesthetic universe, for all its solipsistic majesty, is such a long way from being the be-all, that in the end, you do choose to reach out, you do choose the tentative and the touching over the blinding and the bludgeoning every time.

* * *

Like most great groups, The Smiths left a trail of imitators in their wake. It's as though groups see something that's great, and can't get past the greatness, can only duplicate it. I mean, do you think The Smiths have been a bad influence?

'A lot of groups don't really know what to do, and aren't terribly sure of their footing, and they do mimic, and they do over-estimate and over-utilize their influences. But originality, you must have noticed, is extremely rare, and it's quite natural really. And look at all the singers who copy Madonna.'

But all those groups, like the Wedding Present, with their rather minor version of the pensiveness and wistfulness . . .

'Well, I can only applaud, really, because it is quite an unusual standpoint, still – and anything that hits against the blaring, bloated Bon Jovi mechanisms, I'll . . . stand beside.'

I think there's a rather ill-thought-out assumption that, because you've bared your soul and this fascinating set of problems has emerged, if they do exactly the same their misery, or awkwardness, is going to be as interesting as yours.

'A lot of groups of obviously Smiths-leanings have deliberately tried to trash The Smiths, and all of those groups to my knowledge, have been instantly bottled . . . but I'm always totally flattered and amused when I hear a voice that is . . . indebted.'

This idea that honest, unmediated misery is per se gripping, I think stems from the simplistic notion that your fans identify straight-forwardly with the scenarios in your songs. But how do they connect with such a statistically remote calamity as 'Girlfriend in a Coma'?

'Oh, you'd be surprised! You should read the letters I get. But what are you *really* saying?'

Isn't there something almost aspirational about their identification with such irregular forms of martyrdom? A craving for the hardest hit of self-pity?

'I don't feel they're extreme. If anything, I feel they're understated. I think people live very urgent lives. I don't feel I'm in any sense vaude-villian or melodramatic.'

When writing, haven't you ever doubted that what your vigorous introspection was turning up was going to be of value to someone?

'No, I haven't really. I've always thought I've had a very clear view of what I'm doing. And if things do get slightly dodgy, I think I'll notice.'

Do you think there are limits to the kind of people who get some-thing from what you do?

'Mmmm – but that's true for anybody, really. I'm just pleased that the limits still amount to a sizeable audience. I don't feel the need for more, I don't feel the need to be totally massively global.'

On 'Rubber Ring', you seemed aware that, for many of your fans, the relationship is going to be a temporary if intense, even lifesaving one. Do you think that maybe most of your fans are going through a phase, and that most of them will emerge the other end, and leave you behind?

'Well, it probably is a phase. But if people move on, it's understand-able. In the event that everyone moves on, and I'm left dangling in the recording studio – then it would seem to confirm everything I've ever thought about the cruelties of life!'

It seems to me the only people who do persist in that phase and make something tenable out of an unsatisfied, unsettled life, are rock musicians, and rock critics. But has satisfaction ever threatened to loom in your life?

'It's never been something I've been immediately faced by. It's definitely a possession of other people. I have a very long list of things I want to do.'

Artistic or personal?

'Artistic. Nothing else counts.'

Does a notion of 'artistic growth' have any place in your scheme?

'Not really. Can you give me an example of where that's happened?'

You're right: in rock and pop, it seems people just have their thing . . .

'And they hone it. Or they start bad and merely get better. Artistic growth? I don't really have any ambitions to change in any drastic ways. I'm quite satisfied with how I am.'

You're satisfied with your dissatisfaction?

'Totally. I couldn't be happier. I don't want anything to interfere with this state of dissatisfaction.'

And there'll be an endlessly renewed harvest of dissatisfied young souls filling up this phase which is your constituency, a.k.a. adolescence.

'But I don't consider it to be adolescent. I'm not adolescent, I'm twenty-eight. It's something quite beyond and more complicated than 'adolescence', something that hasn't been thought out yet, but shouldn't be dismissed as "adolescent".'

No, but I have a very high regard for adolescence as an institution; it's a fine way to spend the whole of your life. It's just a handy signifier for a life of restlessness, impatience, and insatiability. But would you prefer 'a questioning life', maybe . . .?

'Yes, something quite like that . . . and that's something that can only aid and assist. I sometimes think it's only the excessively normal elements in the industry who take it all so seriously and maybe I don't – rather than vice versa.'

And you'll grow old (but not up) gracefully . . .

'Disgracefully. I grow old disgracefully!'

* * *

'Did that swift eclipse torture you? / A star at 18 and then – suddenly gone / down to a few lines in the back page of a teenage annual / oh but I remembered you / I looked up to you'

> – 'Little Man, What Now?'

'Fame, Fame, fatal Fame / It can play hideous tricks on the brain.'

> – 'Frankly, Mr Shankly'

One of the best tracks on *Viva Hate* is 'Little Man, What Now?', an eerie, enchanted, rather chilling song in which Morrissey ponders the fate of a young TV actor ('a real person – but I don't want to name names') he remembers from 'Friday nights 1969', briefly elevated to the level of minor celebrity before being abruptly dispatched back into obscurity, never to return – except for an afternoon TV nostalgia show, where the panel 'couldn't name you'. It's another example of Morrissey's unusual awareness of the trajectories of fame, and the ways in which fans use and are used by stars. He's personally experienced the *extremes* of both sides of the double monologue that is the fan/star 'relationship'.

'Fame is the most fascinating subject in the world and I'm keenly interested in speaking to certain people who've had fame and then lost it.'

Was there ever a point when you considered that it might all dry up for you, that you might have to go back to being a nobody?

'I do think about it, but I somehow think, with the intensity of the last five years, that even if, through some dramatic personal desire, I tried to obtain anonymity, it would be impossible. One way and another, I will always be *somewhere* just skating about the edges of global fame, pestering people and throwing glasses.'

Did you *always* crave fame?

'I always had a religious obsession with fame. I always thought being famous was the only thing worth doing in human life, and anything else was just perfunctory. I thought anonymity was easy: it was easy to be a simple, nodding individual who got on the bus. I wasn't terribly impressed by obscurity.'

Did you have a rich sense of destiny and difference?

'I always knew something, shall we say, *peculiar* was going to happen. I think real, true artists do have that instinct.'

From the age of what, nine, ten?

'Much earlier. In some form. I saw a multitude of options and the dilemma was just which one to concentrate on. Obviously, I wrote. At the age of six I compiled a personal magazine every week. I was intensely interested in journalism, and all the things around it, whether it was performing or actually playing records. I intensely envied DJs. To simply sit on this cushion at the BBC day after day and flip on anything they thought was moving – well, I thought that was the most sacred and powerful position in the universe. To me, it was more important than politics.'

You *wanted* to be a DJ?!

'At a tender age, I craved that power – to impose one's record collection on people in launderettes and on scaffolding. But now I think it's such a terrible job that DJs should be the highest paid people in the country. To have to sit in an office all day playing the same records – all of which are awful – over and over and over again – well, it's not funny, is it?! We shouldn't pick on these people. We should send them parcels!'

About this early magazine . . .

'I was only six, so . . . the art direction let it down a bit, really. It was simply the Top 10, then certain pin-ups of artists of my personal choice . . . sketched, in fact, by the editor himself.'

What kind of circulation did it have?

'There was just the one copy, which limited readership somewhat.'

So you quickly became an avid reader and writer?

'I very quickly became obsessed by music papers and pop journalism, and collected them ravenously.'

So did you turn to music as an avenue for writing, or were you driven by musical instincts?

'By staunch instincts of very brittle criticism. Developed through having had this magazine of my own since the age of six, and listening to the Top 30 every Tuesday only to run off instantly to the typewriter in order to compile my own personal Top 30 which totally conflicted with how the world really was. But in my sense, my Top 30 was how the world *should* have been. It was a Top 30 of contemporary records, but the new entries were *very* unlikely, and obviously I favoured certain artists, like T. Rex.

'I can remember writing an extravagant critique of "Cinderella Rockefeller". I was always a totally dissatisfied consumer, aflood with complaints. It seemed to me that the world of pop music, which I worshipped, was there to be altered and corrected.'

That feeling – that pop belongs to 'us', so how come it's blocked up with all this other people's stuff – has been an abiding feeling on the rock 'left' for some fifteen years. (Punk had very little impact on the charts, on what sold.) So Morrissey's infantile gainsaying of pop reality was the chrysalis for indie-pop's wistful, wishful fantasies of a 'perfect pop' returning to oust the impostors in the hit parade.

'I think it's fact, things have reached an unthinkable state, where things are orchestrated entirely by unsympathetic and unmusical hands and ears. The people in key positions are people who don't consider pop culture to have any serious importance whatsoever.'

So you believe pop is, or can be, art – but it's a belief that is only sustained by very rare instances. You seem to have very specific ideas about what constitutes art. The other day it occurred to me that there are maybe two kinds of intelligence in the world: one that's very open, that tries to take on everything, and accordingly gets paralysed by choice; another kind that's narrow, that finds strength by focusing on some things and excluding most everything else . . .

'If I liked everything, I'd be very hard to *understand*. I always found the idea of people who were very hard to please, including journalists who were very critical – I always found they were almost always right when they found something praiseworthy. I find people who are unbudgeably fair quite time-consuming. I find agreeable people immensely disagreeable.'

Is that the idea of *Viva Hate*: that we need bigotries in order to make sense of the world, make it actionable? (The hankering for a punk-style commotion is for precisely such an *illiberalism*, a taking of sides, a new order.)

'Sadly, a lot of people *need* to be told, rather than asked. Also, I often feel I can gain from venomously critical views of me as an artist, more than I can from dithery, sloppily fawning, supportive views.'

Going back to fame, to your intimate knowledge of the processes of identification and obsession . . . having been through various manic fixations, *you* have progressed to being a star, the subject of fixations yourself. Most of your fans, though, will remain condemned to a lonely monologue with their distant idol . . .

'*Condemned* sounds a bit rough . . . but, nonetheless, I can't help but agree, really.'

You encourage the obsessiveness, though, don't you? I remember you once saying you were delighted people sent you underwear, or demands for underwear . . .

'Yes, both! No, I do get lots of very fascinating and fascinated letters, and lots of *fascinating* gifts. I can very clearly understand obsessiveness, and the people who write to me see that I understand obsession and preciousness. And I respond in the same way. I still get very nervous when I meet people I admire . . .'

Like who?

'Avril Angus . . .'

Who?

'Well, exactly – Avril Angus! She acts. I get very nervous when I meet people from the theatre. I think that's a very hallowed, sacred thing to be in. And I still have scrapbooks.'

What does it feel like to see *your* proliferated image about, on hoardings, in magazines, to hear your voice on the radio?

'It's very odd. I was in a shop once, buying scented candles, and on the radio came Steve Wright with a collage of Smiths songs, and I got a distinct chill, almost as though the hand of Death was tapping me on the shoulder, saying: "put yer candles down, it's time to go"!'

About the split . . . there seems to be a desire, on the part of both you and Marr, to represent the end of The Smiths as though there was little or no acrimony involved. But if a band ends, after a period in which the main protagonists hadn't communicated for some three or four months, surely *some* kind of serious conflict was going down . . .

'I expect it's hard to believe there weren't some elements of hatred slipping in and out. I don't think I'd believe that there was no acrimony. But it became a situation where people around the band began to take sides, and there was even a belief that within the audience there was a Morrissey contingent and a Marr contingent. And critics began to separate, and praise one and condemn the other.

'I *personally* did not find this a strain. But I find acrimony and even dwelling on the final events very futile; although in a sense I feel reportable, in another, more affecting way, I *don't*. And I think explanations create their own suspicions that things were much worse than they were. And that's what happened. Because there were so many people around the group, everyone had their own exaggerations, and stories began to breed.'

Was the question of conquering America a problem, Marr being keener to undertake a world tour than you were?

'Once again, this was fabricated. Although I had very little passion to do a proposed world tour, and had less passion than any other member, I always thought my opinion was totally, totally valid. But it's true, if I'd nodded, a world tour would have happened. But I wasn't prepared to become that stale pop baggage, simply checking in and checking out, not knowing where I was or what clothes I was wearing, and quite ritually standing onstage singing.'

The other Smiths had more of a taste for that?

'Not exactly, but they were more realistic and adaptable.'

It wouldn't have been so wearing for them as for you?

'No.'

Do you think Johnny is possibly even *more* into being famous than you are?

'It's very difficult for me to answer that question. People often tap me on the shoulder and ask me that, and it's a general assumption that he must have been. But my general impression is that he wasn't. He had many opportunities to talk to the press, and I was *always* the *only* person who encouraged him to do extra-curricular activities. But I also do become very confused by the *number* of people he does become involved with . . .'

Do you blame Ken Friedman [ex-Smiths manager and now Marr's personal manager] for the split?

'Um . . . I'd rather not discuss that.'

Is it hard to maintain a barrier between your inner self and the worldliness of the biz and its machinations?

'There is a lot that's unavoidable. Money is a constantly draining occupation – trying to deal with it, keep it, *get* it. I find the business side very distasteful, harrowing and soul-destroying. I could talk about tax, which I find quite frightening. But this always sounds like a soft and phoney complaint. Because even though I'm taxed to an extreme and impossible degree, I still at the end have a lot of money. I do get the sense, though, that it's illegal to earn money in this country.'

Surely you're not with Margaret on this one, up there on the guillotine? *Presumably* you believe the disadvantaged ought to be supported and enabled?

'It's very difficult. I always had a very basic view that if you earned money it belongs to you. But that is obviously not the case. People have very slim rights over the money they earn.

'You have to get up very early and concentrate very hard to ever see any of it. The Smiths never earned *any* money touring. We'd come off remarkably successful tours and have to sit down and sign eighty cheques. Johnny and I would just look at each other and all of a sudden get very . . . old.'

Did it feel like it was all getting out of control?

'Oh, it got entirely out of control, totally, *totally* out of control. This, if anything, was the cause of The Smiths' death. Especially the monetary side. We were making huge amounts of money and it was going everywhere but in the personal bank accounts of the four group members. Johnny and I would be walking offstage in the Universal Amphitheater in Los Angeles, after playing an insanely devastating performance, and *instantly* have to sign cheques, while we were still euphoric and dripping with sweat, otherwise we couldn't put our trousers on.

'And finally, I think, Johnny had to back off from that, and put his entire life into the hands of his manager, because there was too much pressure. And there were too many people around the group saying, "pacify me, say something nice, make me feel needed". All people surrounding groups are like that, they need to be needed, they need to telephone you at strange hours to find out if they are still liked and still included. And that's very annoying, because the only two people who needed to be supported were Johnny and me.'

So The Smiths: ye olde story of something unspoilt being strangled by the success engendered by its very novelty; of love, crushed by the wheels of industry. It's the tragedy at the core of rock: how can something essentially private withstand the pressure of going public? Morrissey's answer is to retreat still further into his memories.

The Smiths were prime movers in what you could call the depoliticization of personal life after punk's initial scornful demystification. Remember 1980: 'personal politics' was the phrase that tripped off every lip, groups like Gang of Four ('Love Like Anthrax') and Au Pairs *worked* towards their dream of the equal relationship liberated from the veils of romantic 'false consciousness' – unconsciously mimicking the pragmatism of therapists and counsellors, with their notion of love as contract.

Then 1982: attention shifted to the public language of love, to pop's iconography – the buzzwords were 'the language of love', 'the lexicon of love', 'the lovers' discourse', demystification was superseded by deconstruction and ambiguity.

Finally, with Nick Cave's misogynist agonies, the Jesus and Mary Chain's candyskin classicism, and The Smiths' eternally unrequited gaze, came the return of romanticism in all its purity and privacy. Pop had returned to what it has always been about: the privileging of the personal as *the* realm in which the meaning of your life is resolved. The motor-idea of romanticism – the dream of the redemptive love that will make everything alright, resolve all difference – has, in the twentieth century, replaced religion as the opium of the people.

But it's the dream that continues to speak most deeply to us. And maybe the superstition of love is our last reservoir of spirituality in the face of those 'specialists of the soul' who would seek to *reform* relationships in accordance with their ghastly notions of 'negotiation', 'support', 'partnership'.

I always come back to The Stones when I think of The Smiths, because of the camp, but mainly because of the way each band illuminates their era for us. For The Stones, satisfaction was the goal: everything would be *alright* if we shed the inhibitions that held us back and down. Revolution meant good sex on the 'morrow.

But The Stones were the product of expansive times, The Smiths the product of contracted and beleaguered times. With The Smiths it was a question not of desire but of *longing* – the yearning to belong to or with someone, to belong somewhere. The dream that two half-a-persons can make a whole, fit hand-in-glove. The Stones and their time were all about leaving home; The Smiths and our time are about pining for a home.

It's a sign of the times, maybe, that pop-as-reinvention-of-the-self is something that resonates for fewer and fewer people in the little world that is the music press readership; that the pollwinner, the figure you most identify with, is Morrissey, victim of his past, chained to his memories. And as he says, artists don't really 'develop', they have their act, gift, whatever, and stick with it.

That peal of exile first heard in 'Hand in Glove' still rings true in moments on *Viva Hate*, and no doubt always will, no matter what follows, in the same way that traces of wantonness persist in Jagger's voice beneath all the mannered overlay of time.

As I neurotically double-check if the tape is running, I mutter by way of apology, 'I've had some bad experiences with tape recorders.'

'Oh, I've had some bad experiences with *people* actually . . . you're very lucky.'

Melody Maker, 12 March/19 March 1988

I don't think I was ever truly an uncritical devotee of The Smiths: even at my height of ardour, back when every one of those brilliant early B-sides seemed precious, I could tell when they did weak work (i.e. most of *Meat is Murder*), and rather than love-at-first-listen it was actually *criticism* (a piece by Barney Hoskyns) that unlocked the band's magic and meaning for me (indeed the first few times I heard The Smiths, on those early Radio 1 sessions, their sound seemed rather plain and mundane after New Pop and the lavish lushness of groups like the Associates). Still, in this profile it suited my rhetorical purposes to present myself as a blindly faithful diehard, because one of the things that fascinated me was the way Morrissey the idolizer (the one-time president of the New York Dolls fan club; the sustained icon-ography of those Smiths singles sleeves) turned himself into Morrissey the idol. What was unique was the way the singer codified the themes of loneliness and projection in his songs ('Rubber Ring', for instance, beseeches a fan who's about to grow out of Morrissey-worship, to grow up and leave him behind), in the process coming dangerously close to exposing the circularity and ulti-mate sterility of the syndrome. Morrissey, already relatively old by the time The Smiths took off, surely knew that his teenage belief that he was engaged in 'an absolute tangible love affair' with his idols was delusory, a dead end (unless Mozzer's fans were all supposed to become stars too, with fan-tasmal lovers of their own – the argument of his solo-era song 'Sing Your Life'?). A Pied Piper of teen angst, he knowingly shepherded his flock into this cul-de-sac of loving only the pristine image of a distant icon, rather than risk the mess and compromise of real-life relationships. His disciples came up with a clever twist on the 'tangible love affair' fantasy, though, developing rituals of leaping onstage to kiss and hug the singer. By the early nineties, strategizing how to get from the Mozz-pit on to the stage and achieve a close encounter became the focus of Morrissey fan culture. Those who managed it recalled the Moment of Contact as an electrifying sacrament in which all the repression and unrequited passion of their lives was orgasmically released. Moz-zines like *Sing Your Life* teemed with testimonials: '*I just wanted to stay there forever*', '*a lord up there, his music savagely attacked me*', '*the utmost feeling of ecstasy*', '*I saw God coming down*', '*Morrissey is my life; Morrissey is my death*', '*Morrissey makes reality seem unreal*'. As one fan wrote, '*it is our desire to bridge this distance that keeps us in a state of eternal attraction*': fandom as an ultra-intense state of suspension and deferral, a ploy that allows you live in the ideal, unrequited but thus never dis-illusioned. Which is why all fans need to grow out of Morrissey and *start* their lives.

THE PIXIES

The hollering is all. The Pixies are what's left when all the frustrations and absences that once prompted rock 'n' roll into being have faded away or been catered for, and all that remains is the urge to holler, shriek and whoop it up for the arbitrary, unnegotiable hell of it. They're a poltergeist whose restlessness can never be pacified, the ghost of rock 'n' roll. They throb with an obscure randiness it's difficult to imagine what would *ever* satisfy. A Pixies song is that primal, that post-postmodern.

The Pixies are about . . . no, The Pixies plain *are*, the disfigurement and degradation of language. A Pixies song consists of gnashing, obscure imprecations, rabid interjections, palsied reveries, and the *occasional* lurch into lucidity: 'you're so pretty / when you're un-faithful to me'. Like their Boston neighbours and 4AD labelmates, Throwing Muses, they provoke emotional responses you can't pin down: is that seven feelings at once, or a new, as yet unnamed emotion? They run strange gamuts and achieve peculiar juxtapositions of feeling, one minute haggard, the next luscious. *What's happening?*

An idle glance and you'd take them for a garage group. But this garage is like the Tardis: there's a supernatural amount of space in this rough-hewn, scrapping sound, a wilderness across which Pixies songs careen like tearaway mustangs or stampeded wagons shedding every-thing but their chassis. Along with space, there's a deformed sister to conventional pop geometry.

It's as though the acid-crypt punkadelia of bands like The Hombres or The Groupies has been *possessed* by the spirit of Dada. It's Ubu meets The Gun Club. They rock crooked. Rampaging ruins. 'Wit', 'playful', 'quirky', 'kooky' are all offensively paltry and misleading words to use in connection with The Pixies. It's altogether less suave, more spume-flecked than that. Spooked is a *bit* better.

Their new LP *Surfer Rosa* is a brilliant step-sideways from the more produced trajectory of their recording; it's not so much produced as abased by Steve Albini, the ex-Big Black. The sepulchral, impossibly foreboding 'Break My Body', the deranged shriek-whine 'uh-huhn, uh-huhn' that kick-starts 'Broken Face', the truly gargantuan, holy horny 'Gigantic', the strange soaring and wilting guitars of 'River Euphrates', 'Where is My Mind?' with its crass but genuinely eerie harmonies and its chorus recited in a strange alloy of rueful puzzlement and mild irritation as though Black Francis has simply mislaid his sentience somewhere around the house . . . all these and more have encouraged some pretty uncool behaviour in the privacy of this household recently.

We meet in the well-heeled downtown Boston condo of Mrs John Murphy (a.k.a. Kim, the bassist and sometime – more often please! – singer, on tracks like 'Gigantic') and her obliging husband. Trite as it may seem to some, what's initially intriguing *is* the disparity between these genial unruffled people and such . . . ruffled music: regular Joey Santiago the (incredible) guitarist, David Lovering the drummer with his imminent marriage and his metal-detecting, and the placid centre of it all, chubby Black Francis a.k.a. Charles, the rock 'n' roll shaman.

Only Kim seems inhabited by the same hyperactive energies that dishevel the music, fidgeting, splendidly impulsive, possessed of that unselfconsciousness that seems to characterize young Americans, where a thought no sooner enters the head than pops out the mouth.

Generally, mere transcription cannot do justice to the array of stresses, inflections, manic touches, weird characterizations, in a Pixies (or Muses) conversation: the buggering of syntax, the jaywalking and lane changes within language, the abandonment into inarticulate noises and gestures that is more expressive than conventional eloquence. People have celebrated America as a non-verbal culture, and compared with someone like Green Gartside (where the voice is corseted and coerced by the precision of what's being said), what The Pixies/Muses do, in their music and in their conversation, is to liberate the sensuality, the breath, of the voice. What they want to 'say' will come out, despite the resistance of language, like a geyser. Like talking in tongues.

So are The Pixies their own favourite band?

Charles: 'I *like* it . . . but it doesn't move me enough yet.'

What degree of impact are you looking to match?

'I like Iggy Pop a lot . . . if I can come up with something that powerful, especially the demo stuff, like "I'm Sick of You", then . . .'

Are The Pixies a natural unnaturalness, or was there a deliberate attempt to vandalize the convention? Did you *choose* to jettison symmetry, put in all these gashes and gaps?

'Well, you want to be different from other people, sure, so you throw in as many arbitrary things as possible. So instead of having the typical four-line verse, we'll only sing three lines. Or when we stop for a pause, we won't wait the usual eight beats, we'll go rest for ten beats. Or on 'I've Been Tired', where a four-chord sequence would sound *natural*, we'll turn it into a three-chord sequence, make it trip over itself.'

Like a locked groove.

'Yeah. It's kind of *religious* sounding.'

Like a mantra.

'Yeah, kinda. It's all a question of dynamics. And we only do short songs, which makes things sound even more uneven.'

Obviously with the lyrics, unlike either the confessional songwriter or the social commentator, you don't *set out* to say anything . . .

'Eighty per cent of it's baloney, yeah. It's that T-Rex thing of "if it *sounds* cool . . .". I write the songs by singing a whole bunch of syllables along with the chord progressions, and they become words. A bunch of five words might mean something, or stand for something. But the five words after it, or preceding it, sure as hell won't have anything to do with them.'

Kristin Hersh operates in a similar way, but because her stuff is a stream of *un*consciousness, of dream imagery, you can take it as being riddled with all kinds of meanings she didn't consciously place there, threads you can unravel and perhaps 'read'. Can your words be interpreted at all, or *shouldn't* they be?

'I guess they must have a root somewhere; often the songs are vaguely about something. Like that line "oh bury me / far away / please", it doesn't really mean anything, but it could mean the guy's despondent about being "the son of incestuous union". Or like the whole biblical thing of when the women were menstruating: "go outside the city walls and do your bleeding out there". [I have to say, the connection here eludes me, but this probably says more about the short-circuited synapses of this young visionary than he or I could ever 'work out'.]

'I like David Lynch's movies, his attitude where you don't always explain everything, you just come up with stuff that looks good and sounds good, and you just go with it. And you can look back on it if you wanna.'

Your approach, your thang, reminds me a bit of Surrealist phonetic poetry . . .

92

'It's definitely arbitrary, about going with the immediate. I read this interview with Robyn Hitchcock, he talked about saying something without thinking about why you said it, and because it has a root inside you, it's much more *real*, true to you, than if you think and analyse everything. That made me a lot more confident about automatic writing, or whatever you want to call it.'

It must be a fantastic release.

'*Nothing* beats volume . . . and lights . . . and drunken people.'

Kim: 'If I didn't personally have this release, I wonder *what* I'd do instead.'

It sounds like it should be performed onstage with much loss of inhibition.

Charles: 'We're not good enough players to ad lib like that. We're still kind of static on stage. Kim kind of *twitches*. Dave looks like your baby brother when you think he's dying, but he's just crapping his diapers.'

Well, I suppose the trad gestures of disinhibition just look rehearsed anyway, maybe it's more electrifying and electrified to be rooted to the spot. What's Albini like to work with?

'He's like this brainiac, about six foot tall but only eighty pounds, always reading, always figuring out manuals to see how things work. He's into lo-tech, eight-track, he likes *live*, he hates overdubs.'

Kim: 'He *hates* vocals. We spent days and days on the guitars and drums, and did the vocals in one night. It's like he said: "You're going to do vocals on that song? Well, if you *really* want to . . ." He said that it's the first time he's worked with people who can sing. He *hated* doing the "ri-ri-ri" harmonies on "River Euphrates".'

Charles: 'He's very extreme. It's either "that's great, that's genius" or "that's pussy, that sucks".'

Joey: 'Pussy or non-pussy, that was the studio jargon.'

Kim: 'Everything had to be full throttle. I wish there were more dynamics in it. Every song on the album is produced with the same non-effects, so there's not enough ear-variety.'

Charles: 'I like him because he likes LOUD. All the needles were on red. He totally overloaded the tape.'

Joey: 'He let me use my amp, which was cool. It's this country-jazz amp, which engineers don't like because it's real whiney.'

John Murphy: 'On "Something About You" he put Charles's voice through a guitar, to make it sound all grisly.'

Charles: 'The thing about Albini is that he's so military macho, but he has this *exhaustive* knowledge of gay culture, so you wonder . . . he told us about stuff like "felching", [unprintable, readers, sorry, but if you write enclosing an SAE . . .] and "gerbilling".'

This involves the use of a 'de-clawed, de-fanged, oiled' rodent for the purposes of unnatural pleasure.

'But sometimes the tail breaks, and there are cases where people have to go to hospital . . .'

Charles: 'The *world* is going to end, y'know . . .'

Dave: 'He's part of this network of like minds who circulate videos among themselves, people like the Butthole Surfers. They're into gore . . . Albini has this video of a politician in Pennsylvania who went on a news conference and blew his brains out on air. And videos of people shooting eggs out of their ass, right across the room into another guy's mouth.'

And why 'Surfer Rosa' . . .?

Charles: 'See, there's this nude flamenco dancer on the cover, and 4AD wanted to call the LP *Gigantic* after the song, but decided they couldn't because of the big breasts . . . People might have got the wrong ideas, so I had to come up with something else.'

Something else is what he came up with.

What's this underground that you and Throwing Muses are deemed to be part of?

Kim: 'See, I don't really think there's such a thing as the underground any more. In '81, '82, when the punk thing was really going over here, maybe there was. But now, if you're anything at all, you can get an independent record out, get a video together, maybe get it shown late night on MTV.

'The underground is overground now. Before, though, like with the Stray Cats, nobody in Ohio had ever heard of them, you couldn't get the records, they were never on the radio. I got hold of their stuff by trading cassettes, like they do in Russia. Same with James Blood Ulmer, Captain Sensible, all that stuff . . .'

'All that stuff' – it's interesting how the demarcations and taste hierarchies we have in Britain just don't hold in the States. The local commercial New Wave radio station plays Sinead, Nitzer Ebb, Midnight Oil, Dukes of Stratosphear, Godfathers, Love and Rockets; Mr and Mrs Murphy will introduce me to Aerosmith's back catalogue, but will flip when I play them The Sugarcubes; the Boston nightclub Axis will mix Cabaret Voltaire and Skinny Puppy with ghastly Noo Wave monstrosities that sound like Belinda Carlisle covering the Comsats' 'Independence Day'; Charles will enthuse about his Damned CDs. Everything's topsy turvy.

What makes them most proud about being Pixies?

Kim: 'Okay, this is my own thing, but having lunched and dined with Steve Albini, that we respect human beings. I know that sounds queer, but listening to him rag and rag, he's so sure, and *nobody* can be that sure and not be an asshole. *Nobody* knows what's going on anyway, so how can he actually say "this song sucks" and when he says it, he means it, that's the truth. You *can't* say that.

'When he was ragging on people and cutting them down, that was a bad feeling. An old man and an old lady came in to the diner, and he'd go "they're stupid, they're old, they're dumb", he doesn't even have to look at them, he KNOWS it.'

Charles: 'I like the fact that none of us are rock 'n' roll type people, we're truly naive, so it's very pure. There's not a lot of thought.'

The Pixies put a lot of *thoughtlessness* into their music.

David: 'Just the fact that how we look, how we sound, and what our name is – *nothing fits* together at all, in any aspect.'

Are you particularly interested in the uncanny or freaky?

Kim: 'You mean do we have any *stories*? There's the cake lady. This girl follows the Muses wherever they play, and gives them this food she bakes for them. Cakes.'

Any good?

'I guess so. They eat them. At first they were kinda scared. Every gig they play, she brings food. She was there last night, at the Braddle Theater. A real Bertha. A plain, rather heavy looking girl.'

I saw her. She looks out of time, from the fifties.

'Yeah, always that style.'

Was the desire to escape the fate of your parents, a regular, stolid life, was that a beatnik-impulse behind wanting to be in a rock band?

Charles: 'You mean, trying to rebel against the "leave-it-to-Beaver-ness" of your family?'

Sorry?

'Do you know the TV Show *Leave it to Beaver*? It's a TV show from the fifties, a comedy about the ideal, nuclear family, being an upstanding member of the community, "gee dad, I didn't mean to knock her up", that kind of thing.'

Dave: 'Kids today have all these jokes based on the show, like "How's your Beaver, Mrs Cleaver?", or what's the worst? Um, "Ward, you were a little hard on the Beaver last night." See, Ward is the father and Beaver is the little kid.'

Charles: 'I mean, yeah – both Joey and me went to college in order to be in bands. And we dropped out of college to make a go of it. I don't want to look back and think, "Oh, I wish I'd been in a rock band instead of this." At least have a go.'

Do you think there are singular, definable feelings in your songs?

Charles: 'Hmmm . . . if you're angry, you scream, I guess.'

95

But it's not an anger directed at anyone or caused by anything specific.

'No, it's just for the pure satisfaction of screaming. Just the yyyooOOOOOWWWW!'

Do you think the music sounds druggy?

'I don't know. I don't do drugs. Do you think it does?'

It sounds kind of wired, vaguely trippy . . .

'There's a certain attitude that – although when you analyse it it's all baloney, just volume and entertainment – that "yeah, THIS is what I have to say, everyone else has what they want to say, but THIS is what *I* have to say. It doesn't make a lot of sense, but it's *all* I have, and THIS is it."'

So it's like a preacher testifying?

'Sure. I've been kinda affected by the charismatic Pentecostal thing, which my family was into when I was a kid in California. I grew up exposed to a lot of preaching and righteous rage, and though I've rejected the content of all that, the style has kinda left an impression on me. It certainly left me fucked up, that's for sure.'

Hence all the religious imagery. Was it a really strict sect?

'No, it was pretty American: all handclapping, heaven and hell and sin. It wasn't *quiet*, it wasn't Anglican. It was all "RRRRRREPENT" and "GOD"! I was twelve and religion came over my entire family. But it began to erode when I was about seventeen. No, it wasn't the influence of rock 'n' roll that drew me away, I was always into rock. It wasn't forbidden, if anything they encouraged it.'

The *real* High Priest of rock 'n' roll, talking in tongues as he loves. The religion of the end of religion. And The Word was . . . the death of The Word.

Melody Maker, 19 March 1988

The main thing I remember about this interview was sharing the bed of Mrs John Murphy, later and better known as Kim Deal. Unfortunately I didn't share it with Kim herself but with Tom Sheehan, chief photographer of *Melody Maker*. It was a sofa bed in the Murphys' living room; Kim and her husband had generously rescued us when it transpired that 4AD had neglected to book us into a hotel in Boston. Ah, The Pixies . . . these days they tend to get remembered for their more whimsically tuneful and kitschadelic sides ('Here Comes Your Man', 'Velouria'), such that it can clean slip your mind just how primal and rampant and visceral their music felt early on (especially the dark animalistic vision of *Doolittle*), when they were very much a Dionysian sound of id-energy being vented, as opposed to the light-hearted pop-craft of *Bossanova* and *Trompe le Monde*.

LIVING COLOUR

Living Colour are one of the bands worth *talking about* in '88. The band and its sister project the Black Rock Coalition raise so many questions about race and about rock – where it's coming from, where it can go, what it can *do*. And Living Colour are great to *talk to*. In a year in which vacancy has been the hip demeanour for the rock band in interview, it's refreshing to encounter a group where not only the frontman, but the bassist and drummer, are eager and capable ideologues.

But, despite being in supreme sympathy with their project (the reclamation for blacks of the right to rock, the right for black musicians to be treated as artists as opposed to entertainers), I approach Living Colour with doubts. Their music hasn't really *got* me as yet. They have perhaps three 'moments' – the monolithic moronic metal of 'Cult of Personality' and 'Desperate People', the dreamy despondency of the curious 'Broken Hearts' – but most of their material is a polychromatic purée fusing too many sources too fluently.

Lyrically, everything's a bit too coherent. Issues are *dealt* with, methodically; whereas the rock I dig at the moment is about *not* knowing what you want. But then as Black Americans, Living Colour have very clear ideas about what they want, about what bugs them, and music is clearly a route to self-realization. The white male middle-class flirtations with destabilization, derangement, hysteria, thraldom, just aren't an option.

Does it bug them that critics respond to the black rock issue, and tend to downplay the fact that Living Colour are a band?

Vernon Reid (guitarist): 'Obviously, the Black Rock Coalition and Living Colour are linked. It's a double-edged thing. People taking us seriously as a band is very important. But they also have to take us seriously as people. Outside of playing guitar, bass, drums, those problems in society around race still affect us every day. And people are very comfortable with NO DISCUSSION about race at all.'

Corey Glover (vocals): 'Our experience is of being four black men, it's all we know. So we have to address the question of race. What we'd like to hear now is that we're four musicians as well . . .'

You must be wary also of the danger you might become a cause for white liberals to champion . . .

Muzz Skillings (bass): 'We hope this won't happen. The bottom line is music. But we're also music with a message, we do want to open people's eyes. But it's not a cause.'

Vernon: 'It's not like we're saying: "Living Colour are the definitive Voice of Black Rock". We're *part* of an emerging culture, including everything from Bad Brains to Fishbone to A.R. Kane. And with the Black Rock Coalition we also embrace the issue of a music that's remained unheard, that has never been acknowledged as bona fide rock 'n' roll. Like the Isley Brothers, Funkadelic, Mandrill . . . There are hundreds of majority black rock bands that were never critically or radio-wise acknowledged. And right now, there are hundreds of unsigned black rock bands across the country. They don't fit into the indie college scene, or the mainstream. What we're trying to do is open up a marketplace for black rock. We've faced so many obstacles, but we don't let it immobilize ourselves. Rather we take strength from the fact that we're part of a great tradition of iconoclasts, people that are misunderstood.'

Corey: 'But the kind of message we're trying to put over crosses racial lines. It's for people who happen to be being stepped on, who get lost between the cracks. The song "Funny Vibe" can apply to a black person, but it can also apply to a punk, because he can face the same kind of prejudice.'

Vernon: 'It's a funny thing, cos on one level we're the same as everybody else. But we're different too. Because whether you're raised in a nice suburb, or a shitty precinct, the spectre of racism will get you. It's like a black kid's coming of age involves all the usual stuff – sexual confusion, awkwardness, trying to find out who you are – and this added component, the hassle, the media stereotypes. Hispanic and Asian kids get it too. It gets you through the minutiae, the tiniest things. You go get a box of crayons as a kid, and what freaks me, the crayon called "flesh tone" is this pinkish colour, and you think, "Damn! What *is* this?"'

Have you always been into hard rock?

Corey: 'People ask that all the time, and it's like, "How *could* you? You're *black*!"'

What I mean is, a lot of black kids clearly *aren't* into it and, moreover, a lot of white kids have now *given up* on rock . . .

Vernon: 'I went through a phase of not being into rock, and that was when it seemed like there was no place for *me* in it. The rock I grew up with was Sly Stone, Led Zeppelin, Hendrix, Santana. Radio would play James Brown and Zeppelin back to back, even black radio started to turn on to Hendrix. Then, in the mid-seventies rock became a white-only territory.'

So how did you get back to rock? I know that you're all virtuoso players, you've all been in an incredible range of bands – why choose to focus on a form that seems relatively limited?

Vernon: 'You see, I don't think it *is* limited. Once rock or anything becomes a methodology or genre it's in real trouble. Like with jazz, it was taken in so many different directions by Charlie Parker or Eric Dolphy or Miles Davis, and Ornette Coleman was somewhere else altogether, but it was all *jazz* . . . '

Don't you think there's a case for arguing that rock's strength is actually its inflexibility, its confines? For all the changes over three decades from rockabilly to hardcore, the core of the best stuff has been monotony, lack of subtlety, a certain cretinism even . . .

Vernon: 'But you take a band like Zeppelin, they had weird time signatures, Latin influences, Celtic influences. But it *rocked*, y'know. George Clinton, he turned rock 'n' roll around with "Cosmic Slop", "Superstoopid". Rap's turned rock 'n' roll around. I don't think you can really say that rock 'n' roll has to be basic in order to work.'

William Calhoun (drums): 'And you can find infinity inside the smallest range of chords, like Charlie Parker did.'

So you don't find being a 'hard rock' band, signed to Epic, a constraining format?

Vernon: 'No. Sure, we've *focused* our attention. If we incorporate things from "elsewhere" it's only if it works songwise. Like "Broken Hearts", which has this C&W slide guitar sound over this hip hop beat – but it works as a song. If it didn't – if we put Czechoslovak music next to speed metal – we'd drop it. A lot of that kind of experimentation can be just trite.'

You're playing a style of music that I personally use to get brain-blasted, mentally incapacitated. You use it to raise consciousness. A contradiction?

Corey: 'There's a very popular band whose singer said that he can't listen to U2 cos it drives him nuts to *think* that much. That *makes no sense*! If it wasn't for thinking and people with a conscience, the music that this guy's playing wouldn't be *around* today.'

Vernon: 'One problem I have with the "Oh man, I don't want to think that much" attitude is that it goes hand in hand with . . . sexism, racism, you name it. That Neanderthal "uh, duh" thing is anathema, cos it dovetails with all kinds of ignorance. Plus if you don't think about what's around you, it's gonna come up and *swallow* you.'

Thing is, I suspect most of your audiences here are pretty aware, and there's the danger of preaching to the conver –

Vernon: 'I KNEW you were gonna say that! One thing about Living Colour is we don't project this air of "We've Come . . . To Deliver . . . the Message . . . Because We . . . Being OPPRESSED People . . . Understand". It's only about talking about what's real to us, what we *live* with. Part of which is the question of what we want as a rock band, the dilemmas of becoming well-known, what that can do to you. Part of which is the question of leadership: who should we follow, should we follow anyone at all? Part of which is the question of where "America" is. We write songs about questions we think about *every day*.

'One thing that *interests* me . . . *Melody Maker* has been pretty brutal to us, on the whole, especially that first live review, so it's kinda curious that they would send someone to speak to us . . .'

That review. Well, erm, that was *me* . . .

(In unison): 'OOOOOHHHHH! *That* was YOU!'

They are pretty good-humoured about all this, and the calls for me to be strung up by my ankles are made in a spirit of utmost joviality. I explain that I had been aware of the Black Rock Coalition for quite some time and had come to their London debut with high expectations (something midway between Jimi Hendrix and Bad Brains). Living Colour got the sharp end of my disappointment. The idea of *this*, though, was for a more constructive dialogue. Like, do they never feel that their lyrics are maybe a little too defined, that there's not enough space for the listener to make a creative reading?

Vernon: 'Not enough ambiguity, you mean? I think there's a fair amount of ambiguity in a song like "Which Way is America?", a line like "'we don't wanna crossover, but how *do* we keep from going under?". It's like . . . conundrums. Cos how *do* you answer that dilemma? It's all about questioning what is happening to us.'

Their outlook sometimes makes me think of the British post-punk spirit of demystification. Don't they think mystique, mystification, fantasy, are important parts of the rock experience?

'And we take the fun out of rock, is that it? Ha ha! No, demystifying things is a response to being *mystified*. Bewildered. Like "Funny Vibe", that isn't a statement of policy, it's our *confusion*. How is it that I can be walking out of my door, full of love and understanding for the human race, and some white person sees me and crosses the road. That attitude of "you're a young black male, you're a hoodlum, either you're gonna do something or you already done something". People get killed cos of those attitudes. It's mystifying. I still don't *understand* Howard Beach, y'know. We're just trying to get to grips with the things we have to deal with.'

Having made me question whether my pleasure in the oblivious rock of the moment is a symptom of decadence, Living Colour almost clinch it with a very impressive performance at the Leeds Warehouse that night. They are a blazing, kick-ass entertainment, and this time, what was addled by nuances now achieves heat-haze incandescence. At their best, they offer a kind of benevolently despotic heavy rock. And that underlines the choice that faces them: either coagulate further into moronically monstrous metal, or take on such expanse that they burst the banks of rock.

They've yet to link up with 1988's headlong immersion in the fatuity of love. Living Colour are too *aware* (because they *have* to be) to produce an astigmatic masterpiece of incoherence like *Daydream Nation*. Schizophrenia, chaos, 'the sublime', are luxuries. Like That Petrol Emotion, they're a paradigm of immense potential as yet arrested. At the moment they *represent* themselves too clearly. They are not an ocean. But they could do anything, literally anything. They're attuned to everything that's going on now from Anthrax and Public Enemy to A.R. Kane and The Cocteau Twins. So watch this space.

Melody Maker, 26 November 1988

After this rare (back then, anyway) lapse into fairmindedness, I soon reverted to the original verdict on Living Colour as vented in that live review of their UK debut at the ICA, which ended with the kiss-off 'for the real coming of Black Rock, look to A.R. Kane and Bad Brains'. The substance of my objections was that even at their loudest and most rampaging, Living Colour were always a little bit too exquisite and poised, clearly in thrall to ideals of 'slick' and 'flashy'. Notions of less-is-more and the value of non-virtuosity (Holger Czukay's 'restriction is the mother of invention') don't have an awful lot of currency in black rock. Punk, it seemed, never really happened for these bands (because 'prowess' signifies pride, mastery of your instrument equated with being your own master?). Even Bad Brains, a devastating live experience, were clearly as tautly rehearsed as Earth Wind and Fire or Zapp; their special friction and fire came from cramming astounding musicianship (they'd started as the fusion outfit Mind Power!) within the rigid parameters of hardcore punk.

VARIOUS ARTISTS

Sub Pop 200 (Sub Pop)

Washington State's Sub Pop label sees itself as a guardian of the true delinquent tradition of rock 'n' roll. The '56/'66/'76 axis, the lineage that runs through rockabilly, sixties garage, punk, and between those pivots, Iggy, No Wave, hardcore, and the more dumb-ass metal of the early seventies. The Gospel according to Lester Bangs, in fact, although he eventually dissed all that in an essay called 'The White Noise Supremacists'. Rock's more spacious and galactic forays are clearly, if unspokenly, rejected as defections from the straight and narrow.

For me, all this juvenile dementia has just been transcended by Sonic Youth's *Daydream Nation*. Here, there's nothing so particular or ignoble as an urge, but the *nirvana* of desire dissolving. Daydream nationalists are kids who aren't active enough to be exiles on main street, to be visible dissidents: instead they've *disappeared*.

There's nothing on the *Sub Pop 200* box set that has moved beyond joint-trashing rumpus to reach this kind of rapture, or that understands that last year the coolest thing to be was *asleep*. The Sub Pop roster is divided between those who believe in carrying on the tradition, updating and embellishing it, and those who want to recover the moment before the notion of 'tradition' was even *conceivable*. For instance, Beat Happening's 'Pajama Party in a Haunted Hive' is rock 'n' roll disinterred and jiving cadaverously: it kick-starts with a zombiefied riff and low moans from the crypt, before leaping into lewdly surreal doggerel: 'I'm driving and I'm pumping red / Sting me queen bee sting me drip me honey . . . '. It's the kind of rock sepulchre we haven't been entombed in since the Mary Chain's 'Head'.

But most of the bands on *Sub Pop 200* offer us *renovation* rather than *time travel*. The Fluid, Blood Circus, Swallow and Chemistry Set are firmly in the mould of the Saints and late Iggy: all emphatic, telling guitar blows and anti-heroic bluster, riffs as trusty and blinkered as old warhorses, and raw-cuss vocals. Green River and Nirvana's joint error is to forget that cleverness and dexterity are actually *more* boring than simplistic monotony.

But there is some cracking stuff here. Tad's 'Sex God Missy' is a brutish groin-grind, with tape loops in the middle that gabble like a metal solo. The great-but-not-*that*-great Mudhoney weigh in with 'The Rose', a cantankerous dirge, with the graunchiest guitar tones on all six sides of this compilation. Terry Lee Hale's ostensibly unremarkable folk punk is elevated suddenly by a crater of fretboard fractures where the middle eight should be, making 'Dead I Dead' almost as good as a My Bloody Valentine ballad. Soundgarden's 'Sub Pop Rock City' is a crazed, pervy, twisted blowout like some dream fusion of The Pixies and Dinosaur Jr. And Screaming Trees vandalize Hendrix' 'Love Or Confusion' with results as solar as the original.

Generally, however, *Sub Pop 200* showcases a reading/rending of the past that is pretty limited. Those old and foolish enough to hanker for the next 'revolution' are wasting their time if they're looking here. For the real convulsions are being conducted by the cosmonauts of inner/outer space, not those who hark back to an obsolete model of teenage rampage 'wild in the streets'. Only diehards and record collectors will want to fork out £20 for the eight or nine gems amid all this variable artistry.

Melody Maker, January 1989

Another 'misjudgement' – except, like the house-as-lame-duck comment a few years earlier, it was correct, at that precise point in time: the Seattle sound really *was* a backwards step after My Bloody Valentine/Sonic Youth/et al. I'm surprised I was complimentary to Mudhoney. Witnessing their UK live debut a few months deeper into 1989, I was bored almost literally to tears. Their on-the-surface wildness masked a tame predictability; they struck me as the epitome of a certain sort of archivist approach that turned the garage into a museum. Reviewing the show, I concluded that the band were carving out a future for themselves as the oldest teenagers in town. Sixteen years later, at a festival in São Paolo, I would hear the ageless and immaculate snarl of Mudhoney's Mark Arm once again, only this time fronting the MC5. As for Nirvana, the exact same 'warhorse' metaphor popped into my head reviewing one of their singles a year or so later, me declaring their riffs were fit only for the knacker's yard. But even listening with hindsight-wise ears, the early Nirvana stuff, while vigorous, doesn't sound destined for greatness. The band made a quantum leap when they went for the mainstream's jugular and embraced Butch Vig's grunge-with-gloss production.

THE STONE ROSES

Manchester's The Stone Roses are widely regarded as the most happening band in Britain. Their debut album, *The Stone Roses*, has topped the indie charts, but that in itself is not a particularly remarkable feat, just one they share with all manner of nonentities. So what makes them different?

Their arrogance, for a start. They're not shy of making pronouncements like 'we're the best band in Britain' or 'we're the best band in the world', with a bald, bland conviction that's in marked contrast to the tongue-tied humility of most indie bands. They've haughtily refused the 'sound career moves' that have presented themselves in the form of offers of support slots on major tours (like New Order), on the grounds that they've never played second fiddle to any band, and don't intend to start now. Live, they exude an almost messianic aura, that's perfectly fitting for songs with titles like 'I Wanna Be Adored' and 'I Am the Resurrection'. And where most indie groups search studiously for the most arcane reference points to namedrop, The Stone Roses allude unabashedly to the Beatles, Hendrix, Stones, the Sex Pistols – influences so embarrassingly obvious that by a weird twist of oneupmanship they become the apotheosis of hip. And, of course, the implication is that The Roses are themselves that class of band. They may not be far wrong. In fact, their charisma is so dead centre between the deadpan wit of the Fab Four and the mordant sarcasm of the Pistols, it's uncanny.

For the moment, The Stone Roses wait on the world to wake up to them, and content themselves with being the biggest band in their hometown, Manchester. They're prime movers in a new kind of Manchester scene, a world away from the 'miserabilist' image bequeathed by the bedsit angst of Mancunian legends like Joy Division and The Smiths. It's a scene where a taste for contemporary dance music goes hand in hand with a rediscovery of sixties psychedelics like Pink Floyd, where an interest in drugs like MDMA and LSD meets up with a preference for flared jeans. (Singer Ian Brown gets his flares made up specially to his own expansive specifications, in order to stay ahead of the pack.)

The taste for casual, baggy clothing is emblematic of a new loose-minded attitude, a lust for life that's laidback rather than desperate. 'We hate tense people,' says guitarist John Squire. ' You're only here once, it's not a rehearsal. The tense people are the twats who are only interested in making money and who fuck things up for everybody else.' The Stone Roses loathe the neo-fifties spirit of eighties enterprise culture, the revival of suit-and-tie formality and respectability.

The second mark of difference is that The Roses are a dance band. Where most indie-pop is 'head' music, either an ethereal daydream daze or mindblowing trance-rock that immobilizes the listener in a near-catatonic state, The Stone Roses groove. They *move* the crowd. They say they don't listen to current guitar rock, just house music, dub reggae and seventies funk, and it shows. The only contemporary band they feel any affinity with are fellow-Mancunians and acid-funk lunatics Happy Mondays. It's no coincidence that the Mondays and The Roses are the two indie bands that people who've otherwise written off rock music altogether make an exception for . . .

'We can see their point,' says Ian, 'cos we've been bored of rock music for the last five years. I dunno, everyone I know has always liked rock music and dance music. Punk rock and Northern Soul. So I don't think it's unusual for our fans to be into dance music. Those dividing lines aren't there any more. You can tell when you go to warehouse parties and they play acid house beats but they put Hendrix or the Beatles over the top. They've even started to put our stuff over the top now . . .'

The third factor is that The Stone Roses have brought rage back into indie-pop. On the sugar-spun surface, their songs seem to conform to the poignant introspection that is the indie-pop norm. Look closer, and what appear to be tales of love/hate relationships are in fact poisonous tirades against the establishment. The Stone Roses' cleverness is to have couched the virulence and rancour of the Pistols in the bittersweet lyricism of sixties 'perfect pop'.

Ian: 'If you go home and listen to "Bye Bye Badman" and then imagine it's someone singing to a riot policeman on the barricades in Paris '68, you'll get a picture of what we're about. The song is a call to insurrection. It's important, if you have that aggression, to retain it as you get older. Cos people get mellower as they age. But people like Tony Benn and Michael Foot don't. The current Labour leadership can't compare with them. Labour's outdated and gone, anyway: it's been left behind, it's served its purpose. If you read the Crossman diaries or books about Harold Wilson, it'll tell you that even when a Labour government gets in, it can't actually change the country, or implement its own polices, because of the way the country's set up.

'I don't know what the solution is. I just know there's a lot of people who stay on it, and that gives me inspiration. There's a bloke called Benny Rothman, who lives fifteen minutes from my mum's house, who led the Kinder Trespass, in the thirties, in the hills up above Manchester where local people weren't allowed to go on the land. The first time he went on the land, all these lords whipped him to the ground. The next week he came back with 6,000 people, kids, women, and held firm, and that led to the setting up of the National Trust. And he's now having to organize it all again, cos those lands have been bought by some Americans. He's still there, at eighty, he's never mellowed. People like that you've got to listen to. Not people who scream and shout from fifteen till twenty-two and then stop.

'That's the thing about 1989. You see 11,000 people dancing at a warehouse party, and really it's basically that people are realizing that this is a cruel world and you've got to find people, with similar attitudes, and you've got to stick with them and watch each other's backs. There's so much shit being put out, lowest common denominator garbage on all levels, that I do believe people can only take so much.'

The Stone Roses have stirred up controversy with their venomous attacks on the Royal Family, like Ian's comment in *Melody Maker* that 'we're all anti-royalist, anti-patriarch. Cos it's 1989. Time to get real. When the ravens leave The Tower, England shall fall, they say. We want to be there shooting the ravens.' Have their printed remarks about Prince Charles ('I'd like to see him dead. I'd like to shoot him') engendered any flak or reprisals ?

Ian: 'I had a guy in Shrewsbury spitting in my face, all through the gig, telling me he was gonna kill me, and he was punching people out of the way to get at me. But we've also had a lot of support. Especially in Scotland. They don't really believe in the idea of a United Kingdom up there. Up there, they say Manchester's south of Glasgow, not north of England!'

Where Ian seems extrovert, his creative 'other half', John, is more withdrawn, venting himself more through his incendiary guitar-work. Another outlet is art (his action paintings, 'out and out rip-offs of

Jackson Pollock', adorn the Roses record sleeves). 'The first thing I did for a record was in '85, a collage of broken glass and computer components and stuff. But I've been painting and making things since as long as I can remember: Play Doh, Airfix, Lego and that.' John says this so straightfaced it's impossible to tell if he's taking the piss.

Perhaps the last word should go to Andrew Lauder, head of their record company Silvertone and a man who's been on the cutting edge of music since the late sixties. In the seventies he had seminal bands signed to United Artists like Can, Neu!, Amon Duul II, Hawkwind, Dr Feelgood, and was the man behind controversial punk signings like The Buzzcocks and The Stranglers. Later he set up Radar as the home of Elvis Costello, Nick Lowe, Pere Ubu and The Pop Group. In the eighties Lauder spearheaded the growth of the reissue label with Demon and Edsel. 'I like outlaw bands, ones who want to do things in a different way,' Lauder says. 'I tend to be interested in the bands that record companies find it difficult to deal with. It makes life hard for me sometimes, but that's what makes it interesting too.' The Stone Roses are the latest in Lauder's line of awkward bastards, demanding complete control and more importantly, doing something with it.

Director's cut of piece published in *The Observer* July 1989

That last line rings weird now, given the Roses' struggle to free themselves from their contract with Silvertone, in the process fatally derailing their career and dissipating the momentum they'd built up by mid 1990. But in some ways the enforced hiatus was fortuitous. The Roses were having real problems articulating the mood that had built up around them. In some obscure process, they'd been 'elected' as figureheads. 'In early '89, when we did gigs, you could just feel the people willing you to go for it,' Ian Brown recalled when I interviewed the Roses circa 1995's *Second Coming*. 'Fool's Gold' had been a good if oblique anti-eighties money culture anthem, but 'One Love', the follow-up, was vague and vapid. 'Fool's Gold' was also a sonic testament to the Roses' self-touted relationship with black music, which otherwise could seem somewhat gestural, a component of their myth, e.g. 'Black kids always had something going . . . 1989 was the year the white kids woke up,' as Brown put it in the same 1995 interview. But the group's love of funk and house and reggae was a subliminal presence in the force and feel of the superb rhythm section (Mani and Reni, completely unmentioned in the piece above!). In some ways, this was an extension of their retro-ness, making them more authentically sixties-like than other similarly inclined British bands. Unlike the rhythmically feeble *C86* shamblers, the Roses didn't just pick up on the era's candygirl melodicism, but the fact that *all* sixties groups were dance bands with years of grounding in rhythm-and-blues. So while Primal Scream (a big influence on The Stone Roses) had to weld their psych pop on to a chassis of modern rhythm built by producers like Andy Weatherall, the Roses could directly assimilate the hypno-groove feel of the acid house era into their sound.

THE CARING COLONIALISTS

A Critique of 'World Music'

(written with Paul Oldfield)

The 'world music' phenomenon is everywhere. On TV, we've had programmes like *Big World Café*, *Wired* and the *Rough Guide*; on radio, Andy Kershaw and Charlie Gillett; and in print, *The Wire* magazine, features in *The Face*, and the *NME*'s 'Other Voices' page, while the quality press now tend to replace their former rock coverage with features on WOMAD, on ethnic (usually African) musicians like Salif Keita, Mory Kante or The Bhundu Boys, or on senior pop stars who co-opt global musics or seek out music's 'roots' (U2, Paul Simon, Sting). In 1988, *The Guardian* failed to notice the prolific, progressive reinventions of rock and European electronic music all around and, significantly, nominated The Pogues' traditionalist, Hibernian barroom jaunt as 'LP of the Year'.

What's interesting isn't so much the music and its merits as all the propaganda and rhetoric that surround it. It's assumed that the more Afro-Caribbean or pre-industrial folk musics we listen to, the better. We congratulate ourselves on conquering our ethnocentricity, on rediscovering neglected forms and values, and on finding an antidote to the sterility of pop music. But in fact world music's devotees scarcely discover anything unfamiliar in other cultures. Instead, they've created this 'world' to staunch the crisis of faith in our pop, and have grafted their own very Western, very eighties preoccupations on to it.

World music's disciples fall into two denominations. First, there are the likes of Charlie Gillett, David Toop, *The Wire*, and style bibles like *iD* and *The Face*. This class of people are embarrassed by their one-time allegiance to rock's uncaring, adolescent values. For them, 'world' means maturity, sophistication, open-mindedness and cosmopolitan cool.

The other school of thought wants instead to rediscover the lost essence of rock 'n' roll. DJ Andy Kershaw defines this type. His audience, he's said, are people who grew up with punk/pub rock and are 'bored shitless' now that that moment has passed. So the disparate musics that he plays on his Radio 1 show, such as country and western, bluegrass, go-go, soca, high life, Cajun and Celtic folk, are chosen for their rock-like rootsiness (hence the Afrocentrism of so-called 'world' music), spontaneism and honesty. Fans of this music want a vicarious sense of belonging, of community, *wherever* it's to be found.

But what all these advocates of world music share is the belief that other cultures represent the 'authenticity', naturalness and wholeness that the Western world has forfeited. Modern civilization founded itself on the repression of the 'dark continent' of its own drives and the parallel suppression of 'primitive', apparently less than human cultures. But ever since the psychoanalytic revolution, the West has learned to equate repression with impoverishment. The modern world has convinced itself that it is uniquely 'sick', cut off from passion, instinct and the body. Today *the West* is less than human, and must look to blackness and to tribal people's 'simpler' way of life for models of un-repression, conviviality and natural living (and ethnic musicians must learn to talk in such terms too, if they want to win our approval).

Thus Talking Heads' David Byrne sees America as the land of neurosis and psychosis, and embraces Africa as a repository of mental health (*Remain In Light*, *Naked*). Thus Sting could make a pilgrimage to the rainforests to tell indigenous chiefs that 'the white man is sick. He doesn't understand himself . . . we come to *learn* from you.'

This new orthodoxy is fallacious. *All* culture is an alienation, an act of repression or an altering of nature. The tribal lifestyles that world music fans admire are actually more rule-bound, more repressive, *more* unnatural (ritual, extreme cosmetic surgery, scarification, etc.) than ours. And if they seem 'balanced', if they don't have the ills of deviance, dissent and decadence that we suffer, that's because they've never acquired the very models of individual freedom and growth, self-expression or naturalness that we are so eager to attribute to them.

World music claims to respect diversity and otherness, but it won't finally accept that other ways of living are alien or irreconcilable with ours. Its guiding belief is that we're all brothers under the skin, with a core of 'human' values. Hence the cultural transvestites, like white South African musician Johnny Clegg performing Zulu dances, and hence the efforts of Paul Simon and Peter Gabriel to create a 'rainbow coalition' of musics. Yet the idea of a family of man or a global village is just another Western export to the Third World.

World music is supposed to be a post-colonial phenomenon. Actually it's a more refined form of colonialism, ideological colonialism. Until recently, the West encouraged the developing world to embrace our models of progress and modernity (Coco-colonization, cultural imperialism). But now we've lost our own faith in progress. We believe in preserving other or ancient cultures, and we're embarrassed by the Third World's appetite for pop, synthesizers and TV, by its disregard for the past. So, just as we once foisted our idea of progress on the rest of the world, now we're force-feeding them our ideology of 'heritage'. We've made our culture into a theme park; they must do the same.

We've tried perfectly sincerely to restore the self-respect, self-determination and traditions of other cultures. But simply by teaching them such liberal values, we've annexed them still further into our ways of thinking. As an African musician, Salif Keita, said, 'Africa will never become anything other than what the West wants it to be.'

This makes it sound as if we can't enjoy other cultures without being caring colonialists. But maybe there's another option. Instead of approaching other cultures with humility and attempted fellow feeling, we can submit to the fascination of their irreducible otherness. We can forget Africa and listen to musics that still are a dark continent (Eskimo, Gamelan, shamanic music from the Amazonian jungles). We can listen to ritual or ecstatic music that's a trip out of this world, not just a detour back to our own enlightened values.

Director's cut of piece published in *The Guardian*, 1 September 1989

Although I've since opened up to the continent's charms quite a bit, at the time I did find most Afro-pop distinctly light-on-the-hear (the jangly guitar-playing often reminded me of Johnny Marr's more sunny-and-winsome side). Paul and I were struck by one titbit we uncovered in our researches, the story of a West African heavy metal group who went 'world' when they realized there was a market for it! Mostly what seemed odd was the way 'world' shrank the globe's surface to a wonky-sided polygon whose corners were South Africa, the Middle East, West Africa, Cuba and Brazil. In other words, give or take some rai or Ofra Haza (who turned out to be Yemen's equivalent to Barbra Streisand!), this was an Afrocentric construct, an assortment of Afro-diasporic rhythms embraced as a return to the pure source that originally nourished rock 'n' roll (hence Paul Simon's *Graceland* and its Brazil-oriented follow-up *The Rhythm of the Saints*). Yet 'world' was also post-rock 'n' roll in the sense of renouncing teenage rampage for adult sophistication, adolescent carelessness for grown-up concern (the armchair anti-colonialism of buying *Rhythms of Resistance* to hasten apartheid's fall). As for our counter-proposition of *Other*Worldly music . . . it just felt like there was something more honestly voyeuristic about such barefaced exoticism. So rather Byrne & Eno's 1981 *My Life in the Bush of Ghosts*, based on samples of field recordings and radio emissions, than Byrne's 1989 *Rei Momo*, a foray into Latin American styles like son, samba, salsa, and meringue, made with authentic ethnic musicians.

POSITIVITY

De La Soul, Soul II Soul, Deee-lite and New Age House

There's 'something in the air'. Whatever you want to call it – 'positivity', 'spiritual hedonism', 'good vibes' or 'peaceadelic' – a new zeitgeist is taking shape throughout dance music (which these days, practically *is* pop). People are once again feeling hopeful about hope.

During the eighties, it was rap that set the tone of club culture. Rap's psychology was survivalist, oscillating between delusions of omnipotence and paranoia. At best, the only community that rap could imagine was a strange brotherhood of lone rangers united in ruthless rivalry with each other. But in 1989 (the year the eighties died) the triumphalism that had characterised rap began to wane. Competition and confrontation were displaced by a new unity vibe and laidback sound trailblazed by De La Soul. 'Me Myself and I' dissed the braggadocio and ostentatious materialism of old school rap, which had equated 'being yourself' with the crunch of defeated foes under your stomping feet. In De La Soul's wake came a coalition of Afro-conscious rap groups called the Native Tongue movement (The Jungle Brothers, Queen Latifah, A Tribe Called Quest), all concerned with promoting awareness of community and history.

But the greatest influence on the new positivity in dance culture came from Soul II Soul. Their mellow-but-upful grooves tapped into a public shift in consciousness, a desire to 'move forward' from the divisive eighties towards a brighter, more integrated nineties. People were no longer content with rap's survival in the mean time; they wanted to live, NOW. Jazzie B's litany of gently chiding imperatives – 'elevate your mind', 'free your soul', 'work it out for yourself', 'be an asset to the collective' – aimed to put you on the right track, 'back to life, back to reality'. Where rap staged its individualistic triumphs against a backdrop of anonymous losers, Soul II Soul saw 'getting yourself together' as a contribution to a general amelioration. Individual initiative and entrepreneurialism enriches the community. It's an idea drawn from the Black American jargon of self-realization that underpins such diverse 'buppie' phenomena as the *Oprah Winfrey Show* and *Ebony* magazine.

Soul II Soul have been so successful at being positive role models and community leaders that their influence has been felt across the board in club culture. Perhaps worth singling out, however, is the Talkin' Loud label. The brainchild of DJ Gilles Peterson, it specializes in a dance-oriented fusion of rap, rare groove and jazz, combined with 'motivational' lyrics. The label's slogan is 'talkin' loud ... saying something', and that something mostly consists of variations on the abiding theme of 'aware' black pop: 'I am somebody'. Talkin' Loud's flagship act is The Young Disciples. Their 'Young Disciple Theme' samples Prince's line about 'a gang called The Disciples' from 'Sign O' The Times'. In Prince's apocalyptic scenario, the Disciples were 'high on crack and totin' a machine gun', but these Young Disciples are high on positivity and tote only an armoury of inspirational slogans: 'ever moving forwards', 'good vibes', 'step right on'. The Talkin' Loud aesthetic is firmly grounded in the canon of high-minded black artists: Coltrane, Curtis Mayfield, Stevie Wonder, Gil Scott Heron, Timmy Thomas. It's a pantheon in which black music's more dissolute and outlandish figures (Miles Davis, Hendrix, Sun Ra, Earth Wind and Fire, Michael Jackson, George Clinton) have no place: banished, doubtless, for their excesses of mysticism or frivolity, for not being properly aligned with the community and/or in touch with their roots.

If one strand of positivity has connections to a black pop tradition of uplifting sentiments and upward mobility, another has been shaped by a rather different rhetoric of self-realization: New Age. This input has seeped into dance music via the UK's rave culture. With acid house, the accent is less on community and communication, and more on the communion of Ecstasy (to mangle Baudrillard's phrase 'the ecstasy of communication'). Acid house started out as a means of getting out of your head (the 'let's get mental' attitude). But last year people began to see it as a means of getting your head together. Decadence was supplanted by 'spiritual hedonism'. The word 'joy' (an endemic buzzword in song titles) assumed a special resonance, signifying more than mere physical jollification on the dance floor, but rather a rapture carrying a vaguely mystical charge.

Soon, the shrewder indie-rock bands latched on to the positivity vibe. The Beloved are a typical case. Two years ago they were disciples of New Order's fusion of indie 'miserabilism' with electro-disco. But by late '89, they caught the cusp of contemporaneity with their hit single 'The Sun Rising', which combined a mellow groove (ideal for 'coming down' after the all-night rave) with a hymnal female backing vocal. The video for the next single, 'Hello', prominently featured that emblem of New Age chic, the flotation tank. The album *Happiness* expounded a philosophy of 'subversive affirmation', and was packed with sunny side up sentiments like 'up up and away / hello new day' and 'give the world a message, and the message is "Yes!"'

The Manchester groups have given their own particular spin to the positivity creed, with their buzzword 'baggy'. The Stone Roses have talked of their hatred for 'the tense bastards who fuck things up for everybody else'. This refusal of the uptight formality and go-for-it ambition of eighties style culture is expressed in the distinctive loose-limbed dance and loose-fitting clothes that characterize the Manchester vibe, and in the penchant for flower power imagery. But there's also a Mod input coming through in the post-Manchester scene. The Farm's 'Groovy Train' disses an ex-girlfriend who's traded in her 'attitude' in favour of social climbing, with the kind of class-based venom that characterised The Who's 'Stepping Stone'. On 'Sway', Ocean Colour Scene's enquiry 'do you want a piece of the action?' recalls the Mod rhetoric of Secret Affair and The Jam circa 'Absolute Beginners'.

Mainstream pop has also been affected by New Age positivism. Prince (who namechecked 'positivity' as early as 1988's 'Lovesexy') has spawned a legion of imitators – Lenny Kravitz, Dan Reed Network, World Party, Terence Trent D'Arby (whose last LP was heavily influenced by flotation tank therapy). Sinead O'Connor has shifted from her earlier angst-ridden autonomy to New Age serenity, as signposted in the title of her second album *I Do Not Want What I Haven't Got*. Then there's Neneh Cherry, with her belief in the power of 'positive aggression'. Like De La Soul's 'Me Myself and I', Neneh's 'Buffalo Gals' dissed the gold-wearing, Staggerlee machismo of rap.

Perhaps the culmination of the positivity phenomenon comes with Deee-lite. With their multi-racial/multi-sexual line-up, their fusion of rap, house and seventies disco, and their 'kitschedelic' image, Deee-lite are a Sly and the Family Stone for the age of sampling and computer video. Their *World Clique* album expounds a vision of club music as a kind of pop Esperanto.

Clearly, the positivity explosion is based in a widespread longing for well-being, togetherness, psychic equilibrium. Beyond these personal concerns, it reflects an idealistic hunger for change. The question is: can anything really be changed if the discourse stays stuck at the level of platitudes and their ritual incantation? The problem with the new positivism is that key buzzwords – belief, communication, integration, action, positivity – have become the point at which argument ends. Too often, all this perilously vague language communicates is a fervent belief in belief. If dance music is the new counterculture, it's yet to generate any great lyrical poets: a Lennon, Dylan, Morrison (Jim or Van), who can elevate the level of debate beyond that of the corny old showbiz adage 'accentuate the positive, eliminate the negative'.

Furthermore, some elements of the positivity programme are in direct conflict with the new sense of community. Positivity or 'spiritual hedonism' has its origins in the New Age belief that feeling good about yourself is a real contribution towards improving the world. Change starts from within. New Age thinking locates the problem with the individual, with your attitude. New Age remedies for 'bad attitude' include such dubious techniques as affirmation therapy: incantations (e.g. 'I will get on with my boss'), which if reiterated daily allegedly alter behaviour.

Positivity, too, can sometimes appear to consist of nothing more than a simple gainsaying of negativity: a denial of the existence of limitations, conflict, lack or tragedy. Positivity has little to say about the awkward problem of those who don't want to undergo a change of heart: the power-junkies, anal retentives and sado-crats (multinational corporations, Saddam Hussein, the military industrial complex) who are quite happy to stay 'sick'. From this perspective, positivity seems less like the harbinger of a new culture of resistance, and more like just another symptom of a culture of consolation.

Director's cut of feature for *New Statesman*, 21 September 1990

Missing here: the context, how late eighties prosperity underwrote the optimistic mood, which was further validated by a wave of geopolitical improvement. The staggered collapse of Communist governments across Europe triggered a sense of joyous disbelief – could it be, no more Cold War, no more Armageddon hanging over our heads? – captured on Jesus Jones's positivity anthem 'Right Here Right Now'. As much as the overtly New Agey or nouveau flower child aspects made me cringe (the nadirs being The Beloved's 'Hello', a rave-era 'Reasons to Be Cheerful' list-song, and the 'one happy planet' video for The Farm's 'All Together Now'), a lot of the music made under the sign of positivity was really enjoyable. The charm of things like Deee-lite now has a bittersweet tang, things not having panned out so well for the world (or the group, for that matter). But much more to my taste was the mixture of gladness and madness that developed as rave music's beats-per-minute accelerated and the vibe got harder and heavier. The spreadfreak culture of hardcore fused punk rage and hippie euphoria, and it remains for me the ultimate psychedelic dance music.

RAP'S REFORMATION

Gangsta Rap versus Conscious Rap

A dozen years or more since its birth in the deprived housing projects of New York, rap is now firmly established in mainstream US popular culture. Its influence can be seen on prime-time TV, in the braggadocio of chat-show host Arsenio Hall, or the feisty comedy show *In Living Color*, which cuts between black-on-black satirical sketches and *Do the Right Thing*-style rap choreography.

Rap's effect on mainstream US pop has been as revolutionary as the impact of house in Britain, ranging from the 'swingbeat' of Bobby Brown and Bell Div Devoe (smooth soul galvanized by hip hop rhythm and B-boy attitude) to New Kids on the Block (rap postures emasculated for the teenybopper shopping-mall culture market). Hardcore rap's own presence in the media has increased dramatically. Eight years ago MTV was reluctant to show black artists' videos, no matter how tame, for fear of alienating its mid-American, 'lite-metal' constituency. Now it broadcasts the hour-long *Yo! MTV Raps* daily, timed to coincide with schoolkids returning home.

Rap's expansion has led to something of an identity crisis: different sub-genres claim to be the 'real thing'. The most significant schism is between gangster rap – Niggers With Attitude, Ice T, Boo-Ya Tribe, the Geto Boys – and those groups that argue the genre perpetuates negative stereotypes of black male youth, indeed actively glorifies them.

The principal dissenting faction is the 'Native Tongue' movement of Afro-conscious rap groups (De La Soul, A Tribe Called Quest, Jungle Brothers, Queen Latifah), whose laidback 'hippy hop' sound and peacenik positivity is a deliberate reaction against rap's traditional aggressive ego-mania. Also endeavouring to clean up rap's public image are crossover artists like the phenomenally successful MC

116

Hammer. Musically, his *Please Hammer Don't Hurt 'Em* album takes rap out of the ghetto, polishing and sweetening it for mass consumption (at nearly seven million units, it's the biggest selling rap LP of all time). Lyrically it's all about how to escape the ghetto by following the buppie gospel of positive thinking. The video for the single 'Pray' features Hammer in a run-down area vicar-ishly admonishing gamblers, drunkards and gang members not to waste their lives.

Faced by all these well-meaning attempts at rap reformism, gangster rap has entrenched itself firmly in the ghetto mentality, fended off 'crossover' and stayed true to the street. In practice, this means competing to plunge to new nadirs of misogyny and carnographic imagery, and upping the expletive count. Current market leaders for unpleasant extremism must be the Geto Boys. Based in Houston, one of the most racially divided cities in the US, the group pours scorn on the Afro-conscious groups, with their peace signs, believing instead that 'reality is a knife' and 'we're dead already'. Geto Boys' record company Geffen has refused to release its album, largely because of the track 'Mind of a Lunatic', which imagines the thoughts of a psychopath as he rapes and murders a woman. The Geto Boys' defence is gangster rap's standard get-out clause: 'We write about what we see around us.'

Certainly, there is a case for seeing a parallel between rap's exploration of the extremes of male psychology and, say, Martin Scorsese's films like *Raging Bull* and *Taxi Driver*. In both cases, there's a kind of 'deconstruction of masculinity', in which we vicariously participate in the protagonist's paranoid delirium, only to be confronted with both the bloody external consequences and the inner void at the heart of the male ego. But the question remains: why are we so fascinated by vigilantes, gangsters, boxers, outlaws and other lone rangers? What resonance is there in their (invariably doomed) struggle for autonomy? Perhaps it's the tragedy inherent to the deluded male fantasy that you can be your own master, child of no one.

Hardcore rap's psychology is survivalist, a fortress mentality that veers between delusions of invulnerability and a feeling of being under siege from all sides. What this 'soul on ice' fears most is the thawing warmth of female desire. Gangster rap typically represents women as gold-digging, treacherous 'bitches', or receptacles for male lust.

Some rap groups have found a way round this by deflecting their aggression towards its proper target: the System. Gangster rap's misogyny is sublimated into militancy; its raging erections are replaced by rectitude. The result of this desexualization, however, is an even more frigid, men-only world of righteous rhetoric, urgent communiqués and incendiary slogans. Five years ago, rap's big catchphrase was 'let's get stupid'; now the buzzword is 'intellect'. Groups aspire to the status of prophets or teachers (X-Clan's 'Funkin' Lesson', Boogie Down Production's 'Edutainment', Poor Righteous Teachers' *Holy Intellect* and the group's MC who goes by the name Wise Intelligent). KRS-1 masterminded the rap all-star 'Stop the Violence Movement', whose single 'Self Destruction' addressed the fact that one in twenty-two black men dies of violent crime, mostly at the hands of other black males.

Public Enemy (playing at London Docklands Arena on 3 November) trailblazed this style of righteous rap and remains its most provocative exponent. Public Enemy is keen to promote positive images of black youth as disciplined and aware. But, unlike MC Hammer, the black community that Public Enemy envisages mobilizing is not integrative or upward-aspiring, but oppositional. 'Unity amongst our own kind' is the group's rallying cry. For a while, PE's hyper-consciousness of the race issue spilled over into some distinctly paranoid and off-kilter racial/conspiracy theories.

While the group's interviews are still somewhat perturbing, Public Enemy's musical output has remained crucial. The third album, *Fear of a Black Planet*, saw its early rigid convictions disintegrate into confusion. In a way, *Fear* dramatizes rap's identity crisis, speculating on the nature of 'blackness', wondering who the emergent and insurgent Black Nation can comprehend within its frontiers. Self-hating black men who only date white women ('Pollywannacracka')? Welfare scroungers and bums ('Can't Do Nuthin' for Ya Man')? Black gays ('Meet the G that Killed Me')? On 'Revolutionary Generation', Public Enemy makes a strenuous effort to include women in the struggle, but exposes its own limits with the dubious sentiment – 'It takes a man to make a stand / But understand / It takes a woman to make a better man' – which suggests that women's contribution consists in birthing and rearing good soldiers for the cause.

Oscillating violently between right-on accusations and right-off resolutions, *Fear of a Black Planet* is as dense and uncompromising a work as rap has yet produced. Musically, it captures the chaos of its era with same apocalyptic accuracy that Sly and the Family Stone's *There's a Riot Goin' On* evoked the impasses and moribund ideals of the early seventies. The album's aesthetic strength is its political weakness. It has lots of angry questions. Public Enemy only knows what it does not want. Hence its fetishization of the means (mobilization and militancy), combined with a hazy conception of the end for which the girding of loins is necessary. Live, expect cacophony at the threshold of undanceability, intercut with remonstrance, oratory, imperatives, statesman-like gestures. As grievously flawed as it is, Public Enemy is as politically provocative as pop gets. Just don't expect 'a good night out'.

New Statesman, 2 November 1990

This was a period when hip hop's appeal dimmed for me somewhat. De La Soul et al. were fine but didn't have the visceral impact of Def Jam or Schoolly D, while on the gangsta front NWA sounded kinda flimsy to my ears. So really what kept me rapt by rap through this period (up until G-funk and Cypress Hill basically) was the continuing (mis)adventures of Public Enemy as 'the black Clash'. Simon Frith once wrote that punk was all about the *public* gesture: semiotic terrorism, the use of publicity and controversy as the basic material of artistic expression, a theatre of provocation and staged confrontation. If 'Rebel Without a Pause' was PE's 'White Riot' (the stance and the sound saying: 'black punk, black punk, we want a punk of our own') then 'Don't Believe the Hype' – all about the whirlwind of media panic PE had stirred up – was equivalent to 'Complete Control', a song about The Clash's struggle with the record industry. 'Hype' was hype-ocritical, amping up the very uproar it purported to deplore, but then again, what could be more punk than to goad the establishment, then mock its outrage? In other respects, the righteous rap style sired by PE reminds me even more of post-punk, that didactic strain of conscious-raising agit-prop represented by Gang of Four. I recall a mini-trend for rap videos featuring blackboards and lecterns! The whole idea of 'conscious' recalled post-punk's emphasis on being aware as being *awake:* not lulled into a trance by consumerism or propaganda, but living in a red alert state of constant ideological vigilance. The immediate precursor to PE was a phase in rap where MCs talked about getting stupid: concussive bass, slow beats, marijuana-bleary. Whereas the whole feel of PE – the fast tempos, the paranoid thinking – resembles the amphetamania of post-punk. When rap slowed down again in the early nineties with mellow groups like Brand Nubian, a whole generation of British hip hop fans dived into rave music, their love of PE's speed and attack and riotous blare translating into breakbeat hardcore. These B-boys turned E-boys stripped out the politics and turned PE's state of emergency into the panic rush of rave and jungle.

MADCHESTER VERSUS DREAMPOP

Happy Mondays and Ride

There's a theory that the perception of time is class-related. That's why the counsel of insurance companies and the propaganda of anti-smoking lobbies have greatest impact on the middle classes, connecting with their (self) managerial view of life, their training in forward planning and deferral of gratification. Part of ex-Prime Minister Thatcher's project was to inculcate in the British masses the middle-class discipline of providence, the virtues of belt-tightening and holding out for the long-term dividend. Her method was brutal: systematic immiseration of the working class, through the removal of welfare safety nets, in order to encourage 'initiative' and discourage lazy-ass 'parasitism'.

But a significant portion of the British working class has responded to the challenge of 'enterprise culture' while remaining within the here-and-now time frame. The last decade has seen the explosive rise of a 'black economy'. Proletarian youth in the deprived parts of the country (the inner cities, much of the North) have resorted to all manner of opportunistic means of survival: bootlegging, credit card fraud, petty theft, organizing illegal warehouse parties and raves, drug dealing. It's from this lumpen-prole milieu that Happy Mondays have emerged. Their skills are reactive (the sharp quip, the quick killing) and their pleasures short-term and intense (a quest for 'the buzz' or 'the crack'). The title of their latest album *Pills 'n' Thrills and Bellyaches* (Elektra) sums up Happy Mondays' lifestyle/worldview. If this new psychedelia is a 'holiday from life', it's modelled on the boorishly orgiastic antics of British youth in Ibiza and other Mediterranean tourist spots. No 'politics of ecstasy', no opening of the doors of perception, here; rather a search for 'good vibes', a blurring of vision and slackening of tension, a weekend respite from the alertness of workaday survivalism. Skin up and veg out.

Happy Mondays' sound is a dishevelled slurry of motley influences and dog-eared memories – unconsciously postmodern pop. Wholesale chunks of seventies pop detritus like Labelle's 'Lady Marmalade' and Cockney Rebel's 'Come Up and See Me, Make Me Smile' bob about in a bizarre melange of seventies funk and boogie slide guitar, with the whole thing whipped into 1990 dancefloor shape by DJ-turned-producer Paul Oakenfold. Singer Shaun Ryder rants a guttersnipe version of cut-up: phrases that lodged in his head while stoned in front of the TV, the drivel of acid-casualty acquaintances. Happy Mondays' music never seems to bear any sign of premeditation; it's always here-and-now, what occurred to them or came their way just then.

If Happy Mondays represent the dominant sensibility in UK alternative music, then My Bloody Valentine and their myriad offspring (Ride, Boo Radleys, Lush, Chapterhouse, Slowdive, Pale Saints, etc.) represent the opposing tendency. These bands – known variously as 'shoegazers', 'dreampop' and 'the scene that celebrates itself' – are also obsessed with the here-and-now, the loss of self in the singular moment of rapture. But they're worlds apart from the bleary, slackadaisical euphoria of Happy Mondays. In a way, these groups represent the middle-class response to the quandaries of Thatcher's Britain. Thatcherism's attack on the welfare state has grievously damaged Britain's 'dole culture' (the breeding ground of indie bands). At the same time, Thatcherite culture has turned pop into a reflection of straight aspirations, a normative agent. The utopian dreams of youth culture have been excluded from the centre stage, outflanked and outmoded. And politically, dreams of transformation have shifted from the public to the private sector: personal transfiguration rather than collective progress. Transcendence can only be momentary, tragically confined to the here-and-now.

We're back to time-consciousness and its relation to class. These middle-class drop-outs' special agony is that they can look far enough into the future to see that it has no place for their hopes. At the same time, their rock historical awareness is (over)developed enough for them to feel reproached by the grander aspirations of previous rock eras. So a generation has sacrificed itself to the desolate task of carrying a torch for the impossible dreams of the past. For this vicarious generation, with its unrealized lives and unavoidable sense of lateness, rock's wanderlust has become internalized, turned to daydream. The beatnik idea of 'travelling but never arriving' has become the self-defeating belief that 'it's better to be lost than found'.

Sounds familiar? Husker Du invented all this. Dinosaur Jr gave it an extra spin. Then My Bloody Valentine took that dazed and confused sound, made it even more chaotically ethereal, and added Anglo androgyny and frailty. Ride are the apotheosis of the genre: not because they're its best exponents (that's still MBV), but because they're generic to the point of transparency. Their third EP actually featured songs with titles like 'Dreams Burn Down', and 'Here and Now', while their debut LP on Sire is called *Nowhere*. It's an ambivalent buzzword. 'Nowhere' can signify a plight: lost on the road to nowhere, stranded with no way home. But 'nowhere' is also the site of bliss, to be reached by the paradox of 'going nowhere fast' ('Drive Blind'), or rising above mundane limits into the amnesiac haze of white noise.

Although Ride's music is more classically 'psychedelic' than Happy Mondays', it seems likely that this is because Ride have derived their version of psychedelic experience from other records rather than from drug excess. This is psychedelia as existential posture: disorientation as losing the bearings that would enable you to make your way through the world/make your mark on the world. Or, as one British writer put it, being 'lost in the bewilderness'.

Happy Mondays fantasise about the high life and so hijack the look of winners (flash Italian fashion). Ride dream not of social climbing but of rising above it ALL, and so wear the monochrome uniform of the exile on Main Street. Happy Mondays' music may not be triumphalist like Bon Jovi's blue collar anthems, or MC Hammer's buppiespeak positivism. But it oozes the chancer's confidence in his own cunning, his ability to talk his way out of trouble and into opportunity. Like most indie/college rock, Ride are defeatist. This involves more than simply feeling that they belong to a defeated generation. Their very idea of bliss is bound up with surrender: the dream of being ravished by some total experience (absolute Love, mystic communion) that offers redemption. Compare that with the reprobate Happy Mondays 'on the make, on the prowl' worldview, where pleasure's there for the taking.

Village Voice, November 1990

The time-consciousness and class riff is something that had stayed lodged in the back of my mind from my years as a history student. I've no idea how much credence it ever had within academia, but this is a good example of how I tend to use theory, which involves suspending the question of its ultimate truth and instead using it as a tool, a jemmy to prise open particular recordings or genres. In this case, it offered a useful framework for displaying the differences between the two major trends in early nineties British alternative music: the Madchester baggy sound and the shoegazer scene. One important factor not discussed here is regional rivalry: the baggies all came from the North-West of England, the shoegazers from the Thames Valley (Oxford, Reading, London). Indeed one reason the latter were championed so fervently by the London-based music press was, I suspect, retaliation for Manchester's dominance at the start of the nineties. Shoegaze came directly out of My Bloody Valentine but was also shaped by – no point in being fake-modest here – the climate of writing that enfolded MBV and A.R. Kane (my personal pet group and the guys who coined the term 'dreampop', another name for shoegaze). Of the post-*Isn't Anything* wave, I had the most time for Slowdive, Moose, and occasionally Swervedriver; Ride always struck me as the blandest of the bunch, their mirror image across the baggy divide being The Charlatans (literally mirror image, what with their big-lipped and tousled frontmen). Happy Mondays, I'd loved their early pre-rave records, loathed their brief foray into quasi-pop, then come around again thanks to the Beatlesy slow-shimmer of 'Loose Fit' on *Pills 'n' Thrills* – a manifesto of slack(er)-minded nonchalance similar to their kandy-kolored dole-drifter anthem 'Lazy-Itis' (off 1988's *Bummed*). Overall, though, I'd say it was a pretty slack time for UK rock, which helps explain the next piece . . .

MANIC STREET PREACHERS

Can you feel it? A creeping paralysis accompanying every advance in the obese accumulation of 'good music', a seeping slide into the mire of eclecticism. Don't you feel an urge to purge rising like bile at the back of your throat? And here's Manic Street Preachers, bulimic rockers. Every other band today wants to embroider a corner of 'rock's rich tapestry' (copyright: J. Burchill); every other band is proud to be a torch from a venerated past to a grateful future. Manic Street Preachers are postmodernists too, but fixated on the Year Zeroes of yesteryear, those apocalyptic brinks when rock 'n' roll seemed both to die and to be reborn.

Maybe they're just wistful dreamers trying to retell the Greatest Rock 'n' Roll Story to date (and get the end right this time). Maybe they're no better than Teddy Boys, most likely they've simply looked at the baggy-minded generation, recognized that Happy Mondays and The Farm mirror the age perfectly, and decided that if that is what being contemporary is all about, then they'd rather be out-of-time. Either way – and putting aside for now the merits of the music – nobody is inciting more provocative speculation right now. The ghost of punk, incarnated by these four Welsh boys, must be placated; its reproach, from beyond the grave, at least deserves a considered riposte.

Because so many hate them despite the fact that it'd be easier and crueller to ignore them. Because in the age of tongue-tied inarticulacy and pseudo-mystical gushing without content or context, they're a group to talk to and talk about. Because of the sheer intellect involved (Nietzsche, Situationism, Camus, Kierkegaard, more). Because just when we're all cosily immersed in the diverse splendour of 'our music', here's a band that's put unmentionable concepts like 'boredom', 'rage', 'disgust', back on the agenda.

All this is why I find myself at the darkest Surrey retreat where Manic Street Preachers are rehearsing for a tour and demoing their first and final LP. While singer James Dean Bradfield and drummer Sean Moore (the group's musical heart and beat) are hard at it a couple of floors below, Nicky Wire and Richey Edwards (the brains and beauty) unfurl their giddy whirl of contradictions (naivety and calculation, idealism and cynicism, exhibitionism and shyness). Instead of the obstreperous motormouths I'd anticipated, they're an endearing pair – candid, charming, incredibly bright. Even their most sulphurous putdowns of their peers seem kittenish in those lilting Welsh accents.

* * *

Manic Street Preachers used to define themselves against the boorish hedonism of the post-Mondays groups, with their lumpen pursuit of kicks and retreat from class politics. But these days they find the new aestheticism, the rock for rock's sake anti-stance of the Thames Valley/Scene That Celebrates Itself groups – Ride, Slowdive, Chapterhouse, Moose – even more despicable.

'All those bands are educated and middle class, but all they have to say is, "We don't want to say anything,"' avers Richey. 'A lot of those groups are as wrapped up in musicality as the supergroups of the seventies. There's so much emphasis on pedals and getting the right sound.'

Nicky: 'It's nullifying, there's nowhere you can go with it but into your bedroom. We've done that all our lives, that's the last thing we wanna do. It's an aesthetic of blanking out everything.'

I like a lot of the groups they detest; I know that the lovely new Slowdive EP is an advance where the new Manics is a retreat. But somehow I get more out of 'Stay Beautiful' than any of today's sumptuous sounds. Perhaps it's time for a return to the idea that there's more to rock 'n' roll than just music. Perhaps it's time to start using words like decadence again. Then again, isn't the only real criterion whether a band brings a bit more beauty into the world or not? The Manics think not: bringing more beauty into an ugly world has no value, whereas reflecting the ugliness and trying to rectify it does. They have no interest in expanding the boundaries of sound; they deny the validity of escapism or bliss-out. To them, it's just a middle-class version of the culture of consolation.

'Where we come from, that's what everybody did all the time. Everyone's just a wage slave or a dole slave, and every night you just get bombed out of your head.'

The wallowing, inverted snobbery of the post-Manic proles, the effete, apolitical quietism of the dreampopsters – it's all equally infuriating and inconsequential to the Manics.

Nicky: 'Where we come from in Wales, it's very working class, but there is a tradition of bettering yourself. Our parents never wanted us to go down the pit. Self-education is a really big thing. The work ethic is just massive.'

Manic Street Preachers are self-educated. The group's background was about as claustrophobic and intensive as could be: real blood-brothers, four boys against the world stuff. They've known each other since primary school. Sean moved in with James after his parents split up, sharing bunk beds in a tiny bedroom. This became the proto-Preachers' HQ. Year after year, day after day, they festered together, feverishly devouring the music press, books, videos, records, grabbing hold of every little bit of stimulus they could find.

'People accuse us of having lived vicariously through other people's ideas. Londoners don't seem to understand that in most places in England that is all you've got – the music papers and pop music.'

In their mid-teens/the mid-eighties, they discovered the Pistols; ever since, they've looked desperately for something to match their impact. For a while, they loved Gang of Four and Big Flame, for the lyrics and the attitude, until they realized the music alienated too many people. For the first six months, they adored The Smiths, 'until we realized that there was no point in just standing on stage saying life hurts you'.

For years, the boys bought the records the papers raved about, travelled considerable distance to see groups live, often having to sleep under bridges after missing the last train – but invariably, they were brutally disappointed.

The last few years have been a barren wilderness, according to the Manics. They briefly entertained high hopes of The Stone Roses, after the first *MM* cover story left the impression the Roses were class warriors. Apart from that, they've looked to America, drawing inspiration from Public Enemy (the style, the rage) and Guns N' Roses (the fact that Pistols-influenced hard rock could still sell sixteen million albums). And so they hatched their masterplan, hoping to become the group they always craved for: radical politics plus trad rock riffola plus glam appeal.

Born in the crucible of rock discourse, in a sense the Manics only exist on the pages of the music press – as the catalyst of controversy, lurid news items, a reference point. The Manics take the premeditation of previous manifesto groups (Age of Chance, Sigue Sigue Sputnik) to a new pitch of extremity. So far it's all hurtling ahead as (master) planned: they've got the front covers, a deal with one of the biggest majors in the world, Columbia/Sony, and the new single's been buffed to a commercial sheen by Wham!'s ex-producer. But the Manics have set themselves such preposterously high targets, they're almost guaranteed to fail. Their masterplan is a suicide pact: if the album doesn't top charts worldwide and outsell *Appetite For Destruction*, they're worthless failures. And if it does succeed, they're going to give it all up anyway.

Nicky: 'Whether we sell millions and millions of albums, or we fail abjectly, we'll still have said everything we have to say in one double album. We don't want to look beyond that, because we'd just be treating it as a career. If you throw it away when you're the biggest band in the world, then you're bound to get respect.'

But what will you do afterwards?

'I'm always happiest just living with my mum and dad and my dog. Watching telly and stuff like that. That is my perfect scenario, when I can reach some kind of peace.'

'Suicide pact' seems the right phrase, because underneath this desperate desire to become myth is a kind of death wish: to be frozen for eternity as an immaculate gesture, the image of ultimate cool. What single-mindedness, what marvellous myopia! They blithely consign the rest of their lives to the dustbin, reject the idea of growth, the possibility that in three years' time their ideas might be, *should* be, completely different – 'You're only this hateful and angry once, really.'

And then there's Richey's infamous arm-slashing. What do they think is *at stake* to make such a gesture worthwhile?

'We're completely happy that people despise us, but when you get a writer who should be in fanzines, saying that he doesn't believe we mean it and that we're just a manager's invention, then I got so pissed off that I had to do it. That guy couldn't conceive that people can be so frustrated and pissed off that they're prepared to hurt themselves.'

Pictures of Richey's gashed arm are going to be the basis for Columbia's marketing campaign in the USA. But the Manics say they are ready to be used. Marvellously mixed up, they talk of 'total control' in one breath and of 'being useless sluts' in another. But by all accounts, they're incredibly organized: they send their management a steady stream of plans and proposals, while Columbia say they've never met a group who've known so clearly exactly what they want.

What they want is a Top 40 hit: 'Stay Beautiful' could do it for them. The new single is the first Manics record that's convincing on their own retro terms. It's a quaint but exhilarating salvo of combat rock that sounds rather refreshing in the age of furniture music.

And both 'Stay Beautiful' and its B-side 'R. P. McMurphy' possess a yearning romanticism that hints for the first time that there's soul beneath the Situationist critique. Too often Manics songs are collages of slogans that only briefly flash into poetry: on 'Stay Beautiful', I think I hear the line 'All we love is lonely records', but later learn it's 'lonely wreckage'. 'R. P. McMurphy', a semi-acoustic, worldweary and home-sick lament, is inspired by Jack Nicholson's character in *One Flew Over the Cuckoo's Nest*, and in particular that moment when he tries and fails to lift the washbasin.

Ideally, the Manics' insurrectionary politics would be wedded to the raucous futurism of The Young Gods; at the very least, it ought to be motored by a modern rhythmic undercarriage like EMF. Maybe if they get to work with Hank Shocklee of Public Enemy, they'll get there. But UK teenagers won't groove to their tinny, trad rock rhythms, whose appeal these days is limited to punk veterans. Oh, and Americans, of course.

'Ultimately we just think that rock is the only musical backdrop we can have, cos it's the most popular,' defends Richey. 'The American record company are really keen for us to release records over there. When they talk about us, it's not like they want us to go to the East Coast and blitz the college radio scene, they're talking about us going to the Mid-West, the rock heartland. Which is where we've always wanted to have impact, cos that's closest to our South Wales small-town experience.'

* * *

Manic Street Preachers believe in energy and edge, in an age where the dominant rock aesthetic is bound up with space (dream-space, sound-expanse). They have no interest in listening to Can, loathe Levitation's idea of the return to prog rock. And the Manics believe in the resurrec-tion of rock 'n' roll's most metaphysical and intangible concept: youth. 'Stay Beautiful' is about clinging to your sense of total possibility and 'sense of waste'.

'The only time you really have a chance of doing anything is when you're young,' argues Nicky. 'You're really free, cos you have no responsibilities at all. At school, there's always nutters of a certain age who will rebel against anything. Those people really are just like true anarchy. They'll just do anything to destroy school, which is almost like a prison to them.'

'Youth' isn't compromised by ties, nothing ADULT-erates the terrible lucidity of your desperation, nothing clouds the clarity of your contempt.

'At a certain age, your thought is primed, you're ripe for anything. When you're married and you've got a baby, you've got responsibilities, you can't devote yourself to revolt. You have to resign yourself to making do.'

Sex

You can see their point, up to a point: there's so much to negate – the living death of consumption, cultural necrophilia, mediocrity. But don't they think there's so much to affirm, too: the wonder of being alive, Nature, love. Revealingly, the Manics complain about bands who only write love songs. Don't they believe that love is the great redemptive, transfiguring force? Have they never been in love? They shake their heads. Try it, I say, like a pusher.

Richey: 'Once you fall in love, or get your girlfriend pregnant, or fall into credit, you've got no chance, you've got responsibilities. There's no way you can ever do anything. Once you're reduced to a couple, alone together between your four walls with your TV set, you're cut off.'

It's almost as though they dread comfort, see the spectre of amorous bliss as something that would impair their single-mindedness. Amazingly, at the age of twenty-three, Richey claims to have never had a relationship, and to have only lost his virginity six months ago: 'Sex just never seemed important.' Nicky (twenty-one) briefly had a girl-friend, 'but it was just too scary'. Of all the Manics, it's Sean who's the band's Charlie Watts, having been going steady for eight years.

'At school, we would have done anything to have girlfriends,' says Nicky, heartbreakingly. 'We were just chronically shy. But we're not emotionally developed enough. We're too petty, too obsessed.'

But what about all these lurid tales of groupies? The Manics talk about such soulless encounters as though it's their duty as rock stars to be 'used'.

'Anyway, people underestimate women,' adds Nicky. 'They're more sensitive that that. A lot of them just want to talk about the group, not get pissed and get fucked. We're prepared to do anything, just sit and talk about what we feel and the songs. We'll never refuse anyone.'

It's almost as though they see love as this century's opium of the people, a rose tint that obscures your clear vision of the horror of it all. Being in love is 'just someone to share your boredom with', opines Richey; Nicky adds, 'I think I'll always be happier with my mother anyway.'

129

'N' Drugs

At first, I thought the Manics were trying to resurrect punk's ethics of drug use (ego-and-IQ-boosts like speed are righteous, ego-loss drugs like E or LSD are crap). But although they used speed to fuel their frenzies of reading and letter-writing ('It's really sexless, it helps you concentrate'), the Manics claim they're against addling your mind. Nicky claims never to have touched anything but alcohol, and says he wanted to waste the guy at a London party who said that the greatest pleasure in his life was fixing people up with good gear.

'Drugs just make people more governable,' says Richey. '*The Politics of Ecstasy* is a great read but you look at Timothy Leary now and he's just a vegetable.'

It's the same as their attitude to love: the Manics fear the sweet surrender, the urge to merge. They're too attached to their ego to want to lose themselves. Instead their trip is the rock rebel fix of self-worship/self-hatred. They're addicted to the glamour of ALIENATION (being fucked up, fucking other people off).

'N' Rock 'n' Roll

Yet they know that rock can never be marshalled into a punk-like unity of alienation again, everything's too fragmented. They're on a solo mission, kamikaze style.

'We just want to clear everything away. Maybe after us, music won't seem as important as actually changing the world.'

All they dream of is making a gigantic gesture of repudiation. Isn't that sterile? Isn't negation a dead end?

'No. Because most people's lives are completely sterile anyway. Our attitude is that negation is always better than resignation.'

But don't you think that making people really pissed off with their lives is good up to a point, beyond which it's pointless? Isn't it better to make some space for yourself, find some joy?

'It's really naive, but we really believe that if everybody became conscious of their reality, things could really change. When people stop looking for meaning in sport or music, then things could really change.'

Let's call them 'tunnel visionaries'. They mean it, man. Just adorable.

Melody Maker, 20 July 1991

'Just adorable' is the giveaway: witness the critic having his pants charmed off. I couldn't help warming to Richey and Nicky's passionate bibliophilia and intellectual ambition, nor being flattered that they took the music press so seriously (they confessed they'd jumped to their feet and cheered when they read my panning of Happy Mondays at Wembley Arena). Damping down my reservations about their sonic conservatism, I focused my mind on their ideas and their eloquence, so quenching after the long drought of nothing-to-say mumblers (the latter had initially appealed because they left their music as a blank screen for critical projections but by 1991 I was looking for the musicians to start pulling their weight a bit). The almost-instant impact of the Manics and their enduring appeal testifies to a perennial hunger in the British scene for bands with ideas about *other things* apart from music, groups who gave interviews full of trenchant opinions and provocative stances. In some ways, the Manics were like the last blast, or premature return, of post-punk: not sonically (although *The Holy Bible* made some anguished noises in the direction of Magazine and Joy Division) but in that sense of regarding talk about sound-for-its-own-sake as trivial and decadent. The most post-punk-like aspect of the Manics was their drastic compartmentalization of function within the band: singer/guitarist James Dean Bradfield and drummer Sean Moore composed the music and did almost all the recording; Nicky and Richey wrote the lyrics, organized the design of records and promotional material and did all the interviews. The Manics, of course, immediately reneged on their auto-destruct promise, as they must have always known they would, being indentured employees of a major label who required a return on their investment. Instead, they doggedly slogged their way to stardom by the bog-standard route: touring and releasing singles in numerous formats to ensure chart entry. Their continued existence and predictably controversial opinions used to irritate me no end (there was a pang of embarrassment too for having played a minuscule role in their ascent). *Only in the UK* do you get 'all mouth and no trouser' bands like the Manics becoming genuinely popular, so perhaps it's some weird form of patriotism that now makes me feel a faint twinge of affection for them despite the largely rotten discography. The 4 Realest of them all, Richey, belongs to a select company of musicians I've met (see also: Nikki Sudden, Roger Troutman, Michael Karoli) who are no longer alive.

PAVEMENT

CBGB, New York

Currently the focus of much cultish enthusiasm, Pavement exemplify all that's groovy and all that's grievous about American underground rock right now. Back in 1987–88 American groups had an advantage over their over-theoretical, calculating British counterparts; uncrippled by knowingness, lacking media-bred inhibitions, they were free to fuck about and chance upon the unprecedented. But as the momentum of post-hardcore petered out, self-consciousness crept in. The fatal moment comes when a movement vacillates, decides it's gone too far (witness the backwards step between Sonic Youth's *Daydream Nation* and *Goo*, Butthole Surfers' *Hairway to Steven* and *Pioughed*). Groups began to play it for laughs.

Hence the current quagmire. Pastiche rock like Urge Overkill, Shonen Knife and Pooh Sticks is deemed to be where it's at. Middle-class dropouts fanny about while Public Enemy burn. The sampler and the studio-as-instrument are ignored. And potentially great groups like Pavement sabotage themselves. Pavement suffer from the American disease – a self-deflating fear of appearing to take themselves seriously. A twisted amalgam of shame (at the triviality and futility of being a noisy rock band in 1991) and smugness is the only explanation for singer Stephen Malkmus's inter-song comments: 'I hate to say it – it sounds like a cliché – but can I have more vocals in the monitor?' or (during a technical hitch, in a mock whisper) 'Hey guys, we're losing our momentum.' This ain't life or death, this is just a way of passing time.

A shame, because Pavement could be great. Noise hasn't been injected into pop to such engaging effect since early-to-mid Pixies. There's the same combination of grunge and grace, juggernaut bulk and aching, off-centre harmonies; the same sense of jagged dynamics, Malkmus's voice leaping from guttural to a distraught whinny. Pavement are schooled in the Sonic Youth science of friction, they know how to churn up a smouldering undertow like a fender dragging on concrete. But the songs groove as often as shatter or flail. Unlike so many noise groups, Pavement have feel, a palpable, organic momentum. By the closing numbers, when they're swarming like a horde of fireflies, Pavement are almost sublime.

Yet, for the moment at least, the congenital Amerindie fear of being po-faced confines them to a belittling fanzine context. The ability to be so serious you make a fool of yourself seems beyond American indie groups these days. And so Pavement wield a power they can't conceive of doing anything with.

Melody Maker, 21 September 1991

Village Voice's Joe Levy coined the term 'metacasm' to describe a certain indie sensibility based around an a ironic reinvocation of the hugeness and wildness of pre-punk rock – groups like Urge Overkill, Pooh Sticks, Teenage Fanclub, whose rocking-out came surrounded by invisible scare quotes. Modern examples might include the White Stripes, The Darkness, LCD Soundsystem, Art Brut. You could diagnose it as a defence against the pathos of belatedness, the problem of forming a band today in the face of the mountainous accumulation of precedents. Pavement had a pungent whiff of the metacastic. Yet in another sense, what they did was totally authentic: the knowingness simply reflected their deep knowledge of rock history, while their wry, distanced intelligence and the non-cathartic nature of their music was true to their relatively well-adjusted and comfortable middle-class backgrounds. 'Music isn't life and death for us, and it's hard for me to believe that art can be like that,' Malkmus told me in 1992. 'It's something to fill your day and something to talk about, but to obsess about it seems absurd . . . The thing is, we do "mean" it. For what it's worth. We turn up the vocals, we're not trying to drown out the words in this morass of slackness. There's something there, it's just confused.' The archness rubbed me up the wrong way that first live encounter, but shortly afterwards I fell in love with Pavement's *Slanted and Enchanted*. For a while they and similar lo-fi/slacker groups struck me as blessed relief from the grunge overload, thanks to their richer palette of sound (drawing on Krautrock, The Fall, Swell Maps, Pere Ubu) and their kaleidoscope-tinted, off-kilter refraction of reality. Like the movie *Slacker*, they seemed to contain everything good and everything bad about our generation: the tremendous love and learning when it came to pop culture, the sense of curiosity and wonder, but also an inability to do much more than make attractive mosaics out of the fragments. But when the group stripped away the noise to better expose the song-craft . . . well, I lost interest.

NIRVANA

Kilburn National, London

The only explanation is that a lot of people didn't realize how angry and alienated they really were. Once in a blue moon, a group comes along and fits the zeitgeist like a glove; right now that group is Nirvana. With its oscillation between rage and resignation, its lust for revolution that's immediately crippled by bitter irony, 'Smells Like Teen Spirit' is an 'Anarchy in the UK' for the twenty-something generation. *Nevermind* is a glimpse into the collective unconscious of this blankest of generations, whose fury festers implosively, whose idealism is blocked or dissipated, because neither impulse can find a constructive outlet. The cover of the LP says it all in a single image: a naked infant swimming through uterine waters is lured to the surface by a dollar bill on a fish-hook. Nirvana say: don't do it, kid! Leave your blissful brine for this corrupt world, and it'll be the first and worst mistake of your life.

Nirvana are timely in another sense. After a year in which groups have washed all over you in an increasingly bland and received simulation of ravishment, it feels mighty good to hear something with a bit of visceral thrust, something based around distinct riffs, open-throat haemorrhage, aggression. The Scene groups' strategy of evading reality by evaporating into a dreamtime ether had its virtues; right now, confrontation seems more appropriate than transcendence. Next year, a chasm will open up between the new hard rock/neo-punk and the experimental avant-vanguard (Papa Sprain, Main, etc.): the Scene will simply disappear down this rift. If nothing else, Manic Street Preachers will have had a John the Baptist function, clearing a path for the arrival of Britain's own Nirvana.

Like the Stooges' *Funhouse* or Black Flag's *Damaged*, *Nevermind* turns impotence into raw power, inertia into frenzy, bewilderment into single-minded focus. All this and the prettiest, most plaintive melodies this side of *Doolittle*. If I was seventeen, I reckon Nirvana would be the fulcrum of my universe; a decade after the fact, they still seem like a pretty accurate description of what's going on.

But tonight, Nirvana don't quite happen. Perhaps they're drained by the whirligig of their whirlwind success. I can't quite figure out what's missing. If anything, the sound's too good, replicating the high-gloss rawness of the album, but too cut-and-dried. Nirvana should be this swarming, organic murk. But only intermittently do they find their groove.

All the interruptions don't help. Within songs, Nirvana have the best grasp of dynamics since prime Pixies; as a set, their performance tonight is all fitful faltering and hiatuses of tomfoolery. The first time round, the Vic Reeves-ish skit of having men in white suits come onstage to dust down their gear for blood and saliva is pretty funny. By the third time, the joke's wearing pretty thin. By the time Chris Novoselic is explaining the joke (far from being sloppy slackers, they're 'anally clean, white glove types'), it's threadbare.

When they do shake off the sluggishness, stop goofing around and hit their stride, Nirvana are magnificent. The feral boogie-punk of 'Breed' is a real coition ignition machine. Then there's the despondent rampage of 'On a Plain', a slew of gut-pummelling *Bleach*-era monsters, a blazing 'Territorial Pissings'. By the last encore, you feel Nirvana are finally unleashed, ragin' full on; at the climax, drummer David Grohl inserts his head in the bass drum, and wanders offstage crowned by his own drum kit, a sublime feat of buffoonery that for once feels like a fitting exclamation point, rather than an ironical parenthesis.

Overall, though, I got the sense that Nirvana, wary of their sudden enormity, feel perversely driven to deflate their own importance. At the moment they're uncomfortably poised between their Sub Pop slob-rock past and their future godhood. They seem embarrassed and bemused, it's like their boots are too big for them. Did they seize the time with 'Smells Like Teen Spirit', or did the time seize them? Whatever, power's there for the grabbing. I hope they take the bait.

Melody Maker, November 1991

A precocious intimation of the unease with stardom, with having left behind the womb-like murk and security of the indie-rock underground for the spotlight glare of the pop mainstream . . . something that would torment and confuse Kurt Cobain and play a role in his fatal decision.

Easy to forget just how utterly unexpected Nirvana's breakthrough was . . . I remember arriving in New York early in the autumn of 1991 to stay with my girlfriend/wife-to-be, and Joy saying, 'There's this video MTV are playing, it's *amazing,* you've *got* to see it . . .' And then being slightly incredulous when she said it was by Nirvana (what, that nothing-special group on Sub Pop?). And then being totally blown away. Along with the sheer power of the song and the brilliance of the video, the shellshock came from the fact that we'd never thought that sound – which came out of all our 1980s faves, Husker Du and Dinosaur Jr and The Pixies – had any chance of entering the mainstream, let alone taking it over. The major labels had tried their best, and by 1990 had even signed flagrantly uncommercial underground outfits like Butthole Surfers and Sonic Youth. There'd been a very slight sense of critical mass building (Jane's Addiction's success and then Lollapalooza in the summer of '91), of something swarming outside the barricades. But nobody expected the walls to come tumbling down – least of all the bands themselves. Half of Cobain wanted to be a star, but none of him was prepared for it actually happening.

N-JOI/K-KLASS/BASSHEADS/M-PEOPLE

Kilburn National, London

This being the Deconstruction Records Night, what could be more fitting than a deconstruction of the review? Instead of the singular authorial voice, this review has been reconstructed from my companions' schizo-kaleidoscopic whirl of impressions. This seems more appropriate to the rave experience, since the audience creates the event: that bloke over there doing fishy finger-dancing, or those grimacing goons in bobble hats, are as much a part of the experience as the groups or DJs.

At first, the Kilburn's vibe is too like a village hall, something amplified by M-People's churchy techno-gospel. But the temperature hots up as the soul-mama appeals to 'free free free my body' suddenly plunge several octaves to an *Exorcist* growl and the poly-rhythms seethe pandemonically. Bassheads escalate the atmosphere to something like Nuremberg meets Spurs-at-home, light-beams arcing heavenwards and sampled ovation noises merging with the audience's own uproar. This group really know how to work those bass/biology frequencies. 'Bassheads in your area!' they holler. In your area? Right up yer rectum, more like.

K-Klass are all rump-tremors, electro-lightning bolts, boiling bongos, towering geysers of Moog-like goo; like Cabaret Voltaire's eerie austerity lubricated with sultry pop-juice. N-Joi's juddering bass-quake riffs and volcanic eruptions of pop-soul lava make you feel like Marilyn Monroe standing over the subway vent with her skirt in the air: whoooosh! E(ee), it goes right up you. It's impossible to stay still. The floor is a shiny sea of saucer-eyes; Essex boys lumber like extras in *Bottom*; sixteen-year-olds snort Vicks inhalers because it's supposed to increase the high. Critical faculties scramble, criteria go AWOL. Right about now, we were dancing so hard the writing gets illegible. One friend's contribution to this review is to seize the notepad and use it as a baton to mark time.

So what is the vibe of this techno-rave-acieeeed stuff? It's not exactly funky: there's no dirt, no friction, it's not hip-and-groin centred, but more like a forcefield that has every molecule of your body oscillating. Sanitized dance, maybe (James Brown is Dead!), clinical but crazed, a hygienic heaven. Tracks aren't grooves so much as grids, perfectly interlocking precision mechanisms of staccato judders and spasms. The dancing it inspires, or rather enforces, isn't fluid but all jerks and twitches, like bodypopping but so fast that it appears to be sinuous. Limbs and sequencer riffs, bass-throbs and sinews, interlock so that the whole room becomes one giant 'desiring machine'. Tracks fuse into a single seamless meta-track, pulsating euphoria. Heavenly hell or hellish heaven, let it never end. Nirvana were here a few weeks ago; nirvana was here tonight too. Verdict: a good time was had by all.

Melody Maker, December 1991

Not the first time I did a pill; not even the first rave I went to. But this was the first time I did a pill (one that wasn't a dud, anyway) *at* a rave. So this night was a real turning point, the Magic Moment at which my life changed. I'd been into the music, as *records*, for some years, but for the first time I really understood it as a site-specific and rite-specific culture. Suddenly I was *inside* the music. The coincidence of the rave (closer to an all-star revue than a DJ-oriented party but featuring some of 1991's leading acts from the chart-friendly end of 'ardkore) taking place at the exact same venue where Nirvana played only weeks before is nicely resonant, as if presenting a fork in the road of my pop life. One path was grunge, the resurgent rock I'd fantasized about in that 1987 Husker Du review. The other direction, the one I took, led to years of raving madness, recollected in tranquillity in the form of *Energy Flash*.

My partner-in-crime that evening (and on many, many subsequent occasions) would later during that same journey-to-the-end-of-the-night meet her future husband on the floor at the Ministry of Sound on the other side of London, where we'd headed after the Kilburn National closed. Sadly it would all end in tears.

RRRRRRUSH!

Hardcore Rave and London Pirate Radio

Two weeks ago, Detroit techno pioneers Derrick May and Kevin Saunderson were whining in *Melody Maker* about how UK hardcore is a grisly bastardization of their vision of techno. And it's true that the austere, elegantly minimalist music made by May and his fellow Europhiles has virtually nothing to do with the riotous uproar of hardcore. But far from being 'bastardized', the truth is that just as with acid house back in '88, the term 'techno' became detached from its American prototype, and mutated into a totally different animal. Hardcore is the latest in a long line of great British remotivations of Black American music.

Hardcore only really makes full (non)sense amidst the Dionysian tumult of an illegal rave (otherwise, it's like a soundtrack divorced from its movie). But you can get an idea of the vibe by tuning into London's pirate hardcore stations like Rush FM, Pulse, Destiny and Touchdown. (They also provide an opportunity to tape the latest, obscurest tracks for free.) Self-styled ''ardcore station for the 'ardcore nation', Touchdown seems to be the most regular and have the strongest signal (94.1 FM). From Friday eve to Monday morn, it provides a relentless soundtrack to vibing up before going out, driving between clubs, and recuperating afterwards.

Where the Detroit and early UK techno units like LFO/Orbital/808 State were relatively musically skilled and programmed their own rhythms etc., hardcore is real DIY barbarianism, cobbled together from looped, insanely accelerated breakbeats, asininely simplistic keyboard riffs, dub basslines, and samples of ecstatic vocals sped up to 78 rpm (the ethereal girl-vox of This Mortal Coil, Kate Bush, Dead Can Dance, Pinky & Perky shrieks of soul euphoria, ragga

139

incantations). In isolation, few tracks stand up to intense scrutiny; it's together, as a 'total flow', that they take effect. The feeling is like being plugged into the National Grid. The MCs' staccato patter – "ere we go!', 'let's get rough', '*rrrrr*rush!' all becomes part of the flow. As if the individual tracks weren't crudely collaged enough already, the DJ's mix in rough-and-ready bursts from other records, creating an inexhaustible, interminable meta-music pulse.

No songs here: the keyboard motifs are trite, what hooks you is the timbre of a synth-tone, the colon-deep consistency of a bassline, the epileptic spasm of a beat. Like avant-garde music, hardcore spurns melodic development in favour of repetition, drones, atonal sonorities, found sounds etc. But hardcore's a sort of degraded avant-gardism, an arrested futurism. And that's what's so weird about it: the ideas and effects of DAF, Die Krupps, Cabaret Voltaire, etc. have become pop in the most low-com-denom, plebeian sense.

Most hardcore is trash, then, but it's *effective* trash. Techno's developed beyond music and into a science of inducing and amplifying the Ecstasy rush. The sound is all subsonic bass and ultra-trebly shrillness, bowel-tremor and spine-tingle. Hardcore is a techno-pagan cult dedicated to the worship of speed: not just high bpm, but the amphetamine that most E tablets largely consist of these days. With group names like Risla Bass and song titles like 'We Are E', hardcore must be the most blatantly druggy subculture since acid rock; DJs call out to 'all you nutters rushing out of your heads, speedfreaks out there, you know the score' to send out a 'big shout to everyone who's absolutely trippin' in Hendon', or talk about how they're 'absolutely flying in the studio, 100 mph'. 'Let's go,' chants the DJ, but this is an intransitive acceleration, without destination. 'Hold tight,' he'll cry, like you're on a roller coaster (and apparently, techno is all you'll hear at funfairs these days). Where Detroit techno was spiritual, hardcore is purely about sensation, about an artificially induced state of hyper-real intensity (or, as the title of one track has it, 'Hypergasm').

Crude, mindless, but it's the most vibrant subculture around, and as addictive as crack.

Melody Maker, 4 July 1992

'No songs here' and 'trash' : actually, what strikes me in retrospect is how *musical* the best hardcore tunes were – how cleverly arranged, and how absurdly generous the producers were with hooks and mad catchy licks. A lot of hardcore was insanely *pop*tastic, exploding with fizzy euphoria and showering the listener with melodic shrapnel. 'Trash' partly reflected a lack of confidence in my opinion (as far as techno cognoscenti were concerned, breakbeat hardcore at that point was the lowest of the low, the degradation of a pure and noble artform). But it was also a Lester Bangs-style trans-valuation move, the embryonic stirring of what would soon become a campaign to elevate hardcore to the stature of the 'true' music of its era, just as Bangs and comrades in the early seventies had retroactively hailed sixties garage punk and deposed the post-*Sgt Peppers*/Cream aristocracy of concept album-toting art-rock, blues bores, and assorted progressives.

WASTED YOUTH

Grunge and the Return of 'Heavy'

In 1992, Heavy Rules. All year, the US alternative scene has been dominated by bands who take their cues from the early seventies, when groups like Black Sabbath, Led Zeppelin, Mountain, etc. bastardized and brutalized the blues. And this nouveau heavy rock carries heavy themes. Soundgarden rage against the impasses of life in 'Rusty Cage' and wail about low self-esteem in 'Outshined'. Pearl Jam mingle melancholy with political awareness: their hit singles 'Alive' and 'Jeremy' tackle issues like child abuse and child neglect. Members of Soundgarden and Pearl Jam collaborated for the one-off project Temple of the Dog, and broke into the US Top 10 with an album-length elegy to a friend and band mate who died of a drug overdose.

The most manic-depressive of the lot are Alice In Chains, also in the US Top 10 with their magnificent *Dirt* album. The band's name perfectly evokes their sound, whose ponderous riffs, toiling rhythms and sonorously sorrowful melodies create an impression of struggle against insuperable obstacles. Listening, you feel like you're sinking into the slough of despond (indeed the video for 'Them Bones' is actually set in a slimy quarry). Typical Alice In Chains songs deal with despair ('Down in a Hole'), heroin ('Godsmack') and death: Hamlet's 'alas, poor Yorick' soliloquy rendered in fluent Ozzy, 'Them Bones' says 'we're born into the grave'.

If Black Sabbath are the overwhelming influence on US alternative rock today, it's because the early nineties feel uncannily like the early seventies, when Sabbath's doom-laden songs were the soundtrack to getting numbed-out on depressant drugs – the barbiturates known as Mandies (from Mandrax) in the UK and 'ludes (from Quaalude) in the USA. So what ails the youth of America? The answer can be found in *Teenage Wasteland: Suburbia's Dead End Kids*, by journalist/ sociologist Donna Gaines, which has been hailed by *Rolling Stone* as 'the best book on contemporary youth culture'. Gaines's interest was pricked by the teen suicide craze of the late eighties, and in particular the 1987 case where four teenagers in Bergenfield, New Jersey, gassed themselves in a car. Mingling with a segment of American youth universally known as 'burn-outs', she won the kids' trust and uncovered the harrowing truth about their lives.

Burn-outs 'bomb out' at school, fail to make their grades because they feel they have no future. With the decline of traditional manufacturing employment, the only options for these kids are ignominious service sector jobs, devoid of union protection or prospects of advancement. Persecuted by teachers and cops and despised by their more aspirational peers, burn-outs express their alienation in their scruffy clothes and long hair. As one real-life teenager in the book says, 'no job is worth cutting your hair for'. With little incentive to plan for the future, burn-outs get wasted on drink and dope; some graduate to harder drugs like heroin. They listen to the generation-transcending classic metal of Led Zeppelin and Black Sabbath or its modern successors, the thrash of Metallica and Slayer. Gaines wrote her book in 1990, so she missed the punchline: the mainstreaming of the burn-out aesthetic with the explosive success of Nirvana and the rest of the Seattle grunge bands.

For these kids, the gap between the expectations fostered by the dream factory of Hollywood and MTV, and what they can reasonably expect from life, is huge. The escape routes from this dead end include the anaesthetic/amnesiac coma of drugs, and the one-way ticket 'outa here' of suicide. For some, Metallica's ballad 'Fade to Black' is a nihilistic anthem, its voluptuous melancholy dangerously seductive. (The mid-eighties teen suicide craze was wickedly satirized in the movie *Heathers*, where one character imagines a mass suicide as a 'Woodstock for the eighties'.) The more optimistic burn-outs, the ones with a smidgeon of get-up-and-go, imagine joining the army, or forming a successful rock band: both ways of seeing the world and learning a trade. And so you get the paradox of a band like Alice In Chains, who dragged themselves out of the mire of their native Seattle, and turned their loser worldview into massive success. Even after Bill Clinton's victory, things look bleak for American youth. Paying off the deficit will depress the US economy for years. So you can expect to hear US bands singing the 'born to lose' blues for a long time to come.

Director's cut of piece published in *The Observer*, November 1992

The missing piece of the puzzle here is Joe Carducci's *Rock and the Pop Narcotic*, published in 1990 and therefore, like *Teenage Wasteland*, missing the punchline of grunge, which completely validated Carducci's notion of the 'true' shape of rock history: a hard and heavy lineage running from Muddy Waters through Blacks Sabbath and Flag to . . . Nirvana, Alice In Chains, and Kyuss. (Indeed, when *Rock and the Pop* was republished later in the nineties in expanded and remixed form, the tone shifted ever so slightly to 'told you so' triumphalism.) For Carducci, both the 'politics' and the 'spirituality' of rock happen through the music's kinaesthetics – the frictional interaction of riff and rhythm, tension and release. Carducci analyzes the musical devices heavy rock bands deploy to create abstract-yet-visceral sonic allegories of struggle and perseverance in the face of a 'negative or trying context'. The music's 'powerfully articulated and textured tonal sensations of impact and motion' trigger 'hefty (nondance) motor impulses in the listener'. Carducci further presented metal/punk/hardcore/grunge as partaking of the 'Born to Lose' worldview of the blues and hillbilly traditions in the American South. And he coined the term 'New Redneck' to describe the attitude espoused by the SST label and its flagship act Black Flag, with their punishing regime of no-budget touring and endless rehearsing. As a key figure involved in SST, Carducci knew about this 'work aesthetic' from up-close and sweat-reek personal. With its peculiar blend of almost-collectivist camaraderie and anarcho-libertarian self-reliance, the sensibility was American to the core. And, despite the debt owed and respect given to Sabbath and Zep, these hard-rocking Americans tended to regard British music as effete, the work of Bowie-damaged dilettantes who simply hadn't put in the work.

WELCOME TO THE JUNGLE?

One of my favourite sleights of sampling sorcery last year occurred on a nameless techno track. Suddenly, an all-too-familiar snarl careened out of the mix: 'D'ya know where you are??!!' It was Axl Rose, from G 'n' R's urban paranoia anthem 'Welcome to the Jungle', gloating at your disorientation. Not only did the sample fit perfectly with the track's frenzy, it was a nice joke, because this was 'junglist' techno, and the people dancing almost certainly were so out of it that they *didn't* know where they were.

I don't know where the term 'junglist' (hardcore techno's dominant style for almost a year) originates. Probably from the churning poly-rhythms that define the genre (hip hop breakbeats hyped up to twice their proper pace), which sound like sheer voodoo. But I imagine it's also got something to do with a feeling that 'it's getting like a jungle out there', that in hard times only the hard (core) survive. Recently, junglist techno has developed something akin to a cult of the criminal. A vaguely nefarious aura hangs around the newer pirate stations like Don FM, Index and Lightning. Listen to the MC's coded patter, and you might assume illicit transactions are being conducted. MCs send out shouts to 'all the wrong 'uns' and 'liberty-takers'; sometimes, you hear requests being played for blokes banged up in Pentonville.

Although it's still mostly instrumental, the criminal-minded vibe is seeping into the music, with a spate of tracks with 'bad boy' themes. A big source is ragga, reggae's equivalent to gangsta rap, with its brash insolence and 'rude boy' postures. Junglist is desperate music for desperate times, which is why its two themes are oblivion and crime. British youth want to get out of 'it' (dead-end reality), either by taking drugs or by selling them. The sad fact is that for many kids, the only way they can afford to participate in rave culture at all is to become dealers. And so junglist has become the soundtrack of Britain's underclass. It's sort of appropriate that the sampling aesthetic (taking liberties with other people's musical property) should have fallen into the light-fingered hands of delinquents.

What's weird about junglism is that, having started as a form of techno, it's devolving, inexplicably, into a hyperactive cousin of early US rap. It's not just the breakbeats and outlaw imagery that recall hip hop. Hardcore's cult of bass and spliff as the route to blissful stupor is reminiscent of mid-eighties rap's 'get a little stupid and pump that bass' ethos (before rap got righteous and aware with Public Enemy, etc.). Junglism has even revived scratching and other forms of turntablemanipulating mayhem, long since abandoned by US hip hoppers. Pirate MCs speed-rap self-celebratory gibberish over their cut 'n' mix uproar, just like the earliest rappers.

As the ghetto-ization of Britain's inner city estates worsens, as more and more of the young come to depend on the black economy and petty villainy to survive, it could be that junglism will develop into something more than just party music, just as US rap evolved from its ghetto origins to become a culture. It's even conceivable that it could be politicized, if Tory tyranny extends itself towards the new millennium. But, at the moment, junglism is an anti-culture, locked in a here-and-now time frame, seeing no further than the weekend (and whatever quick killings are necessary to pay for its costly kicks).

No discourse surrounds this music, because even the dance media recoil in horror, cloaking a class-bound snobbery behind talk of a return to 'pure techno' (all electronics, no breakbeats, no squeaky 78 rpm voices). Combining Oi!'s uncouthness, Mantronix's sampladelic absurdism, Mod's speed-freak intensity and avant-funk's eeriness, junglist is a mighty peculiar mutant.

Who knows what it might evolve into?

What counts is that, for better or worse, it reflects what's going on in this country right now. It's the exhilarating, scary sound of a generation going nowhere at hyper-speed.

Melody Maker, 3 April 1993

In 1993, I spent a total of two and a half months in London (the rest of the time I was stuck in New York finishing *The Sex Revolts*) so feel pretty chuffed to have spotted the Next Big Thing ahead of the London-based media. This is a piece about jungle so early it wasn't even *called* 'jungle' yet . . . Well, that's my get-out clause for 'junglist'! Actually, it's true: things *were* semantically cloudy at that emergent point for the scene, people talked about 'junglistic hardcore' or 'jungle techno', it was a flavour not a genre, an adjective or add-on. There's also a poetic-historic right(eous)ness to calling it 'junglist', because that term came first. It was a shout-out captured on Jamaican sound system tapes – 'yard tapes' as they were known when they reached the UK. When the dancehall MC called out to 'alla the junglists' he was addressing people from Arnette Gardens, an area in Kingston nicknamed 'Concrete Jungle'. The junglists' rival gang came from Tivoli Gardens and were known as 'gardenists'! Former slums turned into public housing schemes, Arnette and Tivoli are feared in Jamaica as 'polit-ical garrisons', gang-controlled no-go zones for the police. 'Political', because each area is affiliated to a different party: Arnette to the left-wing PNP (People's National Party), Tivoli to the conservative JLP (Jamaica Labour Party). In the seventies, the PNP was led by Michael Manley, who cosied up to Cuba and used Rasta-style Jah-shall-smite-the-oppressor rhetoric; JLP, headed by Edward Seaga, was pro-America. So there's further righteousness to the association of 'junglist' with anti-colonialist, chant-down-Babylon politics. When hardcore producers sampled the 'big-up all junglist crew' cries from the yard tapes, they inadvertently christened the genre: 'junglist' led to 'junglizm' and then 'jungle', the perfect name for such a densely percussive music, for a sound that oozed tribal energy, voodoo darkness and ghetto-centric menace.

LET THE BOYS BE BOYS

Onyx interview/Gangsta Rap as Oi!

Onyx

Onyx, America's hottest new rap group of '93, describe themselves as 'hard, black and mad'. The New York gangstaz tell us to get ready for the 'Mad Face Invasion'. 'Our symbol is the Mad Face,' says Sticky Fingaz. 'That red "X" in the logo, that's blood drippin', and it stands for all the people that died on the streets.'

Onyx are mad, as in both 'angry' and 'insane', because 'there's nothing to be happy about'. 'It's too late for the world,' says Big DS. 'Whoever got the mark of the Beast is gonna die. The world is corrupt. We're like reporters, y'know? We incorporate in our music what we see in everyday life. What we represent is the anger in everybody's soul. And the insanity too.'

Onyx call the spooky, bad-dream vibe of their sound 'grimee'. 'We incorporate horror and suspense. In the old days of rap, MCs used to battle each other in the park. And that carried over to the audience: if a guy stepped on your shoe, somebody might get shot. So we made "Slam" so you could let out frustrations but still get home and go to bed safe. Slam-dancing was a punk thing but we brought it to the hip hop community. We're telling them that it's alright to jump around and let your frustrations out.'

Onyx's paranoid, besieged attitude comes through in the title of their debut album: *Bacdafucup*. 'That's the mentality we did the album with,' says Fingaz. 'You mad, frustrated, you say: bacdafucup, get away from me!' Big DS: 'Where we from, we don't got no white picket fence, sometimes you don't have a mother or a father, you don't have a lot of money. We can't talk about flowers or butterflies cos that's not our life.'

148

Onyx have a Social Darwinist worldview; capitalism is the war of all against all. 'If you're a squirrel, you gotta steal that nut from the other squirrel to feed your kids.' But their paranoia goes beyond the normal on-edge wariness of the urban jungle dweller; it has an almost cosmological dimension.

'What's coming in the future is Armageddon,' says Fingaz, practically frothing at the mouth. 'And we startin' an army: all the children, age one to age ten. We're training them at a young age, cos right now the army is in jail. The year 2000 is not supposed to happen. 1999, the year before the End, is going to be chaos. No, it's not from the Bible, it's from what I know. It's a feeling. People say "save the world" but it's too late for that. The world is doomed. You're doomed. You're a walking corpse. Me too. To me, truthfully, life is a big waste of time. Everyone in this fucking hotel is gonna die.'

What do you do for fun? I ask, trying to lighten the mood. 'Fuck, smoke weed, write rhymes,' he retorts like a shot.

Onyx, and Sticky Fingaz in particular, have a unique rhymin' style: apoplectic, explosive, ragged with rage. 'It's like we all trying to shout louder than each other, and our voices get hoarse, and that's where you get the "raspy rasp" fashion and the grimee voice. We get hyper, adrenalin's flowing, blood pressure's up. Slow music makes you wanna fuck; our music makes you wanna fight. But we can't have a club of people fighting so that's where the slam-dancing comes in.'

At times Fingaz's delivery's so psychotic he shreds syntax and meter, raps across the beat to the internal rhythm of his own seething fury. 'I'm kind of fucked up, man, cos there ain't enough alphabets in the language to express my thoughts. You know what I wanna do, man?' he adds. 'Swear to God, I wanna rule the fucking world. That's why we're building this army of kids. Cos I don't want the past, I want the future.'

Feeling a mite foolish, I ask if Onyx can never imagine letting down their guard, softening the bacdafucup attitude.

'Sleep is the cousin of death,' says the hitherto taciturn Fredro. 'Word up.'

Gangsta Rap as Oi!

Back in 1991, Chuck D proclaimed the imminent and inevitable demise of 'the negative hardcore' (gangsta rap like NWA) and the triumph of 'positive hardcore' (Public Enemy-style militant/conscious rap). Two years on, the picture looks rather different: judging by their last two albums, PE's muse is ailing, while gangsta is stronger

149

(commercially and artistically) and nastier than ever. Both ex-NWA mainman Dr Dre and Cypress Hill went straight in at Number 1 in the US Pop Album Chart; 1993's big new bad boys Onyx are currently at Number 4 with their single 'Slam'.

If PE are 'the Black Clash' (Chuck D recently made a pilgrimage to Africa, so we may soon hear their *Sandinista*) then the current gangsta resurgence could be rap's equivalent to Oi!. Both Oi! and gangsta share the same kind of pre-political, shortsighted rage; both proclaim their identity as the oppressed, but make no attempt to transcend or evade that identity. And where Oi! was jingoistic, gangsta has its own kind of patriotism: a blacker-than-thou ghetto pride that's very different from the Black Nationalism of Public Enemy or the Afrocentric dignity of Arrested Development. Hence gangsta rap's use of the term 'nigga', which doubles as an affectionate fraternal greeting and an insult. Like Oi! bandnames (The Exploited, Cockney Rejects), gangsta takes the most negative stereotypes of delinquent youth and turns them into a badge of class-bound hostility and defiance.

And Onyx? The 'let the boys be boys' chorus of 'Slam' makes me think of Sham 69, while the male-bonding moshing mayhem of the video clinches the Oi! parallel: hell, there's even a few white punks (members of the thrash band Biohazard) flailing about among all the black skinheads. There's that same combination of faintly homo-erotic camaraderie (cf. House of Pain's boy-sterous lunkhead anthem 'Jump Around') with vicious homophobia. Even gangsta rap's rationale for the violent lyrics is an echo of the standard Oi! get-out clause: 'we only report what we see'.

Further parallels: Oi!'s lager-loutishness is matched by ghetto youth's love of 40 oz malt liquor, an incredibly strong beer that's been blamed for a lot of black-on-black violence. A popular T-shirt in the US right now bears the slogan: 'All I Need is a 40 and a Blunt' (a blunt being an incredibly potent joint). Another T-shirt simply emblazons the word: 'REAL'. Gangsta rap is obsessed with authenticity, which involves a two-fold struggle: first, fending off white consumers, and second, defining yourself against bourgeois art-rap bands (PM Dawn, Digable Planets, The Goats, Basehead), who are seen as pandering to the white college rock audience. Again, this just reminds me of how the Oi! bands hated students and art-punk from PiL to Bauhaus.

As with Oi!, the other side of gangsta's laddishness is misogyny. Masculinity can only be defined against femininity. It's been argued that white supremacist society puts the young black male in a 'female' position (fucked over). And this is why the teenage hoodlums in ghetto-sploitation movies like *Menace II Society* use the word 'bitch' as the ultimate insult against other men. And why Onyx's 'Bichasniguz' threatens a male double-talking backstabber with the ultimate vengeance: 'I'm a-have to pull your skirt up.' In fact, there's been a spate of rap songs in which enemies are threatened with sodomy – dildos up the arse, dicks rammed against tonsils, that kind of thing.

Nasty bizness, for sure. Like Oi!, gangsta is a lumpen-proletarian subculture. Lumpen-prole was Marx's term for the underclass, workers who'd lapsed from the dignity and solidarity of honest toil into unemployment or crime. Marx regarded the lumpen as a counter-revolutionary class, because they preyed on their own kind, and in unstable times were liable to being seduced by fascism or tinpot military dictators. (Hence Oi!'s dodgy neo-Nazi tendencies.) But the big difference between Oi! and gangsta rap is that the music's a whole lot better. In fact, some of the most bizarre and/or radical pop of recent years has come from the underclass: the E-monster pop of Happy Mondays and Flowered Up, the criminal-minded ruffneck avant-gardism of junglist 'ardkore, and the psycho-rap of Onyx and Cypress Hill.

Melody Maker, 4 September 1993

Aesthetic attraction to the 'avant-lumpen', tinged with ambivalence and moral squeamishness, is a thread running right through this book, from Schoolly D's proto-gangsta to Lethal B's grime. (I've often wondered, incidentally, whether Onyx and their 'grimeee' concept had some ancestral role vis-à-vis the genre term 'grime'.) Onyx's moment quickly faded; a lot of hip hop headz found their whole psycho shtick too cartoony to take seriously. A more enduring group with a similar pre-millennial tension/we-are-soldiers-of-darkness vibe emerged a few months later in 1993: Wu-Tang Clan. Through their albums and solo offshoots the Wu deftly walked a line between 'street' and 'art', but somehow I don't think I could have glommed the Oi! thesis on to them. What struck me about talking to Sticky Fingaz (incongruously, the Onyx interview took place in the brightly lit lobby of a fancy Edgware Road hotel) was that this was the first time in my journalistic experience where a rapper's offstage self completely correlated with their vinyl persona. Unlike with LL Cool J, there was no gap, no fall-off in intensity. Which suggests either that rap groups by the early nineties had got wise to the need to 'turn it on' Ted Nugent-style for interviewers. Or that Onyx were actually like that – paranoid-apocalyptic-survivalist – *all the time.*

STATE OF INTERDEPENDENCE

Britain, America, and the 'Special Relationship' in Pop Music

In rock 'n' roll just as in politics, the USA and the UK have a 'special relationship'. Together, they've dominated global pop. Over the decades, rock's centre of gravity has shifted back and forth between each nation. In the sixties it passed from Swinging London to San Francisco, in the seventies from So-Cal soft-rock to UK punk. The rest of the planet has never had much of a look-in.

Musical innovations generally originate in America, and in particular from black music (R&B and soul in the fifties and sixties, funk and disco in the seventies, rap and house in the eighties). But usually it's British bands who respond quickest to Black American innovations, adding a vital element of art-school conceptualism, style and attitude, then promptly selling this repackaged Black American music to White America. This is what happened with sixties white blues, or eighties New Pop (funk and soul given a video-friendly gloss), or nineties rock-house bands like EMF, Jesus Jones, Stone Roses and Happy Mondays.

But just as the 'special relationship' in politics often engenders anxiety among the British (fears that the UK is a US vassal), similarly, the transatlantic traffic in pop is fraught with rivalry and resentment. Right now, the British pop scene is convulsed by one of its periodic fits of anti-Americanism. All year long, there have been murmurings of discontent, which has swelled into a 'Yanks Go Home!' uproar. There are echoes of the anti-American attitude of punk, when the Sex Pistols derided the Lower East Side punk scene in 'New York' and the Clash wrote 'I'm So Bored With the USA'. In this case, though, these bands were purging a bad case of 'anxiety of influence', since they were heavily indebted to their US cousins like The Ramones and Richard Hell. The word 'punk' itself was an American invention.

The current wave of anti-Americanism is slightly different – the British feel deluged by American grunge. From the late eighties until quite recently, most British indie bands had looked to American hardcore and alternative rock, envying and admiring the likes of Sonic Youth, Big Black and Butthole Surfers. American underground bands seemed to have an unselfconscious and intuitive approach that was felt to be preferable to England's traditionally over-theorized and premeditated take on rock 'n' roll. The best British bands of the late eighties, like My Bloody Valentine, took the slacker spirit and neo-psychedelic sound of Dinosaur Jr and Husker Du, and gave it an androgynous spin.

The massive success of Nirvana's 'Smells Like Teen Spirit' and *Nevermind* changed all that. What was once cool and a trifle exotic became commonplace, consensual, oppressive. While Nirvana themselves are still worshipped in the UK, some groups have started to revolt against the horde of grunge bands that have descended on British shores like an occupying army. Even more resented are the home-grown plague of slacker-wannabes who've struggled to emulate the invaders, growing their hair shaggy, mumbling their lyrics, grunging up their guitars. As 1992 turned into 1993, a wave of bands emerged who reject the notion of an 'English curse' (of pretentiousness and preciousness), and instead embrace the idea of being literate, self-conscious, stylised and ironic. They ridicule grunge as mere heavy metal without the glamour.

The most successful and most volubly anti-American of the New Patriots is Suede, who are the big UK pop sensation of 1993. They are currently attempting to conquer America with their first full-scale US tour ... Suede's vocalist Brett Anderson has been outspoken in his disdain for American 'rawk'. Suede's roots are the British art-rock and glam of the seventies (David Bowie, T. Rex, Kate Bush) and the English nostalgia of The Smiths. Anderson sings in an exaggerated London accent, a defiant gesture against the pseudo-American slacker drawl that so many Brit bands still mimic. His fey, flamboyant image and gender-bending lyrics are a resurrection of the English tradition of androgyny and sexual ambiguity, a concerted reaction against grunge's machismo. Earlier this year Anderson appeared on the cover of *Select* magazine beneath the headline 'Yanks Go Home', his lipstick mouth pouting with disdain.

Other bands flying the flag for the imperilled spirit of English pop include Denim, Pulp, The Auteurs and Saint Etienne. Denim and Pulp are both fixated on the tacky, plastic pop of the early seventies, teeny-bop idols like Gary Glitter, Hello, The Sweet. The Auteurs herald a return to literate, wordy songcraft. Singer Luke Haines worships the 'wryness and dryness' of quintessentially English songwriters like Ray Davies of The Kinks. The band's debut album *New Wave* even contained an anti-grunge anthem called 'American Guitars'. Saint Etienne are a stylish dance-pop trio whose delightful, irony-drenched songs, with titles like 'London Belongs to Me' and 'Avenue', often seem like sepia-tinged reinvocations of the Swinging London of the sixties.

The anti-American mood was prefigured by that most England-obsessed singer, Morrissey, formerly of The Smiths. On his 1992 glam-rock-tinged LP *Your Arsenal*, the song 'We'll Let You Know' mourned the fact that 'we look to Los Angeles for the language we use . . . London is dead'. Shortly after the album's release, Morrissey incited controversy when he draped himself in the Union Jack flag while performing at an open-air concert. The singer was criticized for flirting with a symbol associated with neo-fascist skinheads, who have been escalating bias attacks against racial minorities. Another song on the album, 'The National Front Disco' (named after a Far Right political party), heightened the impression that Morrissey was playing with fire.

If there's a sociological backdrop to this mini-movement of bands who are proud to be British, it's that the UK is in the throes of a political, social and cultural crisis. Economic recession, rising crime, deterioration of public services, governmental ineptitude and a sense of stagnation have all fuelled anxieties about where Britain is heading as a nation, what it means to be British. On the one hand, the UK is nervous about merging with its neighbours on the continent in a greater European community; on the other, it feels inundated with American culture, from grunge to Hollywood blockbusters to *American Gladiators*.

The defiant Englishness of this new crop of indie bands is a sort of perversely parochial and Luddite response to global pop culture – everything from Nintendo to sampler-based music like techno (a truly international and rootless music form). Since the future would seem to promise the loss of national cultural identity, these bands turn their backs to the future and rifle the back pages of England's pop glory.

* * *

This transatlantic antagonism often cuts the other way, too: there's a long tradition of American scepticism towards the latest British trends. For some, the UK produces an endless stream of over-hyped 'haircut bands', seen as videogenic, weighted with conceptual baggage, but lacking in musical substance. Suede, for instance, have received a mixed reaction in the US. While the college rock audience, which has always been Anglophile, has responded favourably, the more cutting-edge breed of indie hipsters remain sceptical. And it seems unlikely that Suede's lyrical preciousness and androgynous image will go down well in the rock heartland.

American critics have often suggested that the British lack a natural, 'organic' relationship with rock 'n' roll. There's an Anglophobic tradition that stretches from Dave Marsh, once a fervent fan of The Who but by the early eighties the champion of Bruce Springsteen's all-American populism against the British New Pop invaders like Culture Club and Human League, to Joe Carducci's recent, influential polemic *Rock and the Pop Narcotic*. In his nativist, Anglophobic theory of rock, Carducci argues that British bands quickly lost touch with the blues roots of rock 'n' roll, and that after Led Zeppelin and Black Sabbath, British bands made little contribution to the evolution of the form. In his book, Carducci articulates an abiding, gut-reflex prejudice on the US indie scene: that British bands are rhetoricians rather than rockers.

In recent years, only a handful of Brits have been given the critical red carpet in America. One is Teenage Fanclub, a Scottish raunch 'n' roll quartet who are Americanophile and influenced by the likes of Neil Young and Big Star. Another is My Bloody Valentine, who also initially took their bearings from US underground bands like Sonic Youth and Dinosaur Jr, before radically transforming their sources.

The transatlantic traffic in musical ideas often works by a process of innovation through misrecognition, through a failed emulation of what's going on in the other country. And this traffic is full of unlikely developments, like the way the quintessentially Northern English band The Fall has suddenly and inexplicably emerged as a major influence on a breed of lo-fi indie bands in America (like Pavement), or the way the Sex Pistols have been adopted by US metal bands, with everyone from Guns N' Roses to Megadeth to Motley Crue covering their songs and/or citing their influence. The 'special relationship' between America and Britain generates many ironies. Perhaps the biggest is that grunge, the most American sound of the moment and whose thrall has provoked the insurrection of Suede et al., actually derives from British heavy rock (Led Zep, Sabbath) and British punk. Another irony: the band that throughout the eighties defined American lite-metal, with its glossy riffs and candied harmonies, is Def Leppard, who hail from Sheffield, England.

Mis-appropriation and miscegenation is the way that pop evolves. In view of this, the attempts of bands like Suede and The Auteurs to safeguard the purity of English pop seem shortsighted and futile. Insularity and inbreeding will ultimately condemn British pop to extinction.

director's cut of piece published in the *New York Times*,
5 September 1993

The missing link here is Blur, whose *Modern Life is Rubbish* (a dry-run for *Parklife*) came out in May 1993. Its original working title: *England Vs America*. That same year I wrote a massive piece about Blur's big rivals (pre-Oasis, anyway) Suede and the question of whether they could match their UK impact in America. It was slightly embarrassing to watch Brett Anderson acting all haughty and precious on MTV, or mocking hecklers at their New York debut show with faintly anti-American jibes about 'rawk', or declaring in interviews that 'the US is a thing to be broken, like a disobedient child'. I cringed a little, sensing a nation being rubbed the wrong way, and knowing in my gut that they were destined to join the long line of UK mega-bands like The Jam who make barely a dent in America's consciousness. The problem for Suede, and others that followed in their footsteps, such as Pulp, is that the pop/rock divide they effortlessly crossed in the UK – just like Beatles, Bowie, Roxy, Smiths before them – remained cast-iron in the States. Image flash, androgyny, a healthy dose of contrivance – all the things that are the very spice of pop life in the UK – were anathema to US rock fans, who believed and to this day mostly still believe in authenticity. It would be the 'pop' in the word Britpop, not so much the 'Brit', that would be the problem. As Brett Anderson put it in an interview with me, 'English bands have that feeling of pop about them, but pop is still a dirty word in America.'

MTV

The Revolution Will Not be Televised

I quite like MTV, me. I know I'm not supposed to. As a fan and as a critic, I'm supposed to deplore MTV as architect of the living death of rock 'n' roll, a travesty and a tragedy. MTV: it's the great co-opter, the castrator. Furthermore, so the argument runs, MTV's thrall is co-extensive with the tyranny of video itself, which erodes our individual and idiosyncratic imaginative responses to a song, debasing the abstract power of music by tying it to crass, literal imagery.

MTV's most recent crime is 'killing' grunge by making it mainstream and massive, a pre-fab, off-the-peg look and attitude ripe for the colour supplements and the catwalks. By forcibly overgrounding an underground sound and style MTV, allegedly, has ripped out the heart of American alternative music. But the truth is that the frisson and the uproar of Nirvana's smash-through depended on the medium of MTV for its very possibility. I was in the States when 'Smells Like Teen Spirit' started to shift from 'Buzz Clip' to heavy rotation, and remember a genuine and palpable sense of Event, of a Great Change afoot. For about six weeks, it was thrilling and disorientating to watch a sound (Husker Du, basically) whose marginalization one had become utterly resigned to, suddenly and inexplicably explode into mass consciousness, become meaning-full. It didn't hurt that the video for 'Smells Like' was brilliant, eerie and perturbing, a rare (but not that rare) example of a promo that brings out all the hidden dimensions of a song. The inevitable, rapid normalization/banalization of that sound and vision was pre-programmed into the story; Nirvana always knew they'd be co-opted, that their victory would be their defeat, which was what made the irony of 'Smells Like Teen Spirit' so caustic – the oldest story, the turning of rebellion into money, of rock into light entertainment.

The point is that MTV has become the kind of national pop forum that America has always lacked, the US equivalent to Radio 1 and *Top of the Pops* when they counted for something. I can remember the teenage thrill of suddenly hearing a favourite band invading the public realm – a daytime play for Scritti Politti, DJs gritting their teeth as they introduced Public Image Ltd's 'Death Disco' or 'Flowers of Romance' on TOTP. In a sense, MTV goes against the grain of the times, in that it resists the tendency for rock to break up into a myriad of niche markets and sealed-off genres, a phenomenon that's been called the 'boutique-ization' of the record industry. MTV still depends on outmoded figments and mythical unities like 'youth', 'rock', 'the kids': the illusion that everybody's gathered in the same spot, looking to figurehead artists who will somehow 'explain' them. The Woodstock fantasy. Outmoded, maybe, but still useful, in so far as they make Events like Nirvana possible, or forcibly expose white youth to Black culture (Dr Dre, Ice Cube) rather than simply consigning everything to its niche/ghetto. Of course, in trying to uphold the idea of consensus – of music that means something to everybody, not just its designated cult audience – MTV inevitably fosters a kind of ersatz, 'simulation' rock: the designer grunge of 4 Non Blondes and Stone Temple Pilots. But then, punk engendered the likes of The Vibrators and The Boomtown Rats: pale imitations and bandwagon-boarders is another 'oldest story' in rock. As with punk, grunge's triumph was also its defeat. The crucial ambiguity is that MTV made *both* possible.

If MTV has an 'evil' side, it operates at a level far more subliminal and insidious than the frankly rather quaint concept of 'co-opting' or sell-out. The 'evil' is intrinsic to the medium. MTV is rather like the compact disc, in that it subtly distorts and depletes our relationship with music. For instance, the CD's very convenience not only makes possible, but practically enforces, a shallower and more alienated way of living with music than was the case with the good old vinyl LP. CD-consumers: when was the last time you listened to an album all the way through? The CD's programmability encourages you to rapidly reduce an album to a handful of favourite tracks (which usually means the instantly pleasing ones) and play them over and over; songs that might have gradually grown on you languish in permanent neglect. Remote-control leads to a more fractured relationship with music, like channel-surfing through cable TV. Basically, the CD has made the old way of listening reverentially to an album, living with and learning to love its overall mood, its ebb and flow, not just old-fashioned but almost unrecoverable. What appears to be an increase in consumer choice and flexibility of use has resulted in a diminishment of aesthetic richness: you *use* music, rather than submit yourself to it.

MTV has a similar shrivelling effect on the attention span. There's an internal, inhuman logic to the video medium that's pushing it along a trajectory of quick-cut editing, special FX overload and hyper-stimulation. The result is the same erosion of patience and fracturing of consciousness that's caused by the CD. But the real perniciousness of MTV resides in its last two letters: TV. Whereas radio allows music to be part of life (you can listen while doing your homework, tidying the house, driving the car), MTV makes music-video a substitute for life. MTV is a spectacle, in the full dystopian sense of the word as used by the Situationists: it demands passivity, it pacifies. You sit on your butt and you gawp. Its hyper-real hyper-active imagery is so full of youthful vitality it sucks the liveliness out of your own life. In that sense MTV is anti-rock, or at least anti-rock in the countercultural and punk senses (rock as motivator, instigator, incitement to live NOW).

Ironically, this passive-izing effect is something the people who run MTV seem to want to circumvent, possibly because they still retain vestiges of the idealism of their babyboomer or post-punk youth. MTV attempts to agitate against the spine-corroding, veg-out inducing nature of the medium, by punctuating its stream of visual muzak with bursts of agit-prop: youth-oriented, blipvert-brief public service announcements whose visual flair and wit is far superior to almost all rock-vid (as are the surreal MTV 'idents', i.e. animated logos). The messages – don't be racist, don't hate gays, that sort of thing – are pretty mild, liberal stuff (although, lest we forget, liberal is nearly as bad as 'commie' in some sectors of the US). But they do show that the people who run MTV imagine, perhaps foolishly, that they can motivate and educate the youth.

Then there was MTV's 'Rock the Vote' campaign and the intelligent, intensive election coverage mounted by 'The Day in Rock', the channel's news show. Some pundits credit MTV with winning the election for Clinton by getting the youth vote out; MTV itself seems to share this view, judging by one station 'ident' that cut 'n' mixes video footage of Clinton and makes the Prez drawl a heartfelt 'thank you MTV'. MTV is postmodernism in all its best and worst senses (at one point it actually called itself 'postmodern MTV', possibly following college radio programmers, who sometimes use 'postmodern' as a synonym for 'alternative'). If the self-aggrandising, tongue-in-chic MTV-trailers and gripping exploitation shows like *The Real World* are the good side, MTV-rock is the bad side of postmodernism: a depthless replay of rock's glory years without the resonance, with all the rough edges glossed over. Like Lenny Kravitz's inauthentic authenticity: the way he'll get his bassist togged and wigged up to look exactly like Noel Redding of the Jimi Hendrix Experience, or deliberately use archaic recording equipment to get that 'reproduction antique' feel. Or Matthew Sweet's videogenic purée of Neil Young and Big Star.

If watching MTV is sometimes like traipsing through a museum of rock history, it fits, because MTV is dedicated to keeping the moribund concept of 'youth' on life support. Pragmatically, its survival depends on selling the youth market to advertisers. Ideologically, it needs to promote a youth-consciousness that includes some of the attributes of earlier rock/youth culture (political awareness, idealism, feisty irreverence, grooviness, hedonism) but moulded to fit an age where youth's primary form of self-expression is consumerism, counterculture has become over-the-counter-culture, and political agency is reduced to a T-shirt slogan. Hence, the blatant, barefaced paradoxes of MTV's self-promotion campaign earlier this year: 'the music revolution will be televised'. TV is the antithesis of revolution; nothing radical can happen while you're sitting on your ass, unless you're into transcendental meditation. The idea of revolution being piped through the fibre-optic cable like so much air conditioning is so preposterous, so poignant, you don't know whether to laugh or cry.

And yet, for all that, I quite like MTV, me. Or at least the American version, which is sharper and goofier and has better love-to-hate V-Js than MTV Europe (who follow a placid, soporific 'total flow' aesthetic rather than MTV US's jarring, hyped-up cut 'n' mix). I quite like MTV in the same way that I quite like a can of Coke: they both add a bit of artificial pep to life, a caffeinated glucose blast. I know MTV isn't the 'real thing', that it's bad for me, but at slack moments it gives a buzz, even if over-consumption leaves a bad taste in the mouth and a queasy rumble in the gut. I like MTV's hyper-real, apocalyptic, Baudrillard-ian qualities: the sheer insanity of having a news show called *The Day in Rock*, where world events are seen, if at all, only through the lens of rock, as if music could somehow be a perceptual framework for EVERYTHING. In the sixties, rock was intimately intertwined with the turmoil of the era, it was the medium through which everything was refracted. Watching MTV – the airbrushed, sanitized Bacchanalia of Kravitz's 'Are You Gonna Go My Way', Blind Melon's pasteurized homage to West Coast psych – it sometimes feels like you're living in a ghastly pastiche of the sixties: a world where rock has won, has become the new mainstream, and thereby lost all meaning.

But you can always turn it off. As with all artificial stimulants, use rather than abuse is the key. And there will always be pockets of resistance: the Luddite revolt against hi-tech (the lo-fi underground) or the truly futuristic/nihilistic (rave's anti-videogenic facelessness, where all that counts really is the music and nothing else, nothing at all).

Melody Maker, 16 October 1993

Ah, the good old days, when Music Television actually had music on it! As the nineties progressed, the channel realized that the only way to get viewers to tune in, in a regular and non-desultory manner, was through non-music programming, ultimately leading to the current travesty of an MTV that shows hardly any music videos. Although the station did briefly flourish as the American equivalent to Radio 1, I do think MTV ultimately represented the Death of Rock. Or at least it was rock's co-assassin, the other culprit being the compact disc, with its 'consumer-empowering' enforcement of fragmentary listening. The mode of experiencing/discovering music that characterized the Rock Era (the album-as-artwork and immersive listening experience, the primacy of sound over vision, the Single as Event, the surprises and raptures of radio, the role of the local record shop) began to be eroded from the mid-eighties on. Something else gradually began to take shape as its replacement: a new apparatus of consumption and distribution based around the integration/ subordination of music with/to visuals (advertising, movies, TV), the digitization of sound (eventually leading to iPods, downloading, etc.), a massive decentralization of radio and retail. It's a brand new audio-landscape, in which the uses people make of music and the expectations they have of it are totally in flux.

PJ HARVEY

Think about Polly Harvey too long, and you start reeling. She's a mass, a mess of contradictions. Since she emerged out of nowhere (more precisely, her tiny home town in rural Dorset) at the tail end of 1991, the twenty-three-year-old singer has been the focal point of intense, fascinated scrutiny. No one can quite figure her out. When it comes to the gender map of nineties rock, she refuses to be tied down or placed.

Listen to her band, PJ Harvey, and the immediate impression is that she's the most ferocious, feral she-rebel around, easily surpassing in both songcraft and primal abandon the 'angry woman' bands (Hole, Babes In Toyland, Bikini Kill et al.) that are often regarded as her natural peers. For her part, Polly refuses to describe herself as a feminist and has emitted dismissive snorts in the direction of Riot Grrrl. For hardcore Grrrl-ideologues, this makes Polly a sex-traitor, a collaborator with the boy-rock status quo. But Harvey doesn't care. In songs like 'Rid of Me', she may sound as avenging as one of the Furies, or Glenn Close in *Fatal Attraction,* but in real life, she says she prefers to hang out with men rather than women. And musically all her influences aren't just male they're men's men – Nick Cave, Tom Waits, Howlin' Wolf, Captain Beefheart.

Harvey's desire to be one of the boys goes back to her childhood. 'I spent my life up till I was fourteen just wishing I was boy,' she recalls. 'My older brother was so wonderful, and there were no other girls in the village, so I just used to play with him and his friends. I was a real tomboy. I still do prefer male company. Most of my friends are male. I do love men, probably more than I love women.'

She doesn't seem to know exactly what it is she prefers about men, so I offer a helpful hint. Men tend to relate to each other via an exter-

162

nal, 'objective' entity, a shared obsession – cars, hi-fi, music, sport – which requires expertise, provokes argument but most importantly becomes a means for men to express their emotions, indirectly. Women seem to find it easier simply to talk about their feelings, to relate purely and directly. This strikes a chord with Polly, as she doesn't like the 'girly' way of being together.

'Emotions are something that I don't find it easy to talk about. I'm useless at it. Maybe that's one reason why I'd much rather talk about records or recording techniques or sheep-dipping,' she adds, an allusion to her parents' farm, still a big presence in her life, a sanctuary from rock 'n' roll.

But for all her tomboy tendencies, Polly Harvey's songs derive their savage energy from a conflicted attitude towards masculinity: a mad jumble of envy, admiration, rage, resentment, and above all an awareness of the ludicrousness of machismo's blustery posturing. On PJ Harvey's second album, *Rid of Me*, released earlier this year, there were songs like 'Me Jane' ('Tarzan I'm bleeding / Stop your fucking screaming') and 'Man-Size' (in which Harvey caricatures macho grandiosity, playing the role of a leather-booted thug who struggles to 'get girl out of my head'). *4 Track Demos*, her new album (and the reason the interview-phobic Harvey is grinning and bearing another round of interrogation), contains the original demo versions of the *Rid of Me* tracks plus some new songs, some of which also seem to parody and piss-take male attitudes. 'Easy', for instance, lambastes misogyny ('you can call me devil's gateway'), while 'M-Bike' is the green-eyed lament of a girl who finds herself competing with a motorbike for her boyfriend's affection. Typically, the lunkhead finds it easier to relate to a machine than to a flesh-and-blood partner.

Other times, Polly Harvey seems to aspire to machismo's swagger. '50 Ft Queenie' seems like Harvey's attempt to imagine a female equivalent to the hyper-phallic self-aggrandisement of rock 'n' roll, and in particular the blues tradition of boasting omnipotence (e.g. Jimi Hendrix's 'Voodoo Chile'). In fact, Harvey got the idea from listening to gangsta rap, the nineties successor to the blues. 'I really liked the bragging, the way the rappers say their names over and over. I wanted to write something about a really bolshy character.' Mocking and demolishing the myth of 'penis envy' with the line 'I'm twenty inches long', Queenie 'stomps around a lot', says Harvey. 'She's big cos she feasts on men and that's a good form of protein.'

Another paradox to Polly Harvey is the contradiction between the extreme nakedness of her songs, her apparent compulsion to lay bare her emotions (and frequently her flesh, as on the sleeve of her debut

Dry and on an infamous *NME* cover), and her charming evasiveness in interview. She refuses to explain her songs, and hates the excessive attention paid to lyrics. She's never included a lyric sheet with her albums. 'It seems silly to me, cos they're not poetry, they're not meant to be read. They're meant to be heard with the music. If I buy an album with a lyric sheet, I always end up reading it the first few times I listen, and you don't even listen to the music properly. A song is a song, not a poem or a play.'

While some of her songs aren't confessional but are inhabited by characters, she says: 'They all come from me. It's me imagining myself in that situation, not somebody else.' All her songs are in the first person; she detests the detached, novelistic approach to songwriting, with its third-person vignettes. 'It's too distanced, it's like the writer's trying to protect themselves by projecting their ideas on to a fictional character.'

A final, defining Polly paradox: while her lyrics are acclaimed as taboo-busting (e.g. 'Dry', with its ultimate image of male failure: 'you leave me dry'), and are celebrated for opening up hitherto unexplored realms of female sexuality/subjectivity, musically Polly's a traditional-ist. She makes the kind of music – blues-rock – that she grew up with, quite literally. Her parents were bohemian hippie-ish sorts and she was exposed from a very early age to a constant barrage of rock 'n' roll, blues and jazz.

'The roles were reversed in our house: my brother and I'd get woken at 3 a.m., cos mum and dad would be playing their music really loud in the other room, and we'd get really cross with them. Just recently I've been going through their record collection cos I'd never really listened to it, and I'll play an album and realize I know every single word, even though I never consciously listened to it, because they played it so much when I was young. My mum was a big Bob Dylan fan, they've got lots of blues, Howlin' Wolf, Beefheart, Canned Heat, John Lee Hooker, The Stones.'

Often the children of hippie or hipster parents react against their liberal upbringing and become accountants or investment bankers. With Polly Harvey, it's the opposite: she's followed in their footsteps.

'They never pressurized me to do music, but it's what they always wanted. They were so pleased when I decided not to go to college and do music full time instead. When I was about twelve or thirteen, I did stage a little rebellion against all the blues music around me. I started buying Duran Duran records and U2 and stuff like that. They hated all that.'

But her classic upbringing came through ultimately, most tumultuously with the monstrous, blues-rock stampede of *Rid of Me*. The first time I heard it I was immediately struck by how thunder-quakingly Led Zep the drums sounded, like the ghost of John Bonham in your living room. If anything, the demos and new songs on *4 Track* are even bluesier: the bottleneck guitar on 'Snake', the grinding off-kilter boogie churn of 'Reeling', with Polly veering between a Jagger drawl and a Robert Plant falsetto.

Of *Rid of Me*, Harvey says she wanted to 'get a sound that was as live as possible and a lot of the blues records and the Led Zep records were recorded live. The music is heading even more in that direction, that's what I want the next album to sound like.'

Another reason for the Robert Plant histrionics might be that Harvey's been taking opera lessons for eight months (two retired opera singers happen to live in her village). But if rock opera summons up frightmare images of Meat Loaf or Freddie Mercury, think again. Polly really admires and aspires to the hair-raising, marrow-curdling vocal acrobatics of Diamanda Galas, the avant-garde demon-diva who's closer to a sorceress or shaman than Maria Callas.

But she has her doubts about learning the 'correct' way to sing. 'They teach you how to get the purest sound, how to use your voice without harming it. But the sounds I like aren't "pure", actually come from harming my voice by smoking and drinking too much, so it sounds all gravelly. I'll probably go that direction, towards Tom Waits. I've been smoking again and it sounds good. Good and phlegmy!'

Harvey's heroes, musical (Nick Cave, Waits, Beefheart, Pixies) and literary (William Burroughs), all belong to a particular male tradition of bohemians. The one woman that could fit in well in this beatnik brotherhood, Patti Smith, is someone that Harvey only listened to after she found herself incessantly compared to Smith. What does she like about the psycho-surrealist bad boys?

'It's the only music that makes me feel anything. I'm always looking for extremes in things. That's what I try to do in my music, push something as far as you can take it. Until it becomes almost unacceptable.'

Do you ever worry that you won't be able to sustain this imaginative extremity, that you'll grow mellow and your muse will get tame? Does being happy, or being in love, ever dry up the angst-well?

'Even when I feel really happy, it's never enough. The only way it seems that I can reach "enough" is through music. I've never found a relationship that is "enough". Sometimes when I do feel really happy, I write some of the most horrible songs! It doesn't stop my songwriting at all, I don't need to be tortured and angst-ridden to write.'

Polly is a big fan of French postmodern critic Roland Barthes's

A Lover's Discourse, an exquisite dissection of the delirium and delusions engendered by the amorous condition, an inventory of the neurotic rituals the lover devises to defuse anxiety. 'I just started reading it again. When I read it the first time, I don't think I'd ever been in love. I wanted to read it again and see how different it would be after experiencing the real thing. It's an amazing book. It puts into words things you just can't explain yourself.' She sees certain parallels between what she does lyrically and Barthes's methodology: 'Trying to take things apart, in order to understand them.'

A lot of Harvey's songs are situated in the classic blues combat zone, love's 'killing floor' (a term that originally comes from the abattoir, the place where the unhappy animal gets it in the neck). This fits, as PJ Harvey songs often seem to link carnal desire and emotional carnage. Friction is the word that always springs to mind when I hear her music. Musically, the songs sound somehow itchy. Lyrically, there's a vivid sense of sex as the friction of skin against skin ('Rub Till it Bleeds'). And emotionally, there's a sense of intimacy as abrasion: egos rubbing each other up the wrong way in a confined emotional space.

'I find the music uncomfortable to listen to,' confirms Harvey. 'It's not that enjoyable! I don't play the albums a lot. It's not something you'd put on to relax. It's a friction, an uncomfortable feeling. Which is how I feel most of the time – never quite at ease.'

Harvey suffers terribly from stress, yet paradoxically (that word again!) she clearly thrives on it. Living in London last year drove her to the verge of a nervous breakdown, and even now, on tour, she needs 'stress management'. Then there's the pressure that comes not from mere celebrity but rather from being a cult icon, the focus of obsession and expectation. She's starting to get a flood of weird, intense fan letters. 'A lot of strange letters have found their way directly to the house, addressed to: Polly Harvey, Somewhere in a Small Village, Dorset. And they get there, these days! Some people have started coming to the village too.'

Along with the stress therapy, Harvey is also a bit of a health nut. 'I go through phases of trying different herbal remedies. Sometimes I think they work, sometimes I don't. My mother's always been into that, everything from drinking hydrogen peroxide to rubbing sandalwood on her neck for a sore throat. I'm sure I'll end up just like her, spending all my life trying out new remedies. The funniest one was drinking hydrogen peroxide for a year. She'd read that it's supposed to re-oxygenate the body if you drink a teaspoon a day. She's still alive, but she's got a sore throat, which she blames on the peroxide. Which is where the sandalwood comes in.'

But ultimately, her greatest form of therapy is the catharsis of her own music. 'If I didn't do it, I'd be a big mess. It is a kind of therapy for me, if not for other people. Live, it isn't very therapeutic, unless you've had a very bad day. Sometimes that can work very well: the tension of the day can colour the gig and make it very fraught and intense. But the writing of the songs is the real therapy, rather than performing. Because it's not physical enough, yet. I'm still anchored to one microphone.' She's toying with the idea of expanding the three-piece PJ Harvey unit into a five-piece, so that she doesn't have to play guitar on every song. 'I want to move around at least a little bit. I like dancing, doing physical activities.'

Strangely, for Harvey, performing is not a form of exhibitionistic self-aggrandisement but a peculiar rite of self-exposure.

'In between songs, I do feel quite embarrassed. I do feel very awkward. It's not like I'm showing off, it's putting yourself in a very vulnerable position. It's as much about humiliation as about showing off.'

It sounds like a strange way to make a living. What's the pay-off, emotionally, in making yourself that exposed and vulnerable?

'It's the thrill of it. Like a fairground ride or something. It's very nerve-racking, but when it's a good night, I understand why I'm doing it. It's the biggest high, better than any drug.'

If Harvey gets a sort of erotic buzz from embarrassment, from being in the raw, then I guess the spectator's kick is equally perverse: we're voyeurs, fascinated, but frustrated, because she's a tease and a teaser, and for all her self-revelation, we never really find out what makes her tick. Or, in the words of one of her latest songs, what makes her 'primed and ticking', a human time bomb waiting to go off. But, oh, the suspense is thrilling.

iD, November 1993

The white-on-black relations of admiration/envy and identification/misrecognition running through this book make up a largely male-on-male story: young white men finding something they need in black masculine personae, then exaggerating what are already partly fictions. I was struck by the way PJ Harvey stepped boldly into the flow of this cross-town traffic, both with her blues-rock borrowings and her explicit nod to gangsta rap (very much the nineties equivalent to the original blues: low-down, profane, associated with shady places and all sorts of venal goings-on; a music deplored by middle-class blacks who wanted to advance the race through refinement and respectability). In her games with personae and archetypes, Harvey really was something of a Patti Smith for the nineties, except that where Smith simply lacked for female role models, Polly was male-identified by choice, wilfully spurning the female ancestors and inspirations available to her (among them, Patti).

IT'S A DOGG'S LIFE

Dr Dre and Snoop Doggy Dogg

For months I've been wrestling with my conscience, trying to resist the temptation to buy Dr Dre's *The Chronic*. Dre's a brilliant producer, but the idea of putting extra $$$ in his already-stuffed pockets sticks in the craw. Not only is he an arch-misogynist (the LP closes with 'bitches ain't nuthin' but ho's and tricks'), but worse, he walks it like he talks it (he's just settled out of court in an infamous case where he beat up a female TV presenter).

It's a classic aesthetics-vs-ethics dilemma, one that's bedevilled lit crit and rock crit alike for years. Should Celine's and T. S. Eliot's anti-Semitism affect our estimation of their work? Is it permissible or even possible to ignore the dodgy homophobia of Public Enemy or Buju Banton, and just groove on the butt-quakingly futuristic production? This dilemma is raised to a new pitch of squirming agony by the homicide charge hanging over Snoop Doggy Dogg, for it's largely his lyrical and rhymin' skills that make *The Chronic* so addictive. Of course all this 'bad publicity' served to make his hotly anticipated solo album, *Doggy Style*, even more commercially viable. Gangsta rap celebrates 'real-ness'; by seemingly living out the gun-totin', death-dealin' life he glamorizes, Snoop has proved himself the realest, hardest motherfucker on the block. And so *Doggy Style* went straight in at Number 1, selling more in its first week than the rest of the Top 4 (Pearl Jam, Beavis & Butt-Head and Guns N' Roses!) combined. That's phenomenal. That's sick.

Real-ness is why *The Chronic* ruled rap in 1993. Dre's videos revel in the details of the gangsta good life: sizzling steak barbecuing on a sun-baked Los Angeles afternoon, fridges loaded with 40 oz malt liquor, low-rider cars customized to rock back and forth on their axles.

Lyrically, Dre offers Gangsta's four Ms: megalomania, misogyny, malice and marijuana. This malignant fare is couched in surprisingly mellow, smooth-grooving music (Dre uses real musicians as well as samples). This might confuse whites who equate hardness with noise, but for gangstas, the laidback nonchalance of Dre's jazzy funky tracks fits their ideal for living: cool and in command, suave and serpentine.

So while bohemian jazz-rap got critical kudos, it's Dre's songs that boom from jeep sound systems, and it's his videos that rotate heavy on MTV. With the first single, 'Nuthin' but a G-Thang', MTV used a special effect to censor the blunts and bare boobs, but they couldn't excise the nastiest piece of sexism: an uppity 'sophisticated bitch' gets her comeuppance when some Gs drench her with beer, symbolically soaking her with semen. 'Dre Day' exacted symbolic revenge on a male 'bitch', Eazy E (formerly Dre's partner in NWA and owner of Ruthless, the label with which Dre's embroiled in contractual litigation). The video ends with Eazy as a bum holding a placard that reads, 'Will Rap For Food'; another enemy is sodomized and choked by Dre's dick and nuts 'on ya tonsils'. Eazy retaliated with the 'It's On (Dr Dre) 187 Um Killer' EP. '187' is police radio code for homicide; the video repeatedly flashes a pic of Dre wearing make-up in his pre-NWA pop-rap band back in the eighties; Eazy disses Dre as a 'she-thang', not a real G, as a phony middle-class 'studio gangsta'.

Snoop Doggy Dogg's whole shtick is based on George Clinton's Atomic Dog concept: the born-bad boy who sniffs after bitches on oestrus, runs with his pack (The Dog Pound), and whose bite is every bit as vicious as his bark. Sadly, *Doggy Style* is irresistible: delusions of grandeur and paranoid revenge fantasies have seldom been rendered with such murderous panache, while Dre's grooves are as slinky and P-Funky as ever. My favourite bit: Snoop asks his mirror, 'Who's the top dog of them all?' The mirror replies, 'You are, you conceited bastard!'

Melody Maker, 18 December 1993

More than the original band itself, it was the post-NWA solo careers that really inaugurated gangsta's Thousand Year Reich. From *The Chronic* to 50 Cent, you can trace an unbroken line of seductively smooth and damnably hooky hip hop ('supple and vacant Muzak' is how critic Howard Hampton dubbed Dre's G-funk sound) that cleverly contrived to be both ultra-commercial and doggedly hardcore. Aided by a series of city-based sounds from the Dirty South, gangsta's unflagging dominance has effectively banished conscious rap to a niche market (and an increasingly white one at that, audience-wise at least) on the periphery of hip hop. Those fabulous singles off *Chronic*, along with Ice Cube's 'It Was a Good Day', also marked the definitive birth of rap as an *audio-visual* phenomenon; the records, I suspect, often being bought almost as mementos of the videos, or payback for the enjoyment derived from watching them on MTV. Certainly the songs thenceforth became inseparable from the mini-movies. At their best, the rap promos proved to be an art form in their own right (the likes of Hype Williams becoming genuine auteur-directors). But mostly they became a porno-looping visual muzak of bling and booty (especially after an 'urban music'-dedicated version of MTV arrived called BET, short for Black Entertainment Television). As for Dre and Snoop, they've separately enjoyed uncommon longevity in the usually rapid-turnover rap game, their careers rivalled in duration only by LL Cool J.

AGAINST THE GRAIN

Thinking about the Voice in Pop

Most rock crit doesn't have much to do with rock *as music*. Usually it's amateur sociology, or Eng Lit analysis of lyrics, or biography/gossip. But even those who do grapple with music-as-music seldom get much purchase on the Voice, beyond saying a particular voice is 'great' or 'original', or gushing superlatives. And that's because the Voice is a mystery, defying analysis. It's hard to say why one voice leaves you cold and another pierces the marrow of your soul, gets in your pants, fits you like a glove.

The few who have attempted to 'explain' their preferences often fasten on Roland Barthes's concept of 'the grain of the voice'. The French critic argued that what *got* you about a much-loved voice wasn't what the singer did expressively, it was the *stuff* of the voice itself: its texture, its carnal thickness. In instrumentation, the equivalent of 'grain' is what musicologists call 'chromatics', i.e. not the way Hendrix bluesily bent his notes to express emotion, but the timbre and 'colour' of his fuzz-tone and feedback. For Barthes, an accomplished vocalist who's adept at manipulating the conventional mannerisms of 'good singing' in order to emote can actually be less moving than a stiff, unwieldy singer. The proficient vocalist suppresses 'the grain of the voice' by being too eloquent, too fluent in the language of singing. For 'grain' is the body's resistance to the singer's breath, resulting in 'language lined with flesh': the listener is always reminded, blissfully, that this voice isn't pure soul, but comes from deep inside a specific human body.

But critics often misconstrue 'grain' as synonymous with 'grit'. Aretha Franklin is often acclaimed as a grain-rich singer, but to my ears she's all bombastic virtuosity and pyrotechnic passion. Certainly, the octave-spanning acrobatics and mannered idiosyncrasies of consummate singers like Tim Buckley can astound and enthral, fill you with awe. But often, a weak or limited voice can be more heart-quaking: Barney Sumner, Alex Ayuli from A.R. Kane, even a one-note droner like Lawrence of Felt. Neil Young is a case in point, not just for his torn-and-frayed drawl-whine, but for his guitar 'voice' too: his racked, wrenching one-chord solo on 'Southern Man' communicates more grainy anguish than a century of Clapton's addle-daddle nuances.

Barney Hoskyns' book *From a Whisper to a Scream* is a rare attempt to elucidate the Mystery of the Voice. Hoskyns also cites Barthes's 'grain', but he's a bit biased towards technically superb and Black voices. If the greatest singers combine virtuosity and grain – Al Green, Van Morrison – I'd like to redress the balance and state the case for the deficient, unfluent singer. Like early Morrissey: what struck a deep, carnal chord with miserabilist youth like myself was the lachrymose, mucus-like quality of his voice, so vividly evocative of drowning in self-pity. There's a similarly clotted, inconsolable but luscious, almost edible thickness in Stevie Nicks's singing on *Rumours* and *Tusk*, and in Kristin Hersh's voice on the first three Throwing Muses albums: again, it's the viscosity of the voice, the way it resists the singer's expressive range, that's so blissful. But as Morrissey got 'better' as a vocalist, he became merely plummy in his plaintiveness.

Iggy Pop's voice also declined as it got more singerly. On the Bowie-fied solo albums, Iggy sounds like a cadaverous supperclub crooner, Jim Morrison's corpse. For the real animal you have to turn to The Stooges' first two albums: the Sinatra-on-barbiturates of 'Ann' and 'Dirt', the feral, masticated vowels of 'Loose', and above all, the breath-sucking, beyond/beneath-human gasps at the climax of 'TV Eye' (which get my vote for Greatest Vocal Moment of All Time). Johnny Rotten seldom gets his rightful acclaim as a vocalist, although Dave Laing has pinpointed the gratuitous way he rolled his 'r's and over-emphasized his consonants: a grotesque, thrilling parody of rock aggression. But it's on 'Bodies' that Rotten truly reached Iggy-esque nether limits, gargling lines like 'gurgling bloody mess' to bring home the abject horror of human biology. In recent years, only Kurt Cobain (who's gotta lotta grain) has reached, or retched, such extremity.

Along with a critical language for the mystery of the individual voice, we also lack a history of vocal trends. Why, for instance, has the early seventies blues-rock voice resurged in the last couple of years? Why does it resonate with grunge youth? I'd also like to understand what happened to the black mainstream voice. As soul evolved into 'urban contemporary', rural grit got replaced by jazzily urbane, slimy smoothness. Swingbeat groups like SWV, Bell Biv Devoe, Jade, etc. have eerily futuristic production and kicking beats, but the singing's putrid and pukey (aren't Boys II Men the absolute pits?!).

While swingbeat singing is all elegance and over-expressiveness, rap is a haven for 'grain', in so far as it's vocal but non-melodic. Rhymin' finesse counts for a lot, but for me it's the stuff of the voice that grabs. My current fave is Snoop Doggy Dogg, sidekick of Dr Dre and currently taking off as a solo mega-star despite being charged with murder. Like a lot of black people in Los Angeles, Dogg has a Southern accent, giving his voice a sidling, serpentile quality that's seductive in its menace. Ragga's rasping, patois insolence is also full of grain, harking back to the gruff-but-luscious 'talk-over' voices of early seventies reggae (mainstream reggae singing has gone slick and oily like US soul).

But ultimately you can't legislate about the voice: one person's 'grain' may be another's bland white bread of the soul. When it comes to the voice, preferences are idiosyncratic and unjustifiable. Something in the singer's body resonates inside your body, reopens wounds and triggers pleasure centres, and who can really say why?

Melody Maker, 20 November 1993

This was one element in an entire *Melody Maker* feature package/cover story devoted to Vocal Heroes. Whenever I get misty-eyed about the UK music weekly press as a lost arena of possibility, it's because of the space they gave to pieces like this one. It's hard to think of a mainstream magazine today that would show such indulgence . . .

The grunge voice, I think, was more than just a flashback to seventies blues-tinged heavy rock. Crucially, it's the sound of an old man's voice coming through a young man's body. Think of Eddie Vedder's haggard weariness. Talking of whom . . .

PEARL JAM VS NIRVANA

If numbers count for anything, Pearl Jam wiped the floor with Nirvana. In its first week of release, *Vs* sold five times as many copies as *In Utero* did in its first week: nearly a million where Nirvana shifted under 200,000 units. Pearl Jam also cleaned up at the MTV Video Awards, and got to jam with legendary-survivor-from-the-era-when-music-really-meant-something Neil Young. Of course, unit-shifting and trophies don't automatically equate with kudos or significance. But many of the critics who'd sneered at Pearl Jam as a corporate cock rock scam began to take them seriously this time round, while even Kurt Cobain seems to have retracted some of his bile and acknowledged Eddie Vedder as 'authentic', thus effecting some sort of reconciliation between the pair.

Why have Pearl Jam overtaken Nirvana? Why have they swelled as a phenomenon, where Nirvana appear to have partially succeeded in sabotaging their career? Simply put, whereas Cobain has recoiled from the power that was his for the grabbing when *Nevermind* went through the roof, Vedder has embraced the mantle of Rock Saviour – not greedily or even eagerly (he seems as troubled by stardom as Kurt), but almost with a sense of duty. One example says it all. In MTV News footage from the first *Vs* tour date, Vedder greets the audience: 'How're ya doing?' A pregnant pause. 'Cuz I worry about you guys, y'know?' A massive cheer.

This is Vedder all over: he comes over as a sort of elder brother offering guidance, support and consolation to his faithless, direction-less flock of twenty-something youth. Contrast that with Cobain, who seems stunned by the fact of his mass audience, and thus unable or unwilling to connect with them. Which is why he barely speaks onstage. In recent interviews, Cobain has retracted some of the contemptuous comments he made about the metal kids who bought *Nevermind*, but he's still clearly aghast at the notion of people looking to him for answers or leadership. Probably because he feels just as, or even more, lost and incapable as any of them.

Both Vedder and Cobain grew up fatherless, without a proper male role model (in 'Serve the Servants', Kurt sings: 'I tried hard to have a father, but instead I had a dad'). *Village Voice* critic Ann Powers writes of Eddie: 'the mess he is represents the desire to become a man, something nobody's sure how to do right now'. But where Eddie tries to take on the role of surrogate 'good father' to his audience (with its high divorce rate, so many kids in America grow up in broken homes), Cobain just isn't up to being a mentor. And where Vedder writes songs about neglect and abuse ('Jeremy', 'Alive', and on the new album, 'Leash'), Cobain's voice is the raw, unmediated howl of his own abused 'inner child'. Vedder tells stories (the linked songs 'Why Go' and 'Leash' are about a troubled teenage girl whose over-anxious mum puts her in a mental home); Cobain spews incoherent angst. His cut-up method of lyric-writing works against easy identification, holds out no redemptive vision. And while that makes Nirvana's songs more challenging than Pearl Jam's, it doesn't offer much in the way of catharsis or consolation. Which is what 'the kids' get from Vedder.

Pearl Jam are The Clash to Nirvana's Sex Pistols. Like The Clash, Pearl Jam's vision of rock is humanist, heartwarming, inclusive, and thus deeply traditional. Pearl Jam's success is based on the notion that youth can be marshalled into a unity of alienation, and somehow make their collective power felt. Which is why their music – blues-rock and funky boogie given a glossy, panoramic CD-friendly production – is rooted in the early seventies, the last time people still believed in counterculture. Whereas Cobain's songs fuse the melodic aggression of the Pistols (Glen Matlock was a Beatles fan) with the faithless, proto-punk despondency of Sabbath. Nirvana's point – from 'Smells Like Teen Spirit' through to 'Radio Friendly Unit Shifter' – is the same as the Sex Pistols': rock rebellion is a fraud, it's high time the concept of youth culture was killed off. And so *In Utero* is a self-indulgent, solipsistic record, Cobain singing the millionaire rock star blues. Typically, the only part of being a Rock Saviour Cobain can relate to is being crucified. In that respect, *In Utero* is a bit like the bitterly disillusioned second album Rotten might have made if he'd stayed in the Pistols.

Where Vedder reaches out, Cobain says: 'leave me alone'. The most telling song on *In Utero* is 'Heart-Shaped Box', because it's torn between the regressive fantasy of going back to the womb and the dread of being engulfed. Cobain begs to be hoisted back to sanctuary with his head in 'your umbilical noose'; he wants to be sucked back into 'your magnet tar pit'. While it's probably reductive to identify the 'you' in 'Heart-Shaped' as Courtney Love (mind you, her first love offering to Kurt was apparently a heart-shaped box full of sea-shells), the song does reek of shame about retreating from the world into house-bound hermit-hood. The line about 'meat-eating orchids' is a classic castration-anxiety image (vagina as Venus Fly Trap), but the song as a whole suggests that Cobain would rather be infantilized and emasculated than struggle to be a man.

The title *Vs* is probably meant to evoke conflict and torn loyalties, the kind of inner turmoil that Bataille captured in his declaration: 'I MYSELF AM WAR'. But the point about Vedder – and it's what makes him a Rock Hero in the most conservative sense – is that he doesn't give up the fight. The title of *In Utero* whimpers the exact opposite: it's isolationist, retreatist, defeated by the contradictions of being a rebel-millionaire kingpin in a bankrupt and outmoded rock hierarchy. All this means that Vedder is probably the 'better' human being (at least, more dependable in a scrape), while Cobain is the greater artist. Vedder could never write a song as disturbed and provocative as the near-misogynist 'Heart-Shaped Box', or as pitifully self-absorbed as the me-and-the-missus-are-martyrs-too 'Frances Farmer Will Have Her Revenge On Seattle'. Eddie's too decent, too generous, not petty or pathetic enough. Put Vedder and Cobain together and you'd have something close to a whole human being.

Melody Maker, 25 December 1993

I don't understand what I meant by the last line . . . surely I'd just argued that Vedder was a complete human being (or near-enough) whereas Cobain was a Morrissey-style 'half-a-person'? I felt a twinge of remorse about giving Cobain such a low grade when he killed himself the following summer; although this dereliction of parental duty only confirmed the judgement, no one likes to have spoken ill of the soon-to-be-dead. Vedder and Pearl Jam, of course, slog on as tenaciously as ever, releasing their eighth album in 2006, appearing on VH1's *Storytellers*. Their role model is clearly Neil Young's ornery integrity and refusal to burn out *or* fade away. Pearl Jam's 1994 stand against Ticketmaster's 'virtually absolute monopoly on the distribution of tickets to concerts' in America was the same sort of gesture that Young made with his 1988 anti-sponsorship single 'This Note's For You'. Yet it's the kind of anti-corporate gesture that only makes sense *on* the mass culture stage. When Pearl Jam jammed live with Young on MTV (a heavily symbolic display of the torch being passed between two countercultural generations) it showed their ambition to become 'classic rock' just like Neil, whereas in similar situations Nirvana, tellingly, gestured back to the indie-rock womb-world: bringing the Meat Puppets onstage for their MTV *Unplugged* and covering two of the Puppets' SST-era songs (as opposed to their current major label tunes) or getting UK shambler The Legend (a.k.a. their rock-crit buddy Everett True) to play encores with them on the *In Utero* tour.

THE BEASTIE BOYS

'A lot of people think we planned it,' grins Mike D of the Beastie Boys. 'But if we'd tried to engineer it, we'd probably have failed miserably. It's just luck!' He's talking about the Beasties' peculiar career trajectory – from hardcore punk jesters to massively huge rap-scallions through to their current enviable status as cult band with their own mini-empire (the Grand Royal label and magazine). Most bands who go as mainstream as Beastie Boys did back in '87 – with *Licensed to Ill* and '(You Gotta) Fight for Your Right (to Party)' – either burn out or degenerate into cabaret. Getting back your credibility is a coup, a minor miracle, on a par with regaining your virginity.

The Beasties' early days can be revisited on the just-issued compilation *Some Old Bullshit*, which comprises their hardcore EP *Pollywog Stew* and their hilariously inept proto-rap fumble 'Cookie Puss'. Then the Beasties hooked up with Def Jam and rocketed to success on Rick Rubin's patented blend of funky beats and heavy riffs ripped off Led Zep and Black Sabbath. The Beasties shtick, a Beavis & Butthead avant la lettre melding of metal-kid delinquency and rap megalomania (two brands of teen misogyny for the price of one!), was a guilty pleasure that most of us couldn't resist. Only the po-faced worried about white appropriation of rap: the rest were busy aping the Beasties' ass-waddling strut and Adrock's inimitable nasal sneer.

In reality, the Beasties – Adrock, MCA and Mike D – were only parodying the moronic postures of slob-rock and thug-rap. In truth, they'd grown up as punk-funkateers, and their politics are actually pretty PC. The real Beasties started to come through on 1989's *Paul's Boutique* (*Licensed to Ill*'s flop sequel, which *Spin* proclaimed one of the most under-rated albums of all time), and above all on '92's *Check Your Head*.

'Most people viewed *Paul's Boutique* as a total commercial failure,' says Mike D. 'But it was necessary to get us to where we are now.' By which he means a cult band who sold over a million copies of their last album *Check Your Head*. 'That's one of the beautiful things left about the music industry – you can have these organic, accidental, brilliant occurrences. Despite all the marketing and strategy, there's still gonna be the record that some sixteen-year-old kid'll make for $30 in the basement that'll surprise everyone, completely change the pop world as we know it. And you can't really do that in movies. As for us, all I can say is there's something to be said for holding on to your ideals – if not in the short term, then in the long run.'

GRAND ROYAL: THE LABEL

'I guess the idea of us doing our own label dates back as far back as Def Jam,' recalls Mike. 'Cos when Rick Rubin and Russell Simmons began the label out of Rick's NYU dorm room, we were really closely involved, and were actually instrumental in discovering LL Cool J and Public Enemy. Then as it started to sell a lot of records, Def Jam got less family oriented. It became a big biz label, and we were completely left out. So we always had the idea of doing our own label, it just took us a while to get our shit together.'

Grand Royal was hatched during the *Check Your Head* tour. The Beasties met up with some old friends, Jill Cunniff and Gabrielle Glaser of all-female hip hop group Luscious Jackson. (Drummer Kate Schellenbach had also been in an early incarnation of the Beasties.) 'We'd known Jill and Gabby since our early teens, when we were New York club brats going to see bands like The Slits and Gang of Four. That late seventies/early eighties phase, when post-punk bands were turning on to funk and reggae, is one of the great lost periods of music, and it was when music had its greatest impact on us. It was also the beginning of rap, with Sugarhill Gang, Fearless Four, Treacherous Three, Funky Four Plus One. Anyway, Luscious gave us their demo, and we were all set to make up some excuse, but it turned out to be our favourite thing to listen to on the tour bus.' The demo actually ended up as the first three songs on Luscious Jackson's mini-LP *In Search of Manny*, a brilliant debut for the band and for Grand Royal.

According to Cunniff and Glaser, Luscious Jackson's main affinity with the Beasties is musical. Like *Check Your Head*, *In Search of Manny* fuses live musicianship with lo-fi sampladelic magic. 'We grew

179

up on post-punk, early rap, jazz, reggae. Like them, we're not purists,' says Jill. 'But otherwise, we don't really go along with the Grand Royal programme. We don't wear the same clothes. The Beasties have much more connections with the skate/snowboard scene.'

The influence of early eighties punky-reggae and agit-funk grrl-bands like The Slits, Raincoats and Delta 5 comes through in Luscious Jackson's softcore feminist anthems, like 'Daughters of Kaos', which Gabby describes as 'sort of a fantasy about "if women ruled the world"'. But the vibe is laidback rather than militant, largely because of their slinky rapping-style, which Jill calls 'gabbing'. (Gabby, perhaps understandably, prefers 'blabbing'.) Luscious are currently polishing their first full-length LP, *Uno Mas*.

As for the rest of the Grand Royal roster, the near future should see hardcore rap from DJ Hurricane (formerly of The Afros) and hardcore punk from two Australian bands, Noise Addict and Budd. There'll be a couple of Beastie 'vanity' projects – Adam Horowitz's hardcore band D.F.L., and Mike D's all-drum record (!). Perhaps closest to the Beastie Boys' own thang are Moistboyz (a sideline project by one of wacky-slackers Ween) and 'garage funk' unit The Shackcrew, of whom Mike D says approvingly, 'they record even more badly than we do. To label it funk, might be to insult them, and to insult real funk musicians. They're so out-there, they've got it more together than anybody.'

Beastie Boys' stoned, lo-fi sensibility makes them the missing link between P-Funk and Pavement (the latter are actually pals with Mike D). 'The record company keeps saying stuff like "you guys should do an interactive press kit", and I'm saying "you guys don't get it, we're going the other direction". To me, if something recorded badly on a cassette sounds better than a twenty-four-track CD, I'll put the demo version out. I'd like to get to the point where we're putting out records that people think are just fucked-up demos. One of the things that hip hop's lost, as it's got more refined in terms of studio-craft, is the thrill of sound going through a really fucked-up PA. It's like with Jamaican sound systems – part of the music is the distortion you get from home-made speaker cabinets.'

GRAND ROYAL: THE MAGAZINE

Grand Royal the Label's shambolic, goofy aura carries through to *Grand Royal* the Magazine (which you can find at Tower and at Slam City, the skateboarder shop above Rough Trade in Covent Garden).

'Mike D came up with the idea for a magazine after *Check Your Head*,' says Bob Mack, one of *Grand Royal*'s editors. 'On the album, the Beasties had invited fans to write in for Grand Royal info, which at that stage was just their merchandising company. The response was bigger than they expected – 16,000 kids – and Mike realized that mailing out a newsletter was going to be mighty expensive. So, erm, he decided to pass the cost on to the kids, by doing it as a magazine.'

Mack had worked for the satirical magazine *Spy*, and as a music journalist; he'd got to know the Beasties after 'tweaking them' in an irreverent profile for *Spin*. What was most galling for Beasties Boys was that Mack had cast aspersions on their basketball skills, and their riposte was a B-side track, 'The Skills to Pay the Bills': 'I'm working on my game / its time to tax / I'm on a mission to wax Bob Mack'. Playful enmity became friendship, and then partnership as the magazine became a reality. Highlights of the debut issue include a *Spy*-style investigation of Bruce Lee, and Ad Rock's 'Joey Buttafuoco Fashion Spread', a spoof on the tacky lifestyles of Long Island suburbanites, named after a cheesy character whose liaison with an under-age girl, Amy Fisher, hit the headlines when Fisher shot Mrs Buttafuoco in the head (she survived, but the bullet's still lodged in her brain).

Grand Royal lies somewhere between fanzine and glossy, reflected in its mix of professionals (Mack and some kids from teen-mag *Dirt*) and amateurs. 'Most of our contributors aren't professional, they're the sort of people who should write but who aren't "writers". The Beasties are a bit like that. We've seen glimpses of their smartness before in the lyrics, and the mag is another dimension for it.'

Grand Royal's sensibility is hard to tag: it's not exactly camp, but it's far from devoid of irony. With contents ranging from a report on a convention of KISS fans, to a guide to mid-seventies funk LPs with deceptively superbad covers but ultra-lame grooves, the *Grand Royal*/Beasties 'tude seems close to the 'kitschadelic' bands (Saint Etienne, Denim and Pulp in the UK, Urge Overkill in the US) – a tongue-in-chic, absurdist appreciation of bygone pop tack, combined with a trainspotter-ish record-collector mentality. The downside of this approach is an in-jokey knowingness – precisely the accusation that some level at the magazine.

But the Beasties aren't bothered about that, claims Mack. 'They're into making people take their trip, rather than catering to them. The Beasties have never been about finding out what's happening and fastening on to it. For instance, they've been smoking dope for years, but they'd never make a big thing of hemp like Cypress Hill. Their attitude is 'this is our world, but you can figure it out if you make a little effort'. Exactly like Saint Etienne, in fact – 'Join Our Club'.

The next issue of *Grand Royal* will come out whenever they get their shit together, but one thing Mike D can promise is that it'll contain a 'Top 10 Restaurant Soundtracks'. '4AD bands like This Mortal Coil and Dead Can Dance do very well – that semi-ambient music must be good for the digestion. Unfortunately, *Eric Clapton Unplugged* is the Number 1 restaurant LP worldwide. Often the restaurants that play the worst music have the best food. If you let bad music deter you, you'd miss a lot of good food!'

* * *

As if being head honcho of the Grand Royal empire wasn't demanding enough, Mike D has his own personal business interests, namely the X-Large clothing company he started with two friends, and X-Large's boutiques (in New York, San Francisco and LA, where the Beasties are now based).

'After I'd moved to LA, I started going down to Wilmington, near San Pedro, where all the dock workers get their clothes. Then we figured that if we opened a place in our own neighbourhood selling that stuff – cool work shoes and practical clothes – we wouldn't have to travel so far. Around that time, other kids were starting their own clothing lines, with the same kind of attitude kids had that set up indie labels five years earlier.'

The X-Large style – sort of B-boy meets skatepunk – has caught on with the skate/rap/punk crossover crowd, not just in LA but all over America and even in Britain via Slam City. 'The thing about skaters is they have an open-minded attitude to music – they always wanna hear what's new, so long as it's aggressive. The racial background of the music doesn't matter so long as it makes you skate harder. It could be A Tribe Called Quest or Black Flag.'

THE NEW BEASTIE BOYS ALBUM

Set for May release, but as yet untitled, the sequel to *Check Your Head* expands on the Beasties' innovative soundclash of live music and sampling. 'We might not be a great band for three minutes, but we can always be a great band for three bars,' laughs Mike D. The band's methodology is 'jam & chop' – 'we smoke a joint, play for a bit, then use the best bits and patch it together'. It's similar to the way Can and Miles Davis would improvise for hours, then splice together the choicest grooves and solos into a seamless composition.

As it happens, Miles's early seventies jazz-rock (*On The Corner*, *Agharta*, etc.) is a big influence on the Beasties' new album, along with the 'out jazz' of Archie Shepp and Albert Ayler. 'All this stuff is affecting our music, whether through sample or through osmosis. There's quite a few surprises on the album – on some tracks there's instruments we've never used before, like strings and African drums.'

With their keyboard player Mark Ramos Nishita and percussionist Eric Bobo, Beastie Boys are, to all intents and purposes, a fusion combo – although the word 'fusion' makes Mike wince. 'For better or worse, we end up in that Return to Forever category. But we have to be careful, cos it can easily end up Return to Being Wack.' What prevents them from being a throwback to the days of War and Weather Report is sampling. Beastie Boys combine fusion (blending styles) and fission (postmodern cut 'n' mix collage). Mike D thinks this approach is the way ahead for music.

As for the vibe, 'slow and low', blunted and dusted, remains the Beasties' favourite feel (they're big fans of dub reggae). 'As much as I'd like to think we'll always do something new, there's just something about retarded tempos that we'll always like.'

Are the Beastie Boys even part of hip hop any more?

'Sometimes I'm tempted to say we've gone "beyond hip hop", but really it's just that we're taking hip hop to where it's never been before. You can stretch hip hop a long way before it stops being hip hop. Its appetite and ability to swallow stuff and incorporate influences is infinite.'

GRAND ROYAL – WHAT DOES IT MEAN?

'Biz Markie originally came up with the phrase, and it means something like "Guaranteed Every Time". But in our case, maybe it's really "Guaranteed Fucked Up Every Time"! The only ethos that I would extend to cover the magazine, the label and the Beastie Boys is that it's all about doing stuff that we ourselves are completely inspired by, at that moment – however selfish or "insider" that might seem. There's a lot of references in the magazine that maybe only us and six other people we know would get. And sometimes it's the same with our lyrics. But *Check Your Head* went platinum, so obviously a lot of people get at least some of it. Especially with the magazine, there's nothing objective about it, it's totally subjective. It's the other side of the coin from *Time* magazine writing about pop, explaining it in layman's terms and in such dispassionate language that it's totally meaningless.'

Another big aspect of the Beasties/Grand Royal sensibility – what with the love of *Superfly/Superbad* imagery, afros and rare breakbeats – is that it's the latest twist on ye olde 'White Negro' syndrome. For decades, white bohemians have looked to black streetlife for the exuberance, panache and lust-for-life they can't find in their own culture.

'I'm almost troubled by that syndrome. Right now, with the success of people like Dr Dre, you've got white kids consuming rap and thinking they're down with black culture . . . And they don't really know what black experience is about, they don't have to deal with any of the ramifications of being black. As for us, when we were thirteen and fourteen and went to clubs and heard the DJ mix Big Youth and Treacherous Three with James White or Delta 5, it wasn't like 'hey, now we're finding out what people from another culture are about'. It was just great music. All the kids at my school were into Led Zeppelin and The Eagles, and that was what I defined myself against. So it was more a case of cool music vs uncool music.'

One thing that always puzzles me about white appropriations of black music is the time-lag effect, where you'll get a band like Red Hot Chili Peppers who are totally into Parliament/Funkadelic and outmoded black styles like slap bass, but have a Luddite fear of programmed rhythms and hi-tech. Meanwhile, black musicians, from rap to new jack swing, are embracing technology like samplers, sequencers and drum machines. It seems that white Americans can't get to grips with black innovations until long after the event; at the time they're actually happening, they're dissed as 'disco shit' (which is how most rockers thought of Clinton, James Brown, et al. at the time).

Mike D doesn't quite agree. 'Even if the Chili Peppers are assimilating something old, there's no question that, whether by accident or design, they've come up with something completely fucking different anyway. The Stones did the same thing with Muddy Waters. And with us, we grew up on PiL, Slits, Bad Brains, Funky Four Plus One, and the amalgam of all that was something all our own. Even if we tried to sound black, we'd fuck it up so badly we'd end up with something totally new.'

He's right. Imitation is actually the direst form of flattery (as a lineage of black-wannabe minstrels from Georgie Fame through Mick Hucknall to 3rd Bass amply demonstrates). Purism doesn't just equal 'no fun', it equals 'no future', since misrecognition, miscegenation and mutation are the very stuff of pop evolution. Beastie Boys fuck with their sources every time, guaranteed, and that's why they'll always be interesting.

i-D magazine, March 1994

'. . . which *Spin* proclaimed one of the most under-rated albums of all time'. Erm, weeeell, that, that was *me*: I included *Paul's Boutique* in a Top 10 Under-Rated Records charticle I wrote, alongside Fleetwood Mac's *Tusk* and the Clash's *Sandinista* (which I'd never actually heard all the way through). I confess: a few times over the years I've gotten a sneaky buzz from citing as authoritative reference point an earlier article that was actually me. I further confess: I'd swap the admirable entirety of the Beasties' post '87 discography, even *Paul's Boutique*, just for *Licensed to Ill*. In a heartbeat.

POST-ROCK

Like a clapped-out stretch limo cranked in reverse, today's 'alternative rock' is synonymous with a retreat to one of a number of period genres from rock history. For Primal Scream think *Exile on Main Street*-era Stones. For Suede think Ziggy-phase Bowie. In 1994, just six short years from a new millennium, this is where the money is at: in the musical equivalent of reproduction antiques.

Recently, however, a smattering of British groups, energized by developments in electronic studio based musics such as techno and hip-hop, as well as free improvisation and the avant-garde, have started venturing into a more financially precarious, but aesthetically vital, hinterland-without-a-name. The roll call of futurist honour includes Disco Inferno, Seefeel, Insides, Bark Psychosis, Main, Papa Sprain, Stereolab, Pram and Moonshake, along with such prolific figures as Kevin Martin (Ice/Techno Animal/God/EAR) and ex-Napalm Death drummer Mick Harris (Scorn/Lull).

What to call this zone? Some of its occupants, Seefeel for instance, could be dubbed 'Ambient'; others, Bark Psychosis and Papa Sprain, could be called 'art rock'. 'Avant rock' would just about suffice, but is too suggestive of jerky time signatures and a dearth of melodic loveliness, which isn't necessarily the case. Perhaps the only term open-ended yet precise enough to cover all this activity is 'post-rock'.

Post-rock means using rock instrumentation for non-rock purposes, using guitars as facilitators of timbres and textures rather than riffs and powerchords. Increasingly, post-rock groups are augmenting the traditional guitar/bass/drums line-up with computer technology: the sampler, the sequencer and MIDI (Musical Instrument Digital Interface). While some post-rock units (Pram, Stereolab) prefer lo-fi or outmoded technology, others are evolving into cyber rock, becoming virtual.

* * *

The best way to get a handle on how these groups depart from the 'rock process' is to work from a rigorous model of how the traditional rock 'n' roll group operates. And there's none more rigorous than Joe Carducci's *Rock and the Pop Narcotic*. Carducci may be a bit of a reactionary, but his theory of rock is grounded in a precise, materialist definition of it as music, rather than 'attitude', 'spirit', 'rebellion', or any other metaphysical notions. Rock's essence, says Carducci, is the real-time interaction of drums, bass and rhythm guitar. A group should be a rhythmic engine creating kinetic energy; 'breathing' as an organic entity.

Carducci valorizes the strenuous, collective physicality of performance. His ideal rock process is opposed to the Pop Method, which is studio based and elevates the producer over the musicians. Modern music is a sterile, frigid wasteland because the producer/studio ('cold') has triumphed over rock ('hot'). With a typically American prejudice, Carducci favours the 'presence' of live performance over the increasingly 'virtual' nature of studio music, and prefers the 'documentarian' recording techniques that characterized early seventies hard rock, which were revived by Spot, house producer at SST, the seminal eighties hardcore punk label that Carducci helped to run.

If Carducci has a polar opposite in rock theory, it's that archetypal boffin in the sound lab, Brian Eno. In fact, the art-rock tradition that Eno stands for, and which is crucial to the development of today's post-rock, is something like an egghead version of the Tin Pan Alley pop process that Carducci detests; there's a line running from Phil Spector and Brian Wilson that leads to Eno as clearly as it does to, say, Trevor Horn. Both the Spector and Eno approaches to soundscaping involve using musicians as a sort of palette of textures, as opposed to the rock band's collective toil. Increasingly, the post-Eno approach involves dispensing with musicians altogether in favour of machines.

Another way in which Eno is the prophet of post-rock is his elevation of timbre/texture/chromatics over riffs and rhythm sections; the desire to create a 'fictional psycho-acoustic space' rather than groove and thrust. When he was invited to produce U2 (a group that Carducci reviles as the very model of non-rocking fraudulence) Eno warned Bono: 'I'm not interested in records as a document of a rock band playing on stage. I'm more interested in painting pictures. I want to create a landscape within which this music happens.' As it turned out, this subordination of the aural to the visual was perfect for Bono's 'visionary' vocals, The Edge's stratospheric guitar and the inert rhythm section.

Throughout Eno's own oeuvre, there's a gradual eradication of kinetic energy, beginning with the early solo LPs (with their limpid, uneventful water colours and lyrical imagery of treading water) and culminating in the entropic, vegetative bliss of ambient. The difference between the Carducci and Eno aesthetics is the difference between 'manly' manual labour and 'effete' white-collar brainwork. Carducci actually calls his tradition (the blues-bastardizing lineage that runs from Black Sabbath through Black Flag to Soundgarden) 'new redneck'. By defending the aesthetic of 'heavy' (heavy rock, heavy industry) against studio-concocted 'lite', Carducci wants to protect traditional artisan skills from being usurped by machines (which, in studios as much as factories, are more reliable and cheaper than humans). By contrast, the Enoites embrace technology that empowers the musically incompetent.

* * *

Carducci can't make sense of the pop present, which is based in the soundsculpting innovations of dub, in disco's remixology and hip hop's sampladelic sorcery. His version of rock history also downgrades psychedelia, which was the first music to use multi-track recording to conjure fictional headspace. 'Phonography' (a term that author Evan Eisenberg coined, in his book *The Recording Angel*, to describe the art of recording) bears the same relation to live music as cinema does to theatre. With most rock records, the studio is used to create a simulacrum of live performance, although multi-tracking makes it more vivid and hyper-real than 'live'. But multi-tracking and other studio techniques can also be used to create 'impossible' events, which could never possibly take place in real time. The sampler, transubstantiating sound into digital data, takes this even further – different eras, different auras, can be combined to form a time-travelling pseudo event. You could call this 'magick', you could call it 'deconstruction of the metaphysics of presence' – either way, today's post-rock groups are absconding into this virtual, ethereal realm.

* * *

Post-rock draws its inspiration and impetus from a complex combination of sources. Some of these come from post-rock's own tradition – a series of moments in history when eggheads and bohemians have hijacked elements of rock for non-rock purposes (think of the guitar based late sixties music of The Velvet Underground and Pink Floyd, and a subsequent lineage that includes New York's No Wave groups, Joy Division, The Cocteau Twins, The Jesus and Mary Chain, My Bloody Valentine and A.R. Kane; or the 'Krautrock' of Can, Faust, Neu, Cluster and Ash Ra Tempel; as well as the late seventies/early eighties post-punk vanguard of PiL, 23 Skidoo, Cabaret Voltaire and The Pop Group). Other impulses arrive from outside of rock: Eno, obviously, but also the mid-sixties drone-minimalism of Terry Riley and LaMonte Young, as well as musique concrete and electroacoustic music, dub reggae and modern sampladelic genres like hip hop and techno. Most of the British post-rock groups also explicitly define themselves against grunge, which was Carducci's dream come true: the fusion of punk and metal into an all-American nouveau hard rock.

* * *

For the post-rock groups, Sonic Youth's idea of 'reinventing the guitar' really means un-rocking the guitar; sometimes the next step is ditching the guitar altogether. Disco Inferno's Iain Crause says he always wanted to make his guitar sound like 'actual physical things', such as waterfalls, but in DI's early days (when the group sounded closer to Joy Division and The Durutti Column) he had to do it with masses of effects. It's been said that DI decided to go digital after seeing those samplin', rockin' muthas of invention The Young Gods live. But according to Crause, the real Damascus experience was hearing Hank Shocklee's Bomb Squad productions for Public Enemy. Inspired, Crause traded in his rack of pedals for a guitar synth, which he now rigs up to MIDI so that each string triggers a different sample.

The results can be heard on the astounding LP, *DI Go Pop*. 'A Crash at Every Speed' samples Miles Davis's *Bitches Brew* and Industrial Improv unit God; 'Starbound' samples U2 and children's laughter; while the gorgeous 'Footprints in Snow' samples Saint-Saens's 'Aquarium'. Not that you can tell, since Crause 'plays' these sample-tones rather than merely quoting them. Because he's using a fretboard rather than the usual keyboard, he can use all the guitarist's traditional devices – bending the strings ('It literally sounds like you're twisting the samples,' he says), jamming and improvising. This results in unearthly ninth-dimensional noises that bear no discernible link to the physical acts that generated them. (Perhaps even more disorientating is the group's approach to the drums. They use a MIDI-ed up kit whose pads also cue samples. On 'Footprints', for instance, the tom-toms reproduce the sound of footfalls.)

Crause sees Disco Inferno as a 'virtual reality band'. But what's really interesting about them is the way they haven't totally abandoned the rock process: they combine the physicality of live performance with the wizardry of sampling. (Crause claims that *DI Go Pop* was recorded live, and that the group's future plans include using Marshall amps!)

Other post-rock groups are more affiliated to techno. Insides compose on Cubase, a widely used computer music program that functions as a sort of 'virtual tape recorder', according to the group's J Serge Tardo. 'Cubase allows you to "play" things you couldn't physically play,' he says. Like a sequencer, it 'remembers' a riff, motif or beat and reiterates it in any timbre, whether sampled or derived from a module (a sort of digital library of sounds, no bigger than a Kellogg's Pop Tart).

Insides' non-rock approach dates back to their earlier lo-fi incarnation as Earwig. '[In Earwig] we all played hermetically sealed patterns that overlapped but didn't gel. We'd play separately, in a sense,' explains Tardo. Like systems musicians, Insides weave a tapestry of sound-threads, where Tardo's guitar features as just another iridescent filigree. In fact, he says the greatest influence on his guitar playing is Kraftwerk!

Tardo prefers 'the godlike position of manipulating the soundscape from the outside [the classic Spector/Eno role] as opposed to being in the mix, like a guitarist'. When the group play live, improvisation figures only in the sense that 'you can have a husk of sequencer patterns that you can mutate, like in a dub mix' (an approach that has direct parallels with the live performances of such techno operatives as Orbital and Mixmaster Morris). Performance isn't strenuous in the Carducci sense, but it's mentally draining – 'Like doing somersaults in your head,' says Tardo.

* * *

Like Disco Inferno and Insides, Seefeel are one of those groups whose Year Zero coincides with the arrival of Joy Division and The Cocteau Twins, and whose aesthetic is shaped by the late eighties dreampop of My Bloody Valentine and A.R. Kane. The latter awoke Seefeel's interest in sound-in-itself, which gradually led them to club-based musics such as techno and house. Of all the post-rock units, Seefeel have most avidly embraced techno's methodology; appropriately, they've found a commercial niche in the 'electronic listening' genre (recently performing alongside Autechre and □-ziq), and a home on its premier label, Warp.

Seefeel use a lot of guitars, but only as a source of timbre (all cirrus swirls and drone drifts). If it's mostly impossible to distinguish their guitar textures from the sequenced/sampled material, again it's because of Cubase, which, says Mark Clifford, allows them to 'take two seconds of guitar and chop it into 1,000 pieces, loop it, string it out for ten minutes, layer it and so on'. Similarly, Sarah Peacock's voice is not deployed expressively but used as material; the title track of Seefeel's imminent *Ch-Vox* EP (a one-off for Richard 'Aphex Twin' James's Rephlex label) is composed entirely of her treated and timestretched vocal drone.

Live, the techno process means that Justin Fletcher drums to a click-track, while the rest of the band must keep in sync with the pre-recorded parts. Not surprisingly, this is unrewarding and they'd prefer to dispense with gigs altogether. Clifford's fantasy alternative would involve Seefeel creating an aural environment but not actually being the focal point on stage, which is closer to the process of club DJ-ing than being in a rock 'n' roll group.

* * *

A similar fantasy appeals to Robert Hampson of Main, who reckons 'these could be the last days of gig-going'. He imagines organizing 'a live mix scenario, where we'd be hidden out of sight, behind a desk'; a sort of avant-rock sound system, in other words. Unsurprisingly, Main are primarily studio based, a sound laboratory. With Main, Hampson has returned to the experimental music, based around tape loops and layers of processed guitars, he made before he formed the mid-eighties neo-psychedelic rock band Loop. Main have progressively shed Loop's vestigial rock traces, dispensing first with human drums, then with the drum machine. The percussion on their new LP *Motion Pool* is all sampled, and even this may eventually be replaced with pure ambience.

Hampson is a longtime foe of the sampler, he says, and resorted to it reluctantly. Sometimes he prefers to physically play Main's most monotonous, uninflected, one-chord riffs, because of the minuscule differences in attack and tone this produces. 'To sample the chord and sequence it,' he says, 'would iron out the character, flatten the sound.' As Main drift away from the rock process and the rock mainstream, they inevitably move closer to the avant-garde, finding allies with contemporary improvisers and droneologists like Jim O'Rourke, Paul Schutze, AMM's Eddie Prevost, Thomas Koner, KK Null and Jim Plotkin. A recent North London live showcase for *Motion Pool* made this connection explicit, with Main's two sets split by a free improvisation featuring O'Rourke, Plotkin and Prevost.

* * *

Another key player in this area is Kevin Martin. He runs Pathological Records, leads the post-rock outfits God, Techno Animal and Ice, and participates in the 'supergroup' EAR (along with Sonic Boom, Kevin Shields of MBV and Eddie Prevost). From his own experience as a producer and bandleader, Martin reckons that 'working with technology, you become fond of machine time and fed up with the fallibility of human time'. God is his most traditional project, since it's about combustive improvisation and physical effort, 'the sparks and flashpoints that come from human elements. I see God as a relic of another time, which is why we have images of burnt-out locomotives on the covers.'

God LPs (a new one, *The Anatomy of Addiction*, is imminent) straddle jamming spontaneity and studio mixology. By contrast, Ice and Techno Animal were both conceived with no thought of live performance. For those units, Martin was (like Disco Inferno's Iain Crause) heavily influenced by Public Enemy, specifically the way Hank Shocklee's production situates a song's dynamic in the vertical, not the horizontal: 'The shifting layers of frequencies, not the development of verse-chorus narrative,' says Martin. 'Of course, you could say the same about Jeff Mills or Stakker Humanoid. But Shocklee, on *Fear of a Black Planet*, was the first to use sampling to pile on the intensities, rather than just quote obvious riffs; he took the peaks of other songs, like trumpet solos, and layered them densely.'

Many of his kindred spirits on the avant-rock peripheries – Robert Hampson, Mick Harris, Justin Broadrick (Godflesh/Final) – are embracing digital technology, and Martin thinks that's because digital sound appeals to control freaks. '[These musicians] are a bit solipsistic, they like to control all aspects of what they do. Also, as the audience for adventurous music contracts, they get less interested in playing live, it doesn't pay, and instead retreat to their home fortresses and surround themselves with machinery. I think that connects to what's going on in society as a whole – a process of atomization and disconnection. Digital also appeals because it allows you to break down structure.'

Despite the 'cold' accuracy of digital sound, Martin sees post-rock retaining some kind of primal energy. It's not physical in the Carducci sense, but 'a different kind of friction, the kind that comes with people wanting to interface and integrate themselves with machinery. It's like Lee Perry saying he wanted the mixing desk to take him over, or Can talking about machines having souls. People feel outdated by machinery. So they're taking on technology, but using it to unleash primal energy.'

So perhaps the really provocative area for future development lies not in cyber rock but cyborg rock; not the wholehearted embrace of techno's methodology, but some kind of interface between real-time, hands-on playing and the use of digital effects and enhancement. As

Kevin Martin points out: 'Even in the digital age, you still have a body. It's the connection between "techno" and "Animal" that's interesting.'

The Wire, May 1994

The racial component to this piece relates to the idea of post-rock not as a genre so much as a zone of possibility that re-opens again and again in British bohemian music, with bands attracted to the music of Black America but equally compelled to add something of their own (English quirkiness and whimsy, structural convolution, ideology). With the Canterbury Scene (Soft Machine, Robert Wyatt, et al.) the reference points were jazz and rhythm-and-blues; with post-punk, it was funk, disco, dub; with post-rock, hip hop and techno and jungle . . . The implicit contention: rock *must* keep re-engaging with the black vanguard, embrace its latest advances in rhythm and production, its innovations in expression and mood. If it fails to do this, it will succumb to retro, a self-reflexive and auto-cannibalizing relationship with its own history.

I genuinely thought I was coining a new term with 'post-rock' but as the years went by I kept coming across earlier occurrences. Paul Morley used it in the early eighties to describe something more abstract, the emergence of a new sensibility in which New Pop groups like Haircut 100 and Altered Images would be as valued as Led Zeppelin or Joy Division; being 'post-rock' meant jettisoning rockist assumptions about 'depth', 'edge', 'meaning'. I've also seen 'post-rock' used adjectivally in places like the *Rolling Stone Albums Guide* as a synonym for 'avant-rock' or 'out-rock'. But in terms of what emerged in the early nineties, well, it's true: I *did* supply this floating buzzphrase with a specific referent and something of an ideology (even if precious few of the bands rushed to embrace it . . . quite the opposite, actually . . . and ain't that always the way . . . and perhaps how it *should* be?). I'm astonished by the persistence of the term, the half-life it enjoys in record stores (where 'post-rock' still functions as a section heading), in discussions of music, and even as an identity that bands voluntarily embrace. Amazed, partly, because what post-rock now largely refers to (Tortoise-style fusionoid noodling) is much less compelling to my ears than the first wave of UK outfits celebrated in this *Wire* piece. Pincered between grunge and Britpop, which jointly shrank the horizons of independent music and cut off any hope of financial viability for almost all these groups, they have since become known as the Lost Generation.

SWINGBEAT AND THE NEW R&B

To my ears, swingbeat (a.k.a. New Jack Swing) is a paradoxical mix of seduction and repulsion. At its best, the production on classics like Bell Biv Devoe's 'Do Me' or SWV's 'I'm So Into You' is amazing, an irresistibly compulsive phuture-phunk melange of slick soul melody turbo-boosted with hip hop beats. But everything else about it – the lyrics, the slimy harmony vocals, the video imagery – offends my sensibilities. Swing's sexual politics veer from the graphic, clinical smut-speak of Jodeci and Jade, to the soppy-but-sensible, Mills & Boon meets Oprah Winfrey lovers' discourse of Boys II Men and Tevin Campbell. Above all, the New Jack Voice is nauseating – oily, oozy, jazz-inflected, wobbling like an over-emotional jellyfish.

SWV (Sistas With Voices) offer perhaps the most radical disjunction between reactionary content and radical form. *The Remixes* (RCA/BMG) consists of six tracks from their fab LP *It's About Time* rendered even more eerie and booty-quaking. Brian Alexander Morgan's production makes critics' pets like On U or Weatherall look like lightweights, while lead Sista Cheryl Gamble's voice is so processed and denatured it sounds positively Martian. Highlights here are the tracks where swingbeat pioneer Teddy Riley contributes extra production. 'I'm So Into You' augments the viscous, globular bass-pulse with a guitar-lick from hip hop classic 'Strong Island' and Zapp-style vocoder-scat; the original 'Right Here' only sampled Michael Jackson's 'Human Nature', but this revamp forces SWV and Jackson into close combat, struggling for control of the song. Throughout the LP, though, the Sistas' emotional stance is servile and prone: 'Anything', for instance, whimpers 'when I am weak / baby you make me strong . . . it's all up to you'.

Aaliyah and Blackgirl are post-SWV girl-swing contenders, although maybe that should read sub-SWV. Aaliyah is a protégé of new jack whizzkid R. Kelly, who produced and wrote all the songs on her debut *Age Ain't Nothing But a Number* (Jive/Be!). Basically, it's swing ordinaire, lots of stomach-turning melismatic vocals over tepid beats. There's even a song called 'I'm So Into You' – not a remake of SWV, but melody-wise, a sort of anagram of it. Blackgirl's *Treat U Right* (RCA) offers more identikit grooves and harmonies, and sexual politics that veer from male-ego-massaging ('Treat U Right') to assertive-but-classy ('90s Girl'). 'Chains of Love' is a dubious matrimony-as-blissful-bondage metaphor, while 'Nubian Prince' is Mills & Boon filtered through African American pride.

On the boy-swing front the big news is Blackstreet, the new combo formed by Teddy Riley, the guy who basically invented new jack and whose production pedigree includes such pinnacles as Guy, Bobby Brown, Wreckx-N-Effect, Jodeci and Mary J. Blige. Imagine Riley's studio as a digital crucible in which he melts down all black pop history, then extrudes perfect cyber-funk product. And so *Blackstreet* (Interscope) is full of eighties Clinton bass-farts, Roger Troutman vocoder-bliss, Dre-style cheesy-synths, even the odd Earth Wind and Fire horn-fanfare and a cover of Stevie Wonder's 'Love in Need'. Along with the obligatory 'nuff respect' to The Creator, the sleevenotes pay homage to just about every black musician past and present, but also, bizarrely, to Phil Collins, whose name sits incongruously alongside James Brown, Prince and Ray Charles. The Collins influence probably explains the long, looooong stretch of gloopy ballads that mar this otherwise funktastic release.

Keith Sweat has some fine Riley-produced tracks in his back-cat, but he too has gone all balladic and loverman-ly on his latest, *Get Up On It* (Elektra). From the mid-tempo slow-fuck grooves and Sweat's positively cunnilingual croon, to his spaniel-like bedroom eyes on the cover and phallic poses in the CD booklet, *Get Up On It* (geddit?) is basically aural soft-porn. Typical song-title: 'Grind On You'; typical lyric: 'now that I got you nice and wet / let me ease my way inside'.

One significant development, in the wake of Dr Dre and Domino, is the rise of hip hop so mellow and mellifluous it's merging with the tuffer swingbeat. On *Regulate . . . The G Funk Era* (Island), Warren G shapes up as challenger to his elder brother Dre as a producer of easy-listening gangsta, while his sinuous, soft-spoken rap-style resembles his pal Snoop. The production is glistening and caramel-luscious, all gliding basslines and those thin, reedy, strangely maudlin synth-twirls first heard on *The Chronic*. In many ways the G-funk sound is the nineties black equivalent to the So-Cal seventies soft-rock of The Eagles and Fleetwood Mac; hence the sample of ex-Doobie Bros vocalist Michael McDonald on 'Regulate'. Amazingly, most of the LP is even better than the single.

'Regulate' and SWV's 'Anything' both appear on the *Above the Rim* soundtrack (Death Row/Interscope). From Sweet Sable's groovalicious 'Old Time's Sake' (with its gratuitous product placement for Heineken) through the gamelan hip hop of Lady Of Rage's Dre-produced 'Afro Puffs' to Rhythm & Knowledge's horny 'U Bring Da Dog Out', this is a superb introduction to the increasingly blurry zone between softcore rap and swingbeat. Swing neophytes start here.

Melody Maker, 6 August 1994

Oddly, my interactions with R&B have never had anything to do with how the music is actually *used* by the audience it's aimed at, i.e. courtship grooves in the club, get-your-partner-in-the-mood-music for the boudoir. No, for me, it's all about the new sonic architecture, the textural weirdness, the elegance of form; even the vocals tend to hit me more in terms of an abstract beyond-human perfection than the emotion they supposedly transmit. I don't find much modern R&B that sexy to be honest. Plus the kinds of girls I've dated (including the current occupant of the position) would be unlikely to respond to even something as sublimely sensuous as Al Green. No, the alt-rock equivalent of the slow jam, the seduction soundtrack (for my generation at least), would be things like Cocteau Twins circa *Head Over Heels* and *Sunburst and Snowblind,* Siouxsie & the Banshees' *A Kiss in the Dream House . . .* and a bit later, My Bloody Valentine's 'Slow', 'Feed Me With Your Kiss', 'Soon', 'To Here Knows When' . . .

RAGGA

For the intrigued outsider, ragga provokes the same split response as gangsta rap. You can dig mightily the booty-coercing phuturism of the production, but wince and flinch when it comes to the ideology. Like gangsta, ragga lyrics are all guns, bitches and blunts. Just as fogies lament gangsta & swingbeat as a degeneration from the olden golden days of soul and funk, similarly nostalgics see today's digital reggae as spiritually bankrupt compared to seventies roots and dub. Certainly, Rastafarian militancy/mysticism has given way to a secular, solipsistic worldview, oscillating between sexism and sadism. But sonically, Jamaican pop remains as creative and compelling as ever.

Judging dancehall/ragga by Shaggy or Chaka Demus is like thinking 2 Unlimited are all you need to know about techno. The fierce, far out stuff is the hardcore – that's where you'll find the strangest, staccato-est beats, the starkest productions. *Ragga Ragga Ragga 2* (Greensleeves) is a good entry point for the uninitiated. Ragga is reggae with its fluency turned to erectile rigor (one track here is called 'Spermrod'!). The key factors in this shift to stiff are 1) digital technology; 2) Jamaica becoming a stop-over for the cocaine trade in the early eighties. And so ragga's sound – crisp and dry, all itchy 'n' scratchy computer-game blips and fidgety tics of percussion – sounds like nothing so much as electro, while its palsied rhythms suggest coke-jitters rather than a marijuana-moonwalk.

Fierce competition to be fresher than the rest results in weird 'n' wonderful production gimmicks, like the gastric-rumble bass-sounds on Papa San's Sireen' or the mud-squelch noises on Red Dragon's 'Burning Up' (which fit the lewd lyrics). Like gangsta vis-à-vis seventies funk, sampling allows ragga to simultaneously pay homage and wreak iconoclastic damage to seventies reggae: on Saba Tooth's 'Wap Dem Girl', a tiny wisp of ethereal, rootsical keyboard floats amid the clanking machine-beat, while Lt. Stitchie's 'Wood Fire' is cyber-dub. In fact, ragga is at once futuristic and atavistic: many of its rhythms come from African-based cult religions like Etu, Pocomania and Kumina.

Another excellent introduction to dancehall is *Ragga Sampler Volume 1* (Charm). The standout track is Buju Banton's 'Mind Behind The Wind', which slots the usual gruff, chest-puffed-out bragging amidst undulating tabla-like beats, oddly reminiscent of avant-funk visionary Arthur Russell's 'Let's Go Swimming'. Another highlight: Galaxy P's 'Hardcore', porno-ragga so hyped that its rhythm-mechanism almost seizes up. *Just Ragga, Volume 6* (Charm) showcases several examples of a new trend: duets like Jigsy King & Tony Curtis's 'Any Man Yu Want', which combine the hoarse, coarse vocal grain of ragga with swingbeat's sickly slickness. The contrast of rough lust and oily, unctuous pleading is interesting, and dancehall and new jack have obvious links, production-wise, but I prefer the pure ragga of the Spragga Benz tracks here: the Einsturzende-meets-martial-drums battery of 'Dem Flap', the squelchifarious twitch of 'Gi Wi Di Naany'.

Ragga has generated few artists capable of holding your interest for the length of an album. On Terror Fabulous's *Yaga Yaga* (East West), maestro Dave Kelly's production & beats are subtly inventive but soft-core, and the songs are sweetened with treacly harmonies. Fab's persona is sort of ragga without the aggro: boastful, bawdy ('Water Bed Expert') but never brutal, a ragga LL Cool J instead of a Schoolly D. Where's the Terror? Still, the album does git raw towards the end with 'Mr Big Man' and 'Broke Wine Butterfly', which reprise the epileptic anti-grooves of Buju Banton classics like 'Big it Up' and 'Bogle Dance'.

Much more unsound and exciting are Bounty Killer Versus Beenie Man's *Guns Out* and Ninjaman's *Hollow Point Bad Boy* (both Greensleeves). The ultra-minimal sound (both are produced by King Jammy) is as desiccated, skeletal and 2-D as electro. Beenie's 'Off The Air Bad Boy' and Ninja's 'Write Your Will' each revive the famous Casio-synth B-line of 'Under Me Sleng Teng', the first electro-reggae hit, while Ninja's 'Wap Dem Bubba' is full of wikky-wikky voices. As for the lyrics, they're relentlessly sociopathic, albeit leavened with a macabre wit ('Deadly Medley'). Ninja's 'Hollow Point' takes its title from bullets designed to flatten on impact, mushroom through the body and inflict maximum internal damage (nice one, Ninj!), while he's barely two bars into 'Bad Boy Nuh Cub Scout' before he's namechecked Uzi and Tek 9 ('name brand gun!'). It's cartoon gangsta stuff, perhaps to be taken with a pinch of salt.

Beenie's 'Mobster' is just one of myriad ragga tunes sampled by that strain of jungle I call gangsta-rave. So finally, a word for *Jungle Hits Volume 1* (Street Tuff), which scoops up most of the ragga-jungle cuts that count, from General Levy's roisterous 'Incredible' to Shy FX's bloodcurdling 'Original Nuttah' and 'Gangster Kid'. The compilation's in the Top 3 Album Chart as I write – no doubt about it, this is nineties pop, the sound of young Black Britain.

Melody Maker, 22 October 1994

'Hardcore underground = the avant-edge' was my line at this point, but I do wonder if the best stuff isn't in fact the crossover dancehall. I haven't listened to Bounty & Beenie's *Guns Out* since reviewing it, but Beenie Man's 'Who Am I' – a Top 10 smash and probably my favourite dancehall tune ever – can hardly be accused of a lack of sonic strangeness. Its Jeremy Harding Playground riddim is one of the most stunningly futuristic and uncanny ragga productions of the nineties. Even 'Bombastic' by Shaggy (unjustly slighted here) is pretty extreme if you think about – those insanely deep, *basso profundissimo* vocals.

THE JON SPENCER BLUES EXPLOSION

Irving Plaza, New York

You could call it 'We-Just-Wanna-Rock-Y'Know' Rock. Bands who really do just want to rock are veteran troupes like Motorhead (currently trudging across the States in support of Sabbath) or Dokken. But 'We-Just-Wanna-Rock-Y' Know' bands, that's something else altogether. That's groups like Royal Trux or Urge Overkill, whose apparently 'inane' motivation is really a conceptualist art-rock manoeuvre; they have reached their fundamentalist aesthetic only after years of tortuously exploring and exhausting all the options of avant-rock noise. For Urge, 'rock' = Cheap Trick. For Trux, 'rock' = the terminally unhip but populist Grand Funk Railroad (*Exile on Main Street* now being too tarnished with intellectualism). And for the Explosion (like Trux, an offshoot of Pussy Galore, the ultimate 'conceptual dumb-ass' band), 'rock' is an unholy hybrid of John Lee Hooker, Creedence Clearwater Revival, James Brown and Black Oak Arkansas.

The Jon Spencer Blues Explosion are the toast of Manhattan's hip-oisie. So when, in his Lux Interior/Nicolas Cage in *Wild at Heart* hillbilly/silly-billy voice, Spencer yelps catchphrases like 'I got soul' and 'you sho' got tha funk', the audience shriek back like a teenybopper throng whose collective G-spot has been tickled by Take That. What exactly is this entirely white audience affirming with these histrionics? That indeed they have 'got the funk', since black folks abandoned the genre twenty years ago, leaving it open for gentrification? Meanwhile, true modern funk (swingbeat) and the real contemporary urban blues (hip hop – same tropes of alienation, 'I'm a Man' bragging, pacts with the Devil) are deemed black cultural property, a no-go zone for whitey. Sadly, this stylistic apartheid seems to suit both races in the USA.

The Blues Explosion are at least *aware* of modern black music. They pastiched Dr Dre's synth sound on *Greyhound*, and now here's *Experimental Remixes* – pretty much the first time that US indie-rock has even recognized, let alone embraced, the science of remixology that underlies all modern music, from rap to rave. While it's a shame the Explosion have yet to drop any of this science into their live-in-the-studio methodology, it's a start. It's encouraging because 'we-just-wanna-rock' is precisely the cop-out cul de sac that adventurous US bands run into when they run out of ways of renewing rock from within the gtr/bs/drms format, yet refuse to meet the challenge of sampladelia.

With 'we-just-wanna-rock', it's a question of whether bands can 'fake it so real they get beyond fake'. In the Explosion's case, the 'so real' that redeems them is the rhythm section (i.e. the entire band, minus Spencer's hoodoo-hokum vocals and lyrics). Above all, it's drummer Russell Simins Tha Human Breakbeat Machine who really makes things so swingin' and smokin'. Their boogie-funk groove thang – sort of No Wave gone Redneck, an Appalachian Gang of Four – is so phat and juicy you could swear there's a bass palpitating in the mix, instead of just the two guitars.

For some reason, I always think of *Pulp Fiction* in connection with the Blues Explosion. Both Quentin and Jon-Boy have been critiqued for their blackspoitative dabbling with stereotypes of bad-ass, superfly machismo. Their work shares a strange blend of bloody physicality and ultra-stylised irony, guts and scare quotes. But the deeper affinity touches on the pathos of postmodernism, of living in a 'late' period. Sho' nuff, *Pulp Fiction* is the best American filmic culture can generate at this point in history, but compare it with The *Wild Bunch* or *Taxi Driver*, movies that resonate as opposed to titillate, and there's no doubt we are living in less distinguished times. Similarly, as fun-packed and funk-tastic as The Blues Explosion are, their very eminence is in some sense a subtle indictment of the state of US guitar rock.

Any way you slice it, Spencer's recurrent holler 'for the first time in blues history!' takes some beating for its compacted levels of irony, poignancy, paradox and arrogance.

Melody Maker, 15 July 1995

I spent most of 1994 in London, a return prompted by a mixture of homesickness and not wanting to miss jungle blowing up. Going back to New York for good at the end of '94, I was dismayed by how little seemed to be going on there musically compared with the UK (where not just jungle, but post-rock, trip hop and all manner of electronic music was seething). I even penned a piqued piece addressing the quandary of 'Why American Rock Sucks' for a local zine. This review continued the polemic. Okay, American indie-rock had not been shaken up by rave and electronica like its UK cousin had, simply because that phenomenon never took over the mainstream like it did in Britain. But what about hip hop, omnipresent in America, broadcast via MTV or boomin' from jeep sound-systems on every street corner? White Americans seemed only capable of either ironic flirtation (Sonic Youth's Ciccone Youth side project, the embarrassing cameo of Chuck D in 'Kool Thing') or wholesale emulation; you never got the twist, the white-on-black mutations of sampladelia and looped rhythm that took place in the UK. The only explanation was the fraught politics of race in the US, with white bohemians regarding rap as 'cool' but understandably wary about laying a finger on Black cultural property, whereas Britain's remoteness from this highly charged situation meant that its most quick-thinking bands could respond almost instantly to hip hop's challenge. There was an upside to American indie-rock traditionalism, their antipathy to machine rhythm: the groups really *rocked*, you could go into any bar and you'd hear a better rhythm section than all but the very best British groups. The downside: you never got that shock-of-the-new sensation. As I wrote in an earlier overview of US alt-rock, 'the heart of rock 'n' roll, as the sage Huey Lewis put it, is still beating. But in Britain and Europe, bands are tearing out that heart with an electric claw, rewiring their nervous systems and mutating into cyborg-rock.' When Human Breakbeat Machine Russell Simins was asked what he thought of jungle, he complained that the beats were horrible because there was nothing 'sexy' about them. Reading that, I was disappointed, but not surprised.

BLUR VERSUS OASIS

Right now, the British music scene is convulsed with patriotic fervour. For the first time in over a decade, young British guitar-bands are penetrating the Top 10 of the Singles Chart, barging aside faceless Euro-dance acts and routing the American grunge invaders. This 'Britpop' movement, which includes Blur, Oasis, Elastica, Pulp and Supergrass, harks back to the days when Britannia ruled the airwaves: the sixties (Beatles, Kinks, The Who) and the New Wave late seventies (Buzzcocks, Wire, The Jam). But Britpop's parochial reference points and stylistic insularity, while highly appealing to large sections of UK youth, may pose problems when it comes to exporting the sound to America, where grunge still rules.

By far the biggest Britpop groups are Blur and Oasis, both of whom have new albums set for imminent release in this country. In August, the duel between the two bands over whose single would enter the UK charts at Number 1 made the British national newspapers and TV news. The rivalry between Blur and Oasis is often compared to that between the Beatles and The Rolling Stones, but in fact those sixties giants had a genial relationship and a gentlemen's agreement not to release singles at the same time. Blur and Oasis, however, appear to loathe each other with a genuine and deep passion. Recently, Oasis guitarist Noel Gallagher shocked the pop community when he expressed the wish that Blur's singer and bassist would both 'catch AIDS and die'. Underlying the verbal vendetta is a regional antagonism. Blur are from the South of England and middle class, albeit infatuated with London proletarian lifestyles. From the Northern city of Manchester, Oasis are the genuine working-class article. What both bands have in common is a dedication to resurrecting the lost glory of a quintessentially English pop canon.

Blur's fourth album *The Great Escape* (Virgin) pays homage to the English tradition of music-hall pop, as exemplified by The Kinks, Ian Dury and Madness, who all combined wry, observational lyrics about everyday life with a tragi-comic pathos. Singer and wordsmith Damon Albarn went to drama school, and appropriately most Blur songs are like miniature satirical plays. *The Great Escape* is full of third-person vignettes that caricature English stereotypes. 'Ernold Same', a brief sketch about a conformist commuter crushed by soul-numbing routine, revives pop's tired tradition of 'Mr Jones' songs that jeer at squares. 'Country House', the single that beat Oasis to the UK Number I spot, is about a city gent who retreats from the urban ratrace. Mocking a namedropping poseur, 'Charmless Man' echoes the heavy-handed satire of The Kinks' 'Dedicated Follower of Fashion', while 'Top Man' is a punning portrait of a womanizing thug who's 'naughty by nature / shooting guns on the High Street of Love'.

Despite flashes of wit, there's a condescending detachment and lack of compassion to Mr Albarn's writing that makes his characters hollow and two-dimensional. The singer's bogus Cockney accent, where 'cold sweat' is pronounced 'cow swah', and his perpetual sneering tone, also become irritating with prolonged exposure. Musically, *The Great Escape* manages somehow to be both experimental and dated, favouring the densely detailed arrangements and quirky production effects of groups like XTC and Squeeze, who followed in the tradition of *Sgt Pepper's Lonely Hearts Club Band*. And so Blur's guitar-quartet sound is gussied up with melodramatic strings and chirpy horns, quaint synthesizers and lugubrious pianos.

Oasis's new album *(What's The Story) Morning Glory* (Epic) is also deeply indebted to the Beatles. Singer Liam Gallagher sounds like a more nasal John Lennon, with the joie de vivre curdled to a sour arrogance. Sonically, Oasis are basically a grungier version of The La's, an early nineties Beatles-obsessed outfit from the North of England. While a fervent admirer of La's songwriter Lee Mavers, Oasis's Noel Gallagher has said, of when he first saw that band perform, 'I thought, "he's ripping off my songs!"' In truth, both songwriters are so chronically influenced by Lennon & McCartney that they're basically filling in the gaps in the Beatles' songbook, and inevitably sometimes the same gap.

Theorist Joe Carducci uses the term 'genre mining' to describe such a classic-rock approach. A marginally less hook-laden reprise of the debut LP *Definitely Maybe*, *Morning Glory* suggests Oasis's particular seam of sound is close to exhaustion. By far the best thing on the album is the closing 'Champagne Supernova'. 'Where were you when we were getting high?' taunts Liam Gallagher. 'Some day you will find me / Caught beneath a landslide / In a champagne supernova in the sky.' Like Oasis's previous peak 'Live Forever', this song aches with a lust for glory. Its imagistic metaphors exalt rock 'n' roll as one of the few escape routes for working-class jack-the-lads who want more from life than nine-to-five drudgery.

Outside the narrow, sixties-fixated parameters of Britpop, the UK music scene is generating the most vital and futuristic music on the planet. From the post-rock experimentalism of Laika and Techno-Animal to trip hop's sinister atmospherics and jungle's cyber-funk frenzy, these developments have been overwhelmingly shaped by the rhythmic innovations of hip hop and techno. By comparison, what's striking about Blur and Oasis is their lack of rhythmic power. In Blur's music, the drums are decorative rather than propulsive, while the bass is melodic to the point of being rococo. As for Oasis, the trudging rhythm section is mixed low, allowing the Gallagher brothers' distorted guitars and anthemic choruses to dominate. Far from being a liability, though, this deliberately old-fashioned production style may actually be a big source of Britpop's appeal, at least to those who regard contemporary pop's cult of the beat as a tyranny.

Director's cut of piece published in *New York Times*, 22 October 1995

Hard, now, to recover fully the sense of outrage that this stuff sparked in me at the time . . . This is just one of several critiques I penned, the gist of the argument being 'Britpop = an evasion of the multiracial, technology-mediated nature of UK pop culture in the nineties . . . a symbolic erasure of Black Britain, as manifested in jungle and trip hop . . . the sixties figuring as a "lost golden age" alarmingly analogous to the mythic stature of the Empire for football hooligans and the BNP.' I was struck, interviewing Elastica (my favourites out of Britpop, after Pulp) that Justine Frischmann could only think of one form of black music she liked: ska, i.e. the jerkiest, most New Wavey form of black pop ever! But now, less certain that white musicians have a moral obligation to 'engage' with black music, and with the healing passage of time, I feel a smidgeon of affection for Britpop . . . I do sometimes wonder what it would have been like to actually live in England through it all. Would I have got caught up in the fervour (cf. the World Cup) or just been even more aghast and appalled and feeling like an internal exile?

The prototype conception of *Rip It Up and Start Again* was going to cover the entire period from punk to Britpop, and end with Noel Gallagher's visit to 10 Downing Street: Britpop and New Labour as a content-free replay of the 1960s, Oasis-as-Beatles and Blair-as-Wilson.

PULP

Different Class (Island)

Forget about Blur vs Oasis. The real battle for the 'soul' of Britpop is Blur vs Pulp. The difference between Damon Albarn and Jarvis Cocker is as profound as the gulf between Martin Amis and Irvine Welsh. On one side of the divide you'll find surface-deep verbal flash masking a smug and paltry sense of satire, wherein 2-D stereotypes are set up as Aunt Sallies, mere butts for the omniscient author's superior wit. On the other side: a fluent feel for colloquial language, in tandem with a deep, luminous compassion, the kind of condescension-free empathy that only comes when you've lived and breathed the same (extra)ordinary life as your characters, intimately experienced its cruel ironies and impasses.

This divide runs a little deeper than the merely stylistic (i.e. Albarn's preponderance of third-person vignettes vs Cocker's preference for the first-person confessional mode). It pivots around the question of social background. From the vantage point of privilege, the British class system and its attendant grotesqueries merely afford frightful amusement. But if you're writing from somewhere closer to the bottom of the heap, the stakes are that much higher, the reality of wasted potential and distorted lives all too raw and personal.

If you've tagged Jarvis as pervy poet and sex-maniac, you'll find plenty of titillating ditties on *Different Class*. But the album's title alone (cf. *His n' Hers*) announces that Cocker's broadened his scope, has another axe to grind: social antagonism. If 'Mis-Shapes' is as perilously vague and vacantly uplifting as only a power-to-the-people anthem can be, 'Common People' is infinitely more potent because its populist sentiments are anchored in a specific, one-on-one instance of class combat; the song smarts with the humiliation of being patronized, and takes revenge with gloating glee. The title itself is jarring: I'd forgotten the word 'common' could even be used in that snobbish sense, outside Alan Bennett plays like *A Chip in The Sugar*.

It's hard not to read a subtext into Cocker's diatribe against the female class-tourist who yearns to take a cheap holiday in other people's misery: surely there's a subtle jibe here at those of Pulp's peer-group(s) who've made 1995 the Year of the Fake-Prole Accent. That may just be my animosity runnin' away with me. Then again, Blur seem to look to London prole life as a sort of lost white ethnicity (sixties rock was about the white negro, nineties Britpop is about the posh hooligan). Similarly, Cocker's slumming toff envies the vulgar vitality of the working class, who live in the present tense because the bourgeois virtues of accumulation, investment and deferment just don't pay. But even as he rubs her nose in the fact that she'll 'never get it right', Cocker never hides the real motor behind the vitality of prole life and leisure: desperation. 'You'll never watch your life slip out of view / and dance and drink and screw / cos there's nothing else to do.' Cocker is Irvine Welsh's 'A Smart Cunt': too clever not to see through the tawdry safety-valves and inverted snobberies that hold the working class together in dismal contentment with their lot, yet perversely loyal to his social and regional roots. Musically, the low-rent-Roxy swirl of 'Common People' has the same quality as Cocker's singing. In straining for but not quite reaching an epic pitch of grandeur, it attains – à la Kevin Rowlands, Marc Almond, Band of Holy Joy – another grandeur, all the more touching and stirring in its all-too-human fallibility.

Then there's 'Sorted For E's & Wizz' – the kind of sympathetic but double-edged snapshot of the UK's dance/drug culture that Albarn & Co couldn't muster in a million years. Cocker's lyrics are exquisitely nuanced in their ambivalence about rave culture; his Syd Barrett-like nursery-rhyme pathos and post-E disenchantment are truly poignant. 'Is this the way they say the future's meant to feel? / Or just twenty thousand people standing in a field?'; Jarvis has been in that field, knows all about oscillating back and forth between utter immersion in the rave dream and a creeping sense of hollowness and futility. All that idealism and energy mobilized and expended, for what? A revolutionary affirmation of our common humanity, or just a massive evasion of post-Thatcherite reality? Cocker refuses to pass verdict on rave, his stance captured in a phrase of perfectly poised ambiguity: 'IT DIDN'T MEAN NOTHING'.

With the exception of 'Monday Morning' and 'Bar Italia' (two songs frantic with dread vis-à-vis the eternal return of the working week's bludgeoning drudgery), the rest of *Different Class* returns to trad Jarvis terrain – from the heavy-breathing vocals of 'Pencil Skirt' (about a creep who preys on his mate's fiancée when he's not around) to the Scott-Walker-in-Brel-mode melodramatics of 'Live Bed Show' (a bed's eye view of a woman's derelict love life) to the almost self-parodic 'Underwear' (a very Jarvis word, that). In this typically furtive vein of lugubrious lust and dingy desire, 'I Spy' is the stand-out: Cocker casts himself as a sort of sex-bandit who 'specializes in revenge', and whose reprisal for childhood humiliations takes the form of fucking his way up the class ladder. Better still, and surely the next single, is the futuristic-sounding 'Feelings Called Love', close to a Cocker manifesto on the mysterious workings of the heart and the loins. Love is a volcanic disruption ('it's not convenient . . . it doesn't fit my plans . . .') that shatters 'chocolate boxes and roses' notions of romance with its messy urgency. 'It's dirtier than that,' pants Jarvis, 'like some small animal that only comes out at night.' Speak for yourself, mate!

Like all Pulp-related discourse, this review is unavoidably Jarvis-centric. A quick word about the band: Pulp are just about the only Britpopsters whose sound – a sort of shabby glam-rock tinged with the glitterball-grandeur of 'I Will Survive' era disco – can't really be tagged to specific sources. Perhaps simply because they've been around for so long, they've arrived at a sound at once richly evocative of a quintes-sentially English pop past and yet as irreducible, idiosyncratic and NOW! as, say, The Smiths in their heyday. Pulp, in fact, are The Smiths if they hadn't been so appallingly disco-phobic. Pulp, then: not so much the jewel in Britpop's crown, more like the only band who validate the whole sorry enterprise.

Melody Maker, 28 October 1995

Confession: I once scorched Jarvis's flesh. It was in the bar area at an Elastica gig in Camden, I must have been gesticulating with a cigarette in my hand, there was a tell-tale *hissssss*, a tiny gasp, and I turned to see a familiar figure scurrying away with a furtive air, clutching his wounded paw, too fast for me to proffer apologies. What a way to treat your absolute favourite UK pop star of the 1990s!

R&B: THE SOUND OF 1997

Timbaland and Magoo

'Up Jumps Da' Boogie'
Welcome to Our World

Aaliyah

'One in a Million'

Missy Elliott

'The Rain (Supa Dupa Fly)'
'Sock it to Me'
Supa Dupa Fly

Queen Pen

'Man Behind the Music'

Blackstreet

'No Diggity'

The most sonically astonishing and pure-pleasure-intensive music coming out of America in '97 was the stuff spawned in the rumpshaker interzone between uptempo pop rap and hard R&B/swingbeat. Teddy Riley and Timbaland out-shone, out-avanted and out-funked 'proper' hip hop (and revealed Wu-Tang Clan producer the RZA to be a one-trick pony), while the videos' sub-hallucinatory ultra-vivid colour schemes, fish-eye distortions and Dali-Barbera surrealism made hard-core rap's monochrome fetishization of the 'real' seem drab and done-to-death overnight. (Busta Rhymes, take a bow also.) From Big Beat to speed garage, Puffy to Missy to nouveau ska, this was a year of good times music; overnight, the entire darkside paradigm of pre-millennium tension and blunted paranoia was jettisoned, consigned to the pop-historical scrapheap, leaving the likes of Wu-Tang, Tricky and techstep looking like Jeremiahs out of work and out of step with the zeitgeist. Maybe it's just a knock-on effect of the economic boom, or just an inevitable reaction against post-grunge/post-rave gloom, but the pleasure-principled party-hard ethos felt like a blessed relief, a welcome injection of energy.

Highlights: Aaliyah's Timbaland-and-Missy produced 'One in a Million', with its jungle-at-ballad-tempo stop-start beats twisting your torso and stuttering triple-time kickdrums pummelling the solar-plexus (and Aaliyah's thankfully restrained when it comes to swingbeat's cardinal drawback, excessively nuanced and melismatic singing); Blackstreet's 'No Diggity', a sublimely inventive blend of roots 'n' future, featuring the most exhilarating enunciated utterance of the year – Queen Pen's 'we be the baddest clique' (a slice of super-slurred slan-guage so succulent she just had to slip it to us one more time on her solo debut 'Man Behind the Music'). Above all, Timbaland & Magoo's 'Up Jumps Da' Boogie' – every cranny of the mixscape infested with eerie nuances, grating drone-loops, lewd squiggles and funky quivers; cyber-funk as an animated audio-frieze of gratuitous grotesquery. And let's not forget that strange subliminal lyric that goes 'see the white man scared / of the black man's power'. This R&B/swingbeat/'urban contemporary' stuff is the blackest shit on the planet, with the possible exception of ragga – no white producers, no white influences; wigga rap fans who get off on the radical chic of Wu-Tang just don't get it at all. As a white bohemian/lapsed socialist, I still find the designer-label commodity-fetishism and conspicuous consumption, the Hennessy-swigging and Rolex-brandishing element, a bit hard to handle – but even that gives it a weird sort of transgressive late-capitalist edge, a la Bataille's sumptuary-expenditure-without-return/will-to-extravagance.

Favourite Records of 1997 for *Blissout* website

I always think of 'One in a Million' – which actually came out in 1996 but lingered – as the turning point, the historical hinge opening the door to a whole new era of black American pop.

But black genres generally evolve in small increments, a steady flow of innovation that tends to blur the sense of drastic breaks or sudden giant steps forward. So just as pivotal in its own way was a track from a year before 'One in a Million': TLC's 'Waterfalls'. Produced by Organized Noize, this 1995 monsterhit pipped 'Million' to the post by being the very first R&B track I can think of where you wanted to sing (or at least vocally mimic) the drum patterns – that schlurpppting fibrillation of clusterfunk beats at the end of each bar – as opposed to the melody. 'Million' then took this to the next stage, stripping away almost everything but the beats and the gorgeously multi-tracked vocal arrangement, turning the song into a duet between the drums and the singer.

RONI SIZE/REPRAZENT

New Forms (Talkin' Loud/Mercury)

Its day in the British media limelight past, jungle is now in disarray. Riven by schisms – the white industrial sadomasochismo of techstep versus the populist boisterousness of jump up – the scene has lost much of its black audience to yet another new London sound: speed garage, soulful house music turbo-boosted with sub-bass and rude-boy ragga samples. Meanwhile, increasingly divorced from the dancefloor and its dissensions, album-oriented drum & bass (jungle's respectable cousin) is firmly established as an art form and industry in itself, winning a pop audience that has never experienced the music in its proper context of DJ rewinds and MC chatter.

Leading the pack of impending major label debuts (Adam F, Dillinja, Krust, 4 Hero, Source Direct, to name just a few), Roni Size's *New Forms* is to '97 what *Timeless* was to '95 and *Logical Progression* to '96. It's this year's consensus electronica album, the double-disc *magnum opus* garlanded with critical acclaim and hyped with the dubious sales-pitch 'if you only buy one jungle album this year . . .'. Roni Size and his Bristol-based Reprazent clan (DJ Die, Krust, Sov) have even won the UK's prestigious Mercury Music Prize – a seal of approval that will doubtless doom jungle as outsider chic. Some scene insiders are already complaining that the fusion-flavoured *New Forms* is mere coffee table jungle-lite.

But then white bohemians (myself included) have never truly grasped why the likes of LTJ Bukem glimpse utopia in the jazz-funk of Lonnie Liston Smith and Roy Ayers, why Goldie flips out for the fuzak of The Yellowjackets and mid-eighties Miles Davis. *New Forms* is a timely reminder that elegance can be a form of rebellion for the black working class (not just straightforward upwardly mobile aspiration).

From Earth Wind and Fire and Chic to today's G-funk and nu-R&B, the regal panache and sheer slickness of sound communicate a kind of defiance, a refusal of your allotted place in the social pyramid. Like Notorious B.I.G./playa rap's commodity fetishism (Hilfiger, Cristal, Rolexes, Hennessy, Lexus et al.), *New Forms*' sonic luxury – stand-up bass, lush strings and jazzed cadences – proclaims: 'Nothing's too good for us.'

Yet often when electronic musicians attempt a synthesis of sequenced sound with 'musicality' ('real' vocals, 'live' playing), the result is an embarrassing mish-mash; witness the worst bits of *Timeless*. If *New Forms* mostly escapes that dire fate, it's because Size/Reprazent are minimalists where Goldie is a maximalist (I quail at the prospect of the G-man's forthcoming forty-five-minute track 'Mother' recorded with a thirty-piece orchestra). Steeped in the Bristol confluence of dub reggae and hip hop that spawned Massive Attack and Tricky, Reprazent understand that the real 'jazz thing' going on in drum & bass doesn't involve sampling electric piano licks or hiring a session musician to noodle out a sax solo. Rather, it resides in the rhythm section – the tangential relationship between the hyper-syncopated breakbeats and the roaming, ruminative but always visceral bass. Strip away the stereo-panned streaks of abstract tone-colour and the Pat Metheny-style guitar glints from 'Matter of Fact' and the track is basically a ricochet-rimshot drum solo (albeit one painstakingly constructed over days of red-eyed computer-screen toil rather than played in real-time and in a real acoustic space).

The first disc of *New Forms* contains all the 'big tunes', as well as the most overt nods towards jazz: the double-bass-driven 'Brown Paper Bag', the title track with its tongue-twistingly sibilant scat-rap from Bahamadia, and the gorgeous singles 'Heroes' and 'Share the Fall', both graced by the torch-song croon of Onalee. 'Share the Fall' isn't as good a song as 'Heroes', but it's better jungle. Singing inside your flesh, the *beat* is the melody, its rolling tumble of rapid-fire triplets making you step fierce like a bebop soldier.

Disc Two of *New Forms* is more cinematic and soundtrack-to-life oriented, achieving a widescreen feel and Technicolor sheen rivalled only by Spring Heel Jack. 'Trust Me', for instance, sounds like it might be woven out of offcuts from Dudley Moore's symphonic jazz score for the sixties movie *Bedazzled*. Truer to jungle's anonymous funktionalism, the tracks on Disc Two strip away song structures and 'proper' vocals to reveal a music of lustrous details. Drum & bass is an engineer's art, oriented around specifications and special effects, timbres and treat-ments. What you listen for is the sculpted rustle and glisten of hi-hat

213

and cymbal figures, the contoured plasma of the bass, the exquisitely timed placement of horn stabs and string cascades. You thrill to the music's murderous finesse – intricacies and subtleties designed to enhance the ganjadelic mind-state but which are so nuanced and three-dimensional that they stone you all by themselves.

After techstep's explosive psychosis and dirty distortion, *New Forms* offers implosive anxiety and obsessive-compulsive cleanliness of production. Tracks like the eerie, menthol-cool 'Hot Stuff' modulate your metabolism like the impossibly refined neurochemical engineering and designer drugs of the next century. New forms, for sure – but in Roni Size/Reprazent's music, the clash between the ghettocentric exuberance of the breakbeats and the opulent arrangements of the studio also forges new emotions: tense serenity, suave unease, fervent ambivalence.

Spin, November 1997

A turnaround for me – having spent the previous couple of years complaining about drum & bass's obsession with 'jazzual' vibes, well-appointed arrangements and slick production, I started to get more of a feeling for the aesthetics of elegance. In truth, alongside the ruffneck menace and bass-bruising minimalism, there was always a side to jungle that involved supreme daintiness and neat-freak finesse. It's a different kind of rush – the tingle you get from the nimble, glancing panache of a jazz-inflected synth-chord. This dialectic between crudity and refinement, exuberance and savoir-faire, is integral to black music history; it runs all the way from blues to crunk, and correlates to class divisions within African American society and to dilemmas of crossover and assimilation. The issues are contentious enough for black musicians, critics, and fans. When white folk, with their various projections and misunderstandings enter the picture, things can get real fraught. 'Nothing's too good for us': a lick nicked off Adorno, from one of his infamous diatribes against jazz (a music I strongly suspect he'd only encountered in the dilute form of Benny Goodman-style swing). The 'sample' reappears in the next piece . . .

FEMININE PRESSURE

2-Step and UK Garage

If you live in London, perhaps you've scanned the FM spectrum and come to a halt at a pirate station whose sound you can't quite finger or figure. It's got house music's slinky panache, but the rhythm's wrong – too fitful and funked-up, and besides, there's an MC jabbering over the top, jungle-style. Maybe it's jungle, then – but then again, maybe not: too slow, too sexy. Sometimes it's a bit like American R&B – except it sounds druggy, the wrong kind of druggy: like Timbaland on E.

So what is it, this genre-without-a-name? It's the latest in a series of mutations spawned from London's multiracial rave scene, the next evolutionary stage beyond speed garage (itself a swerve sideways from jungle). And the new style does have a name, albeit an unsatisfactorily dry, technical one: '2-step', increasingly a general rubric for all kinds of jittery, irregular rhythms that don't conform to garage's traditional 4-to-the-floor pulse. Somebody really should coin a more attractive name, though, one that captures 2-step's lipsmacking lusciousness. Because all the juice squeezed out of jungle by the post-techstep school of scientific drum & bass has oozed back in the succulent form of 2-step.

* * *

'Truthfully, jungle stemmed from house music. It has a reggae influence, but it's still house,' MC Navigator from jungle pirate Kool FM insisted back in 1994. Three years later, jungle returned to the source, when its rude bwoy spirit and rhythmic science violently possessed the body of garage (the most soulful and songful form of house), in the process creating a new London scene.

Jungle's relationship with garage actually went back some way. Instead of techno clubs' ambient chill-out rooms, the second room at jungle clubs usually bumped to garage; pirate radio stations often programmed garage shows for mellow moments in the weekend (Saturday morning, Sunday afternoons). It was on these pirate shows that DJs started pitching up their garage imports (artists like Masters At Work, Kerri Chandler, Todd Edwards) to 130 bpm, giving them the extra 'oomph' required by the London jungle audience. DJs favoured the dub versions of the US tracks, says Spoony of DJ collective The Dreem Teem, because 'not having much vocal element, you could play the dubs faster without them sounding odd'; these near-instrumentals also left gaps for the MCs to do their stuff. Soon the DJs started making homegrown garage trax that sounded like their pirate shows – faster than the US sound, with jungalistic sub-bass, dub-wise FX, and ragga chants timestretched so that the vocal fissured and buckled like the wings of a metal-fatigued Boeing 707.

This UK underground garage also radically intensified the aspect of the New York sound that most appealed to jungle-reared ears: intricate percussion patterns, highly textured drum sounds, and above all, the skippy, snappy, syncopated snares and busy, bustling hi-hats that make garage much more funky than regular house. Reticular and metro-nomic, house is 'banging' or 'pumping'; polyrhythmically perverse, garage is all bump 'n' flex, twitch 'n' grind. But house and garage are both underpinned by a 4-to-the-floor kick drum that pounds mono-tonously on every bar.

2-step transforms garage into a kind of slow-motion jungle – a languorous frenzy of micro-breakbeats, hesitations and hyper-syncopations; moments when the beat seems to pause, poised, and hold its breath. In its simplest form, it does this by removing every second and fourth kick from the 4-to-the-floor pulse, creating a lurch-ing, falter-funk feel. More adventurous 2-step producers program irregular kickdrum patterns that syncopate with the bassline, akin to Timbaland's double-time or triple/quadruple/quintuple-time kicks. 2-step has actually taken the 'speed' out of 'speed garage', or at least the sensation of velocity, because removing two out of every four kicks subtracts that steady-pulsing energy. The effect is similar to the way the dub bassline in jungle used to run at half-time under the frenetic breaks. Indeed, some 2-step tunes have a ska or rocksteady-like skankin' feel.

To compensate for the energy-deficit, 2-step producers hype the funk by making every element in a track work simultaneously as rhythm, melody and texture. Organ vamps, horn stabs, keyboard pads, vocal licks, all interlock like cogs with the percussion patterns, which are processed through effects until the rhythm track alone offers an ear-tantalizing panoply of textures: crunchy, squelchy, spangly, woody, spongy, scratchy. These tactile timbres combine with the twitchy triplets and syncopations to create weird cross-rhythm effects – nicks and barbs that seem to snag your flesh and tug your body every-which-way.

'The rhythm track is not just the backing for a song any more,' declare Dem 2, the Thurrock, Essex-based duo of Spencer Edwards and Dean Boylan, whose nubile nu-funk anthem 'Destiny' was the UK blueprint for 2-step. 'The beats, the various instrument voicings, and any vocals within a track all carry equal amounts of importance – any one can be the hook that sticks in the mind.' Although Dem 2 correctly argue that you can hear this rhythmelody/texturhythm simultaneity at work across the gamut of contemporary dance music, it's undeniable that UK garage mostly assimilated this knowledge from drum & bass; many of the leading 2-step producers did their apprenticeship programming jungle. But right now, it's hard to imagine any drum & bass producer building a groove as seductively sleek and springheeled as 'Destiny'.

This is ironic, because 2-step is in many ways a reassertion of the jungle influence in reaction to the alarmingly rapid crossover of first-wave speed garage, which simply proved too attractive to mainstream house clubbers. 2-step is a semi-conscious attempt to make garage 'a London thing' (even an East London thing) again, rather than a short-lived nationwide fad. The similarity with jungle comes across in the way 2-step DJs mix. 'With traditional garage and house, the underlying beat and instrumental arrangement is more continuous and pulsing,' says 'Bat' Bhattacharyya, the resident 2-step expert on the Internet discussion forum ukdance. 'New York garage is designed so that the DJ mixes in a new track with a slow continuous fade-up. But 2-step, like hardcore and jungle, is far more amenable for chopping and cutting with the cross-fader – the sort of hip hop techniques you can't use with a house pulse-beat, cos it sounds funny.'

You can also hear the jungle ancestry in 2-step's low-end seismology, which has evolved way beyond the wah-wah/'dread bass' that drove speed garage in '97. Listen to pirates like Freek, Mission or Smooth, and you'll hear bubbling B-line melodies, chiming bass-detonations, and pressure-drop booms that have nothing to do with house as hitherto known. The baleful electro-dub rumble, plinky melody-riffs and migraine-wincing synth-tones of Steve Gurley's remix of 'Things Are Never' by Operator & Baffled hark back even further than jungle – it's just one of a number of tunes that flash back to the bleep-and-bass era of Unique 3/Nightmares On Wax/Sweet Exorcist/LFO/Forgemasters, that dawn-of-the-nineties moment when the British merged house and reggae for the first (but not last) time.

* * *

If jungle really did stem from house, as Navigator claimed, the true continuity between the two genres is not rhythmic or textural: it's the use of vocals (almost always absent in techno). At a rough guesstimate, maybe two-thirds of hardcore/jungle anthems between 1991 and 1994 relied on sampled diva vocals as primary hooks. Producers lifted them from old house or R&B classics, or from CDs packed with a cappellas recorded specifically for sampling. While there's no diva refrain equivalent to the ubiquitous, endlessly revisited 'Amen' break, certain classic vocal phrases were reworked time and again, with producers using similar techniques to breakbeat manipulation: acceleration, pitch-shifting, timestretching, looping, filtering and so forth.

When techstep achieved dominance in 1996, vocal samples began to disappear from drum & bass. But the house-hardcore-jungle continuum of diva-worship didn't end, it just branched sideways into speed garage. You can see it in the career of Steve Gurley. As a member of Foul Play, he sampled diva vocals from SOS Band and Kleer for tracks like 'Finest Illusion' and 'Open Your Mind'; going solo as Rogue Unit, he crafted a gorgeous drum & bass revamp of 'Say I'm Your Number One', a 1985 hit for Brit-soul chanteuse Princess. Today, Gurley is a leading 2-step producer, doing damage with torrid diva-driven tunes like his remix of Lenny Fontana's 'Spirit of the Sun'.

Traditional New York garage privileges the classy vocal, draping its melodious melisma over the groove. In contrast, 2-step producers subordinate the singer to funktionalist priorities, slicing 'n' dicing the vocal samples into staccato, percussive riffs that interlock with the groove to create extra syncopations. 'Vocal science' is Bat from ukdance's term for this vivisection of the diva, which effectively transforms the singer into a component of the drum kit. 2-step's vocal trick - nology has resituated garage on the other side of house's great divide: songs versus 'tracks', melody versus rhythm 'n' FX. Right from the start, there's been a tension in house between veneration of the Big Voice (Darryl Pandy, Robert Owens, Tina Moore, CeCe Peniston, et al.) and a more pragmatic 'trackhead' approach that uses anonymous session-divas as raw material (Todd Terry and Nitro Deluxe creating stammer-riffs by 'playing' the vocal sample on the sampling keyboard).

Jungle producers like Omni Trio took these crude techniques to the next level of sophistication, moulding and morphing diva vocals into a sort of passion-plasma, a body-without-organs fluid. Then, just as the hypergasmic diva was fading from jungle, 'vocal science' flickered back to life somewhere else – US garage, of all places. On his remixes of St Germain's 'Alabama Blues' and his own tracks like 'Never Far From You', New Jersey producer Todd Edwards developed a technique of cross-hatching brief snatches of vocals into a melodic-percussive honeycomb of blissful hiccups, so burstingly rapturous it's almost painful to the ear.

Todd Edwards's music had an extraordinary impact on London's emergent speed garage scene. If anyone in 2-step picked up Todd's baton and ran wild with it, it's Dem 2. 'Destiny' features an android-diva whose plaintive bleat is so tremulously FX-warped that for months I thought it went 'dance t' th' beat' instead of 'des-tin-eee'. Dem 2's 'Don't Cry Dub' of Groove Connektion 2's 'Club Lonely' is an even more ear-boggling feat of robo-glossolalia. This 1997 remix sounds like the missing link between Zapp's vocoder-funk mantra 'More Bounce to the Ounce' and Maurizio's dub-house. Snipping the vocal into syllables and vowels, feeding the phonetic fragments through filters and FX, Dem 2 create a voluptuous melancholy of cyber-sobs and lump-in-throat glitches: 'whimpering, wounded 'droids crying out in desolation!', as Spencer Edwards puts it.

'You can add a different soul that wasn't there' is how Dem 2 describe this kind of vocal remixology. 'Deconstruction' is not too strong a term, for what is being dismantled is the very idea of the voice as the expression of a whole human subject. 'Instead of the "organic" female singer of early garage, you get a legion of dismembered doll parts,' says journalist Bethan Cole, who's writing a book about the diva in dance music. On tracks like Dem 2's remix of Cloud 9's 'Do You Want Me' or Colors featuring Stephen Emmanuel's 'Hold On (SE22 Mix)', the vocal – a paroxysm of hairtrigger blurts and stuttered spasms of passion – doesn't resemble a human being so much as an out-of-control desiring-machine. What you're hearing is literally cyborg – a human enhanced and altered through symbiosis with technology.

2-step's vocal science has intersected with the anti-naturalistic studio techniques of American R&B, whose producers have long been digitally processing vocals to make them sound even more mellifluous and diabetically ultra-sweet. US R&B tunes are routinely given a 2-step remix these days. Two early, superior examples are The Dreem Teem's sublime transformation of Amira's 'My Desire' into a gamelan-tinkling tumble of undulant percussion, and the sultry menace of First Steps' remix of 'Telefunkin'' by British diva-wannabes N-Tyce. Alongside such official remixes, there's been a spate of bootleg revamps of R&B

anthems like Jodeci's 'Freak 'N You'. The heavy-rotation pirate smash of 1999 is Architechs' unofficial 2-step remix of Brandy & Monica's 'The Boy is Mine', which resurrects hardcore's infamous sped-up chipmunk vocals by whipping the duetting divas into a creamy warble of wobbly, high-pitched melisma. But 2-step's favourite R&B goddess is Aaliyah, whose Timbaland-produced 'One in a Million' has been extensively pillaged. Best of the bunch is Groove Chronicles' 'Stone Cold', which samples a handful of vocal phrases ('you don't know / what you do to me', 'desire', and other splinters of yearning) and deploys them to create endlessly fresh accents against the groove. The original song's mood is totally subverted: what had been a devotional paean becomes a baleful ballad of sexual dependency, with Aaliyah digitally dis-integrated into a multi-tracked wraith of herself, stranded in a locked groove of desolated desire.

* * *

Hang out at a garage shop like Rhythm Division in East London, and chances are you'll hear one of the blokes behind the counter say 'the girls love that one' in reference to certain tracks – like Doolally's Top 20 hit 'Straight From the Heart' or the duo's pirate smash/UK Number 1 'Sweet Like Chocolate', released as Shanks & Bigfoot. In most dance scenes, this comment would be a diss. Take the unwritten boy's own constitutions of techno and drum & bass, where overt melody, explicit emotion and recognizably human feelings are regarded as 'cheesy', conventionally poppy – in a word, *girly*. For the UK garage scene, though, 'the girls love that tune' is a recommendation. There's a striking deference to female taste. Pirate DJs dedicate tunes 'to the ladies' massive'. And most DJ/producers share Ramsey & Fen's opinion: 'When the girls start singing along to a tune like our own "Love Bug", it gets the guys hyper! If the ladies love it, they all love it.'

Feminine Pressure is the name of an all-female garage DJ crew. In a very real sense, UK garage is organized around the pressure of feminine desire; a key factor in the scene's emergence was when women defected en masse from the junglist dancefloor, fed up with the melody-and-vocal-devoid bombast of techstep. 2-step garage bears the same relation to jungle that lover's rock did to dub reggae: it's the feminized counterpart of a 'serious' male genre. Like 2-step, lover's rock was a UK-spawned hybrid of silky US soul and Jamaican rhythm, that restored treble to the bass-heavy frequency spectrum and replaced militant spirituality with romantic yearning. Pirate MCs send out shouts to couples cuddling at home ('or even engaged in horizontal activities'). The mic' chat can get seriously lewd, in the beyond-suggestive, explicit style of modern R&B; on one station I heard an MC rap 'to the ladies, undo my zip / and you'll find I'm well equipped'! There's even a pirate station called Erotic FM.

2-step is lover's jungle; it's also hardcore for grown-ups. Ravers who were teenagers during the 1989–92 era are now in their mid-to-late twenties, with jobs, marriages, even kids. At Rhythm Division, I saw a guy behind the counter bottle-feeding a six-month-old baby, who seemed utterly unperturbed by the thunderous B-lines booming out of the speakers; later that day I picked up a flyer for a club that boasted it was 'the very first rave with a genuine crèche for the children – with registered child minders, 5 quid per child. So there's no excuse, bring the fucking kids.' Rather than abandon the drug-and-dance lifestyle, the first rave generation is finding ways to accommodate it to their new adult circumstances – coupledom, relative affluence. The garage remakes of hardcore tunes like Jonny L's 'Hurt You So', the samples from Shut Up And Dance's 1989 '£10 to Get In' redeployed in Some Treat's 2-step anthem 'Lost in Vegas' – these represent not so much old skool nostalgia as a celebration of continuity. Hardcore to 2-step, the subcultural infrastructure of pirate radio/specialist record stores/dubplates/etc. abides. The dress code, crowd rituals, and other elements have evolved; MCs , for instance, now superimpose a smoov R&B patina over the junglist's creole hybrid of ragga patois and Cockney patter. But the subcultural project is the same as it ever was: the creation of 'vibe'.

'Vibe' is UK garage's biggest buzzword – from Aftershock's classic 'Slave to the Vibe (Dem 2 Remix)' to garage dons Tuff Jam's 'Unda-Vybe' remixes, from MC chants like 'I've got the vibe to make you hyper' to Da Click's 'Good Rhymes', an MC-anthem that culminates with a rollcall of the scene's key players, all of whom 'got the vibe'. But isn't 'vibe' just one of those nebulous buzzwords, like 'street' or 'real', used to evoke blackness? Yes, but it's also what everyone (except maybe chronic hermits or Detroitphiles) are looking for from music: that palpable forcefield of tribal energy generated by the perfect convergence of music, drugs, technology and popular desire.

'Vibe' works through evolution rather than revolution: producers simultaneously giving the people what they want and slyly seducing them into wanting things they've never had; DJs pulling off the same trick through sheer sleight of mix, all the while carefully avoiding a lapse into disparate (vibe-less) eclecticism. And 'vibe' only really occurs when music is a component in a subcultural engine, an urban folkway with its own privileged sites and rites. Its musical methodology may be postmodern, but 2-step garage has no truck with techno notions of the post-geographical or transcending the local – hence the recurrent variations on the old hardcore themes 'just 4 U London' and 'London sum'ting dis'. Like jungle, 2-step is heard at its utmost through a big sound-system, by a body surrounded by other bodies (the massive). Which is why 2-step, like most hardcore dance styles, can sometimes sound flat when heard as an isolated twelve-inch, outside the DJ's mix, without MC chat or the participatory clamour of the audience. If you want to 'catch the feeling', the next best thing to being there is to tape pirate radio transmissions for free; third best is buying a mix-CD like the Ramsey & Fen mixed *Locked On, Volume 3*, probably the finest introduction to the full span of UK garage.

* * *

Compared with the anhedonic severity of its estranged cousin drum & bass, one of the most striking things about speed garage is the scene's relentless emphasis on pleasure. The names of clubs, labels and pirate stations evoke melt-in-your-mouth, sensuous indulgence – Cookies & Cream, Nice N' Ripe, Chocolate Boy, Ice Cream, Pure Silk, Twice As Nice, Bliss, Lush FM – and mirror the sonic penchant for warm, organic textures and thick, succulent production. Garage's fetish for 'niceness' and luxury – champagne-and-cocaine, designer labels, 'rude bimmers' – has a long history in Black British dance culture, going back to the pre-rave dancehall and R&B scenes. The most charitable reading of such 'living large' is that it's a refusal of your allotted place in the class system, an insistence that 'nothing's too good for us'. A more hostile viewpoint would argue that garage's opulence is mere hyper-conformism, deluded mimicry of the high life.

Either way, cocaine is the perfect signifier for garage's ambivalent politics – not only because of its associations with prestige, but because it's a drug that stimulates the appetite for all pleasures, and because the dynamics of its use (insatiability, basically) offer a kind of parody of consumerism. Sonically, garage seems to fit cocaine like a glove: the playa-pleasing patina of deluxe sound, the fidgety, febrile beats that feel itchy with desire. The 'cocaine ear' favours bright, toppy sounds – hence garage's harsh glare of crisp hi-hats, shrill brass, glossy synths and trebley vocals.

Horny-making coke has changed the vibe in other ways, encouraging a return to the sexed-up, dressed-up mores of pre-rave clubland. The shift from Ecstasy to cocaine represents a kind of Fall from paradise, with rave's androgynous asexuality displaced by re-polarized gender roles and rapacious sexuality. And although the standard image of the coke-head is of a chatterbox who finds himself endlessly charming, the effect in clubland has been to replace loved-up bonhomie with charlied-up hauteur. 'On coke, you don't feel the need to talk cos you've got so much brilliance within yourself,' says Bethan Cole. 'But there's no E-like empathy, it's a hollow feeling.' You can feel the difference in the music – the gaseous diva vocals of hardcore mirrored the swoony, boundary-melting intimacy of Ecstasy; 2-step's staccato vocal stabs accentuate coke's cold, brittle glitter.

Drug phenomenologist David Lenson describes almost too vividly the 'third stage' of cocaine intoxication, 'hypersexuality', a frenzy in which desire is unable to focus on any single object (kinky sex, grandiose fantasies, other drugs) for more than a few seconds before flitting off elsewhere. Ultimately, the mania fixates on cocaine itself – desire-for-desire. Not far beyond hypersexuality lies the paranoia and undead delirium of 'stimulant dysphoria'. Whether anybody on the garage dancefloor regularly reaches hypersexuality is beside the point – the music's own internal dynamic is pushing it into the twilight zone. Often hidden on B-sides or released on white labels that circulate for only a few weeks, 2-step is producing some fiendishly fucked-up tunes that merge twisted vocals, convulsively DJ-unfriendly beats, and svelte-but-sinister textures. Easier-to-find pinnacles of darkside garage include DJ Richie & Klasse's 'Madness on the Street', productions by Skycap like their '97 classic 'Endorphin', and 'Plenty More' b/w 'Get It' by rising producer Chris Mac – tracks whose unsettling blend of brittle and supple, desperation and desire, show how the pursuit of pure pleasure can take music to some pretty strange places. Dem 2 also look set to probe 'a darker, deeper electro direction' in 1999, what Dean Boylan describes as 'Gary Numan meets Tina Moore'; the duo are also starting an overtly experimental label called Purple Orange. For now, check their alter-ego US Alliance's 'Grunge Dub', with its angular anti-groove and gibbering, strung-out vocal (like a crackhead Bobby McFerrin).

The original 1993 darkside hardcore was a catastrophic plunge, the first rave generation succumbing to E-induced malaise en masse. With garage, though, it's more like 'darkness' is a normalized component of the scene, a zone some cross into if they overdo the stimulants, perhaps even a phase of any given club night (after 4 a.m., say, when some of the clientele has crossed the optimal threshold of enjoyable wired-ness, or reaches a weekly apprehension of the void at the heart of the hedonistic lifestyle). In fact, dark garage existed right from the earliest days of the London scene. K.M.A.'s 'Cape Fear' combined breakbeat rhythms, ominous 'video vocals', and destabilizing 'bass warps' that triggered crowd pandemonium the very first time the tune was played out, in late '96. 'You could see the goosebumps rising on everybody's neck, the hair standing on end,' says K.M.A. producer/vocalist Six. 'The crowd erupted, they were so confused about what just happened they forced the DJ to rewind the track.'

The anecdote recalls the early stunned responses to the body-baffling pitchshifted beats in 'Terminator', the Goldie tune that pioneered darkcore. Six talks like Goldie, declaring 'my music is like a movie' and 'I see myself as a painter, a surrealist painter'. After following 'Cape Fear' with another moody, breakbeat garage anthem, 'Kaotic Madness', Six tired of K.M.A.'s darkside reputation and decided to go in a smoother, more 'musical' direction – just like Goldie did circa 'Angel'. The result was 'Re-Con Mission EP', whose highlight track 'Blue Kards' meshed disjointed emotions, phased vocals, bluesy guitar, and asymmetrical beats to create one of 1998's most exhilarating sonic (con)fusions. What's exciting about 'Blue Kards' and the other dark 2-step tunes that have surfaced in the last year is that the music often sounds like a hybrid where the grafts haven't wholly congealed. Sometimes, it sounds 'wrong', but only in the way that 1993 darkcore sounded not-quite-there-yet. If you want seamless, fully-realized fusion, listen to drum & bass, a style that has arrived at a definitive version of itself and accordingly spent the last two years scratching its head wondering where to go next. 2-step sounds like it has a whole world of places left to go.

The Wire, April 1999

For a good two or three years back there, 2-step was *the thing* for me, one of those ultimate musics that hits all your buttons. Its vital balance of elements recalled the glory days of hardcore and jungle: futurism vs tradition, tracks vs songs, dark and light, masculine and feminine, bass and treble. The latter was particularly crucial: the genre's big innovation was its discovery that extreme treble can be as intense as extreme bass. The sensation induced by all the high-pitched melisma, pizzicato strings-y sounds, and sheer production gloss was head-spinningly effervescent, as though you had champagne running through your veins instead of blood. Then again, that's an old 'ardkore trick: cut the mid-range, drop the bass *and* boost the treble. Like hardcore at its height, 2-step was POPtastic. But at the time of writing this piece, early 1999, give or take a few medium-sized hits, 2-step had yet to really break out of the underground; it was like pop music in waiting, exiled, poised on the threshold of the mainstream. By the end of that year, though, and all through 2000, 2-step completely dominated the UK charts – an exhilarating anschluss, even for someone watching from the opposite side of the Atlantic, like myself.

The on-line re-incarnation of this piece originally came with insanely extensive footnotes, mostly pursuing myriad threads of minutiae, but a few thoughts seem worth resurrecting here. The first is that around this time I started to feel a bit like an ethnomusicologist, someone documenting the folkways of a 'vibe-tribe' (to borrow a song title from hardcore heroes Phuture Assassins). In my case, I was one of those anthropologists who live with the tribe and get too emotionally involved, compromising their objectivity. The other thoughts relate to cocaine. I read about how central nervous system stimulants, when heavily abused, can cause a delusion that insects are crawling under your skin, and this just reminded me of the itchy-and-scratchy anxiousness of 2-step, its percussive tics and chitters. Reputedly cocaine use is also often accompanied by an obsessive-compulsive attentiveness to *small things*, which might explain the miniaturization of detail in 2-step production, its micro-rhythmic clicks and finessed intricacies.

KING AND QUEEN OF THE BEATS

Timbaland and Missy Elliott

Although history tends to focus on glamorous vocalists and visionary songwriters with something to say, black pop's evolution is as much about changes in rhythm and production. From the house sounds of Motown and Philadelphia International to the Chic Organization's streamlined disco style and George Clinton's mini-empire of funk bands, it's a history made not by sacred cow artists but by session musicians and backroom technicians: musicians, producers, arrangers, engineers and, not least, their machines.

Typically, an up and coming producer taps some unforeseen potential in the latest technology and, for a couple of years, rewrites the rules of rhythm. In the mid-eighties, Janet Jackson's producers Jimmy Jam and Terry Lewis drafted a new blueprint for dance pop, using drum machine beats and synthesized basslines to build angular, abrasive grooves. By the end of that decade, producer Teddy Riley installed a new paradigm, marrying R&B's mellifluous melodies with hip hop's aggressive beats and sampled loops to create the style known variously as new jack swing or swingbeat.

In the last two years, Timbaland and Missy Elliott have reigned as unchallenged king and queen of the beats. Producing and writing for a stable of protégés that includes Aaliyah, Ginuwine, Nicole, Total and Playa, they have scored a run of hugely successful smash singles on both the R&B and pop charts. Missy Elliott has also written hits for artists like Brandy, Mariah Carey, SWV and Whitney Houston, and can reportedly demand $100,000 per song. Ruling producers have hitherto tended to remain behind the scenes (Jam & Lewis) or subsume themselves in a band identity (Teddy Riley now operates as part of the harmony group Blackstreet). But

Timbaland and Missy Elliott have pushed themselves forward as stars. Timbaland released a collaboration with rapper Magoo called *Welcome to Our World* in 1997 and a solo album proper late last year; Missy Elliott has just released her second album *Da Real World*, the sequel to 1997's platinum selling, Grammy-nominated *Supa Dupa Fly*.

The real testament to Timbaland and Elliott's hegemony, though, is the massive influence they've had on other R&B and rap artists. If imitation is the sincerest form of flattery, the duo ought to be feeling pretty good about themselves. Instead, they seem rather embattled. Only a few minutes into *Da Real World*, Elliott is lambasting all the producers who have copied Timbaland's distinctive jittery beats and stop-start grooves: 'beat biter, dope style taker . . . you just an imitator, stealing our beats like you're the one who made them'. That style really came together on Aaliyah's late 1996 hit 'One in a Million', which was written by Elliott, produced by Timbaland, and typifies their collaborations in the way the beat is as hooky as the melody. A ballad built around a push-me-pull-you groove, the song introduced many of Timbaland's trademark tricks: syncopated bass drums stuttering in triple-time spasms, irregular flurries of hi-hats, and skittery snares. As with earlier rhythmic innovations, from seventies funk to nineties jungle, the Timbaland sound practically enforces a new kind of dancing, full of twitches, jerks and tics. You can see it in Missy Elliott's videos like 'Beep Me 911' and the current 'She's a Bitch', where the choreography resembles a kind of geometrically precise epilepsy and sometimes recalls the body-popping style of eighties breakdancing.

Alongside their massive influence on American R&B, Timbaland's twitchy beats have caught the ear of British electronica artists. On their new album *Surrender*, The Chemical Brothers sampled a vocal hook from Nicole & Missy Elliott's 'Make it Hot' for their track 'Music: Response', transforming the sexual come-on of 'I got whatcha want / I got whatcha need' into a DJ's boast. In London, a whole scene and sound has emerged called 2-step, based around the merger of Timbaland's hyper-syncopated drums with jungle's booming bass and house's succulent synth licks. The respect that Timbaland and Missy Elliott have received in the electronica field shows that although the duo are classified as R&B, their skills at digitally manipulating rhythms and creating eerie sounds make them among the most accomplished and innovative electronic artists on the planet. Indeed, critics have long suggested that Timbaland's asymmetrical grooves owe something to jungle; Timbaland has denied this, but does give the nod to electronic artists like Prodigy, Tricky and Bjork, whom he's sampled a couple of times.

Like techno artists, Timbaland and Elliott are obsessed with the future. They are determined that their records sound avant-garde and futuristic, and they're infatuated with special-effects-laden science fiction movies like *The Matrix*. The title of Missy Elliott's new album comes from a pivotal line of dialogue in *The Matrix*: 'welcome to the real world'. Both Missy's music and her Hype Williams-produced videos have a hallucinatory quality. *Supa Dupa Fly* is a shapeshifting phantasmagoria of sampled sound, where unlikely sources (baby's gurgles, birdsong, insect-like chitters, horse whinnies and dog barks) are transformed into polyrhythmic devices. Listen closely, and beats turn out to be made from gasps or giggles, and a bassline is moulded from the human voice. It's headphone R&B, and like electronica, it's most inventive on the level of rhythm and texture, rather than songcraft. 'Hooks on songs are more major than verses. People hardly remember verses,' Elliott told rap magazine *The Source*. For the most part, Elliott's vocal hooks are delivered in a style midway between singing and rapping, and generally work percussively as much as melodically. She specializes in devising complex vocal arrangements that interlock with the rhythm tracks like cogs. Timbaland and Elliott also pepper their tracks with tiny, almost subliminal vocal riffs – onomatopoeic noises and nonsense chants, half-spoken ad libs – which add to the rhythmic density of the music.

Da Real World arrives at a critical moment for the Elliott/Timbaland dynasty, when the duo's influence remains endemic but their own momentum shows signs of flagging. They've maintained their profile in 1999 with Elliott penning the R&B smash 'Where My Girls At?' for diva trio 702 and Timbaland producing Ginuwine's second album and the hit track 'Jigga What?' for rapper Jay-Z. But Timbaland's solo album was generally received as a disappointment, and some wonder if his production skills peaked with last year's astonishing Aaliyah hit 'Are You That Somebody?'. It's an abiding dilemma for pop innovators. Do you repeat what was so successful before at the risk of adding your own self-plagiarism to the melee of clones and copyists? Or do you struggle for self-reinvention at the risk of alienating your audience? This quandary has undone many artists in the past. Synth-pop pioneers Kraftwerk, for instance, became paralysed by the enormity of their own influence and the challenge of staying ahead of the state-of-art.

Da Real World sees Elliott and Timbaland struggling to come up with fresh twists to their formula. Sonically, *Da Real World* marks a shift to a harsher sound that Timbaland has called 'real dark, real ghetto'. The new style includes bombastic quasi-orchestral riffs, booming sub-bass, and stiff, angular beats, all of which sometimes recall Curtis Mantronik's productions for T. La Rock and Mantronix in the late eighties, but is more likely a nod to the current popularity of New Orleans bounce, an electro-influenced style of rap. Persona-wise, Elliott has swapped the playfulness of *Supa Dupa Fly* for a pugnacious 'street' attitude and a dramatically increased level of profanity. Abandoning *Supa*'s kooky surrealism and free associational lyrics, Elliott has penned a series of tough-talking songs: 'You Don't Know' threatens a girl who's trying to steal her man, 'All 'N My Grill' reprimands a deadbeat live-in lover who won't pay his way and 'Hot Boyz' is a hormone-crazed paean to sexy roughnecks who tote machine guns, flex Platinum Visa cards and drive expensive jeeps. The harder, ghetto-centric sound and lyrics smack somewhat of a calculated attempt at repositioning Elliott in a market where 'real-ness' is back in favour thanks to rappers like DMX and Jay-Z.

Coming from a debut artist, *Da Real World* would be garlanded with acclaim. But given the expectation that Missy and Timbaland would rewrite the rules of R&B again, the album is anti-climactic. *Da Real World* peaked at Number 10 on the pop charts and rapidly slid to Number 22. Furthermore, Missy Elliott's audience seem unconvinced or, worse, alienated by her image tweak. The first single off the album, 'She's a Bitch' – a strained and tuneless attempt to project bad attitude, with a baleful monochrome video markedly different from the polychromatic psychedelia of the earlier promos – only reached Number 30 on the R&B charts. For an artist of Missy Elliott's stature and track record, that's a flop.

But then the rap and R&B marketplace is cruel even by pop standards; brand loyalty barely exists, artists are only as hot as their latest track. So are Missy and Timbaland going to go the way of other ex-pioneers, like Jam & Lewis? Elliott has her own major label-funded imprint Gold Mind and a long line of protégés waiting in the wings. Timbaland might want to consider a strategic retreat from the spotlight in order to concentrate on crafting tunes for his proven hitmakers Ginuwine and Aaliyah, and to R&D some new gimmicks (he's talked about creating beats built from the sound of a stylus skipping on a scratched record). Perhaps the greatest solace for the duo is that there's no powerhouse producer threatening to usurp their throne. (Although there might have been a hint of Oedipal anxiety when Timbaland recently gave his seal of approval to a young pretender: Swizz Beatz, who's crafted beats for Jay-Z and for his own outfit Ruff Ryders). At the moment, there's an interregnum in R&B – everyone's waiting for the new king of the beats to take over.

Director's cut of piece published in the
New York Times, 1 August 1999

Swizz Beatz did indeed have a large moment there – Eve's slinky, sultry 'What Ya Want' and 'Gotta Man' eclipsed 'She's a Bitch' that summer of 1999, while hits from DMX and The Lox showcased Swizz's more typical sound, a crude-but-effective formula of muddy bass thump, kickdrums like low blows and nagging sub-melodic hooks played on cheap-and-nasty digital synths that gave off the clinical whiff of eighties pulp movie soundtracks, videogame muzik and ring-tones. But the real challenge came with the rise of the Neptunes – Pharrell Williams and Chad Hugo, who were once in a band with their Virginia Beach neighbour Timbaland. Now they jostled with the podgy producer for control of the Black American BeatGeist, pushing a stiff, starker style that harked back to eighties electro's drum machine sound without ever seeming explicitly retro. On tracks like The Clipse's 'Grindin'', The Neptunes got *this close* to ungroovy rigor mortis and utter non-musicality but still managed to swing. Timbaland refused to be ousted from the throne, though, producing hit after hit, if nothing quite as landmark or rulebook-shredding as 'One in a Million' and 'Are You That Somebody' (he talked in interviews about using Aaliyah as a 'probe', a way of testing out his most extreme ideas). In 2006 he was widely hailed as Artist of the Year (for his production of Justin Timberlake and Nelly Furtado) although this really said more about chart pop's dearth of invention and spark than Timberland having scaled new heights. Missy Elliott likewise survived the stumble of *Da Real World*, triumphing with 'Get UR Freak On', 'Work It' and many more, and remaining wealthy enough to fritter her fortune on expensive customized sneakers worn for just one day before she discarded them.

HATE ME NOW

Puff Daddy and the Player Hater Syndrome

A couple of songs into Puff Daddy's new album *Forever* there's a comic interlude, a skit about people phoning the 'Player-Haters Anonymous Hotline'. One caller confesses that he's fallen off the wagon and has been 'hatin' today . . . all week as a matter of fact'. Another, distraught and at the end of his tether, warns the hotline counsellor that he's got a key in his hand and is on the verge of scratching 'this motherfucker's Bentley'.

The rapper CJ Mac's new album *Platinum Game* features the comedy interlude 'Hating Game', a spoof on the television show 'The Dating Game' in which each contestant is asked how he would react if he discovered his woman in flagrante delicto with CJ Mac. And on her debut album *Ruff Ryders' First Lady*, Eve, goes one step further with the parody track 'My Enemies', in which she mocks the trend of songs about players and player-haters itself.

The 'player', a sort of dandy megalomaniac, and the 'player-hater', the non-entity who resents the player's ostentatiously opulent lifestyle, are twinned concepts that have dominated the imagination of mainstream rap for the last few years. The player persona was originally codified and popularized by The Notorious B.I.G. – real name Christopher Wallace – the rap star who was murdered in a drive-by shooting in 1997 and who is the main cash-cow of Puff Daddy's label, Bad Boy Entertainment. Player signifies a top dog, the big shot who calls the shots. But it also evokes the idea of a playboy, someone who visibly basks in the wealth and prestige of being a winner. Where that earlier archetype of rap masculinity, the gangsta, focused on the means of wealth production (crime) and all its drawbacks (paranoia, the constant possibility of death), player-oriented rap emphasizes the leisure and pleasure aspects of the lifestyle: the fine women, the conspicuous consumption of luxury goods, the clique-ishness of associates and hangers-on. The realities of where the 'paper' – slang for money – comes from are deliberately kept hazy; the player might be a hustler, a wheeler-dealer businessman or an entertainer, it doesn't really matter.

What does count is being seen to be living large, which is what The Notorious B.I.G. communicated so successfully in the videos for the hit singles from his 1994 debut album *Ready to Die*. In the videos for hits like 'One More Chance' and 'Juicy', The Notorious B.I.G. is the epi-centre of a Hugh Hefneresque milieu in which champagne is sipped like soda and white accountants discreetly handle B.I.G.'s business affairs leaving him free to . . . play. Into this Eden of languid luxury crept trouble, though, in the snake-like form of the player-hater. In hip hop parlance, to 'hate on' somebody is to resent, envy, badmouth and scheme against. Following the initial massive success of The Notorious B.I.G., subsequent Bad Boy releases increasingly conjured a vision of player-haters as a swarming mass of green-eyed small fry.

Notorious B.I.G.'s second album, 1997's *Life After Death*, acknowl-edged this one drawback to the player lifestyle with songs like 'Mo Money Mo Problems' and 'Playa Hater', while Puff Daddy's debut *No Way Out* featured 'Been Around the World', with its boastful chorus 'been around the world / and I been player-hated'. On *Harlem World*, the debut by Ma$e (Bad Boy's Notorious B.I.G. surrogate), player-haters became a dominant lyrical topic with songs and skits like 'Lookin' at Me', 'Wanna Hurt Ma$e?', 'Hater' and 'Niggaz Wanna Act'. The closing 'Jealous Guy' sees Ma$e hoarsely crooning a rule from his 'New Pimp Testament' – 'you can't be a player, and hate the players – that don't make no sense', which translates as only losers feel bitter towards winners.

Although Bad Boy's commercial success and influence on hip hop peaked at the end of 1997, the player-hater concept coined by the label has continued to proliferate through the rap scene like a virus. Examples from this year include Nas's 'Hate Me Now', Big Hutch's 'Player Hater', B.G.'s 'Don't Hate Me' and Tear Da Club Thugs' 'Why Ya Hatin'?' as well as albums like Willie D's *Loved By Few, Hated By Many*. The Beatnuts' current hit 'Watch Out Now' jeers 'you wanna hate me / cause your wife wants an autograph / from the look in her eyes I can see she wants more than that'. According to the player's twisted logic, stealing other men's women is just what players do. It's the cuckold who is being perverse by begrudging the player for doing what comes naturally, what the cuckold would do if he was in the player's shoes.

Player-hating is bizarrely similar to Nietzsche's concept of ressentiment: the hostility of the oppressed towards their superiors. He diagnosed and denigrated those feelings as mere self-defeating rancour and impotent rage. The difference is that the hip hop player is a self-made aristocrat, a former member of the underclass who's raised himself from its ranks and seized his chance to 'shine'. The ressentiment of those you have left behind is an integral element of the player fantasy. Indeed a retinue of haters is an essential accoutrement of success, just another status symbol alongside the Versace furs, platinum Rolexes, Mercedes Benzes, diamond-encrusted jewellery and endlessly flowing Cristal and Hennessy. Because Puff Daddy represents himself as the ultimate player, a sort of hip hop Donald Trump and 'black Sinatra' rolled into one, it figures that he's got to have the most haters. Moving well beyond the lighthearted jibes at player-haters on his debut album, *Forever* presents a beleaguered Puffy, bewildered and wounded by the resentment stirred up by his relentless rubbing of his success in the world's face.

On the album's bombastic intro track, he declaims: 'I will look in triumph at those who hate me . . . Though hostile nations surround me, I destroy them all in the name of Lord.' This mogul-as-martyr shtick climaxes with a direct quote from Jesus as he's being crucified: 'Lord forgive them, for they know not what they do.' It's not the only time on *Forever* that Puffy compares himself to Christ; one song includes the line 'I'm on the run like Jesus'. What's striking about these messianic allusions is that earlier this year Combs got into serious trouble in a dispute that involved a similar self-identification with Jesus Christ. As a guest-rapper on Nas's player-hater-themed single 'Hate Me Now', he consented to be filmed for scenes in the video of the two rappers being crucified. Regretting this decision, he asked Nas's manager Steve Stoute to remove the crucifixion imagery before it was aired. When the video was shown on television unchanged, an enraged Puff Daddy and two of his minions visited Mr Stoute in his office on 15 April, and roughed him up. Although no charges were pressed by the victim and accounts of the incident conflict, the Manhattan District Attorney's office is still considering prosecution.

If he doesn't actually believe he's Christ, Puff Daddy reckons he's pretty tight with him – judging by 'Best Friend', a bizarre and saccharine serenade to Jesus that samples Christopher Cross's sentimental soft rock ballad 'Sailing' and uses the gospel backing vocals of the Love Fellowship Choir. It's one of *Forever*'s few glints of joy. Unlike Bad Boy's earlier pleasure-centred albums, *Forever* makes the player's life seem like a trudge through a vale of blood, sweat, and tears. What exactly does a twenty-nine-year-old tycoon with an East Hampton mansion and a many-tentacled business empire (including record, management and publishing companies, restaurants, the magazine *Notorious* and the Sean John clothing line) have to complain about? Mostly, it's those pesky player-haters. When Puff Daddy's not boasting, he's bleating: in 'What You Want', about hangers-on who hang out with him only for the reflected glory, about 'bitches, hands out, grabbing / niggers, hating, scheming, and backstabbing'. In the catchy 'Do You Like It . . . Do You Want It', Puff Daddy discovers a new woe of the over-achiever: the ennui of those whose triumphs come so thick and fast that victory is no longer a thrill. 'Where do you go from here when you've felt you've done it all / When what used to get you high don't get you high no more? . . . When you expected to win, they ain't surprised no more?'

As the album proceeds, Puffy's paranoia escalates. In 'Is This the End', he describes himself as an enemy of the state over a backing track that sounds as frantic as a panic attack, while 'Reverse' dramatizes a defiant Puffy as 'me against a million, billion of y'all motherfuckers'. Finally, his persecution complex flowers with the closing track 'PE 2000', a remake of Public Enemy's 1987 classic 'Public Enemy No. 1'. With a video that depicts the rapper pursued by a sinister black helicopter, and lyrics that beseech 'let me ask you what you got against me? / Is it my girl or is it the Bentley?', the song replaces Public Enemy's political militancy with Puffy's trademark blend of self-aggrandizement and self-pity. The original song was the opening salvo and statement of intent in a career that revolutionized hip hop; although they were just starting their career, Public Enemy's paranoia-in-advance was justified, as their controversial opinions were set to make them lightning rods. Posing as a homage, 'PE 2000' might really be an exorcism of Public Enemy's spirit, at a time when the group's political consciousness has been almost totally marginalized from mainstream rap culture. And the hubris of covering the song invites unflattering comparisons: not just between Puff Daddy's weak rapping and self-pity and Chuck D's authoritative cadences and charismatic gravitas, but between the imaginative poverty of the Bad Boy worldview and the Public Enemy vision. Thanks to Bad Boy, but also more gangsta-aligned labels like No Limit and Cash Money, mainstream hip hop has reverted to its pre-1987 days when rapping largely comprised 'talking on myself' (i.e. boasting) and rappers sported gold chains. Jay-Z's current single 'Girl's Best Friend', for instance, is a love song to diamonds.

Where 'Public Enemy No. 1' spoke for the man in the street, 'PE 2000' invites the rap fan to identify with the man cruising in the Silver

Bentley, brooding over the astonishing fact that money and power does not bring peace of mind.

Transforming the eternal war of the players and the player-haters into a monument of kitsch paranoia, *Forever* ought to sound the death knell for the player ethos. But rap fans continue to find vicarious enjoyment in the player fantasy, where being hated is the inevitable price for being one of the few who make it in a system that otherwise guarantees anonymity and poverty for most. This is the fantasy structure of rap in the late nineties, where the top hip hop radio station Hot 97 advertises its own Player's Ball multi-artists concert in between commercials for tele-cash loans by phone ('to help you through tough times . . . payday comes today'), two-for-a-dollar cheeseburgers and anti-heroin ads. In 'Diddy Speaks!', a mawkish, mumbled interlude on *Forever*, Puff anatomizes the mechanism of this fantasy-identification process; he explains that his full-throttle quest for success wasn't just selfish, that he was 'doin' it for all of us'. It's as if he's saying that what really hurts is the ingratitude of the player-haters who have forgotten that he is their representative and stand-in.

Director's cut of piece published in the *New York Times*,
10 October 1999

A meme circulated in hip hop from the late nineties onwards: 'don't hate the player, hate the game'. It's appeared as a lyric in countless rap tunes and as a maxim in innumerable interviews. (See also the related concept, 'game': if you've 'got game' it means you're endowed with mojo, moxie, chutzpah, the seducer's gift of the gab.) 'Hate the game': it's a tiny chink of enlightenment in the wall of false consciousness, just a hair's breadth from saying 'this isn't personal, our conflict is structural, based in systemic and radically dysfunctional unfairness: a competition in which winners are over-rewarded out of all proportion and everybody else is a loser'. And maybe two hairs' breadth from saying, 'let's change the rules'. Except for the (self) confidence trick that keeps on being pulled: everybody believes, deep down, they can play and win. That ideological sleight is why rap is as American as apple pie and capitalist to the core. It was almost inevitable that a rapper would come along *called* The Game. And when he arrived, a protégé of Dr Dre and 50 Cent, his stardom inevitable . . . it just seemed to seal finally the fact that rap as 'black folks' CNN' (Chuck D) and a movement of emancipation had long been displaced by rap as entertainment industry and as a career structure for self-advancement on the individual rather than collective level. The Game's lyrics were self-reflexively about his career trajectory, his moves. He even caught the collective → individual shift with his song 'Dreams', which equated the civil rights movement with his own 'war to be a rap legend': 'Martin Luther King had a DREAM / Aaliyah had a DREAM . . . So I reached out to Kanye and I brought you all my dreams.' Still, we should thank him really, because for once it was possible to hate the player *and* the Game.

FOR THE LOVE OF MONEY

Lil Wayne, Cash Money and New Orleans Rap

Two words say almost everything you need to know about Cash Money, the New Orleans label that has pretty much ruled rap in 1999: Mannie Fresh. Not just because he's the producer who programs, engineers and plays nearly every instrument on records by the Cash Money roster (Juvenile, B.G., Big Tymers, Hot Boys and Lil Wayne). But also because the surname Fresh is like a flashback to the old skool era. 'RZA said that in the South, we was still livin' like it's 1985,' Juvenile told *Rolling Stone*. 'At first I was pissed off, but you know what? In a way, it's kinda true.'

Fresh's sound returns to that point in the mid-eighties just before rap was totally transformed by digital technology, and imagines a sort of 'What if . . .?' alternative future where drum machines and synths, rather than looped breakbeats and sampled licks, remained hip hop's building blocks. This alternative future is actually what transpired as reality throughout much of the South. The brittle rigor of 'Planet Rock' electro, traded in by New York rap producers in favour of sampler-assisted retro-funk fluency, survived and thrived as Miami Bass and New Orleans Bounce – party-oriented styles organized around 808 bass-booms, call-and-response chants, and crisp 'n' dry programmed beats.

Like its Crescent City rival No Limit, Cash Money has gone from local hero status to nationwide dominion by merging bounce-influenced rhythms with gangsta rap. The bounce element is what gives Fresh's drum programming its hop, skip and bump – those rat-a-tat-tat snare rolls and double-time hi-hats that feel simultaneously frisky and martial. He's effectively using drum machines to build his own brand-new breakbeats, rather than depleting further the exhausted seam of archival seventies funk. But although he doesn't sample, Fresh is into surreptitious plagiarism, ripping off everything from S.O.S. Band rhythm patterns to lite-classical's pantheon of schlock. I wouldn't be surprised if Fresh's tinny toy-synth renditions of over-familiar melodies are inspired by cell phones that offer a select-your-favourite-ringing-sound range of Mozart/Chopin/Tchaikovsky-type themes.

Alongside Fresh's sly steals and his manifest drum-machine virtuosity, there's another factor that gives Cash Money records their edge over No Limit's. At first I thought I was hallucinating the reverb-smudged Balearic house piano in Juvenile's 'Spittin Game', the brief burst of Roland 303 acid house bass-wibble in Lil Wayne's 'Loud Pipes'. But no, it turns out that Fresh used to work with legendary Chicago house producer Steve 'Silk' Hurley. Which helps explain the eerie technoid flavour of Juvenile's 'Ha' and B.G.'s 'Dog Ass', and the spectral echoes elsewhere of early Todd Terry, Belgian hardcore, Sheffield bleep 'n' bass, hip-house, Uberzone. (In fact, a bizarre, unacknowledged convergence took place between rave and hip hop/R&B this year, audible in the snaky techno-pulse writhing inside Ja Rule's 'Holla Holla', in the angular stab-riffs driving Ginuwine's 'What's So Different' and Destiny's Child's 'Bugaboo'.)

From the tinkling timbales in 'High Beamin'' to the jungle-at-mid-tempo mashed snares of 'Remember Me', the rhythm programming on Lil Wayne's debut album *Tha Block Is Hot* (Cash Money/Universal) is like a drum choir – precise yet joyous, a symphony of syncopation. Overall, *Tha Block* is Fresh's most accomplished and intricate production so far, so riddled with stereopanning subtleties and sonic witticisms it verges on 'headphone bounce'. Alongside the mock-classical flourishes (pseudo-string ostinatos, synth-horn fanfare, harpsichord), there's a pervasive jazz-lite flavour, courtesy of bassist Funky Fingers and Mannie Fresh's own guitar (at times redolent of the echoplexed ripple of folkadelic minstrel John Martyn, or the plangent lacework doilies spun by ECM jazzbos Ralph Towner and John Abercrombie). This relaxed, jazzual vibe overlaying the fierce beats reminds me of when jungle tried to go all 'musical' and 'intelligent'. It exudes a sort of cheap expensiveness, a nouveau riche sheen. And in this context, that's perfect, because Cash Money is – no duh! – all about the Benjamins, baby.

Mercenary and aesthetic impulses have never been at odds in black pop; you can't map white bohemian complexes about materialism on to breadhead seers and business-savvy anarcho-surrealist shamans like Lee Perry and George Clinton. Indeed, 'getting paid' has a sort of liberating charge in itself, given the history of black artists being short-changed and swindled by the white music biz. Which is why it's not just Cash Money founders Ron and Brian Williams, plus friends and family, who are buzzed by the label's $30 million distribution deal with Universal – a pact that allows Cash Money to retain ownership of its recordings.

Still and all, there's something faintly disheartening about the fact that the Cash Money worldview is fundamentally no different from Schoolly D back in 1986. The terminology goes through subtle inflections (gangsta □ playa- □ thug □ baller) but the underlying arche-type abides: Stagger Lee, the sexy sociopath who recognizes no limits to desire. Cash Money have popularized their own term, or at least one filched from a group of 'gangsta-ass, killin'-ass niggaz' attending their shows: the 'hot boy'. Gold-mouthed, FUBU-clad, ice-wristed, camou-flage bandanna-sporting, untamed. One measure of the term's currency is Missy Elliott's lust-stricken thug paean 'Hot Boys', *Da Real World*'s best track and effectively a free radio advert for the Cash Money super-group Hot Boys (Juvenile, B.G., Lil Wayne and Young Turk).

Since the label's rappers appear on one another's records in all manner of multiple cameo pile-ups (no guests from other labels, though – why bother boosting non-clan members?), every new Cash Money release is essentially another Hot Boys album. Anti-pop fogey Theodor Adorno would have called this 'pseudo-individuation' and 'part-interchangeability'. And Mannie's inexhaustible Fresh-ness aside, you *are* basically buying the same record each time; the lyrics reshuffle a lexical deck – riding Hummers, chasing paper, spilling brains, sipping Henny, bashing heads (a.k.a. splitting wigs!), wifey-stealing, flossing, twenty-inch chrome rims, choppers (AK-47s), blow jobs from avid 'hos – into slightly different patterns. The effect, and possibly the subcon-scious intent, is numbing: murda-Muzak, an ambient moodscape that doesn't melt your defences, but hardens the character armour.

There are a few chinks on *Tha Block Is Hot*, rare glimpses of fragility that suit Wayne's high-pitched, mannish-boy drawl. Breaking his own no-cussin' rule, 'Fuck tha World' is a baby-gangsta's blues, Wayne sounding like Tupac in hoarsely mawkish 'Ain't Mad'/'Dear Mama' mode as he frets about losing his stepdad Rabbit to the gun and fathering his own girl-child, all before his seventeenth birthday. 'Up to Me' is a touching love letter to Rabbit, who taught Wayne 'game' even though he himself lost. Bone Thugs 'n' Harmony-style, Wayne imag-ines meeting his pa at heaven's gate – this, despite Rabbit clearly being no angel and *Tha Block*'s staggering inventory of mortal sins and broken commandments (Thou Shalt Not Leave Your Neighbour's

Wifey 'Tasting My Rubber'). The Hot Boys' *Guerrilla Warfare* also lets the façade of invincibility drop just once, with the uncharacteristically subdued 'Tuesday & Thursday', which advises the smart thug to keep a low profile on days when the police task force is on the warpath.

The forlorn vulnerability and cowed anxiety of these songs stand out all the more because of Cash Money's usual ebullience and exuberance. Strip away the socioeconomic and racial details, and Cash Money's live-for-now voraciousness is sheer Romanticism. When Hot Boys boast 'we on fire', they're speaking the same Dionysian language as nineteenth-century literary critic Walter Pater, who exhorted his readers 'to burn always with this hard gemlike flame'. Mind you, Pater probably didn't have in mind sporting a mansion's worth of diamond and platinum on your wrist. But twentieth-century Romantic Georges Bataille would relish lines like 'my Rottweilers drink Moët', or Wayne bragging about buying Cartier watches for every member of his crew.

Celebrating such wasteful aristocratic pursuits as gambling, dandyism and potlatch (extravagant gift-giving), and denigrating bourgeois thrift and caution, Bataille exalted 'a will to glory' that impels us to 'live like suns, squandering our goods and our life'. His language and hip hop's converge in contemporary rap's highest superlative: 'blazing'. It's the kind of existential incandescence that Jarvis Cocker captured in Pulp's 'Common People', with his image of lusty proles who 'burn so bright and you can only wonder why'. For Cash Money's 'uptown shiners', though, the joie de vivre is edgier – the kind that accompanies being ready to die.

Village Voice, 30 November 1999

'"Getting paid" has a sort of liberating charge in itself' – compare with the uncomprehending comments about Eric B & Rakim's 'Paid in Full' in the Public Enemy interview. It's a long and rocky road to enlightenment, for sure.

Lil Wayne is still going strong: in 2004 he guested on Destiny's Child's 'Soldier' (rapping about how 'Cash Money is an army') and at the end of 2005 released his fifth album, the critically-acclaimed and platinum-selling *Tha Carter II*. He's also majoring in psychology at the university of Houston. In 2006, Lil Wayne cockily claimed that he was now a better MC than Jay Z – and many rap pundits concurred with him. Mannie Fresh parted company with Cash Money in late 2005.

STREET RAP

Ja Rule – 'Holla Holla' (Murder Inc), Snoop Dogg – 'B Please' (No Limit), JT Money – 'Who Dat' (Freeworld/Priority), Cam'Ron – 'Let Me Know' (Untertainmnent), Jay-Z – 'Jigga What' (Rock-A-Fella), Lil Troy – 'Wanna Be a Baller' (Universal), Tru – 'Hoody Hoo' (No Limit), DMX – 'Ruff Ryder's Anthem' (Ruff Ryders)

For some reason, the stuff that sparks me most in current hip hop isn't the 'undie' (indie label/underground) stuff that's supposed to be superior and what someone 'like me' should be into – Quannum, Divine Styler, turntabilism, Mos Def/Black Star, Rawkus. No, it's the tunes that are big on BET (for non-American readers, the black MTV) and Hot 97 (the rap equivalent of KISS FM in London), the singles that have the flash videos and the albums that get glossy double-page adverts in *The Source*. Ruff Ryders, Cash Money, Murder Inc., Violator, Hoo Bangin' . . . the stuff known variously as street, hardcore, gangsta . . . that sells shitloads but isn't really sell-out, crossover pop-rap.

Why? Any or all of the following reasons might apply . . .

(a) The impurism of street rap ('if it works, steal it') guarantees more sonic thrills and surprises than the purism of undie rap. Fidelity to the old skool by definition implies a degree of familiarity and staleness; it's about resurrecting what you loved before, preserving in aspic something that's bygone, been and gone. (Break it down and 'old school' ought logically to signify something pretty unappetizing – 'old', past and past-it; 'school' – a place of detainment and education.) Undie/indie rap's codification of the genre is a denial of the hybridity and makeshift quickwitted opportunism that originally sparked hip hop. Lyrically predictable and repetitious (not to mention offensive, nihilistic, socially irresponsible and in thrall to false consciousness), street rap generates more sonic surprises than

240

undieground rap, perhaps because it has to be responsive to the motility of popular desire, rather than to a definition of what proper hip hop is.

(b) There's an off-putting connoisseurial vibe to the indie-rap milieu – the encrypted lyrics, the oblique scansion, the fetishization of 'flow'. Rather than being the artistically valid and spiritually solvent alternative to gangsta rap's bankruptcy, undie rap's lofty aura is really just another male superiority complex. It's 'look how deep I am' instead of 'look how hard I am'; basically, just the bourgeois-bohemian version of rap's fundamental psychological mode – male paranoia, endlessly oscillating between delusions of grandeur and a persecution complex. Instead of the gangsta rapper's violence, the undie rapper wields his gnosis, his arcana, his oracular penetration, his coding and decoding skills. (Encrypting his own utterances, lest they be too easily understood; decoding the conspiracies that underpin and organize white diss-topian reality, a.k.a. Babylon.)

(c) This gangsta versus conscious, street versus underground schism maps on to a similar one in dance culture – the cognoscenti-oriented scenes (Detroit techno, deep house, acid jazz/down-tempo/Mo Wax/Talkin' Loud, etc.) versus the hardcore undergrounds (jump up jungle, speed garage, filthy acid-tekno, gabba, etc.). It's actually a three-way division – you have main-stream crossover stuff (Will Smith, Coolio, etc./cheesy trance, handbag house) i.e. stuff that appeals to non-rap fans or non-dance fans; the connoisseurial elites; and somewhere in between the hardcore street scenes. The latter seem to me to be where all the vibe comes from. In a crucial paradox, the hardcore street scenes are populist but anti-pop. Their populism takes the form of tribal unity against what's perceived as a homogenous, blandly uninvolving pop culture. They're about the 'massive' as opposed to 'the masses'. But unlike the connoisseurial cliques or experimentalist ivory-tower cloisters, the hardcores are about innovative music with real 'social energy' mobilized behind it.

(d) I'm just a philistine.

Fave Records of 1999, *Blissout* website

Like 'authentic' and 'authenticity', the word 'street' was something the sharper music critics had learned to flinch from – the concept was yukky, cringingly passé, the trigger for knee-jerk squeamishness. In the introduction to his 1997 book *More Brilliant Than the Sun*, Kodwo Eshun wrote a brilliantly blistering critique of the way black music tended to get written about in terms of 'roots' and 'soul', the streets and the ghetto; he argued that these socio-historical ways of looking at music domesticated and contained the future-shock of black 'sonic fiction', re-familiarizing it via the language of humanism and heritage. But while it's true that such 'street' talk was too often a set of journalistic clichés masking a condescending attitude towards black creativity, there's a kernel of truth there that can't be blithely brushed aside: the material realities of exclusion, disadvantage and exploitation that simultaneously hamper and energize all forms of underclass music (black *and* white). The real problem with attempts to forcibly pension off the concept of 'the streets' is its persistence within black music culture itself, from NWA's declaration 'you are now about to witness the strength of street knowledge' at the start of 'Straight Outta Compton' through The Lox's album *We Are the Streets* (the band also appealed directly to 'the streets' – hardcore rap fans – when campaigning to be released from their contract to Bad Boy, in order to return to the Ruff Ryders label and get back to having a more 'street' sound than Puff Daddy gave them) to dancehall and grime's imagery of gutter and gully. Staying true to 'the streets', a place compounded of reality and fantasy, clearly continues to mean something to these youth. 'Kids on the street' sounds like something a social worker or an *NME* circa 1977 punk journalist would talk about. But the notion is more than just a cliché: people who don't have huge roomy apartments or nice suburban houses actually *have* to hang out on the streets, that's where a lot of this music is actually *heard,* and it's why rap labels have 'street teams' handing out promo CDs in order to build a street buzz. Hence my attempt to renovate the concept, to work through the embarrassment that clung to it (which probably dates back to The Clash's tower block chic and seventies music press notions of 'street credibility'), to recover both its point and its threat.

WE ARE FAMILY

The Rise of the Rap Clan and the Hip Hop Dynasty

When rapper DMX accepted a trophy at the Billboard Music Awards last year, he took the stage flanked by a squad of fellow artists from the Ruff Ryders label. It's hard to imagine anyone in rock doing this – Trent Reznor, say, menacingly surrounded by the roster of his label Nothing. But in hip hop, such shows of collective strength are growing more common, as rap labels increasingly style themselves as families. Like the mafia families whose Hollywood mythology has so influenced gangsta rap, these labels compete to dominate the lucrative hip hop market, and in this symbolic war of clan against clan, loyalty is exalted as the supreme value.

The two biggest forces in contemporary rap, the Yonkers-based Ruff Ryders and the New Orleans label Cash Money, both ferociously project a sense of clan identity, through logo-based regalia and unity-themed songs and album titles such as 'I'm a Ruff Ryder', 'Ruff Ryder's Anthem', Eve's *Ruff Ryders' First Lady*, and 'Cash Money is an Army'. Cash Money also has a supergroup, Hot Boys, composed of the label's biggest solo stars – Juvenile, B.G. and Lil Wayne. As it happens, both labels are literally family businesses: Ruff Ryders was started by the brothers-and-sister team of Darrin, Joaquin and Chivon Dean, while Cash Money was founded by brothers Ron and Brian Williams. As if in recognition of their similar ethos, the two labels have joined forces for a massive rap tour currently crossing the USA.

Although crews, cliques and posses have always been part of hip hop lore, rap's dominant lyrical mode has hitherto been first person singular. But in the last year or so, ego has been eclipsed by what you might call 'wego', the collective triumphalism of Ruff Ryders' 'We in Here' or Hot Boys' 'We On Fire'. In the wake of Cash Money and Ruff

Ryders success, other labels are presenting themselves as families or Cosa Nostra-style syndicates. 'You Are About to Witness a Dynasty Like No Other' proclaims the sticker on Jay-Z's new album, referring to his Roc-A-Fella label's protégés Beanie Siegel, Memphis Bleek and Amil, while Murder Inc. has combined its roster into the Hot Boys-style supergroup The Murderers.

The idea of the rap group as a blood-brotherhood was pioneered in the mid-nineties by the Wu-Tang Clan, the ten-strong band of MCs centred around producer the RZA. While the lyrics and cover art self-mythologized the group as warrior priests wielding arcane knowledge and encrypted language as weapons against power, the Wu-Tang Clan simultaneously operated as a shrewd entertainment corporation, signing its members to solo deals with different record companies and diversifying into all manner of Wu-branded merchandizing offshoots: clothing, a comic book, a website, the videogame *Wu-Tang: Shaolin Style*. So iconic was the Clan's logo at the group's 1997 height of prestige and popularity that rap paper *The Source* could feel secure about using it as their cover image, rather than a recognizable celebrity face.

Wu-Tang's branding strategy was taken further still by Master P's label No Limit, whose assembly-line turnover of releases all have instantly recognizable cover art (garishly hyper-real 'ghetto fabulous' tableaux created by design team Pen & Pixel) to match the identikit New Orleans gangsta sound of the records. Ironically, the Pen & Pixel look has been appropriated by countless second-division hardcore rap labels, hoping to get accidental sales from fans picking up unheard what they assume is a debut from the latest recruit to the 'No Limit army'. Master P also goes in for diversification in a big way, building a business empire reputedly worth $361 million through No Limits toys and clothing, and a series of inexpensively made straight-to-video movies.

Influenced by Master P's acumen, Cash Money and Ruff Ryders have their own movies in production. And both labels have imitated No Limit's strategy of market saturation and hitting while you're hot. DMX has released three albums in barely more than eighteen months, and the first two months of 2000 have seen a flurry of Ruff Ryders debuts from The Lox and Drag-On, with a new Swizz Beatz compilation and Lox-man Jadakiss's own solo album soon to follow.

Ruff Ryders and Cash Money have built their empires using techniques that are now predictable procedures in the rap business. Reinforcing the all-for-one, one-for-all clan image, rappers from the same roster guest on one another's tracks; new artists are introduced to the public through cameo appearances in the single/video by the label's established stars. Cash Money have taken this twin strategy of cross-promotion and artist-development to the furthest extreme. Other rap artists will feature R&B singers or big-name rappers from other labels on their tracks in order to add more-stars-for-your-money sales appeal. But Cash Money's tracks never feature outsiders – the 'guests' are always only other Cash Money artists.

Still, it would be incorrect to suggest that hip hop's family values are just an ideological gloss for business realpolitik. The family is basically a microcosm of socialism, based around the same ideals like sharing, altruism and self-sacrifice for the greater good. Effectively, the rap clan works as an enclave of collectivism within capitalism's rapacious cut-throat competition, and as such it offers solace and security in what would otherwise be a desolate moral and emotional void. Ruff Ryders' catchphrase 'Ryde or die' divides the world into a starkly opposed them and us: people you'd kill versus people you'd kill for/die for/ride into battle alongside. Taken from a 'blacksploitation'-era cowboy movie, the name Ruff Ryders recalls the going-out-in-a-blaze-of-glory romanticism of Sam Peckinpah's *The Wild Bunch*.

Lyrically, DMX avoids two of gangsta rap's staples – flaunting wealth and abusing women – to focus almost exclusively on loyalty, betrayal and retribution. His yearning for a surrogate family is expressed through an obsession with dogs strikingly different from the incorrigibly lecherous canine persona adopted by George Clinton circa 'Atomic Dog'. DMX's use of the term 'dog' to refer to himself and his clique stems from admiration for the way wild dogs run in packs and domesticated dogs give their owners unconditional love. In song after song, DMX insists, 'I will die for my dogs.' He imagines this canine fraternity becoming a kind of pedigreed dynasty: 'My dogs, the beginning of this bloodline of mine.'

DMX's doom-and-gloomy imagery – album titles like *It's Dark and Hell is Hot*, songs like 'The Omen' – has as much in common with angst-racked industrial and heavy metal artists such as Nine Inch Nails, Marilyn Manson and Korn as with other rappers. A crucial aspect of his Gothic imagery is what the philosopher Michel Foucault called ' the medieval symbolics of blood', as seen in the title of DMX's second album *Flesh of My Flesh, Blood of My Blood*. Thicker than water but easily spilled, 'blood' is a highly charged word in DMX's vocabulary. Its ambivalence condenses gangsta rap's violently polar-ized emotions, the way it's forever oscillating between love and hate, loyalty and skulduggery, unity and dog-eat-dog struggle.

Gangsta rappers have found a reflection of these hot-blooded passions in Hollywood's mafia films, whose families disregard the broader society's morality and instead cleave to a privatized morality: a neo-medieval ethics of loyalty and revenge that operates only in the domain of kith and kin, plus bondsmen unrelated by blood but who have sworn fealty to the clan. With its code of honour among villains and its family structure, the idea of the mafia resonates with hardcore rap partly because of the way it maps on to the street realities of gangs and turf wars. But it's also because the idea of family offers a kind of unity that seems more tangible and grounded than allegiance either to the abstract, remote and problematic entity known as the United States of America, or any of the various forms of African American nationalism. In rap, patriotism contracts to the compact and plausible dimensions of a clique, and usually one tied to a place – a project (like Cash Money's Magnolia neighbourhood in New Orleans), a borough, or at its most expansive, a city.

The cinematic representation of mafia history in films like *The Godfather* and *Goodfellas* often involves an ultimately fatal tension between family loyalty and business logic, as medieval values imported from Sicily collide with American capitalism. Clan elders are disrespected, bad blood sets brother against brother, rival families feud and go to war, because conflicts arise over the new market opportunities represented by drugs. In rap too there's a tension between the rhetoric of 'til death do us part' fealty and the provisional, contractual reality of business relationships. Although The Lox were originally members of the Ruff Ryders milieu, the trio eagerly became henchmen of Puff Daddy, who signed the group to his Bad Boy label, altered their name (originally the Warlocks), persuaded them to tone down their hardcore street style, and coached them in writing radio-friendly songs. But when their debut album for Bad Boy failed to make them rich, the Lox defected, re-plighting their troth to Ruff Ryders, and releasing the ghettocentric *We Are the Streets* this January. Other examples of rappers shifting allegiances between different labels/cliques include ex-Death Row artist Snoop Dogg signing on as a No Limit soldier and Eve originally being a protégé of Dr Dre's Aftermath label before affiliating to Ruff Ryders. All this suggests that rap operates less like feuding clans and more like sports, another lucrative entertainment industry based around symbolic warfare, where top players are hired guns and transfer their loyalties at the drop of a cheque.

Still, for some at least, the thick-like-blood rhetoric is for real. DMX, in particular, regards loyalty as a transcendent value. In a hyper-capitalistic world where market forces tear asunder all forms of solidarity and everybody has their price, he claims: 'They do it for the dough / Me I do it for the love.' In a skit on his third chart-topping album . . . *And Then There Was X*, an unidentified hanger-on declares he'll do anything to get the money he desperately needs. DMX issues a stern reprimand: 'Dog, you got to think about loyalty first, know wha' I'm saying? You got loyalty, money will come. You got a lot to learn.'

Director's cut of piece published in New York Times,
12 March 2000

I recall my *Melody Maker* comrades the Stud Brothers slipping the concept of 'amoral familialism' into a feature, apropos of not much. Apparently it's a term that Italian sociologists devised to explain the persistence of clan-like structures (the Cosa Nostra) in their society, which they diagnosed as a symptom of the relative weakness of both nationalism and state power in Italy (the country being a relatively recent creation compared with other European states). There is perhaps an analogy to be drawn here with the erosion of a sense of black nationalism in America after the sixties, and the resurgent atavism of neo-medieval clans filling the vacuum. Gangs are quasi-families, providing a surrogate paternal function in many cases. In another medieval echo, they are also aristocracies of the street (sometimes consciously framing themselves that way: the Latin Kings). The aristocratic and royal dynasties that established themselves way back in the Dark Ages were originally nothing more than gangsters seizing power and land, subjugating populations and turning them into peons; a gigantic protection racket. The playas of the Middle Ages, these thugs in shining armour squandered wealth in potlatch display – finery, feasts and lordly vices like gambling and hunting. 'Bling' means living like a king.

ROOTS 'N' FUTURE

The Disappearing Voice of Reggae

One of my absolute favourite pieces of dubbed-out roots singing is Linval Thompson on the King Tubby-mixed song 'Straight to Babylon Boy's Head'. Thompson sings: 'From I was born in this world / My mama always tell me / That Babylon is a-wicked . . . Babylon drink rum / Babylon eat pork / Ride on dreadlocks . . . If you don't believe me, just look in the Bible . . . Babylon have to face / the Judgement Day.' Now, I had a bit of bacon only the other day, and although I think 'Babylon' is a handy nickname for the multi-tentacled malevolence of globalizing capitalism, the Good Book is just another book for me, not God's truth. Listening, rapt and swoony to roots songs like this, I feel simultaneously involved and detached, attracted and repelled.

Altering slightly the words of 'Panic' by The Smiths reveals the paradox of my roots infatuation: 'The music that I constantly play / Says nothing to me about my life.' Yet I love it to death anyway. How can it happen, such violent cathexis, this flooding intimacy of pleasure, this beckoning? It's surely mediated by all the cross-cultural baggage of projections and preconceptions, but it doesn't feel like it – it feels like an instantaneous spark of connection, almost pre-cognitive. It's tempting to talk vaguely about inarticulate speech of the heart, about pure spirit cutting across all barriers. Morrissey, who once declared 'all reggae is vile', actually provides my only clue. There's an uncanny vocal resemblance between Thompson and The Smiths' frontman – the fey flutter and lambent grain – and a similar emotional attitude: a mixture of rejoicing in the fallen-ness of the world and confidence in the singer's elect righteousness. The cultural specifics of the expression (Thompson's Old Testament imagery versus Morrissey's mish-mash of

Genet, Oscar Wilde, Patti Smith, et al.) seem to have no overlap what-soever, but the inner core of feeling is very close: a protest against reality, a feeling of exile, nostalgia and homesickness for somewhere that never existed.

* * *

How better to open a meditation on the white romance with Jamaican music than with a record guaranteed to induce cringing from a higher percentage of reggae connoisseurs than any other? I'm talking about The Clash's 1977 single 'White Man in Hammersmith Palais'. Whatever you think of its rabble-rousing punky-reggae, this song remains interesting because lyrically it's actually about the projections and mystifications that inevitably occur when white folks *identify* with black music (as opposed to simply consuming it). In the song, Joe Strummer attends an All Nighter at London's Hammersmith Palais venue featuring such 'first time from Jamaica' stars as Dillinger and Delroy Wilson. But the performances – 'showbizzy, very Vegas', Strummer recalled years later – frustrate his expectations. Instead of 'roots rock rebel' fighting talk, 'it was Four Tops all night / with encores from stage right'. The transracial identification felt by punk rockers towards roots rockers – captured earlier by The Clash in 'White Riot', with its admiration/envy towards the blacks who fought back at 1976's over-policed Notting Hill Carnival – collides with a different reality of Jamaican pop culture (entertainment/escapism), leaving Strummer demoralized and confused.

Roots reggae is now almost exclusively valued for dub's legacy of studio techniques. These include dropping out the voice and certain instruments, often stripping down to just drum and bass; the extreme use of echo, reverb and delay to create an illusory spatiality; signal processing treatments that 'texturize' the instruments (making the cymbals, say, splashy, or the snares metallic-sounding); the addition of sound effects like thunderclap, sirens and animal noises. Using this arsenal of effects, the dub producer transforms the original version of a reggae song into a decentred near-instrumental in which the human voice appears only as a ghost of itself.

Today's hipsters revere dub reggae as a black psychedelia, focusing on the production's hallucinatory and disorienting qualities. Which makes it disorienting in itself to go back to the mid-seventies roots heyday and discover that reggae fans, black and white, actually looked to reggae music for 'a solid foundation' (as The Congos sang it), for certainty and truth, militancy and motivation. The Clash's phrase 'roots rock rebel' neatly condenses how Jamaican music was seen both by rock culture and by reggae itself. Reggae was anti-imperialist: Rasta's Pan-Africanism connected with the period's post-colonial struggles, from the Communist MPLA in Angola resisting a South African invasion that was covertly supported by the USA, to the Patriotic Front liberation forces in white-controlled Rhodesia (Bob Marley later headlined Zimbabwe's 1980 Independence Celebrations). Reggae was anti-capitalist: Rasta's rhetoric of judgement day for Babylon's plutocrats was harnessed by Jamaican Prime Minister Michael Manley, whose socialist government enjoyed increasingly warm relations with neighbouring Cuba. This in turn led the USA to try to destabilize Jamaica via an International Monetary Fund cash squeeze, the smuggling of guns into the country to fuel warfare between politically affiliated gangs, and other dirty tricks (including, some believe, CIA assistance to the people who attempted to assassinate Bob Marley in 1976). Finally, reggae was anti-fascist. British reggae bands like Matumbi and Steel Pulse provided much of the soundtrack to benefit concerts thrown by Rock Against Racism and the Anti-Nazi League, organizations that had emerged to resist the growing street presence of the National Front (the far right political party whose anti-immigration, pro-repatriation stance had become disturbingly popular in late seventies Britain). All through this era, Jamaican icons brought radical chic to countless student digs in the form of posters and album sleeves: Pete Tosh, a Che Guevara with natty dreads and black beret; dub poet Linton Kwesi-Johnson, creator of catchy ditties like 'fascists on attack / we gonna drive them back / we gonna smash their brains in / cos they ain't got nothing in 'em.'

Even before punk, rock culture had seized on reggae as the 'rebel beat' of the seventies, a much needed dose of authenticity at a time of post-countercultural stagnation and retreat. Bob Marley was lionized by many rock critics as a Caribbean Bob Dylan. In Greil Marcus's rundown of the best records of all time at the end of *Stranded* (a 1980 collection of essays by leading American rock critics that he edited), the Wailers are compared to The Stones: 'Get Up Stand Up' was 'the real "Street Fighting Man"', Marcus declared. UK punk rock itself has been interpreted (by Dick Hebdige in his classic *Subculture: The Meaning of Style*) as partly based in the yearning for a 'white ethnicity' equivalent to the Rastafarians (who were highly visible on Britain's urban streets by 1975). UK punks, argued Hebdige, saw themselves as exiles on high street, trapped in a Babylon burning with boredom.

During the half-decade from 1977–81, reggae vied for supremacy with funk as the musical template for progressive post-punk groups. After the Sex Pistols' break-up, John Lydon formed a new group,

Public Image Ltd, based around a bass-heavy and dub-spacious sound, the dread vision of his lyrics riding the deep rolling basslines played by his friend John Wardle, a blue-eyed Londoner who had reinvented himself as Jah Wobble. A year later, The Specials spearheaded the racially integrated 2-Tone movement, fusing social realism with the amphetamine-twitchy rhythms of sixties ska; their Midlands neighbours UB40 (like the Specials, a mixed-race band) dolefully hymned the integrationist Martin Luther King (rather than repatriation proponent Marcus Garvey) over dole queue skank riddims. And always, always, there was The Clash: hiring dub producer Lee Perry to work on 'Complete Control', covering Willie Williams's 'Armagideon Time' and Junior Murvin's 'Police and Thieves', and pulling off a convincing roots reggae facsimile of their own with 'Bankrobber' (Jamaican producer Mikey Dread at the controls). Jamaica, formerly a British colony, responded to all this sincere flattery from the Empire's bastard children with songs like Bob Marley's 'Punky Reggae Party': 'The Wailers will be there / the Slits, the Feelgoods and the Clash.'

Punky-reggae bands like The Clash, The Ruts and The Specials were the mainstays of Rock Against Racism's anti-Nazi festivals, along with homegrown UK roots outfits like Aswad. Reggae was central to RAR's vision of a multiculturalist Britain. But although socialists approved of reggae's socially conscious lyrics, stand-up-for-your-rights rhetoric and resilient rhythms, they were never really able to integrate dub's topsy-turvy sonic overturnings with its conception of reggae as a straightforward protest against injustice. In neo-Marxist academia and left-wing activist circles alike, there was a certain uneasiness about drugs, partly because of a preference for clear-minded rationality, and partly because linking black subcultures with drug use was felt to be crypto-racist. But the real problem was the passionate religiosity of reggae – the absolute centrality of Rastafarianism to the roots worldview. It's possible to translate Rasta beliefs into socialist terms, treat them as allegory, mythic narratives of dispossession and deliverance. Just don't do it in front of a true Rasta believer. When ethnologist John W. Pulis attempted such a dialogue, his Western liberal relativism was swiftly dispatched: 'Only *one* reality . . . na *views* . . . I-and-I no deal with *kon*-sciousness, I deal wit' truth.'

Today, a totally different white hipster discourse frames reggae, emphasizing elements downplayed in the late seventies but (inevitably) suppressing others. Today the talk all revolves around ideas of dub as deconstruction (of the song, of the metaphysics of musical presence); the producer as mad scientist, sorcerer, dark magus, trickster; the notion of dub as a postgeographical virus that has long since drifted away from its Jamaican roots and infected other genres – jungle, house, hip hop, post-rock; the idea of dub's sonic instability, its ambush-like bombardment of effects and sonic surprises, offering what writer/musician Kevin Martin calls an 'education in insecurity'.

One of the earliest essays to conceptualize 'black science fiction' or 'Afro-futurism' was 'Brothers From Another Planet: The Space Madness of Lee "Scratch" Perry, Sun Ra, and George Clinton' by John Corbett (which appeared in his 1994 book *Extended Play*). Corbett portrayed these artists – with their fantastical aliases, bizarre costumes, and kooky cosmology – as renegades against reason, pop-guerrillas deploying black 'folly' to disrupt and undermine white 'sanity'. In their cosmology, 'space' is the polar opposite of earthbound common sense: Sun Ra claimed he was born on Saturn and was the Ambassador of the Omniverse; Perry described himself as 'the firmament computer'; with Parliament-Funkadelic, Clinton imagined a Mothership landing to take black people to a better world. All three artists use language – myth, riddles, encryptions – to unravel 'common sense' and reveal 'the truth' concealed within. At the same time, Ra's self-mythology and quasi-etymological 'word equations' and Perry's punning, paranoid talk resemble the prolix, delusional flow of the schizophrenic, especially those autodidacts who bolster their persecution complexes with hours of library study and arcane research.

Corbett's Afro-Futurist analysis oddly neglected the music in favour of the construction of persona. This omission was rectified by David Toop's probing (in the 1992 essay 'Cut 'N Mix' and later in his book *Ocean of Sound*) of the origins of modern remixing in the dub techniques invented by Jamaican producer King Tubby at the dawn of the seventies. By the end of that decade, either by migration of ideas or by parallel development, disco and dance music had absorbed dub's deconstruction of the song. Producers and remixers effectively de-composed songs, disassembling them into 'into modular and interchangeable fragments, sliced and repatched into an order which departed from the rules of Tin Pan Alley . . . Songs became liquid. They became vehicles for improvisation, or source material . . . that could be reconfigured or remixed to suit the future.'

Developing these twin notions of dub as the ancestor of modern remixology and of the dub version as the Song's spectral/skeletal alterego, Ian Penman wrote about Bristol trip hop artist Tricky and his debut album *Maxinquaye* for *The Wire* in 1995. Highlighting Tricky's debt to the 'smoky logic of dub', Penman coined the term 'tricknology' to describe these techniques of studio sorcery. The neologism's submerged allusion to the trickster gods of West African mythology crystallizes a crucial strand of Afro-Futurist polemic: the fusion of science and religion. Or as Penman put it, 'dub's tricknology is a form of magic which does indeed make people disappear, leaving behind only their context, their (t)race, their outline . . .'. Finally, Kodwo Eshun's 1997's book *More Brilliant Than the Sun* provided the emergent Afro-Futurist consensus with its canon, its manifesto and its lexicon. The subtitle 'Adventures in Sonic Fiction' pinpointed the idea of dub as hallucinogenre, dub as a set of studio techniques for generating phantoms and phantasmagoria. Rejecting the traditional approaches to black music favoured by journalism or cultural studies – which fixate on soul, roots, the streets, real-ness, the ghetto – Eshun proposed to gleefully jettison the socio-historical approach and focus instead on both the materiality of music as it rhythmically impacts the listener's 'bodymind' and on music's insubstantiality, its ability to tantalize the mind's eye with mirages and figments.

All this theorizing has been paralleled by, and has often drawn inspiration from, a range of concurrent musical activity, stretching from New York's 'illbient' scene (artists like DJ Spooky and Sub Dub) and Brooklyn's Wordsound label (Spectre, Dubadelic, et al.) to the numerous dub-related supergroups and collaborations orchestrated by Bill Laswell, to American post-rock outfits like Tortoise and Labradford, through to the dub-informed house music released on the German labels Basic Channel, Chain Reaction and Burial Mix. What all these strands of dub theory and dub practice share is the exaltation of producers and engineers over singers and players, and the idea that studio effects and processing are more crucial than the original vocal or instrumental performances. According to Kevin Martin, whose *Macro Dub Infection* compilations drew widely across the scattered field of music activity delineated above, 'it's almost like musicians are accessories to the process now . . .'.

This contemporary shift in focus has also altered the way people look at the past. In the old days, writing about reggae focused largely on the singer/songwriter/frontmen – figures like Marley, Toots, Burning Spear's Winston Rodney, Michael Rose of Black Uhuru, and so forth. There was acknowledgement of the importance of a producer like Lee Perry (although this might have something to do with his eccentricity, and the fact that his vocals appeared on some of the records he produced), or a rhythm section partnership like Sly Dunbar & Robbie Shakespeare – but little in the way of substantive analysis of what they did. Today, a near-complete reversal has occurred, with producers and engineers usurping the status of auteurs. In the last decade, thousands of words have been spilled on the wizardry of Perry or Tubby, but surprisingly little on reggae vocalists or the role of drummers, bassists, rhythm guitarists, keyboardists, et al. in building kinaesthetic moodscapes (a.k.a. grooves). The mystery of 'skank' has failed to provoke a downpour of eloquence – the way different riddims pull you into their flow, entrain your limbs in their gait, tune your cells into their vibration. This is understandable, given the difficulty of writing about rhythm with any specificity (mind you, it's just as tough to go beyond generalities and talk about a specific auteur-producer's signature, to isolate exactly what it is that gives one dub engineer, or jungle producer, his singularity and superior rank).

One strange side effect of this new focus on the producer, though, is that a crucial facet of reggae has been almost totally forgotten: the fact that it actually involved people *saying stuff*. Lyrically, most seventies roots reggae was as plainspoken and bluntly demagogic as Pete Seeger or the Tom Robinson Band. This is not to say that the shift in how reggae has been conceptualized – from 'the sound of politics' in the seventies to 'the politics of sound' today – hasn't opened up exciting ways of thinking about the music; indeed, it was originally a necessary corrective to the exhausted post-punk over-emphasis on messages and meaning. But today's focus on reggae's technicians and the machines they operated has effectively de-politicized and de-spiritualized a music that in its original context was 'part journalism, part prophecy' (James A. Winders). At the extreme, there seems almost to be a subconscious desire to erase Jamaica in all its knotty cultural contradictions. So Calvin Johnson, founder of the Olympia, Washington, indie label K Records and frontman of Dub Narcotic Sound System, can blithely declare: 'I never saw dub as a type of music, but as a process. The fact that it originated in reggae is inconsequential.'

* * *

The totem and touchstone for this form-not-content version of reggae is Lee 'Scratch' Perry. As the new consensus about dub has solidified over the last decade, he has been elevated to become the auteur-producer par excellence, at the expense of some of his less flamboyant yet more consistent peers (King Tubby, Keith Hudson, Jack Ruby, Augustus Pablo, Tommy Cowan, Joe Gibbs, Harry Mudie, et al.). Perry is often contrasted with Bob Marley by critics of the Afro-Futurist persuasion: the two are almost like a binary pair, conceptual twins, with Perry always bigged up as 'mad scientist' producer-genius and Marley always denigrated as dull 'n' worthy statesman. Strikingly, two critics who contrast Marley-ism (reggae as text/truth/soul/roots) with Perry-ology (dub as texture/fiction/technology/deracination) use almost exactly the same metaphor to chastise Bob and exalt 'Scratch'. In his Tricky meditation, Penman mocks Marley as 'an olde worlde flat-earth icon'. In his brief Perry chapter in *More Brilliant Than the Sun*, Eshun praises Scratch's location 'far from Rastafari's flat-earth metaphysics', in effect arguing that dub logic is at odds with the faith-based worldview that Marley made world-famous.

Apart from the ethnocentrism of this Rastafarianism as flat earth theory analogy used by Penman and Eshun (odd, given the Afro-Futurist tendency to valorize voodoo, alchemy, Gnosticism, and other magickal and superstitious beliefs), it's misleading to imply that dub and roots reggae can be understood separately from that strange Jamaican religion. For starters, Rasta's sacred burru drums – bass, funde, repeater – are embedded deep in reggae's rhythmic matrix. Perry himself is a devout, if eccentric, Rasta. He produced and often had an instigating conceptual role in scores of songs with titles like 'Psalms 20', 'Zion's Blood', 'Dread Lion', 'Sodom and Gomorrow', 'Feast of Passover', plus numerous topical social comment tunes like Max Romeo's 'War in a Babylon' and Junior Murvin's 'Police and Thieves'. Even a seemingly whimsical Perry lyric like 'Roast Fish and Cornbread' is actually about ital, the dietary guidelines that are crucial to righteous Rasta living.

Lee Perry's sonic achievements are mighty but I can't help suspecting some dubious ulterior factors behind the adulation of Scratch. One is simply that his work is such fertile ground for critical analysis: Perry's syncretic cosmology of superstitions, science fiction, and pulp movies, his is-it-schizophrenia-or-performance-art-that-never-stops eccentricity, his delirium of wordgames and puns, will support a micro-industry of dissertations, seminars and museum exhibitions, for decades to come. One example is a late entry to the Afro-Futurist argument, Erik Davis's 'Roots and Wires', which appeared as a liner note to *Death in Light of the Phonograph: Excursions Into the Pre-Linguistic*, a CD by Paul D. Miller (a.k.a. DJ Spooky). The essay is an exhaustive inventory of the buried meanings and ancestral traces in Perry's oeuvre that has the unfortunate effect of transforming this outrageous character into an almost-saintly figure. The other reason for the Perry Cult is, I reckon, because the tomfoolery and quirked-out levity of much of his output offers a blessed reprieve from the sheer earnestness of roots reggae, which is often literally sermonizing, all parables and chapter-and-verse.

Dub's tricknology, as we've seen, is often linked to the trickster gods of West African animism (spirit-worship). But Rasta itself is not pagan. It has little in common with Haitian voodoo, Cuban santeria or the other Africanized remixes of Catholicism. Instead of a panoply of spirits disguised as Catholic saints, Rasta has just the one God, the stern patriarch of the Old Testament – not someone with whom you can cut deals, as you can with voodoo's spirit-gods, the loa. If anything, Rasta is Afro-Protestant, sharing with mainland America's fundamentalists an emphasis on close reading of the Scriptures (devout Rastas read the Good Book for an hour a day) and a millenarian belief in an End of Time whereupon the righteous get transported to the promised land. Bob Marley believed 144,000 true believers would be taken to Ethiopia: the exact same number that some born-again Christians believe will ascend to heaven in The Rapture. Blood and Fire may be the name of Britain's leading roots reggae reissue label, but before that it was the slogan of the Salvation Army (which itself could almost be the name of a roots band, come to think of it!). In addition to Rastafarianism, Jamaica actually has its own local versions of Pentecostalism and Baptism, either as straightforward transplants (the Revival church) or Africanized, dance-trance versions such as Pocomania. The ecstatic fervour of a Poco congregation is reputedly what inspired a passing Lee Perry to slow down ska's rhythm, in the process inventing rocksteady and reggae.

Rasta also resembles some of the revolutionary and Gnostic heresies of the Middle Ages documented in Norman Cohn's *The Pursuit of the Millennium*. These anarcho-mystical sects were rabidly opposed to the established Roman Catholic church; bizarrely, anti-papist sentiments are often expressed as crowd-rallying cries in modern dancehall reggae, and Perry himself recorded a song about Vatican procedures for the accession of popes called 'Bafflin' Smoke Signals'! Rasta's belief in Haile Selassie, His Imperial Majesty of Ethiopia, as the Messiah recalls those medieval sects documented by Cohn whose utopian hopes involved the resurrection of a king or emperor who would be saviour of the poor and scourge of the corrupt (false kings, the clergy). Rastafarianism also owes a lot to Judaism – the kosher-like ital laws, the taboos about menstruation, and above all the Exodus saga of a people uprooted and enslaved (first by the Egyptians, then by the Babylonians) but struggling to return to their homeland. (Rasta's own version of racial envy goes: 'Black Zion! We want a Zion of our own.') Transmitted via reggae, this mythic narrative resonates with dispossessed peoples across the world, from aboriginal Australians to Native Americans (roots reggae is hugely popular on the reservations, rivalled only by death metal!).

Because of its anti-institutional tendency and its trust-in-Jah fatalism, Rasta never summoned the will-to-power to actually create the theocratic society it basically proposes. To grasp how weird it is that such an anti-modern creed has been so influential over Western youth culture, though, imagine the following alternative history scenario: the parallel universe where post-revolutionary Iran generates a form of popular music so globally inspirational it spawns its own Ayatollah-friendly bands along the lines of The Police and UB40. Both Rasta and Islamic fundamentalism are anti-imperialist, anti-America and opposed to ungodly Western liberalism – from women's reproductive rights (Rasta decries birth control and abortion) to homosexuality.

Which brings me to what prompted this essay in the first place: the gap between my intense pleasure in and (for want of a better word) 'identification' with roots reggae, and the glaring fact that my experiential framework and worldview are utterly remote from the Rastafarian's. John Peel once described the sound of Misty In Roots, his favourite homegrown UK reggae group, as 'medieval'. Rasta's liberation theology is a disconcerting weave of revolutionary and reactionary, and its paradoxes are intrinsic to dub's own musical double-feel of pre-modern and postmodern. Dub is Jamaican psychedelia, but it is also Jamaican gospel – it simultaneously offers an adventure playground for the perceptions and 'a solid foundation', the bedrock certainty of faith. Maybe its uncanny power has something to do with precisely this 'impossible' warp 'n' weft of two different modes of consciousness. Because reggae has penetrated Western culture so deeply and feels so familiar, it's easy to forget that Jamaica is still part of the undeveloped Third World. Reggae is a membrane between pre-industrial antiquity and hi-tech futurism. (Hence Perry's own magick-meets-sci-fi imagery of 'vampires' and 'bionic rats'.) Rastafarianism's idea of time itself jars with Western linear progress. History is conceived as a loop (homeland-diaspora-homecoming), and Zion, the end of history, is constantly accessible in the now as an entranced-dance epiphany.

Dub's aura of Eternity and timelessness has a lot to do with marijuana (a sacred herb for Rastafarians). Stoned, the listener hears all forms of music with increased fidelity and dimension. But dub's echo-drenched spatiality is *designed* to be enhanced by marijuana. The drug also weakens the interpretive and associative functions of the mind, and diminishes both memory and future-focused anxiety; the combined effect is to enable the listener to become utterly absorbed by the present moment, 'lost in music'. Dub reggae turns sound into incense or fragrance, filling the gaps between listener and speakers. Swathed in this 'holy smoke', the Rastafarian glimpses Zion through his ears. Indeed, dub reggae often seems to work through a kind of abstract impressionist pictorialism: the golden horizons and mirage shimmer of an Abyssinia of the stoned mind's eye; patient processional rhythms suggesting freedom trains, the stoic trek of exodus and return.

* * *

The trajectory of dub & roots after its late seventies peak corresponds to a familiar syndrome: the black popular music (designed for dancing) that gradually turns into highbrow art, its past cherished and conserved by white curators and archivists, its present sustained by a mostly white vanguard who rarefy the music and place it firmly on the cerebral side of the mind/body dualism it once so successfully dissolved. You can see this syndrome recurring through the histories of jazz, soul, funk, old skool hip hop. Often running in parallel to the avant-garde abstraction option, there's a purely antiquarian approach – the pointless fidelity of trad jazz or digital dub (digi-dub).

The first casualty of the bohemianization of dub wasn't the usual one (danceability), it was the voice. Dub and dub-influenced music in the nineties almost always consists of instrumentals. At best, you get love songs to dub reggae, rather than love songs to Jah. At worst, you get a music that is all effects and no affect. The symbiosis and synergy between roots and dub is a bit like Swiss cheese. Without the holes, the cheese is less eye-grabbing but it still works on a basic nutritional and flavour level. But the holes, on their own (i.e. tricknology abstracted and decontextualized) are nearly nothing. For sure, Tubby's dubs of singers like Linval Thompson and Horace Andy are more thrilling than the originals: hole-some is better than wholesome. But Tubby needed material to go dub crazy with in the first place. The same applies to more recent tricknologies like 'breakbeat science', the techniques of computer editing, recombining and processing seventies funk drum patterns that are used in jungle. The science needs something to manifest itself through, the flesh and sweat and hands-on, played 'feel' of legendary beats like 'Amen' or 'Think'.

The glory of Jamaican music in the 1970s was that it worked on all these different levels: science, emotion, politics, spirituality. (And being dance music, it was physical, sensual, sometimes sexy.) But the mostly white musicians and critics who have become the guardians of dub reggae have focused on just one facet of the music as 'the legacy'. At its most reductive, Jamaica's gift and inspiration to the wider world of music is brought down to certain production mannerisms involving tape echo, reverb and phaser.

This separation of dub from reggae – a process of dematerialization and decontextualization – is not unrelated to the fact that, for many white listeners, the Jamaican musical narrative comes to a dead stop in the early eighties. Most people who worship the roots & dub era have a surprisingly total lack of interest in the last two decades of Jamaican music. It's a common opinion that the rise of dancehall and digital reggae (a.k.a. ragga) was the death-knell for whatever was good about Jamaican music culture. Even dub fans who are passionate about such intensely digitalized and computer-based musics as hip hop, jungle and house make the anti-digital argument, arguing that 'feel' and 'warmth' and 'soul' disappear from the post-roots music era. Regardless of these arguments, it is a bizarre, implausible notion that somehow the community of knowledge and creativity that had marshalled itself in seventies Jamaica – the songwriters, singers, DJs, producers, engineers – should somehow vaporize, punctually, circa 1982; that the well of inspiration would just dry up. But this is what most dub/roots fans apparently believe.

Another reason white hipsters stopped paying attention to Jamaica in the early eighties was that the roots narrative had seemingly run its course: Marley was dead, other leading 'culture' bands had fallen into a platitudinous rut. The 'dancehall' ethos that replaced Rasta spirituality – based in 'slackness' (ribald, coarse and ultra-explicit sex talk), materialism and ghettocentric realism – jarred with the white liberal hipsters' values but lacked the radical chic that had compensated for Rasta's uncomfortable reactionary elements. Dancehalls – the buildings or enclosed lawns where sound systems played and competed with each other in the soundclash – had always been the primary location for reggae performance. When 'dancehall' became a distinct genre in the mid-eighties, supplanting roots reggae, this was a classic example of 'black flight': the local Jamaican audience abandoned reggae, a sound that had been globalized by the success of Marley, Third World, and others, and co-opted by white rock musicians like The Police, and retrenched around a new sound that was much more localized in its appeal and reference points, impenetrable to outsiders. The word 'dancehall' itself emphasized the primacy of the dancefloor, the power of the crowd or 'massive', and implicitly, the black working-class Jamaican-ness of the culture. And the music itself was highly successful at driving off whitey. Its manic machine-beats were incompatible with relaxing home-listening, unlike the leisurely-tempo'd skank riddims. The lyrics and vocals were almost hieroglyphic in their opacity to the outsider: harshly exaggerated patois and Jamaica-specific references replaced Marley-style 'one love' universalism. Increasingly, dancehall had less and less in common with reggae musically – its jarring, palsied beats were actually more African than reggae, a digitalized reversion to pre-ska rural folk rhythms like etu, pocomani and kumina. Paralleling the slick and shiny digital sound of dancehall, the roots era's preference for earthy, natural-looking garments gave way to glossy man-made fabrics and a fashion sense based around the most expensive designer labels; natty dreadlocks were replaced by the close-cropped 'baldhead' look or angular, sometimes dyed haircuts (for men) and multi-coloured hair extensions (for 'dancehall queens').

For those fans who had idealized reggae's authenticity, its organic and earthy qualities, and its revolutionary credentials, the emergence of dancehall was profoundly depressing. Essentially, dancehall glamorizes the ways of Babylon: commodity-fetishism, synthetics, heterosexism, capitalism's war of all against all. With Reagan-admirer Edward Seaga ruling the country and the IMF restructuring its economy along neo-colonial and monetarist lines, Jamaican pop culture looked away from Africa to America. There was a revival of enthusiasm for the Hollywood bad-boy mythologies (cowboy and mafia movies) that had been so popular in the pre-Rasta 'rude boy' phase of sixties ska, and an increasingly reciprocal relationship of influence between dancehall and Black American gangsta rap. Another crucial factor was Jamaica's becoming a stop-over for the cocaine trade in the early eighties. Dancehall ragga's crisp, haze-less sound and jittery rhythms replaced reggae's stoned skank. Cheap cocaine defined dancehall's brash, braggart vibe, and partially explain its hypersexuality (from songs about 'punanny' to sexually explicit rump-wiggling dances). And the grim realities of the drug trade and gang warfare provided much of its subject matter, in the form of the 'gun talk' genre. This ragga end of the dancehall spectrum is characterized by a faithlessness verging on nihilism: 'Africa nah go make me bullet-proof,' as one rude boy put it, scorning the dream of Zion.

Almost inevitably, given the failure of Seaga's Reagan-Thatcher style policies to trickle-down as promised, and the increasingly neo-colonial vassal-state status of Jamaica, there was a resurgence of roots-and-culture ideas in the mid-nineties. Dancehall had its own Rasta stars like Sizzla, Luciano, Tony Rebel, Anthony B., plus rude-boys-turned-righteous like Capleton and Buju Banton. Even arch-gangsta Ninjaman was reborn as Brother Desmond. For the first time in a decade, dancehall stages were trod by singers dressed in Ethiopian military uniforms, with their dreadlocks stuffed inside woolly 'tams', and wielding sceptre-like walking sticks: 'rods of correction' that symbolized the Rasta singer's role as apocalyptic 'warner', scourge of the wicked. But despite this partial revival of 'consciousness', white hipsters didn't recover their interest in contemporary Jamaica, but remained fixated on the golden age of dub, whose sonic footprints can be seen across the spectrum of modern dance music, from chill-out techno to progressive house and drum & bass to trip hop

Others have tracked the migration of dub techniques through the last twelve years of UK dance culture. But another syndrome has also been going on that has attracted far less critical attention: the diffusion of the roots vocal itself, the raw material that was originally dubbed up into flickering ghosts of itself. From the start, UK rave culture has been defined by a compulsion to fuse house with reggae and hip hop: the bass pressure of bleep techno outfits like Ital Rockers and Unique 3, Meat Beat Manifesto's 'Radio Babylon', Moody Boys' *Journey Into Dubland* EP with its Hugh Mundell 'got to be free' clarion, the Ragga Twins' fusion of dancehall jabber and hardcore techno blare. You could argue that UK rave was in large part the direct transposition of Jamaican dancehall culture into Britain – the competing sound systems, the all-night parties a.k.a. 'blues' in shady, unlicensed premises, the dubplate specials, the bass worship. As hardcore rave evolved into jungle, vocal samples from roots singers and dancehall chatters like Dr Alimantado, Leroy Sibbles, Eek-A-Mouse, Snaggapuss, Barrington Levy, Cutty Ranks, Anthony Red Rose, Topcat and many more became endemic. Imported 'yard tapes' of Kingston soundclashes provided a wealth of catchphrases from unidentified MCs – 'get ready for dis, for dis, for dis', 'special request', 'come with it my man', 'get mash up', 'champion sound a-way' – which were endlessly re-sampled and still crop up in today's UK underground garage and 2-step tracks, killer vibe undiminished.

There's a vast amount of writing on the role of DJs and producers in dance culture, but hardly any discussion of the MC's crucial role in the hardcore/jungle/garage continuum: the way the mic' controller operates as a kind of membrane between the expressive and the rhythmic, the social and the technological. The MC vocalizes the intensities of machine-rhythm by transforming himself into a supplement to the drum kit. At the same time, he relays the will of the dancefloor's massive's back to the DJ in the form of the demand 'rewind, selector!': the audience clamour for a record to be spun back to the start. The MC is also the most stubbornly ineradicable Jamaican trace persisting in UK rave, permeating the music both as samples from ragga records and as live partner to the DJ. (Confusingly, in Jamaica itself, the MC, the person who talks over records, is known as the DJ; the person who spins the records is known as the selector. Here I'm sticking to the hip hop and rave use of MC to designate the mic' controller/master of ceremonies.)

The crucial role of the MC shows how contemporary Jamaican music has had as huge an effect on dance culture as dub. Intriguingly, that influence is largely on the level of vocals and language rather than rhythm or production. In UK underground garage, the gruff, booming dancehall vocal provides the yang to the yin of the diva's ultra-trebly vocals. But the ghettocentric grain of the patois voice also works as a kind of simultaneously textural and ideological counterweight to garage's aspirational gloss and opulent production. Sampled from dancehall tracks or live-and-direct on the mic', the MC voice is a residual trace of non-assimilated Jamaican otherness; it's some 'this is where we came from' grit to offset garage's 'this is where we're going' slickness.

UK garage is really an improbable four-way collision between gay American house, homophobic Jamaican ragga, East London ruffneck jungle and uptown US R&B. It's the sonic embodiment of a British identity in flux, under the triple attrition of American pop culture, European unity and colonial chickens coming home to roost. Hence the 'reverse assimilation' effect caused by the Caribbean population in the UK; diasporic peoples unsettle wherever they settle. Fulfilling the promise of Smiley Culture's eighties dancehall smash 'Cockney Translation' – which compared Jamaican patois with Cockney rhyming slang patter – generations of West Indian immigrants have other-ized the 'true' Britons, seducing the young into speaking a creole tongue and making them unfamiliar and alarming to the parent generation. Hence such anxiety symptoms as Ali G.'s popularity and the articles last year in the quality newspapers arguing that rap radio DJ Tim Westwood got what was coming to him when he was the target of a drive-by shooting. The papers made a great deal of the fact that Westwood, the son of a bishop, uses hip hop slang and speaks in a Jamaican accent. (Which he doesn't – it's Bronx B-boys he strives to be down with, not Kingston ragamuffins!) The subtext was pernicious, though: not so much 'to your own self be true' authenticity but 'stick with your own kind' apartheid.

In this undeclared *kulturkampf*, UK garage fights back with rhythm and melody. Artful Dodger's 'Re-Rewind (The Crowd Say "Bo! Selector")' and Oxide & Neutrino's 'Bound 4 Da Reload' both took dancehall slanguage to the top of the pop charts. On the *Warm Up* EP, MCs Shy Cookie, Sweetie Irie and Spee reinvent the Englishness of canonical literature and period drama in the form of 'Millennium Twist' – Dickensian dancehall starring an updated Fagin from the musical *Oliver!* instructing modern urchins how to duck 'n' dive Y2K style. The chorus goes 'L.O.N.D.O.N, London / That's where we're coming from'. The paradox of London dance culture is the way it combines total openness to external influence (the one-way alliance with American R&B; the enduring ties with Jamaica) with a fierce sense of local identity. London's endless permutational flux also illustrates something that offers a partial solution to my quandary about how I could possibly love Rastafarian roots reggae so much. Somehow music, even when targeted at a very specific community and tailored to a precise and rather inflexible worldview, drifts out of the hands of those who 'own' it and gets under the skin of those it was not intended for and whose world it does not describe. It still may not belong to you, but, strangely, you can belong to *it*.

Drastic remix of a piece first published in
The Wire, September 2000

The reason I 'versioned' this piece was to apply for a grant from an American organization handing out money to help authors with writing projects. Hence the working title I gave the document in my computer, '$7000 bucks please'. I presented the remix as a sample chapter from a book to be titled *White On Black*, a phantom project whose imprint can be detected here and there in *Bring the Noise*. (And no, I didn't get the grant.) Along with going against the Afro-Futurist grain (which by then had settled into a rather cosy consensus), what seems most timely – or even ahead-of-its-timely – is the final section on the burgeoning role of MCs in UK garage, which damn-near glimpses grime on the cultural horizon.

EURO

Trance Music and the People-Pleasing Power of 'Cheese'

Trance rules the world's dancefloors with a white-gloved fist. Occasionally, though, voices of dissent pipe up to insist, 'That's not real trance, that's Euro.' Uttered with a disdainful wrinkle of the nostrils, the E-word is code for 'cheese', for dance music that's too close to conventional chart-pop. And these grouches have a point – the original early nineties trance was harsh, trippy and coldly cosmic, and it almost never featured vocals or normal song-structures. Although it was drug music and people raved to it, in some ways the first-wave Teutonic trance from Berlin and Frankfurt was born as a reaction against rave – or what rave had degenerated into (all goofy kids TV show samples, pianos, anthemic choruses). As much as purist Detroit techno or progressive house, the original trance was intended as a stripped-down, sombre, cheese-purged purification of techno.

Between 1994, when first-wave trance's hipster credibility was usurped by drum & bass, and 1998, when trance's popularity resurged dramatically off the back of the Mitsubishi phenomenon (the return of reliably high-quality Ecstasy), the music changed substantially. Borrowing elements from commercial house (hands in the air break-downs and crowd-inciting drum rolls) and from Balearic (the spangly MDMA-friendly textures and wistful refrains popular in Ibiza every summer), trance reinvented itself as the populist softcore option – cheesy and proud of it. It became Euro-trance, and as far as connoisseurs were concerned, an abhorrent thing.

What makes it Euro? Maybe it's that there's too much Aha and Erasure in the mix. The hallmark of this music is an indecent amount of melody (remember, there's an inverse ratio between tunefulness and deepness in dance culture), a hint of melodrama and operatic-ness.

Rhythmically, the Euro element comes in with the nu-trance's debt to a style of music that will probably never enjoy the hipster rediscovery afforded electro or disco: Hi-NRG. Huge in gay discos all through the eighties, this genre is defined by a butt-shaking rhythm that is best conveyed by the words 'Blue Monday'.

Alongside the shameless mozzarella content, trancephobes always accuse the music of lacking 'funk' and 'soul' – of being too white, basically. The 'funkless' accusation is pretty incontestable. It goes back to Giorgio Moroder, whose productions for Donna Summer pioneered the first all-electronic dance music: Eurodisco. Moroder deliberately simplified funk's clustered beats into an even flow of metronomically regular pulsations, all synched to the unsyncopated 4-to-the-floor kick-drum. Rhythmic children of Giorgio, trance DJs like Paul Van Dyk emphasize seamless transitions between tracks, creating the sensation of surging through a frictionless soundscape. And without friction, where's the funk?

The 'soul-less' accusation is unfair, though – if anything, trance can be too E-motional. Besides, there is a European soulfulness to trance, a quality that descends from the serene glide of Kraftwerk's 'Autobahn' and 'Neon Lights', both hymnal songs about falling in love with the modern world while in motion through it. Listen to today's trance, and you think of the pristine, hygienic beauty of a modern unified Europe – the high-speed trains, the autobahns, the pedestrian-only boulevards of city-centre shopping districts, the noiseless moving walkways of airports. It's why Euro-trance flourishes wherever the romance of streamlined, sterile modernity holds sway, from Hong Kong to São Paolo (the most European of Brazil's cities).

It's also why this music, so rootless and synthetic sounding, comes from the Old World. On a recent vacation in Tuscany, I started to understand how the ancient stuff everywhere – medieval hilltowns, cobbled streets, palazzos – could feel oppressive to young people. I'm sure it's got something to do with why Italian kids have long favoured shiny man-made fabrics and shiny machine-made music. Italian pop radio plays nothing but Euro (that, and the occasional Bon Jovi tune, pop-metal at its most glitteringly inorganic), and it's perfect precisely because it doesn't fit the picturesque landscape of olive groves, sunflower meadows and ruined farmhouses scrolling past your car windows. In the land of terracotta, plastic has a liberating future-buzz about it.

The Italian contribution to rock is not huge, but they did play a significant role in the history of house and techno. Moroder came from the northern province of Tyrol, culturally poised between Italy and the German-speaking world. The style of post-Moroder electronic dancepop known as Italo-disco was popular in Detroit, where they called it 'progressive' – artists like Klein & MBO and Alexander Robotnik. Robotnik's 'Problemes D'Amour' was actually the first dance track to use a Roland 303 bass-synthesizer, the basis of acid house and a staple of trance. Later, Italo-house – all tingly-rush-inducing piano vamps and shrieking divas – by artists like Black Box and Starlight was hugely influential on the British rave scene. Even today, Italian producers like Tigino & Legato more than pull their weight when it comes to fuelling Ibiza's midsummer blissfest.

All of which brings us back to my original point, the puzzling fact that the word 'Euro' is an insult, when 'in the beginning' European-ness was the quintessence of cool. Detroit techno, for instance, began as a scene of affluent black teenagers who defined themselves through their obsession with all things European, from music to fashion. It's not inaccurate to describe techno and house as white European music that black Americans 'got wrong' – a sort of reverse parallel with the emergence of rock as a white misrecognition of the black blues. Detroit cognoscenti fetishize the obscure Italian records that Carl Craig and Derrick May spun at high school 'socials' in the early eighties (along-side tracks by Yello, Depeche Mode, Liaisons Dangereuses and other Euro exotica). But they have no interest in, and nothing but contempt for, contemporary Euro, which has clear ancestral links with that music.

'Deep' is a buzzword in dance culture, code for the sort of cognoscenti-pleasing subtleties that ensure the music will never cross over because it's not instantly appealing or anthemic enough (see also 'dark' and 'progressive', two other praise terms that virtually guaran-tee a lack of blatant tunefulness and overt emotion). The opposite of 'deep' is 'cheesy', basically anything people-pleasing. It's worth remem-bering, though, that the Italians have had centuries of experience with using just the right amount of cheese – think risotto, pasta, pizza. Too much and it's inedible, nauseating. Too little, and it lacks flava. The same thing goes for dance music: 'cheese' adds savour and pungency. When dance producers get too tasteful, the result is music that is completely taste*less*.

Director's cut of column for *SonicNet*, 2000

The seed for this piece was a visit to a trendy techno store in New York, where I innocently asked where I might find a particular record (Da Hool's 'Meet Her at the Love Parade'), only for the guy behind the counter to grimace and suggest 'try the cheese section'. Not long after this I started getting into trance quite a bit (a development that surprised me, on account of having in '93 volubly backed jungle against trance, when the latter was very much deemed the thinking person's post-rave sound). I began wondering about the embarrassment that recurs in dance circles whenever the music gets 'too white'. Often this complaint means 'too rocky' or 'students have starting coming to the clubs, oh no' (as with Big Beat), but in the case of trance it was specifically about a deficiency of funkiness and soulfulness. The idea that 'European-ness' had no place in dance music seemed not only PC and sycophantic towards black culture, but historically unsound. Surely trance and gabba just had a different, but equally valid, kind of energy from funk-derived or dub-bassed rhythmatics? These were fun ideas to play with for a while, but in the end I couldn't spend too much time in these 'metro-nomic undergrounds', as joyous (fluffy trance) or intense (gabba, psy-trance) as these scenes could be. Without the boom-boom-bap, without syncopation or swing, dancing to those kinds of strict time-sequencer pulses and march beats felt too much like hard work.

MILES DAVIS

Live-Evil, Black Beauty: Miles Davis at Fillmore West, In Concert: Live at Philharmonic Hall, Dark Magus: Live at Carnegie Hall, (Columbia Legacy reissues)

'Can the ocean be described? Fathomless music . . .' intones Conrad Roberts in a slightly hokey paean to Miles midway through *Live-Evil*'s 'Inamorata'. I know what he was getting at, though, vis-à-vis Miles Davis's early seventies output. No music makes me feel more inadequate or induces a stronger feeling of temerity – for 'description', however floridly imagistic, always seems like a reduction, and 'explanation' can only ever be a foolhardy projection.

In his brilliant 1983 essay 'The Electric Miles', Greg Tate argued for Davis's early seventies music (still languishing in critical neglect when Tate wrote) as a sort of simultaneous culmination/dissolution of the jazz tradition. Fifteen years on, it's tempting to align the electric Miles with aesthetic kinsmen outside the jazz lineage: the 'oceanic' tendency in post-psychedelic rock that encompassed Tim Buckley's *Starsailor*, Yoko Ono's *Fly*, Can's *Tago Mago/Future Days/Soon Over Babaluma* trilogy, Robert Wyatt's *Rock Bottom*, John Martyn's 'I'd Rather Be the Devil' and 'Big Muff'. To varying degrees, all this music was animated by the same impulse that drove Miles, a quest for a 'One World' music, a fissile fusion of jazz, funk, rock, Indian music, electroacoustics. To varying degrees, all this music shared the same split methodology that underpinned Miles's Teo Macero-produced studio albums of that era: freeform, unrehearsed improvisation followed by extensive studio-as-instrument post-production and editing in order to sculpt jams into coherent compositions.

As with the aforementioned avant rockers, chromaticism – rather than melody or harmony – is what the electric Miles is all about. David Toop notes in *Ocean of Sound* how Stockhausen inspired Miles to organize his music around 'textural laminates and molten fields of

268

colour'. But it was Jimi Hendrix who hipped Miles to the chromatic potential of distortion and effects processing; during this period Miles played his trumpet through a foot-controlled wah-wah unit, guitarist Pete Cosey deployed an arsenal of effects pedals, and percussionist Mtume spiced the polyrhythmic paella with exotica like log drums and kalimba. As a result, Miles's music of the early seventies is as livid as a tropical disease, as lurid as the patterns on a venomous snake, as lysergic as his own cover art (Mati Klarwein's Afrodelic fantasia, Corky McCoy's Fauvism-meets-Blacksploitation street scenes of superfly guys, true playaz and fine bitches in hot pants and high heels).

Getting back to Miles's kinship with the post-psychedelic starsailors and aquanauts, the music of *Dark Magus*, *On the Corner*, *Agharta*, et al. offers a drastic intensification of rock's three most radical aspects: space, timbre and groove (by which I mean something altogether more machine-like/mantric than jazz's freeswinging drive). Making what he imagined was a sideways shift towards the pop mainstream (ha!), Miles actually achieved a culmination of rock's trajectory towards kinaesthetic abstraction, a.k.a. the textured groovescape.

The music on these four double albums seems like excerpts from some continuous monster jam that lasted from 1970–75, when an understandably shagged-out Miles collapsed and retreated into coke-addled hermitdom. *Black Beauty* and *Live-Evil* are both from 1970, and feature the instrumental line-up of the *In a Silent Way* and *Bitches Brew* era (Chick Corea, Dave Holland, Jack DeJohnette, et al.). The music is a darkside counterpart to Can's halcyon flow motion universe. Miles's ocean is no coral-reef arcadia or wombadelic paradise, but altogether more murky and miasmic, full of rip-tides, treacherous currents and chthonic undertow, not so much Jacques Cousteau as E. A. Poe ('Descent into the Maelstrom').

It's a realm of grace and danger. On *Beauty*'s 'Directions', Chick Corea's Rhodes keyboards dart and dilate like shoals of poisonous jellyfish; Dave Holland's bass sustains terrific tension (although his sound seems monotone and two-dimensional compared to the plasma-morphic, pulse-sculpturing of Michael Henderson – the missing link between Larry Graham and Bootsy Collins – on the later albums). 'Miles Runs the Voodoo Down' begins with the brontosauran heavy rock gait of Mountain, swiftly comes to a seething roil – like magma in a caldera – then subsides into an amazing drumless interlude of itchy-and-squelchy insectoid interplay. Lacking the grotto-like recessive depths of the Macero-sculpted studio version, *Bitches Brew* is over-run with scrofulous, scurrying detail, then unravels into a post-fever stillness of necrotic ambience. On *Live-Evil*, highlights include the discombobulated, three-legged falter-funk of 'Sivad', the eldritch timbre poem 'Little Church', and 'What I Say', shifting from strident freeway boogie (imagine James Gang jamming with Art Ensemble of Chicago) to an amazing drumspace interlude before careening back on to the two-lane blackstop.

By 1973's *In Concert*, Miles's group was the *On the Corner* en-semble that included Michael Henderson, guitarist Reggie Lucas, drummer Al Foster and electric pianist Cedric Lawson. The album was a stop-gap release, offering loose and intermittently inspired versions of 'Right Off' from *A Tribute to Jack Johnson*, the awesome sitar-laced acid-funk of *On the Corner*'s 'Black Satin', plus previews of 'Rated X' and 'Honky Tonk' from the next studio album *Get Up With It*. Even the Corky McCoy artwork reiterates the ghettodelic imagery of *On the Corner*, testifying to Miles's determination to reach out to a young audience of black funkateers.

Throughout this period, Miles was infatuated with Sly Stone's music; in the sleevenotes for *Dark Magus*, saxophonist David Liebman tells of how Miles made him listen over and over to one track on *Fresh*. From the Family Stone's polyrhythmic perversity, Miles seems to have derived a model of musical democracy. But by *Dark Magus*, Miles and co-conspirators had gone several steps beyond Sly's utopian funkadelic commune or Weather Report's genteel 'everybody solos, nobody solos' equality; this music was far more turbulent, closer to mob rule or a flash riot. By this point, conventional structuring principles have long since been smelted down by the infernal heat generated by the ensemble, leaving just riffs, vamps, blips and blurts of sound, and irregular escalate-and-ebb dynamics that resemble the feverish struggle between a body and a contagion, or a soup shifting between simmer and boil. This is a music strung out between spasm and entropy.

In mob rule, there are no ringleaders, but certain troublemakers stand out from *Dark Magus*'s crowded mix: Pete Cosey's writhing spirals of lead guitar agony; Mtume's rattlesnake lashes of percussion and random eruptions of drum machine that recall Can's 'Peking O', Reggie Lucas's scalding, staccato rhythm guitar, etching itself into your brain like a branding iron. And of course, Miles's slurred, smeary trumpet, breaking out across this music's flesh like weals and blisters. Miles sounds poisoned, like he's siphoning pus from a soul-turned-cyst.

'Can the ocean be described?' was Roberts's rhetorical question. I think of chaos theory (*Dark Magus* as demonic Mandelbrot) and Deleuze and Guattari's rhizome ('musical form, right down to its ruptures and proliferations, is comparable to a weed'). I think of post-Deleuzian cyber-feminist Sadie Plant's description of the information ocean as 'an endless geographic plane of micromeshing pulsing quanta, limitless webs of interacting blendings, leakings, mergings . . .'. I reckon Miles was half in love with, half in dread of, the 'female' will-to-chaos, the mutagenic, metamorphic life force, exalted by Plant in her book *Zeroes + Ones*; that's why Miles's misogynist nickname for oceanic flux was 'bitches brew'. I think also of the Afro-diasporic baroque that is wildstyle typography, then remember Greg Tate got there first with his description of Miles's 'scribbling blurbs of feline, funky sound which under scrutiny take on graphic shapes as wild and willed as New York subway graffiti'. Finally, I think of the word 'protean', which derives from the name of a shapeshifting sea god. That's what Miles was, in his electrifying Electric Period: a Modern Proteus.

The Wire, October 1997

The only piece in this collection taken out of chronological sequence, because it sets up the next piece: an interrogation of the very assumptions (the equation of boundary-crossing and genre-blurring fusion with a utopian, One World impulse) that underlie my Electric Miles paean, with its libidinized imagery of alchemy, mutation, mongrelization, contamination, infection, intoxication . . .

PURE FUSION

Multiculture versus Monoculture

It's funny when you suddenly become aware of a tic within your own writing. It's a reflex I share with a fair few other popcult commentators: using the word 'purist' as an insult. I go further and frequently use the coinage 'impurist', which *sounds* like it ought to be pejorative, as praise. Behind the tic, there's a broader reflex: the impulse to celebrate artists who draw on a wide range of influences, based on the assumption that mixing up genres is intrinsically more progressive than a narrow focus on one stylistic path.

Increasingly dissatisfied with this glib assumption, I almost want to perversely defend purism as an aesthetic strategy – if only because such a lot of ostentatiously border-crossing work is actually far less impressive than it thinks it is. Think of Bill Laswell, leftfield music's most assiduous networker, continually convening one-off supergroups that unite P-Funk keyboard players with free jazz hornsmen with African guitarists with hip hop turntablists with dub producers with . . . well, you get the picture. The idea is similar to Jon Hassell's notion of the Fourth World (Western hi-tech modernity meets atavistic ethnic spirituality, to each other's mutual enrichment) but Laswell's panglobal superjams almost invariably end up a horrible mish-mash. Then there's those other perpetrators of lameness in the name of hybridity: the 'ethnotechno' school of world music sampling electronic outfits like TransGlobal Underground, Banco De Gaia, Loop Guru (who actually had a few moments, admittedly), Juno Reactor . . .

Trouble is, most of the music I like is hybrid, and its hybridity is high on the list of reasons why I rate it. This raises the question of why some fusions work and others remain composites of disparate sources without any vital spark. The language for judging success or failure in this realm is entirely metaphorical. Successful hybrids invite the imagery of alchemy or metallurgy (crucibles, amalgams, melding, smelting, and so forth), or the essentially similar language of cooking (bouillabaisse, gumbo, melting pots, etc.). Bad hybrids, like lumpy purées or unsuccessful cakes, are subject to the ultimate put-down: 'the end result is somehow less than the sum of its parts'.

Good musical hybridity, like good cooking, might be where you can still detect every element's distinctive flavour, but the flavours have interpenetrated each other – a perfect balance of heterogeneity and mixture (as opposed to the homogenized taste of a perfectly smooth purée). Then again, music isn't really like cooking – there's no reason why you can't have artists who make a whole dish out of the sonic equivalent of flour, or salt. (And you do – virtuosos of monochromatic concentration like Plastikman and Pole). And yet there's hardly any positive terms in pop critical discourse for fanatical focus or fixated perseverance. Fruitless displays of undistinguished versatility (a.k.a. being a jack of all trades and master of none) always run better with reviewers, few of whom seem to be equipped for listening closely to the subtle modulations of purist genres based around an aesthetic of the 'changing same', to misuse Amiri Baraka's phrase, the groove that just keeps on keepin' on, yet absorbs you with its endlessly shifting inflections and accents. Look at dance magazines, and you will see reviews that approvingly list an artist's forays into genres other than the one whose section they are actually reviewed under. Stylistic inconstancy, generic treason, and dilettantism are, paradoxically, almost supreme values. And often the writer gestures at a vague enemy allegedly outraged by these border-crossing forays and illicit mixtures: the purists.

Why is 'purist' such a potent insult? I think it relates to the word's etymological echoes (puritanism, and its related tropes of squeamishness, prudishness and closemindedness) and its semantic traces from other, genuinely reprehensible bodies of thought: eugenics, racial purity, cultural hygiene. 'Impurist' music, or what in an earlier age they called 'fusion', allies itself with a more virtuous bunch of concepts: multiculturalism, miscegenation, cosmopolitanism. It's especially heartwarming to ally yourself with words like these right now, when European politics is muddied by upsurges of ethnic anxiety about pollution and mixture: Le Pen, Haider and similar ultra-nationalist figures in Belgium, Romania and Norway; racial attacks on migrant workers, asylum seekers, immigrants. While British neo-fascist parties have declined in recent years, the UK's general population remains deeply divided over issues of multiculturalism and European unity;

there was a storm of outrage when a government-funded independent report on multiculturalism declared that the concept of 'Britishness' was latently racist owing to its imperial echoes.

One of the figures involved in drafting that report was Stuart Hall, pioneer of the cultural studies movement at Birmingham University in the 1970s. Paul Gilroy, one of Hall's former associates and, like him, a Black-British theorist about postcolonialism and hybridity, made his own contribution this year to the multiculture debate with *Against Race: Imagining Political Culture Beyond the Color Line* (also published, in the UK, as *Between Camps*). If the book has a crux, it's the fatal ambiguity of the word 'culture' itself – which simultaneously has an organic, biological resonance (growing plants, germ cultures, etc.) yet also signifies the antithesis of earthy natural-ness (the civilized, the non-instinctual, the artificial, the sublimated). The first aspect of 'culture' connects to notions of blood ties and their inevitable companion blood-letting: tribal warfare, ethnic cleansing, Balkanization or 'Rwanda-ization', the rhetoric of roots and homelands, struggles over mother tongues and state control of language.

Aiming to de-biologize the concept of race, reveal it as a pseudo-scientific figment, Gilroy – just like a music journalist – has his set of bad terms and his set of good terms:

essentialism/primordialism/unanimism/fraternalism/ethnic absolutism
versus
syncreticism/transculturalism/cosmopolitanism/diaspora.

There are no pure races, cultures, or art forms, Gilroy contends; everything is always already hybrid, contaminated by the other.

Gilroy acknowledges dance music as one of the bastions of contemporary 'transculture'. And interestingly, club and rave culture are where the discourse of purism versus hybridity is most heated. This is partly because the culture's primary focus isn't individual artists, as it is with rock, but styles and scenes. Because this is the level on which it's most productive to talk about stuff, a huge amount of discursive energy goes into cultural taxonomy, into identifying genres and subgenres like species; into tracing the genealogy of genres, the family trees and evolutionary pathways of different sounds. Yet individual dance artists are typically praised for *departing* from their chosen genre and taking on ideas from other styles.

Genre has a phantom trace of the concept of the genetic, and almost all the language used to discuss music has connotations of miscegenation: mix-and-blend, mutation, mongrels, the imperative to avoid incestuousness (the downside of all close-knit scenes) and instead widen one's gene pool. Either that, or it's the language of horticulture: grafts, hybrids, cross-breeds, grass roots. Typically, a new genre is discovered and hailed for its distinctiveness. But if it's not careful, this scene will soon become castigated for being purist, for not embracing influences from other genres. Rare indeed is the scene that can maintain for any length of time an equilibrium between self-consistency and flux, absorbing outside influences without flaking off into subgenres or offshoot tribes (with the hype-hungry media eagerly hastening this process in order to have something to write about).

Perhaps the privileging of aesthetic mingling as supreme value echoes the broader 'project' of club and rave culture, the premium it sets on social mixing. (Itself an echo of rock 'n' roll's original subversiveness – cross-town traffic between different races, the phantom threat of miscegenation that aroused the white Southern establishment's fears of 'negrification' and 'jungle rhythms'.) In dance discourse, a club that draws a mixed crowd is always good; all kinds of scenes echo the credo of pirate station Kool FM, 'it doesn't matter what your class colour or creed, you're welcome in the house of jungle'. Scenes lose their vibe, it's generally believed, when the mix becomes unbalanced (drum & bass, it's said, lost it when there were too many boys on the floor, the girls driven away by techstep's distorted noise and mechanistic stomp). The exhortation to mix up the styles, keep porous your genre boundaries, has an ethical charge to it: as if somehow an artist could singlehandedly resurrect the lost unity of rave, a unity shattered by, you guessed it, the purists, the schismmakers. Hence the unanimous praise for Basement Jaxx and Armand Van Helden, paradoxically taken as exemplars of their genre (house) yet praised for attempting to leave its borders at every opportunity.

There's a reversibility to dance culture's pro-hybridity rhetoric, for when the 'purists' (who do exist, and are often reactionary) talk about protecting their genre from its debasers, their language takes on unfortunate eugenic associations. Detroit techno pioneer Derrick May described breakbeat hardcore (the music that evolved into jungle) as a 'diabolical mutation' and declared, 'I don't even like to use the word "techno" because it's been bastardized and prostituted in every form you can possibly imagine'. His contemporary Eddie Fowlkes described European rave in terms of the 'cultural rape' of Detroit, and later put together a compilation of 'proper' Detroit-affiliated techno called *True People*. As Barbara Stafford argues in *Body Criticism: Imagining the Unseen in Enlightenment Art and Medicine*, 'the hybrid posed a special problem for those who worried about purity of forms . . . and unnatural mixtures . . . The metaphysical and physical dangers thought to inhere in artificial grafts surfaced in threatening metaphors of infection, contamination, rape and bastardy.'

Then again, the extent to which these aesthetic issues map on to real-world politics is confusing, to say the least. In the case of Detroit techno versus UK hardcore rave, the irony was that these British kids (white, black, mix-race) who were 'corrupting' techno were doing so by mixing it with elements from other forms of black music that the Detroit pioneers (all African American) disdained: hip hop's break-beats, dub reggae's bass, dancehall's rowdy vocals. In the cultural politics of Detroit, class division transected racial allegiances: the arty middle-class black kids who invented techno were Europhiles who despised hip hop as ghetto music, and feared its fans from the projects. Hardcore/jungle, as a hip hop/techno hybrid, represented the return of Detroit's repressed – which is why Detroit and Detroit-aligned artists resisted the breakbeat revolution for as long as possible.

Then again, is what I cherish about hardcore/jungle, and find relatively lacking in most Detroit techno, really about the former's hybridity and the latter's purism? Mixing disparate elements together guarantees nothing. There's a whole realm of bland blending out there, which Gilroy acknowledges when he refers to the banal forms of rootless cosmopolitanism in which 'everything becomes . . . blended into an impossibly even consistency'. Why is this kind of hybridity so lacking in interest? Is it the scent of tourism – safe encounters with an Other that reassuringly turns out to be harmless, or even the Same? I'm thinking of the world music phenomenon, where white Westerners like Paul Simon discovered the primal innocence and raw spirit of fifties rock 'n' roll alive and kicking, clad in the exotic ethnic flesh of Soweto or Bahia. The edge-less aura of these hybrids has something to do with their top-down nature, as opposed to more lateral/reciprocal/rhizomatic interactions. The slumming, inspiration-starved, albeit often genuinely enthusiastic, respectful and well-informed rock stars (David Byrne, Peter Gabriel) who seek aesthetic rejuvenation from outside Western pop can be contrasted with the sort of hybrids that emerge spontaneously through long-term proximity of different populations. Think of London's dance culture, which goes back long before rave to when Jamaicans first imported their sound system culture of heavy bass pressure, 'blues' (illegal all-night parties) and ganja. The result has been a continuum of creole music: lover's rock, Soul II Soul's 'funki dread' sound (imported American soul meets reggae, but only in London), breakbeat hardcore and jungle, today's UK underground garage and 2-

step. Or take Bristol, another UK city with a long-established multiracial presence, but which produced its own quite differently inflected cross-breeds: The Pop Group's dub-funk-jazz charged version of postpunk, trip hop, Roni Size/Reprazent. All of these hybrid sounds have an element of evolutionary randomness about them, and reflect not just sonic recombination but social exchanges, reciprocal transfers of behaviour and ideas. Compare these slowly spawned hybrids with the fusions hatched in laboratory-like conditions by the likes of Bill Laswell. The organic versus synthetic metaphor is perhaps too loaded, but there does seem to be a difference here between interbreeding/grafts and cut 'n' paste/collage, a contrast possibly analogous to the difference between analogue and digital. Where the first set of hybrids (jungle, 2-step, etc.) are productively contaminated with the mess of everyday life and street knowledge, the second set has an unmistakeable aura of sterility, the academic.

Ultimately, these are musical values, aesthetic failings, though: lack of 'spark' or 'vibe' or whatever other vital intangible it is that animates music. And perhaps the whole debate over purism versus impurism is based on the mistaken belief that you can map aesthetics on to politics, find a straightforward equivalence or correlation between worth in one realm and the other. Dick Hebdige, the famed subcultural theorist (and contemporary of Stuart Hall and Paul Gilroy), once described the development of UK pop music as 'a phantom history of British race relations'. I've long concurred with this view, but now I'm not so sure. The racial narrative – above all, the white romance with black music – is just one of many threads in the tangled tapestry of pop culture, and the picture gets confused by a host of other factors and struggles: class, gender, technology. Furthermore, as pop/rock grew older, it started to develop its own internal politics, engage in purely aesthetic struggles, and go through shifts based on a self-reflexive relationship with its own accumulating history (the postmodern feedback loops crystallized in the famous phrase 'pop will eat itself'). Working out what a given piece of music, or a particular trend, correlates with in terms of the outside world is hard enough, let alone a specific strand of political reality such as race relations.

Take, for example, the recent issue of *Melody Maker* that featured a cover story headlined 'UK Garage – My Arse!' and the sub-headline 'Alternative Rock Fights Back'. Depicted on the cover is a black man with a striking resemblance to garage superstar Craig David, sitting on the toilet listening to a Walkman with his trousers around his ankles, a piece of toilet paper in his hand. The back story to this is the bursting of Britpop's bubble. The giddy mood of jingoistic triumphalism that consumed the entire UK indie-rock scene – bands, fans, journalists – for a good three-year period 1995–97, had now curdled to bitter dismay, as the pop charts became dominated by American R&B and rap, plus the homegrown house/jungle/R&B hybrid known as UK garage a.k.a. 2-step. *Melody Maker*'s cover could be seen as a petulant fit of impotent rage from a magazine whose sales had shrivelled to a pathetic 30,000 copies a week.

My initial response, as UK garage fan and *MM* veteran of the days when the magazine put Public Enemy on the cover, was to squeal 'racism!'. The explicit equation of UK garage, a multiracial scene dominated by black musical values, with shit connects unhappily with a little-known dirty secret about the UK music press: market research by IPC, the conglomerate that owns both *Melody Maker* and its rival *NME*, discovered that the large market segment of casual readers who pick up one paper or the other depending on who's on the cover wouldn't buy issues that featured black faces on their covers. As reprehensible and sad as the 'UK Garage – My Arse!' cover was (the first black man on *MM*'s cover in living memory), though, I'm not utterly convinced that indie-rockers' antipathy towards 'that garage crap' is really racist. It's a mixture of discontents and repugnances: aesthetic disgust (the smooth, shiny UKG production transgresses indie-rock's values of sonic shabbiness), gender bias (UKG connotes girly, pop values like singalong melodies, diva soulfulness, lyrics about sex and romance), class affiliation (garage's working class dress-to-impress fashion and fetish for expensive designer labels versus middle-class students' dressed-down scruffiness), rock snobberies about the superiority of lyrics/persona over rhythm/production. Add to that the stinging feeling of being marginalized, a sense of being the underdog, and you have the ingredients for ressentiment. Racism – more on the level of ignorant, stereotyped ideas about black music cultures than hatred – acts as a glue that coheres all these different strands of antagonism together. In other words, it's exactly the same complicated tissue of reactionary and nostalgic impulses that lay behind Morrissey's attitudes to dance music.

Another way of looking at these relationships between aesthetics and politics is to find the least black-influenced music around and see if it correlates with racism, as it ought according to this logic. So take gabba, the hardcore techno subgenre – one of the most ferociously purist forms of music around, and 'white'-sounding to most ears. Gabba has been persistently smeared with a Far Right association for years – because of the lack of 'blackness' in its rhythmic feel, the aura it emits of a rampaging mob, and the fact that many of its fans have

278

short cropped hair. As a fan of some of this stuff, I'll tell you straight up that there's definitely an aesthetic quality to it that verges on the fascistic, or at least the dark side of the Dionysian: an amphetamine-wired aura of blitzkrieg, sinister pageantry, sturm und drang. Does this cyber-Wagner bombast have any intrinsic politics, though? (Marcus Garvey was into regimentation, drill, uniforms, too.)

Dig deeper, and you discover that while gabba has a skinhead following in some parts of Europe, it is also the soundtrack of choice for Far Left anger – for anarchists, squat-dwelling and free party organizing renegades. Even in Holland, where some of the big gabba labels felt the need to clarify things by putting 'Gabbers Against Hate and Racism' slogans on their record sleeves, you discover that many of the leading DJs started out spinning hip hop. Some top gabber DJs – Holland's Darkraver, the UK's Loftgroover – are actually black.

But let's focus on one gabba god, German producer Marc Acardipane (a.k.a. the Mover and about twenty other alter egos). Probably the most accomplished producer in the genre, and perpetrator of some of the most Vikings-going-berserker sounding gabber so far, Acardipane is also a big hip hop fan. His formative techno influences are from black Detroit artists Suburban Knight and Underground Resistance, and he also made some early breakbeat-driven rave tunes and jungle tracks. So we're not dealing with a guy with a closed mind or ears. The Mover's decision to pursue such a purist, narrowly focused music path is entirely aesthetic, and entirely productive: he has created a vast, frequently astounding body of work.

There are purisms in music that are reactive and reactionary. They couch themselves in terms of a return to something that's been lost – an original vibe, 'funk', musicality, emotion – or as honourings/resurrections of some bygone golden age (acid jazz and seventies fusion; deep house's yearning for the Paradise Garage and the lost eclecticism of seventies underground disco culture). You could call this kind of purism 'fundamentalist' perhaps, gesturing at its religiosity, its attitude of keeping the faith. But other purisms are forward-tilted, emergent, and in some senses self-generating. This kind of purism seems to coalesce in response to the centripetal pull of a strange attractor, shedding off the residues of other styles and honing down to an aesthetic essence: think of how jungle emerged from the messy chaos of hardcore rave, and how jungle further refined itself into jump-up and techstep. Perhaps there is an optimal point in the arc of any purist music, after which the self-refining minimalism becomes anorexia – the style eating away at itself. (This is what happened to drum & bass after it perfected itself circa 1996; to gabba once it had gone beyond a certain extremity of beats-per-minute and distortion and exhausted all the possibilities within its very enclosed terrain.)

The Mover's purism is the forward-leaning sort. Title-wise, his tracks often refer to a private mythology based around the apocalyptic future; an obsession with the year 2017 that maybe relates to this idea of an exponential arc of intensification (sonic, techno-cultural) hurtling towards a singularity in the near future. If Acardipane were to dabble more in mixing styles or broaden his textural palette beyond the few colours of which he is master, his work would only lose its power, its fanatical focus. There is an undeniable aura of zeal in the music, which begs the question again of its real-life correlates, if any. The 'fascism' in this music is the desire, enflamed by the music but also satisfied by the music, to merge with a collective vastness ('Into Sound', as one Acardipane track is titled; see also titles like 'Hall' and the Cold Rush label slogan 'music for huge space arenas'). This is also the desire to merge with the rave massive: mobilized but aimless, united but apolitical. In a sense, this music isn't about but simply *is* the desire for mission, insurgency, destination, destiny, singlemindedness, a mobilized and rampaging unanimity; rage without object, belief without creed. And it suggests that fantasies of purity relate to our ancient desires for the absolute. When you come to think about it, music is just about the healthiest, safest place to deal with such longings.

Director's cut of piece written for *Springerin*, December 2000

It's amazes me how artists still get a round of critical applause for adding genre X to genre Y, and a bleedin' ovation if they throw genre Z in there too. Why, only in the last week I've seen pieces praising Diplo and Kid 606 for basically being consummate style hoppers, magisterial magpies. This sort of thing never ceases to play well with reviewers: gadfly eclecticism, leaping between styles from album to album, proliferating an endless chain of side-projects and collaborations (not so much rhizomatic as simple networking). Border-crossing forays of this ilk have become an almost completely meaningless gesture. In this digital age, anything can be spliced to anything else at the click of a mouse, and all musics are almost instantly accessible. So you can explore an Other-ly music without effort or risk – there's no venturing into shady clubs or dangerous neighbourhoods, no need for actual fraternization with the Other. Nowadays musicians don't even need to meet to collaborate, they can back-and-forth music files through the web.

Yet there did used to be a liberating charge, a subversive buzz, to the bringing together of styles that were meant to be kept separate . . . the emergence of new hybrid genres (from punk-funk to jungle) seemed to echo on the collective, public level the kind of epiphanies we experience as individuals, in private . . . a line of taste is crossed, a prejudice overcome, there's the vertigo of horizons expanding. The question remains: what are these musical breakings-down and breakings-through worth, if nothing outside the realm of culture ever changes? They seem to be worth something, something more than nothing . . . but maybe that's a faded echo or hangover from the era of genuinely volatile and transformative fusions.

And in the following piece I revert to the default position – lambasting insularity (Brit-rock) and praising an 'all gates open' approach (Radiohead circa *Kid A*).

RADIOHEAD VERSUS BRIT-ROCK/
THOM YORKE INTERVIEW

What went *wrong* with British rock? Surveying the current panorama of mediocrity, it's hard to recall a more barren time. The last four years' output of UK guitar-based music makes the early seventies – that fabled hiatus of stalled stagnation between sixties supernova and punk renewal – seem like a period of staggering abundance and diversity. (Which it actually was, if you think about it: the official rock history gets it wrong, as it so often does.)

What *happened* to the culture that produced bands like Roxy Music, Joy Division, The Fall, the Banshees, The Specials, Associates, Human League, The Smiths, My Bloody Valentine (and that to-name-just-a-few litany includes neither obvious Mythic Greats nor the myriad mavericks that brighten the corners of Brit-rock's pantheon) – bands who each created their own aesthetic universes and singular pop languages. Now steel yourself and scrutinize the standard-bearers of recent years: Gomez with their amiable pastiches of bygone Americana; Manic Street Preachers, the People's Choice after years of dogged slog, peddling overwroughtly arranged New Wave melodrama queerly redolent of the Boomtown Rats or Pink Floyd circa *The Wall*; Catatonia, Stereophonics, Gay Dad, and other inkie cover faves offering what apparently passes for star quality, singing, and songcraft in this blighted isle. The sense of doldrum, of living through undistinguished times, is completed by the steady drizzle of solo albums and post-breakup projects from the debris of Madchester and Britpop – Butler, Squire, Brown, Coxon, Ashcroft.

Why does British rock continue to come up empty? Obviously, Britpop shoulders much blame – for its nostalgic jingoism and implicitly racist flight from contemporary multiculture; for the way it sanctioned derivativeness and grave-robbing necrophilia; for its anorexic, anachronistic fetish for the snappy three-minute ditty (as if the seven-inch single was still the culture's prime format). Most pernicious of all is the damage done to the ideal of independent music by Britpop's Make it Big at All Costs ethos, which made the pursuit of innovation for its own sake unfashionable, even faintly ludicrous. If The Stone Roses started this tendency (citing only the most obvious influences, like the Beatles, as mark of their ambition and self-regard) and the Manics turned it into ideology (so that having obscure influences or experimental impulses became the sign of defeatism/elitism), it was Oasis who made it orthodoxy. Their sole *raison d'être* was to be Big, to create a sense of Size that we could all bask in. And so empty boasts about seeing no reason why this band shouldn't be as big as the Beatles became compulsory for the kind of bands that exist to fill up one-page features in the weekly music papers. Since major labels alone have the clout to make bands that big, the result was a massive withdrawal of energy and interest from the independent sector. Look at the indie charts now, and you'll find a motley coalition of drum & bass and techno records, death metal albums and other micro-genre niche-markets, and pop stars who happen to go through independent distribution. The kind of diverse but unified independent music culture that in 1988 could sustain an A.R. Kane album at Number 1 for four weeks doesn't exist any more.

By now, though, there should have been the backlash, seeds of regeneration budding if not blooming. Britpop's bubble burst quite a while back (Pulp's *This is Hardcore*'s unexpected shortfall, the bloat and crapulence of Oasis's *Be Here Now*), and the gold-rush A&R blunders have puked up their dismal debuts and in many cases already been downsized from the rosters. But apart from the odd cult-figure-in-waiting (your Badly Drawn Boys) and veteran shapeshifters (your Primal Screams, Saint Etiennes, etc.) this unprecedented inspiration-drought continues. Why?

Dance culture done it. Dance culture was the worst thing that ever happened to British rock. Not just because its unparalleled enticements permanently hijacked the greater portion of rock's potential audience (even in its lamest, most edge-less form – trance and hard house – clubbing beats gigging by an unbeatable margin). But because the electronic arena has sucked up a good 90 per cent of the musical intellect available. Brit-rock ails because this country's sharpest musical minds are dedicated to making instrumental, non-band music. Why should the Eno-type inspired non-musicians bother with all the friction and hassle of being in a band when they can implement their ideas quickly via compliant, near-infinitely flexible machines? Dance culture and its home-listening oriented adjuncts even hold out the possibility of making a few bob.

As a result, rock has been left to people with the worst motivations: fame, exhibitionism, the desire to make music like they did in the good old days (the sixties, punk/New Wave). Or it's left rock to people with something to 'say': the quote machines, the would-be poets. 'All mouth, no trousers' has been Brit-rock's cardinal liability since the post-punk era, when attitude, self-salesmanship and music-paper-friendly gift of gab became more important than instrumental skill or sonic vision.

For most of the nineties, the ferment of post-rave music made the mounting failure of Brit-rock easy to ignore. So why not just dispense with rock and be done with it? Because dance has its own downside – what you might call 'all trousers, no mouth'. The problem with funktional ravefloor fodder and *Wire*-magazine type abstraction alike is that it is so sheerly sonic, about the materiality of rhythm and texture and nothing else. Whereas the genius of British pop has always been the way that sonix and discourse, music and ideas *about* music, have meshed and cross-catalyzed each other. It's not that dance music is meaningless. It can even 'say' stuff about the world outside the club's walls, through vocal samples, rhythmic tension, bass pressure, atmospherics. But the feelings dance music communicates tend to come in primary colours, without shading or ambivalence. Mostly, it has the vicarious quality of the drug experiences it's generally designed to enhance: blasts of euphoria, impersonal forcefields of energy that you can plug in to. It can be hard to connect the weekend's sensation-rides and artificial highs with everyday life. Which is why the late nineties saw lots of people who'd been through the rave adventure suddenly feeling stranded in an emotional void. I really noticed it in 1997: friends hitherto exclusively of the electronic persuasion were suddenly listening to albums by bands like the Verve and Spiritualized. Above all, they were listening to *OK Computer*. That album had the ravishing textural splendour required to seduce ears used to electronica's lavish sonic palette, but it also contained the complicated emotions, spiritual nourishment and solace that rock at its best has always provided.

In a sense, dance music has been Britpop's accomplice, its partner in crime – together they have created a fatal split in British pop culture, separating musical innovation from all the other stuff that the UK has always excelled at (stylization, attitude, arty pretentiousness) and without which, music is 'just' music. A great British rock record in the

Y2K would have to fuse the severed halves, reconnect sound and significance, get the balance right between mouth and trousers. A great, fully contemporary rock record would have to rival the vivid colours, spatial weirdness and rhythmic compulsion routinely available in the realm of electronic music, but combine them with the kind of interiority and potential for individualized response that surface-and-sensation oriented, collective-high-inducing dance rarely reaches. *Kid A* is such a record . . .

Uncut, November 2000

Platinum and gold. The walls of Courtyard Management's office are lined with discs commemorating prodigious feats of unit-shifting in far-flung territories of the globe. Located in the somnolent Oxfordshire village of Sutton Courtenay, Courtyard is the nerve centre for one of the world's most successful bands. But all previous triumphs (*Kid A* winning the Grammy for Best Alternative Album, the anointing of *OK Computer* as Best Album of All Time by the readers of *Q*) surely pale next to the ultimate accolade: getting on to the cover of *The Wire*.

Seriously, though, maybe your first thought on picking up this issue of *The Wire* was 'whatthafuck?!, and maybe that's an understandable reaction. After all, Radiohead are a group who have chalked up multi-platinum sales in fifty countries. I haven't done the maths (I'm not that crazy) but it does strike me as perfectly conceivable that the total career sales of every single other artist featured in this current issue of *The Wire*, totted up, still might not match the global sales of *OK Computer*, Radiohead's biggest album. And there is a potent argument that a band with this kind of commercial heft and such a degree of mainstream consensus of praise behind them simply has no place on the front cover of a magazine known for championing mavericks and margin-dwellers.

But Radiohead, I will argue, have earned it. Consider the facts: late last year, three albums rejuvenated the moribund concept of 'post-rock', Sigur Ros's *Agaetis Byrjun*, Godspeed You Black Emperor's *Lift Yr. Skinny Fists Like Antennas to Heaven!*, and *Kid A*. All three tampered with post-rock's increasingly pro forma formula in signifi-cant ways: Godspeed bringing political angst to this generally abstract and dispassionate genre, Sigur Ros adding human songfulness to what's usually instrumental mood music, *Kid A* doing a bit of both. But only one of this 'post-rock reborn!' triumvirate entered the UK and US album charts at Number 1. Now its sister-record *Amnesiac* – drawn from the same sessions as *Kid A*, indeed at one point the two records were set to be a double album – has repeated this extraordinary feat.

What's fascinating, and unprecedented, is just how Radiohead pulled off this violent swerve from the path seemingly mapped out for them (*OK Computer* had left them only a step away from becoming the biggest rock band on the planet), and instead plunged into *Wire*-friendly terrain. For whether it's Autechre-like glitchtronic contraptions like 'Pull/Pulk Revolving Doors', the Scott Walker-scored-by-Penderecki balladry of 'How to Disappear Completely', the *Spirit of Eden/On Land* vapourscape of 'Treefingers', the Faust-meets-Mingus interstellar overdrive of 'The National Anthem', or the Alice Coltrane-infused haze of 'Dollars & Cents', Radiohead are currently operating as mainstream ambassadors for many of the things this magazine cherishes.

Asked to ponder this mystery, Thom Yorke – Radiohead's singer and by all accounts its aesthetic tillerman – shrugs it off as simply not that remarkable: 'Maybe we just took some sort of left turn.' Relaxed and healthy-looking, he barely resembles the gaunt ghostfaced figure that appears in the *OK Computer* world tour documentary *Meeting People Is Easy*, harrowed by the endless grind of interviews/meet-and-greets/photo-shoots/soundchecks/ligs. Nor is he the prickly, blood-from-a-stone interviewee of legend. There are moments, though, where it does occurs to me that 'genial, laidback, unassuming' might just be another shield: a slyer strategy of self-protection than the old fools-not-gladly-suffered persona.

'Downplay everything' seems to be the new Radiohead media relations policy – the canny pre-emptive disarming of any accusations of auto-hype or delusions of avant-grandeur. So Yorke suggests that *Kid A* was 'not as much of a radical gesture as some said'. And guitarist/multi-instrumentalist Jonny Greenwood, speaking by phone from Spain a few days later, claims Radiohead just picked up where they left off with *OK Computer*. 'With us, it's never going to be a case of "let's tear up the blueprint and start from scratch".' When the *Kid A* reviews came out accusing us of being wilfully difficult, I was like, "if that was true, we'd have done a much better job of it". It's not that challenging – everything's still four minutes long, it's melodic.'

Such self-effacing professions of modest ambition are rather at odds with the impression given by Radiohead in the press blitz around *Kid A* last autumn, which painted a picture of a band almost tearing itself to bits in the struggle to achieve total aesthetic renewal. Yorke spoke of how he'd even contemplated changing the name of the band in order to make a break with Radiohead's past recordings, towards which he felt utter alienation. Instead of self-destruction, Radiohead eventually settled on self-deconstruction: discarding or tampering with the two things that the band was most celebrated for by fans and critics alike, the guitar sound, and Yorke's singing and lyrics. *Kid A* is largely devoid of guitars (Jonny Greenwood preferring to play the Ondes Martenot proto-synth, arrange a string orchestra, even play the recorder). And *Amnesiac*'s slight-return-to-rock is not going to get the fans transcribing fret fingerings and posting 'guitar tabs' up on their webzines, as they did with *OK Computer*. As for Yorke's singing, on *Kid A/Amnesiac* studio technology and vocal technique are both applied to dyslexify his already oblique, fragmented words. Yorke has said he will never allow the lyrics to be printed and that listeners are expressly not meant to focus on them.

Radiohead's not-such-a-radical-shift-really line is also belied by Yorke's evident glee at the way *Kid A* upset his 'peers' in the Brit-rock aristocracy. 'We're extremely chuffed because two days ago Jonny did an interview with a Brazilian newspaper and the first question was "What do you think of Noel and Liam from Oasis saying *Kid A* was 'a monumental piece of cowardice'?" I don't even know what that means, but who cares, we were like "YES! we've finally pissed them off!" Lots of people took massive offence at *Kid A*. We got it from the weirdest sources, like Shirley Manson from Garbage. She wrote this pure bile, like: "How fucking dare they? They're not the Velvet Underground! Who the fuck do they think they are?!" What was the other one? Oh yes, even better – the singer from Texas said "If they're going to make music only for themselves, they can fuck off back to their bedrooms!"' This creates a nice image for me: the notion of Shirley Manson and Sharleen Spiteri secretly craving to make music influenced by Mingus or Messaien, but denying themselves out of some sense of duty to their fans or the world at large. 'Exactly! For the benefit of humanity, Texas exist . . .' Yorke cackles uproariously.

Clearly, *Kid A* was clearly taken as some kind of stinging reproach by a number of underachieving and deeply compromised Britpopsters. 'We've obviously riled them in some way,' agrees Yorke. Perhaps the 'cowardice' comment from the Gallagher brothers is related to Britpop's core ideology of make-it-big-at-any-costs, a rhetoric of shooting-for-the-charts which denigrated the old indie-rock ideals as defeatist, obscurantist, even elitist. Not only did *Kid A* resurrect a different concept of ambition – artistic growth as opposed to sales bloat – but it interfered with Radiohead fulfilling their 'proper' destiny: becoming a U2-circa-*The Joshua Tree* megaband.

* * *

A brief history of Radiohead: how they got here from there. Formed in Oxford by five school friends, the group first grabbed attention with 'Creep', a single that on its original release in Britain did nothing, but became a massive hit in post-Nirvana America when modern rock radio programmers picked up on it. In many ways, the 'grunge ballad' sound of 'Creep' and its stance (maladjustment and ressentiment akin to the outcast protagonist of 'Smells Like Teen Spirit') did make Radiohead an English equivalent to Nirvana. The two groups had similar influences and idols (Pixies, R.E.M., Sonic Youth), were fuelled by similar distaste for phoniness and plastic-ness, and faced similar accusations of wallowing in misery. But the crucial word there is 'English': you can imagine Kurt Cobain, if he'd chosen to live, probably going the unplugged troubadour route, stripping down his sound to let his plaintive songs stand naked and alone, forlorn and folky. You could never imagine him doing a *Kid A*, plunging deeper into studio science. Therein lies the vast, enduring gulf between American and British ideas of rock.

By 1995's *The Bends*, the English art-rock element was starting to come to the fore. Pop musicians and movie stars started turning up to their shows; stoners and lapsed ravers turned on to the sheer drug-conducive luxuriance of their sound. But it was 1997's *OK Computer* that really transformed Radiohead into the rock band it was okay for electronica headz to dig. It was also the album where Yorke and Co. started to complicate the anthemic-ness of their earlier music in earnest. Although it's not immediately evident on the surface of the record, the spaciousness of songs like the rippling, radiant 'Subterranean Homesick Alien' was influenced by deep immersion in Miles Davis's *Bitches Brew*.

A sort of semi-concept album about technology and alienation, *OK Computer*'s sheer magnitude – of sound, thematics, aspiration – served time on Britpop, replacing its laddish anti-intellectualism and vacant hedonism with the glamour of literacy and angst. Noel and Liam are right to feel goaded: Radiohead are the anti-Oasis, and *OK Computer*'s massive popular success, eclipsing the Gallagher Bros' cocaine-blighted/bloated *Be Here Now*, announced the closing of an entire era of Brit-rock. Touring and promoting the album for much of 1998, though, convinced Yorke that it was still too enmired in rock tradition, too epic. 'It was still pressing all the correct buttons,' he says. When *Q*'s readership infamously voted *OK Computer* the Best Album of All Time (an error of passion that is at least preferable to unfurling yet again the sanctioned pantheon of *Pet Sounds/Revolver/Astral*

Weeks/London Calling), Radiohead had become rock icons in the most old-fashioned sense – the singer as seer, oracle, figurehead, spokesperson. 'I tell you what's really ridiculous . . . going into a book shop and there's all these books about yourself,' Yorke says of the multiple cut-and-paste Radiohead biographies that came out in *Computer*'s wake. 'In a way, it feels like you're already dead. So you've got a kind of licence to start again.'

Worn out by the experiences documented on *Meeting People is Easy* (like touring America's infamous 'shed circuit' of 10,000 capacity, corporate-sponsored venues) and the self-consciousness feedback syndrome induced by being over-interviewed and reading pseudo-psychoanalytical interpretations of his work ('people presume everything you write is completely personal . . . it feels weird, like someone walking over your grave'), Yorke spiralled into a black period of confusion and creative block. 'Melodies became an embarrassment to me,' he told *Select* last year; he hated the lyrics he was coming up with. Even the sound of his voice made Yorke nauseous. 'It did my head in that whatever I did with my voice, it had that particular set of associations. And there were lots of similar bands coming out at the time, and that made it even worse. I couldn't stand the sound of me even more.' Embarking on the fraught, spasmodic sessions for *Kid A/Amnesiac*, he 'got really into the idea of my voice being another one of the instruments, rather than this precious, focus thing all the time'.

This instrumentalization of the lead singer was just one facet of a total deconstruction of Radiohead as rock band, instigated by Yorke. As guitarist Ed O'Brien put it, the members had to learn 'how to be a participant in a song without playing a note'. In a sense, every member became a Eno-like figure, a non-musician producer/catalyst, abandoning their designated instrumental function and grappling with unfamiliar sound-generation devices as if they were toys, with a child-like wonder and joy. 'It's not about being a guitarist in a rock band, it's about having an instrument in front of you and you're really excited by it,' says Yorke. 'It's like with Jonny playing Ondes Martenot on . . . just about everything! We couldn't stop him! We had to beg him to play guitar on "Morning Bell".'

Greenwood says the Martenot obsession dates back to hearing it used in Oliver Messaien's Turalinga Symphony when he was fifteen. 'I spent years reading all these descriptions of them, I couldn't even find a photograph, and then two years ago I finally got hold of one, and they're fantastic. The best way to describe it is a very accurate Theremin that you have far more control of. The most famous use of Martenot is the *Star Trek* theme, and it sounds like a woman singing. When it's played well, you can really emulate the voice. I get annoyed with electronic instruments because I reckon the Martenot is a bit of a peak.'

With producer and 'sixth member' Nigel Godrich gradually coming round to the new approach, Radiohead embarked upon all kinds of Eno-esque oblique strategies: working on dozens of songs at once, moving on to something different as soon as it got boring or blocked; splitting into two groups engaged in different activities. 'It's like you're dabbling, but at the same time, when something really comes off, it's all down on tape,' says Yorke. 'Nigel's really into the idea of capturing a performance, even if we're doing pure electronic stuff. So it's never like we just program stuff and let it run. There always had to be something else going on, processing in real-time.'

Holger Czukay's jam/slice/splice approach to producing Can was another model. 'Dollars & Cents', one of *Amnesiac*'s highlights, was edited down from an eleven-minute improvisation. 'It was incredibly boring,' laughs Yorke, 'but it's that Holger thing of chop chop chop, making what seems like drivel into something coherent.' Then orchestral strings – arranged by Greenwood and recorded in Dorchester Abbey – 'were added to give it a sort of authority'.

No strangers to the studio craft of overdubbing and effects, on *Kid A/Amnesiac* Radiohead finally and utterly abandoned the performance model of rock recording and went fully into concocting sonic fictions using the mixing desk as instrument. Answering a fan's query on Radiohead's spinwithagrin web forum, Greenwood talked about being obsessed with 'the whole artifice of recording. I see it like this: a voice into a microphone on to a tape, on to your CD, through your speakers is all as illusory and fake as any synthesizer – it doesn't put Thom in your front room. But one is perceived as "real", the other, somehow "unreal" . . . It's the same with guitars versus samplers. It was just freeing to discard the notion of acoustic sounds being truer.' Speaking on the phone, Greenwood says the idea was influenced by reading a book on recording called *Repeated Takes*. 'The more concerts we do, the more dissatisfied we get with trying to reproduce the live sound on a record. In a way, it can't be done, and that's a relief really, when you accept that, and recording just becomes a different thing.'

The most striking departures from the real-time three-guitar band sound are pieces like *Kid A*'s title track (with its exquisitely wistful music-box chime and melted-candle Yorke vocal, it's worthy of Curd Duca or Boards of Canada) and *Amnesiac*'s 'Like Spinning Plates', whose disassociated drift reminds me of Robert Wyatt's *Rock Bottom* updated for the IDM era. 'Plates' is partly built from an earlier song called 'I Will' played backwards. Says Yorke, 'We'd turned the tape around, and I was in another room, heard the vocal melody coming backwards, and thought "that's miles better than the right way round", then spent the rest of the night trying to learn the melody.'

Although some have accused Radiohead of jumping on the electronica bandwagon, Yorke says his interest in Aphex-type music actually pre-dates the band's 1983 debut *Pablo Honey*. 'When the Warp thing was first happening, I was really into things like Sweet Exorcist's "Per Clonk". It sounded really amazing coming out of an enormous PA system. All that Warp stuff made the bass bins blow with their turbo sounds.' Studying Art and English at Exeter University in the early nineties, he even participated in a techno-influenced rock group called Flickernoise as a sideline from Radiohead, but found working with sequencers too frustrating. After the *OK Computer* tour, though, utterly burned on music containing guitars and singing, Yorke bought the entire Warp back catalogue and started ordering obscure IDM records via the Internet. For a long while during the *Kid A* sessions, he was totally uninterested in melody, just into exploring texture and rhythm. The result was tracks like *Kid A*'s 'Idioteque', which sounds like a PiL/'Death Disco'-style twist on 2-step garage but is actually 'an attempt to capture that exploding beat sound where you're at the club and the PA's so loud, you know it's doing damage'. On *Amnesiac*, the dirty 808 bass of 'Pull/Pulk Revolving Doors' invites you to re-imagine Yorke's mid-eighties adolescence – not pining indoors to *Murmur* and *Hatful of Hollow*, but doing graf and breakdancing in deserted shopping centres alongside LFO.

* * *

All this mixing-up sounds very 'post-rock' – unsurprisingly, a banner behind which Greenwood, ever so courteously, declines to rally. More tellingly, it's also very post-punk: the Lydon-esque rhetoric of leaving rock for dead ('I never wanted to be in a fucking rock group,' Yorke told *Spin*), the post-Eno/dub embrace of the studio, the forays into electronics, black dance rhythm, jazz. Radiohead are possibly the very last of a generation of bands formatively influenced by the 1979–81 moment. Too young (all early thirties) to have experienced Joy Division/Magazine/etc. as they actually happened, they encountered it through the time-honoured 'older brother syndrome'. Or in the case of Jonny and Colin Greenwood (Radiohead's bassist), an older sister. 'It was that cliché of having the older sibling, whose record collection you kind of acquire,' says Jonny. 'Even five years out of date, her music was much better than what the kids at our school were playing to each other.' I tell Greenwood he's very lucky: in my day, the 'wisdom' passed on by older brothers was of the 'Clapton is God'/'Genesis rule' sort (thank God I was the first-born in my family).

Greenwood's guitar sound – more audible on *Amnesiac*, which has a couple of Smiths-y tunes but is nothing like the back-to-normal-Radiohead-business it was touted as – is firmly in the post-blues, non-riff lineage that runs from Tom Verlaine through Will Sergeant/The Edge/Johnny Marr/Terry Bickers: that plangent dazzle-ripple-chime. 'Our guitars are more clitoris substitutes than phallus ones – we stroke them in a nicer, gentler way,' Greenwood once said; when I bring this up, he says he nicked the line from Slowdive, another Thames Valley group. 'I think guitars are over-idolized as instruments. All the guitarists I've ever liked have had the Bernard Sumner approach. It's about not practising. I like what Tom Waits said about only ever picking up an instrument if he's going to write a song.'

Radiohead's very name comes from an obscure Talking Heads song, and *Remain in Light* was a life-changing event for Yorke. Not just musically but lyrically too. 'I'd listened to it endlessly but never looked at the words, and when I finally did, it really freaked me out. When they made that record, they had no real songs, just wrote it all as they went along. Byrne turned up with pages and pages, and just picked stuff up and threw bits in all the time. And that's exactly how I approached *Kid A* . . . Jerry Harrison, their keyboard player, turned up to one of our gigs, just walked into the dressing room. Poor chap, after we realized who he was, he got grilled for hours on *Remain in Light* – "are there any loops or did you just play it all?" And they played it all, even though it sounds like tape-loops. Do you know the story about "Overload"? They'd read about Joy Division for the first time in NME, thought "that sounds interesting", and decided to do a tune based on what they thought Joy Division would be like, never having heard them!'

* * *

Two other things about Radiohead also strike me as very post-punk. First is their quiet but steadfast insistence on 'total control', which recalls PiL's (largely rhetorical) notion of itself as a 'communications company' using a major label's marketing muscle but essentially being autonomous. In Radiohead's case, 'total control' encompasses not just the licence-to-indulge that underpins *OK Computer/Kid A/Amnesiac*, but a host of other aspects: the way they've kept their operational base outside London; the obsessive attention to detail that goes into their artwork (*Amnesiac* comes encased as a hardback library book, complete with much-stamped slip; inside, there are lavish colour plate illustrations by Yorke's alter-ego Tchocky and university pal Stanley Donwood); the group's website (also designed by Donwood) via which Radiohead maintain direct contact with its fans. Shrugging off the PiL analogy ('we could never do a record on a par with *Metal Box*, let alone *Flowers of Romance* . . . and I'm no Lydon: I can't keep up the attitude!'), Yorke likes to stress that their independence-within-the-corporate-mainstream is precarious, dependent on the massive success of *OK Computer*. Greenwood admits 'we are a little fascistic in how and where our music is heard, but then we can be. If we were struggling, I'm sure we'd sell our music to anybody just to carry on.'

The other spirit-of-'79 quality is Radiohead's relentless bleakness, an alienation that is never entirely private, sourced merely in individual neurosis. Reversing the old post-punk dictum, one might describe it as 'the political is personal'. Yorke has described *Kid A*/*Amnesiac* as being about 'bearing witness'. The things witnessed range from the connivings of politicians ('You and Whose Army?' is about Blair, based on direct encounters that came about through Yorke's involvement in the Jubilee 2000 petition to write off Third World Debt) to a wider sense of the world as simultaneously ever more over-controlled and out-of-control.

You can pick up this feeling from the lyrics: oblique images of running out of future, Darwinian dog-eat-dog struggle, cannibalism, an emotional 'Ice Age coming' (an unwitting echo of Margaret Drabble's famous novel *The Ice Age*, widely regarded as BritLit's counterpart to punk in its capturing a mid-seventies UK moment of malaise and crisis). More than the words, though, it's audible as a certain tenor, even timbre, of voice. 'You and Whose Army?' offers words of defiance in a voice that sounds like all the fight's been kicked out of it (which is why it works in 2001, where an update of 'Stand Down Margaret' would seem facile). Yorke is literally voicing (rather than articulating) contemporary feelings of dislocation, dispossession, numbness, impotence, paralysis; widely felt impulses to withdraw and disengage that are perfectly logical, dispirited responses to the bankruptcy of Centrist politics, which ensure that everyone remains equally disenchanted and aggrieved.

'It's all so part of the fabric of everything, even the artwork,' Yorke says, referring to the recurring, Art Brut-like schizo-scrawled motifs of Grim Reapers and Weeping Bears. 'I couldn't really say it directly so much, but it's there – the feeling of being a spectator and not being able to take part. I was really conscious of not wanting to use a sledgehammer to bang people over the head with it. It's pretty difficult to put into songs. In a way you have to wait until it's a personal issue or experience.' Jubilee 2000 was when it became personal. The petition's presenters, a group including Yorke and Bono, were outwitted by the

G8 politicians, who denied their desired worldwide-front-page-guaranteeing photo opportunity in front of the conference's building. 'We were made to walk down the back streets, and it was fucking surreal – we had these German military police escorting us down a tiny pedestrian shopping street, we're carrying this fucking banner, surrounded by bemused shoppers.'

Playing off Greenwood's love of Penderecki, you could describe *Kid A*/*Amnesiac* as a Threnody for the Victims of Globalization. Yorke says that spending three years in the UK after a lot of time touring abroad was a big influence: reading newspapers, noticing the discrepancy between mainstream pop culture and what was going on 'out there'. Three members of the band read Naomi Klein's anti-corporate bestseller *No Logo*, and at one point it was rumoured that *No Logo* would be the album title. Talking about the upsurge of anti-globalization dissent, Yorke defends the movement from charges of ideological incoherence and being merely reactive. 'That's how it's always dismissed in the mainstream media, but that's because it's this coalition of disparate interest groups who are all pissed off because they've been disenfranchised by politicians who are only listening to corporate lobby groups or unelected bodies like Davos. It's not based on the old left/right politics, it's not really even an anti-capitalist thing . . . It's something far deeper than that: "who do you serve?" It's a new form of dissent, a new politics, and the point is that the most important political issues of the day have been taken out of the political arena. They're being discussed by lobby groups paid for by, or composed of, ex-members of, corporations. And they spend a lot of effort trying to exclude the public, because it's inconvenient.'

Yorke cuts himself short with a self-deprecating 'I could go on like this forever, but I don't know what the fuck I'm talking about really!' He's fully aware of music fans' traditional scepticism and low tolerance for pop stars who speak out (Sting and the Rain Forest), and conscious of the contradictions of Radiohead as dissidents bankrolled by Parlophone/EMI/TimeWarner/AOL. 'We're screaming hypocrites. No, we are!' He also acknowledges that platinum-in-fifty-territories Radiohead are arguably the hip face of globalization. Recalling Coca Cola-sponsored MTV events they played in Mexico and Thailand back when 'Creep' was a heavy-rotation video, he says 'it was a weird feeling because you are right at the sharp end of the sexy sassy MTV eye-candy lifestyle thing that they're trying to sell to the rest of the world, make them aspire to. It's fair enough to question it. Unfortunately, if you're interested in actually being heard, you have to work within the system.' He slips into a comedy Nazi accent: 'Zey haff Kontrol!'

If Radiohead are a love-or-hate proposition – and they do seem to induce violently polarized responses – a lot of it is down to Thom Yorke's voice, the dolorousness that is its natural tone-and-texture. 'Miserabilist', 'whinging', 'tortured': these are the kind of adjectives hurled by the hostile. Fans, in contrast, tend to talk of 'beautiful sadness'. This split response is reminiscent of how Morrissey divided listeners in 1983 into those who found his voice nectar to the ear or nails-on-blackboard grating. The parallel is apposite in so far as 2001 feels a lot like 1983: mainstream pop relentlessly glossy and upful. The conditions that made The Smiths (or R.E.M., in Reagan's America) necessary as a counterweight to the Wham!s have returned.

The anguished timbre may be an acquired taste, but Yorke is an amazing singer. What's especially impressive about *Kid A*/*Amnesiac* is the way he operates as an ensemble player, another colour in the band's palette. Bored with all the standard tricks of vocal emoting, Yorke decided to interface voice and technology and develop what he's called 'a grammar of noises'. The first two tracks on *Kid A*, 'Everything in Its Right Place' and the title track, are especially striking in this respect, almost a declaration of intent: the words drastically processed in order to thwart the standard rock-listener mechanism of identify-and-interpret (the very mode of trad rock deep-and-meaningfulness that *OK Computer* had dramatically revived).

'The real problem I had was with the "identify" bit,' says Yorke. 'Even now, most interviews you do, there's a constant subtext which is "is this you?". By using other voices, I guess it was my way of saying obviously, it isn't me.'

Turning the voice into an instrumental texture, other-izing it via effects, allowed Yorke 'to sing things I wouldn't normally sing. On "Kid A", the lyrics are absolutely brutal and horrible and I wouldn't be able to sing them straight. But talking them and having them vocodered through Johnny's Ondes Martenot, so that I wasn't even responsible for the melody . . . that was great, it felt like you're not answerable to this thing.'

Another vocal treatment Yorke resorted to was auto-tuner – most famous from Cher's 'Believe', but widely used in R&B as an intermittent glisten of post-human perfect pitch added to particular lines or words. 'We used auto-tuner on *Amnesiac* twice. "Pakt Like Sardines", I wasn't particularly out-of-tune, but if you really turn up the auto-tuner so it's dead in pitch, it makes it go slightly – [he makes a nasal, depersonalized sound]. There's also this trick you can do, which we did on both "Pakt" and "Pull/Pulk Revolving Doors", where you give the machine a key and then you just talk into it. It desperately tries to search for the music in your speech, and produces notes at random. If you've assigned it a key, you've got music.'

Elsewhere, Radiohead's 'vocal science' bypassed digital state-of-art for antiquarian technology and the sort of ad hoc boffinry redolent of the things Lennon and George Martin got up to at Abbey Road (Yorke confesses that *Revolution in the Head*, Ian MacDonald's book about the recording of every single Beatles song, was his 'bedside reading all through the sessions for the albums'). On 'You and Whose Army?', the muzzy vocal – which sounds like Morrissey sliding into a Temazepam coma – was an attempt to recapture the soft, warm proto-doowop sound of forties harmony group The Ink Spots. 'We hired all these old ribbon microphones, but it didn't work because you need all the other gear, like the old tape recorders. So what we ended up using is an eggbox! And because it's on the vocal mic', and the whole band's playing at the same time, everything on the track goes through this eggbox.'

Radiohead also used a device called the Palm Speaker on 'You and Whose Army?', creating a halo of hazy reverberance around Yorke's vocal. 'The Palm Speaker is something else that Monsieur Martenot invented, to go with the Ondes,' explains Greenwood. 'It's a bit like a harp with a speaker in the middle of it. The strings are tuned to all twelve semitones of an octave, and when you play a note in tune, it resonates that specific string and it creates this weird kind of echo that's only on those pitches.'

On *Kid A/Amnesiac*, Yorke performed his vocals knowing the kind of spatiality it would be moving through: the effects are always 'live', audible to him through headphones. 'Nigel Godrich is very into this idea that if you're going to do something weird with a track, you make it weird there and then, rather than doing it in the mix afterwards, because the effect changes the way people play. They'll play to it. And that's really inspiring, because it's like having a new instrument. If you've got an incredibly cool reverb or something on your voice, suddenly you're really excited about what you're doing again.'

* * *

The vocal tricknology on *Kid A* was perhaps the most offputting aspect for many listeners, prompting accusations of emotional withdrawal and a refusal to connect with the audience, or the absurd, frequently heard charge 'there's no tunes on the album' (actually, almost every track is structured like a song, and hauntingly melodic). The mixed response *Kid A* garnered in the UK revealed how the Britpop era has weakened the rock audience's ability to handle anything not blatantly singalong. At its lowliest (Oasis) Britpop was barely more than amplified busking, disregarding the studio's sound-sculpting potential and relegating rhythm to a menial timekeeping role, low-in-the-mix like they did it in the 1960s. Call it the new philistinism: as Greenwood commented acidly circa *Kid A*'s release, 'People basically want their hands held through twelve "Mull of Kintyre's".'

Surprisingly, the more trad rock America gave *Kid A* an almost uniformly rapturous reception. Two exceptions were *New Yorker* rock columnist Nick Hornby, who complained that the album was simply too demanding for grown-ups exhausted by work/parenting and accused critics who raved about *Kid A* of thinking like sixteen-year-olds, and Howard Hampton in the *New York Times*, who dredged up that hoary old 'it's just like the mid-seventies again' scare tactic, a scenario in which Radiohead are the new Pink Floyd and it's high time we had another punk rock.

The Pink Floyd analogy has dogged Radiohead since *The Bends*. And there are parallels, for sure: the concept album flavour of *OK Computer*, the lavish artwork (there's a secret booklet concealed inside *Kid A*'s CD case), their obsessive attention to track sequencing the albums to work as wholes, even the fact that both bands came from Oxbridge towns. Despite a dearth of real sonic similarity, Radiohead are often described by journalists as Floyd-influenced, which Greenwood fears may have stemmed from interview comments 'from about five years ago, when I heard *Meddle* for the first time and liked half of it. And I felt a bit ripped off, because when I was at school, the popular post-punk myth was that Floyd were rubbish.'

I'm hardly a fan of that group post-Syd, but it's worth at least querying why 'Pink Floyd' is such an enduringly potent insult, such an instantly discrediting reference point. Johnny Rotten may have famously scrawled 'I Hate' on his Pink Floyd T-shirt (but why did he own one in the first place, I always wonder?), yet of all the pre-1976 dinosaurs, Waters & Co. were arguably the least decadent, corrupt and aesthetically bankrupt. *Wish You Were* (1975) contains anti-record biz sentiments that anticipate punk; *Animals* and *The Wall* are as bleakly no-escapist and apocalyptic in their view of modern society as anything from the post-punk vanguard. At one point in the mid-seventies, Floyd even planned making an entire album using household implements, a gambit that would have surpassed in advance *Flowers of Romance*, *Vibing Up the Senile Man*, Nurse With Wound . . . not to mention Herbert.

There's a case for arguing that 1977-style three-chord punk was just a back-to-basics blip in the continuum of UK art rock, and that 'progressive' pretty much resumed in the form of post-punk, albeit shaped by some new sonic prohibitions/inhibitions. Before 1977, figures like Eno and Wyatt collaborated with proggy types like Fripp and even Phil Collins. After punk, some of those early seventies art rockers fitted the new rules of cool (Eno producing Devo, No Wave, Talking Heads; Wyatt playing with Scritti and recording for Rough Trade). Others didn't, seemingly for almost arbitrary reasons: Peter Gabriel, Kate Bush (whose *The Dreaming* now seems a lot more successful at more or less the same game as *Flowers of Romance*).

Perhaps the Pink Floyd comparison has less to do with any real stylistic parallels and more to do with the vein of inverted snobbery that runs through British rock culture, one symptom of which is an abiding discomfort with the notion of 'art rock' itself. 'Too fucking middle class, that's our problem!' says Yorke. Radiohead met at the same Abingdon public school, where several members had classical music training of varying kinds; most went on to university (Cambridge in Colin Greenwood's case). But what are their qualifications in the university of real life? What right do they have to 'moan' about anything? How can such polite, well-educated, well-brought-up, diligent, meticulous young men be 'rock 'n' roll'?

One of the things I like about Radiohead, though, is that they seem comfortable with their middle-classness: not proud, conscious of the issue of privilege, but at the same time not adopting Mockney accents or concealing the fact that they read books. (*Amnesiac*'s title, for instance, was inspired by something Yorke read in a book about Gnosticism.) Even the fact that Greenwood went AWOL from the original interview at Courtyard's office in order to watch the first day of cricket at Lord's seems part of their authenticity. (It reminds me of how Lloyd Cole used to be mocked in the music press for being into golf, whereas The Cure's Robert Smith could get away with talking about Camus because he was madly into football and therefore a 'good bloke'.)

'People distrust learning, don't they?' muses Greenwood. 'Not to compare ourselves with him obviously, but there's all these stories of Miles Davis going to the Juilliard academy and poring over classical scores in the library. That side of Miles is glossed over a bit in favour of the living-on-the-edge stuff. But it just makes me love him even more, the idea of him wanting to get musical inspiration from everything and everywhere.' For his part Yorke attacks what he calls 'the noble savage idea of creativity' as 'a really destructive myth' and 'a trap' for the artist.

'At one point, I started to believe that if you sit down and analyse what you're doing, worry about it, then you're not being your true self. But, for instance, Mark E. Smith is not a noble savage – he's a fucking intellectual. With us, though, there's this suspicion of calculation all the way through what we do. Where does this come from, the idea that if you sit down and think about something you can't be emotional in any way? Maybe it's some sort of punk hang-up.' Punk was indeed the great era of prole-ier than thou street-cred and downwardly-mobile accent-slippage. Then again, think of Glen Matlock – forever ridiculed for being middle class, a mummy's boy, a Beatles fan – and think how crap the Pistols were when he and his tunesmithery were expelled. Jerry Dammers was the son of a vicar! So let's hear it for the bourgeoisie – perpetually disavowed, but they've always played their part in rock's story.

'Sometimes, I think they're right about us,' muses Yorke. 'Sometimes we do over-think things.' He thinks that's why accusations of humourlessness are often directed at Radiohead, despite the fact that in interviews they're perfectly witty chaps. 'People used to throw that at The Smiths all the time, but Morrissey obviously had a sense of humour. Even something as dark as "How Soon is Now" has a quippy element.' Imputation of sense-of-humour deficiency is one of the classic levelling weapons in the arsenal of English anti-intellectualism, used to deflate anything radical ('bloody humourless feminists') or pretentious and arty. 'How dare Radiohead take themselves so seriously?' is the subtext of much of the animus against *Kid A/Amnesiac*: witness the *NME* album review that began with the words 'the unbearable heaviness of being Radiohead'. But it's precisely the group's re-invocation of art-rock earnestness, and the refusal of levity and frivolousness that is actually dissident in our pop culture right now, pervaded as it is with post-*Loaded* bluff blokey cheer, heterosexualized camp (from Robbie Williams to all the eighties nostalgia programmes), and won't-get-fooled-again cynicism that aims to trivialize intensity or vision-quest of any kind. Yorke says he can understand the demand for light entertainment, though. 'The reason people are so into escaping is there's a fucking lot to escape from. In a way, the last thing anyone needs is someone rubbing salt in the wounds, which is sort of what we're doing.'

The Wire, July 2001

There has always been something slightly uncool about Radiohead. I'm not talking about the name (redolent of that undistinguished pre-Britpop era of semi-noisy guitarbands like The Catherine Wheel) or even about the superfluous 'h' in Yorke's Christian name. It's more to do with the way Radiohead leave all the hipster credibility stuff to the Sonic Youths and Stereolabs and instead lay their wares out on the stall marked 'importance'. It's this that makes them 'middlebrow' – a self-seriousness that flashes back to the earnestness and solemn sense of artistic entitlement that characterized progressive rock. The symbolism and conceptualism, the hankering for deep-and-meaningful. But you know what, middlebrow is fine. The greatest music, in fact, ends up in that category, if not by design then certainly by acclamation. Like it or not, Love's *Forever Changes*, Van Morrison's *Astral Weeks*, Velvet Underground, Miles Davis, even Can and Neu! are middlebrow nowadays. Even Sonic Youth, despite their best efforts, have become pretty middlebrow. With rock music, there's two alter-natives to middlebrow. Either you go esoteric, become one of those uber-hipsters who claim that Faust is for lightweights and the real hardcore Krautrock is Dyzan or Annexus Quam . . . if you follow that path you'll end up listening to a nonstop audio-diet of cassette-only noise from the Pacific North West, New Zealand lathe-cut ten-inches and Smegma live albums . . . your living room will resemble Thurston Moore's. The other option is the inverted snobbery route (Stock Aitken Waterman as the most crucial musical force of 1980s UK pop . . . Girls Aloud better than Arctic Monkeys . . .). So you see there is no real alternative. Embrace it: the history of rock greatness *is* that middling region where experiment and accessibility, song and space, co-exist. Hooray for middlebrow! Or at least for *upper* middlebrow (Radiohead, Bjork, Chemical Brothers, David Bowie, Kate Bush, et al.), as opposed to lower middlebrow, which is Coldplay.

2-STEP AND R&B CRITIQUED

Did this piece on 2-step for *Vibe* – they were looking for illustrations so I sent the few club and rave flyers I'd gleaned. Owing to some clerical error I got this hefty package back from them through the mail, containing my flyers plus tons of others they'd procured by means unknown. Sometimes it's only when you confront a culture in concentrated bulk form that you realize how crap it really is. I mean, these flyers were so relentlessly tacky, so cheaply put together, so lacking in rave-era humour or wackiness. Pix of horrible cheesy-looking birds in flash scanties, images of champagne flutes and similar nouveau riche imagery. Tack-eee! A real turn-off.

I'd had my 2-step anti-epiphany earlier in 2000, though – doing another feature on UK garage, as it happened, this time for *Spin*. I expect this isn't especially uncommon: feelings of cognitive dissonance when you love a particular form of music yet are confronted with the 'social energy' that fuels the music and is essential to its very existence, and find it grim, dismal, in all ways irredeemable, just a drag to be near. Field-researching the piece in clubs like Liberty's and Twice As Nice, I found myself wondering why on earth anyone would voluntarily expose themselves to the toxic atmosphere of tension, incivility and snooty attitude that permeates these events. I mean, my excuse was I was being paid to be there, and got in for free – why would you actually pay – queue for ages, and then pay hard-earned dosh – to experience such sustained unpleasantness? UK garage's collective superiority complex is the antithesis not just of rave but of house culture: uptight, alpha-male, peacock, skrewface, people looking down their charlyed-up noses at each other, imagining themselves hot-shit cos of their costly garments – the fatuous circularity of paying tons of money for clothes that are desirable simply because they signify you paid tons of money for them. Why would anybody want to waste their precious leisure time in such a no-fun, merriment-free space? People who are into this lifestyle (as opposed to the music, which you can sort-of-but-not-really separate from the subculture) are people who . . . well, not to put too fine a point on it, their consciousness is fucked. When you compare UK garage to hardcore rave, you're talking about a real, measurable deterioration in intensity, electricity, idealism and all-round worth: a fall from paradise into the vice and viciousness of a world where the prospect of any other mode of existence, any better way, is unimaginable. Hardcore knew the rave dream was 'just a dream', but it still clung on to it. Whereas UK garage culture's very foundation is the post-rave relapse into dream-less cynicism, accommodation to 'reality'.

Thing is, I think most people in the scene, in their heart of hearts, know this. At Liberty's, for most of the night there were more people in the old skool jungle side room, where the DJ played fevered 1993 darkcore classics like Potential Bad Boy's 'Let's Go'. You could see people moving to the old music, eyes shut, and just tell they were dying to 'brock out', trying to dance their way back into that explosive euphoria; they were yearning for the release, feeling it still in their nerve-memories, but blocked, trapped, stranded. I can't imagine ever ceasing to be obsessed with the latest sounds to come out of London pirate radio; at the same time, I equally am unable to find anything worth endorsing about UKG as a subculture or A Way of Life. Essentially, UKG is about glamorizing the ways of Babylon. There's a word here I'm grasping for, it's on the tip of my tongue – could it be 'counter-revolutionary'?

* * *

Funny, 2000 was the Year of R&B for so many people (meaning they finally woke up to it, of course), but I can hardly think of a single killer R&B tune that really knocked me out. I mean, there was Destiny's Child's 'Say My Name' and 'Jumpin'' – but they're both from an album that came out in 1999. They're not even the best tunes on that album – those would be the first two singles, 'Bills Bills Bills' and 'Bugaboo', both massive hits and both released in 1999. A lot of critics actually voted for the Destiny's Child album in the 2000 end-of-year polls, seemingly oblivious to the fact that the album came out in midsummer 1999. (Or was it even earlier? I'm not sure.) It is therefore a piss-poor argument for 2000 as a fantastic year for R&B.

'Independent Women', on the other hand, is a fantastic argument for 2000 as a piss-poor year for R&B. Around about the eleventh

hearing, the song finally revealed its melody to me, but it barely constitutes a song, and the arrangement and production still seem flaccid and
nothing-special. It is also attached to a really *really* bad movie. (I
haven't actually seen it, but some things you just know, you know.)
Could it be that the expelled/downsized members of Destiny's were
actually crucial to the chemistry in some barely fathomable way?

What about the rest of this year's R&B crop? I can barely remember
any of them. 'Case of the Ex' was neat but the rest of Mya's album is
bogged in slow-jams and maturity-bids. Kandi stepped out from her
background song-doctor role (TLC's 'No Scrubs', Destiny's 'Bills Bills
Bills', other angry-diva sub-feminist anthems) and revealed why she
shoulda stayed in the background (a little something to do with having
no vocal presence whatsoever). Hmm, what else? Seemed like there
was just endless faceless loverman trios/quartets in the post-Boys II
Men/Jodeci mould, all unctuous vocals and slow-jam tempos – cloying,
glutinous, characterless, audio soft-porn. Talking of which, Sisquo's
'Thong Song': shurely shome kind of cultural nadir? I'm really scrap-
ing my memory-barrel here: was Pink's 'There You Go' this year?
Pretty good but so much better as Sovereign's tuff 2-step bootleg . . .

Beyond the lack of great songs, production ideas, and the over-
saturation of that Timbaland/She'kspere stop-start beat thing (with
supastars like Janet Jackson and Jennifer Lopez further diluting the
weak brew – and may I just digress for a moment, and ask whatthafuck's up with Janet's teeth – in every video, she looks like an ad for
denture cleaner, this eerie pearlescent glow, like she hasn't got individual teeth just this unstriated band of tooth enamel. Creepy! Her body
looks really weird too – Japanese-prisoner-of-war-camp levels of exer-
cise fighting against her natural shape, winning, but at what *cost*. And
that strange, perturbing bra that makes it look like she's got a pair of
buttocks transplanted on to her chest. Shudder!), beyond the sheerly
sonic disappointments . . . I have to tell you, I'm feeling a little bit of a
value gap. It's sort of a cross-the-board antipathy that goes from R&B
to all the white-out teen-oriented versions of blackpop from Britney
to the legion of boy bands . . . As pop music goes, on a certain level,
it's irresistible . . . but mainly in the sense that a conquering army
subjugating all in its path can be said to be hard to resist.

The remorseless, ruthless, invincible precision with which this
vidpop is programmed, edited, choreographed, groomed . . . definitely
verges on the militaristic. And the 'artists' involved, whether it's
Aguilera or Aaliyah or whoever, are like figments spun into existence
by squadrons of technicians – make-up artists, hair stylists, lighting
crews, postproduction special effects, recording engineers who tint and

pitchshift the vocals, chop up the best takes down to single words and re-stitch them together ... The amount of energy and effort and money and micro-management that goes into one two-second shot in a video, or one bar of the record, it's staggering ... These stars are cartoons, robots, ciphers, logos, branding devices ... and while I suppose there's a sort of Baudrillardian hyper-real/post-human/simulation-pop buzz to it ... I dunno, is it backward of me to prefer the early eighties New Pop era? Where there was a striving for glamour yet at the same time the charm of all-too-evident flaws and fallibility and untampered, untreated fleshly reality – I'm thinking of Altered Images or Human League ... or going back further, Marc Bolan (who, with just a mane of corkscrew curls and some glitter on his cheek-bones, was more otherworldly and alien than any of today's digitally enhanced pop stars). This faux-animation element to modern vidpop, the way that the choreography and filming techniques are designed to make humans move in ways that resemble the characters in videogames, is why you've got this spate of pop groups taking the next logical step and hiding themselves behind cartoons: Gorillaz, Daft Punk's anime-style promos and robot shtick. William Gibson's *Idoru* – the purely computer-generated star-as-figment – is just around the corner.

I'm also, gotta admit, starting to feel a certain intellectual exhaustion with the whole rhythm-as-the-star, rhythm-as-melody approach. When everything else about a record sucks – the song, the star, the cultural ramifications – maybe a 'dope beat' alone ain't sufficient. Rhythm, melody, lyrics, compelling persona ... It's not entirely unprecedented to have the whole package: Sly Stone, Prince, P-Funk – there's even a few white examples I can't be bothered to list.

Perhaps what I'm imagining in the back of my brain is some kind of eventual revolt against the utter victory of 'black' musical values (rhythm-and-production as more important than song/lyrics; nouveau riche/aspirational, licking-the-arse-of-the-status-quo lyrics/attitudes) and the return with a vengeance of rock pretentiousness/bohemianism. Simon Biddell has been banging on about 'vision' as a concept that needs to be reintroduced to the critical lexicon – the idea of being transported, by music as well as by lyrics and charisma, into an individual's very particular view of the world – and citing the likes of Beefheart, Mark E. Smith, Sly Stone, Peter Hammill as exemplars. And in a lot of ways I kind of concur, if only out of boredom, desire for an all-change: a massive movement of sonically over-reaching and lyrically over-ripe art rock would be just the ticket right now. (Some would say that's what the best of modern hip hop is anyway – today's art rock

304

– and maybe they're right – which reminds me, you gotta hear the Cannibal Ox album.) Of course, as Biddell concedes, the idea of 'vision' leads back down the perilous path towards auteur theory, the expressionist fallacy, and so forth . . . But maybe it doesn't have to be so backward: Radiohead, for instance, have shown that you can have the vision thing and the riddim thing at the same time. PiL, Roxy Music, Can, Joy Division – all utterly bang-up-to-date rhythm-and-production wise, all utterly vision-ary. And there was this great moment in the late seventies/early eighties, when people tried to fuse punk and disco, 'white' and 'black', in really suggestive ways. How did we ever learn to settle for less, adapt to the split consciousness of liking parts of things but not the whole?

From Unfaves of 2000 overview, *Blissout*

Frustrating as it was being a 2-step fanatic on the wrong side of the Atlantic, experiencing it through the records and through pirate radio tapes (sent by friends or recorded by the dozen on rare visits to London) allowed me to maintain a self-protective veil of semi-ignorance about the lived reality of the scene. The few experiences I'd had in London clubs on those visits were oddly flat, thanks to the disconcerting mismatch between the music's effervescent joy and the crowd's subdued and slightly sour atmosphere. I had a far funner time at New York's fledgling 2-step scene, where the vibe was amiable and enthused; the dancing was also much more energetic and fluidly expressive than the taut shoulder/hip/butt shaking you saw in the UK. Best of all, there was none of that UK garage snooty hauteur or conspicuous consumption. In London clubs like Twice As Nice and Cookies & Cream, I recall seeing a guy walking around with the neck label of his Moschino shirt pulled out from under his sweater, so you could be sure of seeing how much he'd spent, another guy wearing a T-shirt with the logo 'Dolce & Gabbana is Life', and two blokes who literally flashed their cash (a fat wedge of twenty-pound notes) in my face with a jeering 'we've got loads of money'. But in New York the scene had a totally different demographic (bourgeois bohemian: edge-chasing Anglophiles, non-aligned hipsters), so not a drop of champagne was to be seen. Sadly, after a year or so of looking tantalizingly close to taking off, the New York 2-step scene foundered on the contradictions of being based entirely around import records.

In the R&B critique (as in the Radiohead piece) you can see the line of thought developing that led me to *Rip it Up and Start Again*.

FAVES OF 2000: DANCEHALL

Elephant Man, *Comin' 4 You!* (Greensleeves); Capleton, *More Fire* (VP); Beenie Man, *Art & Life* (Island); Various Artists, *The Biggest Ragga Dancehall Anthems 2000, Greensleeves Reggae Sampler 21, Doorslam* (Greensleeves Rhythm Album #3); *The Biggest Ragga Dancehall Anthems 99* (all Greensleeves); Various Artists, *Strictly the Best 23, Dancehall 101* Vol. 1 and Vol. 2 (both VP); Various Artists, *Massive B Presents: Yard Bounce* (Massive B)

This goes up front not because it's necessarily the stuff I extracted most pleasure from this year, but because it's the stuff that surprised, confused and did my head in the most, forced me to think hardest . . . and this year, that seemed more important than mere enjoyment . . . (That said, I can't actually think of many things I enjoyed more than this stuff.) A lot of the thinking related to the quandary of whether I can have any place in this music, any real relation with it . . . It's not even a black/white thing, as with hip hop – dancehall is so relentlessly Jamaica-local in its references; lyrically it's almost indecipherable. For a white liberal, it is also a culture, strung out between Rasta's Afro-Protestant fundamentalism and its inseparable polar opposite, rude boy/Staggerlee ghetto-nihilism, that it is impossible to affirm or be comfortable with – the ritual battyboy-bashing incantations, the misogyny, the gun talk. And yet, and yet, the sheer physical compulsion and force of sonic surprise demands attention, deserves excitement.

Can't claim to have 'mastered the field', or even come close. Jamaica has the highest per capita rate of musical production in the world, and given dancehall's insanely frantic turnover of riddims and versions, its scores of production squads and hit-factory studios, keeping up with the genre would be a full-time occupation, involving much time in cramped basement record stores with hundreds of seven-inch singles (amazingly, what the DJs still use – they don't even mix) stuck on the walls . . . So, like any dabbler, it's compilations for me.

306

If it seems like there's been a creative upsurge in dancehall, I'm aware it's almost certainly an optical illusion caused by my not really having paid attention since the last time ragga grabbed my ears, circa 1994. That was back when jungle was synonymous with ragga samples, and this time round it's partly through the endemic use of dancehall vocal licks in 2-step garage that my dormant interest's been revived. Often it's the exact same MC chants and catchphrases, originally from yard tapes, re-used for the Nth time – 'get ready for dis, for dis, for dis', 'special request', 'get mash up', – a sort of sampladelic folk-memory archive for the hardcore continuum. Then there's all the 2-step collaborations with dancehall stars (Glamma Kid, Lady Saw) and the MCs with a strong ragga influence to their patter (Richie Dan, Splash, etc.).

More and more, I am coming round to the idea of rave, at least in its London-centric hardcore/jungle/garage sense, as an almost straight transposition of dancehall culture into the UK: the dubplates, the champion sounds (pirates largely replacing the sound systems, as sounds on the airwaves), the cult of spliff-tastic bass frequencies, the role of the MC (which you don't get in house, techno, trance) and his glorious nonsense; the sense of manor and local identity. Then there's the whole dancehall/hardcore thing of renegade capitalism a.k.a. resistant micro-capitalism: white labels and illicit raves, studios/labels based around record stores (like M-Dubs's Sugarshack Recordings being in the back of their Hounslow record shop); the balance between avant-gardism and pleasing the massive. In Jamaica, the dubplate system works in a different fashion to UK hardcore/jungle/garage. Because they compete in 'soundclashes' against each other, sound systems need a constant turnover of fresh dubs to sway the crowd and slay their rivals. At each of Kingston's many recording studios, there's a bustling traffic in killer and filler tunes alike (sounds can't fire all their best shots too early; they save the most devastating ordnance for the final stretch of combat). Established stars and hustling aspirants alike chant patois-rich raps over currently hot riddims; in return for these vocals-for-hire, the champion sounds pay anything from US $25 to $3,000.

Another typically Jamaican attitude that seems to have migrated into the hardcore/jungle/garage continuum is that weird mix of idealism and pragmatism – a sort of arty experimentalism untrammelled with modernist/bohemian complexes about money-making or selling out. Read *Wake the Town and Tell the People*, Norman C. Stolzoff's useful analysis of Jamaican dancehall culture, and what emerges is a native genius for transforming economic constraints into creative opportunities. Sound systems, for instance, first emerged in the 1950s when the burgeoning tourist trade priced live bands out of the popular market; DJs playing records (then imported American R&B) filled the void. Thrift was partial inspiration for two crucial innovations: the recycling of rhythms, and dub. Producers realized they only had to pay session musicians for a single performance if they put instrumental dub versions on B-sides, or released 'one riddim' albums featuring different songs and singers over the same groove.

Similar implacable financial logic led to today's ragga, where drum machines and digital technology enabled the downsizing of human players altogether. It's really only the raucous, overbearing presence of the MCs (confusingly known in Jamaica as DJs; the guy who spins the record is the selector) that has concealed for so long the fact that dancehall is essentially identical, in terms of its means of production, to house/techno/jungle/etc.

Beyond these affinities and its subordinate role as a pantry full of patois vocal licks sampled by junglists and 2-steppers, dancehall has its own forceful claims upon our attention as the Other Electronic Music. Its digital rhythm science can easily rival the art-techno fraternity when it comes to bio-mechanical this-must-be-wrong-but-it-works weirdness. Just check the madcap creativity of Beenie Man's 'Moses Cry' (on Greensleeves' *Biggest Ragga Dancehall Anthems of 2000* double-CD) for sounds as futuristic and aberrant as any avant-techno coming out of Cologne. Produced by Ward 21 & Prince Jammy, its asymmetrical groove is built from palpitating kickdrums, garbled rave-style synth-stabs, and an eerie bassline that sounds like a human groan digitally mangled and looped. Or check the quirktronica pulsescape underpinning Beenie on 'Badder Than the Rest', or Elephant Man's amazing '2000 Began' from *Comin' 4 You!* – basically acid techno a la Plastikman.

It's easy to overlook dancehall's sonic strangeness, though, because the performers' personae are so domineering. The mix seems lopsided, in-yer-face voices battling with the beat to control the soundscape, and crushing the rest of the music (strangulated samples, perky videogame-style blip-melodies) into a skinny strip of no-man's-land in between. The ragga voice, jagged and croaky, is a form of sonic extremism in itself. Dancehall's got to be the only form of modern pop where the typical range for male vocals is baritone to basso profundo. Obviously related to the culture's premium on testosterone and disdain for effem-inacy, ragga's ultramasculinist bombast sounds simultaneously absurd and intimidating. From some DJs, like Buccaneer, you'll even hear a Pavarotti-esque warble, hilariously poised between portentous and preposterous. Elephant Man's own voice is a pit-of-belly boom that opens up like an abyss of menace, enhanced by a sinister, serpentile lisp. Combine this sort of gravelly machismo with typical lyrics about exit wounds and tonight being the opposite of your birthday (i.e. your 'deathnight') and you've got some seriously chilling Staggerlee business. 'Replacement Killer', a series of boasts about how cold-blooded Elephant is, actually utilizes death-rattle gasps as functioning elements of the beat. No surprise, then, that there's a mutual trade pact between dancehall and gangsta rap (which has escalated since Jamaica recently got wired for cable and now has exposure to BET and MTV). US rap terms like 'playa hater', 'my dogs' and 'making cheese' now crop up as brief blips of relative cipherability amidst ragga's hieroglyphic code-flow of opaque patois. And increasingly dancehall artists interpolate direct lifts from current rap hits. On *Comin' 4 You!* 'One More' is based on DMX's 'One More Road to Cross', 'E-L-E-P-H-A-N-T' rips a Dre/Snoop chorus, and the album's fiercest cut 'Somebody' rides the clanking rampage of the Yard bounce riddim, a fusion of dancehall with the New Orleans bounce style popularized by Cash Money Records. (The Yard bounce CD features seven versions of that riddim, created by Bobby Konders of Massive B, including Bounty Killer's 'Fire With Fire', Burro Banton's 'Phenomenum 1' and Lexxus's 'Ride With Me' – a sequence, culminating with the Elephant Man version, that has been played with shameless incessant-ness on Massive B's dancehall show for Hot 97 in New York.) You also get dancehall artists doing remakes of rap hits, where they treat the original as just another riddim and do a totally different vocal lick over the top: Elephant Man's got one based on Ludacris's amazing 'Southern Hospitality'.

With six appearances on the Greensleeves best of 2000 compilation, Capleton reaffirms his supremacy over the dancehall already established by last year's awesome *More Fire* LP. Like Malcolm X, he belongs to the syndrome of the self-reformed Staggerlee; like Buju Banton, he's a raggamuffin who turned Rasta. But Capleton's sanctimony doesn't sabotage his records because instead of soothing roots reggae visions of 'one love', he concentrates on Old Testament-style wrath and Armageddon: Jah as the ultimate Enforcer, the Don of dons, smiting the corrupt and ungodly. The gloating relish with which he wields the brimstone imagery of divine retribution (he fits this Rasta street preacher archetype known as the 'warner') is as vindictive and venomous as ragga's ultraviolence. Capleton's righteousness and Elephant Man's ruthlessness are flipsides of the same cultural coin; God's fire simply replaces gun fire. Even though he's a 'good guy' now, Capleton still sounds like a rude boy. That ragga/Rasta dialectic is fascinating to me, because in dancehall they aren't seen or felt as opposites but complementary: it's similar to the way that even the most cold-blooded, heartless, murda-mad, ho'-banging rappers always give praise and thanks to God despite their ungodly, vice-ridden and vicious lifestyles. Dancehall can appear to merely mirror and perpetuate 'reality' (soundclash slanguage, all 'sound boy killers' and 'burial' tunes that finish off the rival sound, reflects not just the routine violence of Kingston, but capitalism's war of all against all – harsher in this postcolonial corner of the globalized world than most). But the culture still contains flickers of utopian hope for a better way: selectors will cut from a toast about murderous revenge to a conscious song about redemption in the blink of a cross-fader. In the mix, these contradictions – reveling in Babylon's corruption versus dreaming of Zion – achieve an uneasy co-existence.

Back to the music . . . Basically, there's too many insanely inventive, rhythmically ferocious tracks on all these comps to get into close description. One thing I can't get my head around just yet: the one riddim album. Even when the riddim is hothothot, like Doorslam, twenty different versions from DJs and singjays in a row riding the exact same groove, well it's a bit of a mindfuck. (Although it is a good way of appreciating the skills of each vocalist: the groove functions like one of those mechanical bucking broncos where you can pretend to be a rodeo cowboy; each MC finds a different way of riding the beat.)

Another thing I've found increasingly intriguing is the music of the non-Jamaican West Indies, e.g. digital soca and calypso. At its best, it's really demented-sounding – like the happy hardcore of the Caribbean. I've heard a soca version of Soft Cell's 'Tainted Love'. Strange bhangra influences, at times – apparently one legacy of the British Empire is the way East Indians migrated to the West Indies. And we can't forget dancehall's great crossover artist – not Shaggy (although that 'wasn't me' tune is catchy-as-fuck) but Beenie Man. Whose latest album *Art & Life* produced the gorgeous R&B-dancehall crossover hit 'Girls Them Sugar' featuring the lovely Mya, the ominous New Orleans-style gangsta-bounce of 'Original Tune', and hardly any 'pure' ragga. And why should it? Dancehall and the other genres of the 'Black Atlantic' diaspora have long entered into relations of fruitful mutual contamination. From techno-ravey-drum & bassy ideas infiltrating the E'd up world of American hip hop, to 2-step's non-reciprocal love affair with US R&B and borrowings from dancehall and roots reggae, to the rumours about Timo Maas's 'Doom's Night' remix being a huge smash in Jamaica, more and more the borders between all the different street musics become meaningless – thanks to digital technology and the near-instantaneous way that musical ideas migrate these days. (Dancehall itself is a diaspora, with outposts from Brooklyn to

London to Miami to Toronto; almost as many Jamaicans live outside the island as on it.) What has emerged through all this criss-cross traffic is a single unified bass-beats-bleeps culture, a transatlantic confederacy of hardcore sounds.

Blissout, 2000

My favourite dancehall tune of 2000 isn't on this list because I was unable to identify it until somewhat later – an incredibly boisterous and rhythmically uproarious (snares that seemed to explode under your feet) track by T.O.K. called 'Chi Chi Man'. It turned out to be an incongruously joyous-sounding diatribe against homosexuals (chi-chi man = gay man), its hella-catchy chorus promising 'blaze the fire make me bun them . . . Chi chi man fi dead that's a fact.' I'd like to say the drying-up of my obsession with dancehall came about as a direct result of discovering what this song was about. It didn't (although I couldn't bring myself to buy the T.O.K. CD). No, I just burned out on dancehall through over-exposure; also, the quality seemed to deteriorate sharply in 2001, especially with an overdose of tracks based wholesale on American hip hop, the MC-ing simply superimposed over the imported beats.

After ragga, the next major stop in the hipster chase for ruffneck exotica was baile funk a.k.a. funk carioca, basically Brazilian dancehall (they call the parties 'balls', that's what 'baile' means) in its spirit of gangsta raucousness and graphic lewdness, but musically drawing more on Miami bass and electro. Exciting for a moment or several, but I realized that beneath the surface of local difference I was basically listening to the same thing as dancehall or any other form of 'shanty house'. That's what blogger don Matthew Ingram a.k.a. Woebot calls the panglobal web of hardcore street sounds – reggaeton, Baltimore breaks, kwaito, Desi, etc. – which are all based on unlicensed sample thievery, creole bastardization, sub-bass meets subaltern pressure, and worship of the female posterior. The vibe in all these musics mixes rudeness (ruffneck rowdiness) and cheesiness (blatant steals from mainstream pop, Euro-rave, etc.). It's the (un)changing same of world-is-a-ghetto music, made by bwoys and gyals from 'hoods where nobody wants to go (in Brazil they call them favelas; in America, projects; in Kingston, they're 'gardens' or garrisons; in the UK, estates . . .). The beats shift but the underlying substructure is basically identical, and it's an almost structural fixture that there will be bourgeois-bohemian hipsters who realize the liveliest party vibes comes from the lumpen-proletariat. Somewhere between dancehall and baile funk, though, I felt like I had chased a certain 'street beats' line to its end point. You can accumulate a mountain of knowledge in the effort to understand (and mine is a molehill compared to the deeply informed passion of people I know who are real dancehall or funk carioca experts) but when the music remains so alien to your world, and in many ways opposed to it, you can find yourself wondering what you're doing. Well, I did.

HISTORIA ELECTRONICA

The Case for Electronic Dance Music Culture

Every so often, people ask me: 'Why are you so into electronic music and this whole dance culture thing? What's it all about? What makes it different?' Some add a slightly combative edge to the question, pointing out that there's always been 'dance music', and that anyway people will dance to any music if they like it, even a group as overtly non-funky as The Smiths or R.E.M. If they're really sharp, these people also point out that almost all pop today is 'electronic', using synthesizers, sequencers, sampling and digital editing software like Pro Tools, or processing 'natural' acoustic sounds like the human voice or drums through effects, filters and studio sorcery of all kinds. And after all, what's an electric guitar if not an electronic instrument?

These are all good points, but the fact remains that electronic dance culture is a distinct entity. What follows here is my attempt to sketch the broad foundational principles that give electronic dance music its coherence as a defined cultural field. Not every exponent of this music, not every scene or genre, fits each single criteria, and some actively flout 'the rules'. But taken en masse, these parameters define a kind of 'field of possibility' within which the vast, variegated sprawl of electronic dance exists. For sure, it's a terrain with porous boundaries, through which seep influences from neighbouring areas of music. Sonically, the most influential of these neighbours are hip hop, avant-garde electronic experimentalism, industrial and dub reggae. In terms of attitudes and values, rock in all its various forms, from psychedelia to punk, has had most impact on electronic dance culture. From full-on rave madness to self-consciously avant-garde experimentalism, electronica has become the inheritor of rock's seriousness: its belief that music can change the world (or at least an individual's consciousness), rock notions of 'progression' or 'subversion', the conviction that music needs to be more than entertainment. Yet at the same time, the founding principles I sketch below frequently challenge and dismantle rock ideas of how creativity works, what defines art, and where the meaning and power of music is located.

1) Machine music

Dance music isn't unique in being obsessed with technology: rock has its share of songs hymning cars, while guitars are fetishized as noise-weapons. But electronica goes further by defining itself as machine-music. This is upfront in the genre name 'techno', and it comes through in the reverence for specific pieces of equipment: drum machines like the Roland 808 and Roland 909 to antique synths like the Moog and Wasp. You even have artists naming themselves in homage to gear: House of 909, 808 State, Q-Bass (a pun on the Cubase programming software). And you can see the cult of machinery in names that sound hyper-technical, robotic, or like models of cars or computers: Electribe 101, LFO, Nexus 21. Electronic musicians also love to describe what they do as scientific research, imagining the studio as a sound laboratory.

Electronic music is driven by a quest to find the most radical or futuristic-sounding potential in brand-new technology. And that involves essentially (re)inventing the machines: producers are always claiming the first thing they do after acquiring new gear is to throw away the instruction manual and start messing around. Often creativity entails abusing the machines, employing them incorrectly. Mistakes – sometimes genuinely accidental, sometimes 'deliberate errors' – become aestheticized. This is a pop echo of the twentieth-century classical avant-garde's project of pushing the envelope of what is conventionally regarded as 'music', via the incorporation of noise-sound and environmental sonorities.

You can hear this in the contemporary genre of 'glitch', where artists like Oval and Fennesz make radically beautiful music using the snaps, crackles and pops emitted by damaged CDs, malfunctioning software, etc. In dancefloor genres like speed garage and jungle, you can hear the same approach in the deliberate misuse of timestretching, a digital effect that allows a sample to be compressed or prolonged in duration without its pitch going up or down. Previously when producers speeded up a vocal sample to fit the ever-faster tempos of dance music, the effect was squeaky and cartoon-absurd, like the vocalist had inhaled helium. Timestretch was invented to enable producers to achieve pleasanter, more 'musical' results, but ironically it's been seized on for the opposite effect: stretching out a vocal until the sample cracks up, creating a terrifying metallic rattle like a stuttering robot.

Even when machines aren't being used in ways never intended by the manufacturer, electronic dance music aestheticizes the mechanistic and industrial-sounding – sonic attributes opposite to the traditional musicianly premium on hands-on 'feel' and nimble dexterity. In electronic music, the cold precision and uninflected regularity of drum-machine beats and sequenced basslines aren't considered unmusical or lacking in 'swing'. Riffs tend to be angular rather than curvaceous; timbres are blatantly synthetic and artificial-sounding (unlike in pop music, where synthesizers are mostly used to inexpensively simulate acoustic instruments like horns or strings). The very inhuman aura of electronic music is part of the culture's obsession with the future, whether that is conceived as a utopia of streamlined pleasure-tech, or a dystopia of surveillance and automation.

A lot of electronica is not 'played' in any traditional instrumental sense, but is assembled using computers. Riffs are 'step-written' one note at a time on a sequencer (sometimes resulting in note-patterns that would be unplayable by human hands). With the ever-more complex 'virtual studio technology' software that's available, you can 'draw' the music on a computer screen as a visually represented waveform; sonic material can be endlessly edited and recombined, layered and subjected to all kinds of treatments and effects. As a result, what you hear rarely correlates with physical human actions in the way that the sounds in rock music (even heavily studio-manipulated and overdubbed rock) still correlate to recognizable manual gestures. So you rarely visualize a person or band when you hear electronic music. Some find this unnerving, an erasure of humanity, but for others it frees up the imagination: the music becomes a intricate, maze-like environment, or an abstract machine taking the listener on a journey through a soundscape.

2) Texture/rhythm versus melody/harmony

Another aspect of electronica's break with traditional musicality is the way that processing is more important than playing; the vivid, ear-catching textures matter more than the actual notes played. For conventionally trained musicians, the chord progressions and harmonic intervals used in electronic music can seem obvious and trite. But this misses the point, for the real function of the simple vamps and melody lines is as a device to display timbre, texture, tone-colour, chromatics. That's why so much electronica uses naive child-like melodies that sound like a music-box's chimes. Complicated melodies would distract from the sheer lustrous materiality of sound-in-itself; the pigment is more important than the line. Recent technology like DSP (digital signal processing) and 'plug-ins' (the computer age equivalent to guitar effects pedals) allow for a fantastical palette of timbral colours.

In electronic dance, every element works as both texture and rhythm. Beats are filtered to sound metallic, crunchy, spongy, shiny, wet. Melodic units are mostly simple, little vamps and riffs that work as rhythmic cogs interlocking to form a groove. And rhythm usurps the place of melody. In much of this music, it's the drum patterns – off-kilter breakbeat arrangements in drum & bass, intricate hi-hat figures in house and garage – that are the hooks, the most memorable element of a track. Each year the rhythmic subdivision of time gets ever more fantastically complex: micro-syncopations, asymmetrical patterns riddled with hesitations, multiple tiers of polyrhythm. Factor in DSP treatment of the beats and the spatial distribution of drums across the stereo-mix, and the result is a kind of rhythmic psychedelia.

3) You're so physical

With almost everything in the music working as rhythm, electronic dance is supremely physical music, engaging the body's psychomotor reflexes and tugging at your limbs. But this doesn't make the music 'mindless'. Rather, electronic dance music dissolves the old dichotomy between head and body, between 'serious' music for home-listening and 'stupid' music for the dancefloor. As Kodwo Eshun argues, at its most sophisticated electronica makes your mind dance and your body think. There is a kinaesthetic intelligence in this music that involves your muscles and nerves, and which is seen at its utmost in the extraordinary grace and fractal fluidity of the dancing style, 'liquid', that's popular at American raves. Yet still you get people who uphold a dichotomy between music for listening and music for dancing. Actually, a good dancer is 'listening' with every sinew and tendon in her body.

Electronic dance is intensely physical in another sense: it's designed to be heard over massive club sound systems. Sound becomes a fluid immersive medium enfolding the body in an intimate pressure of beat and bass. The low-end frequencies permeate your flesh, make your body vibrate and tremble. The entire body becomes an ear.

4) Against interpretation

Electronic music appeals to the mind in a quite particular way, however. Not by engaging the listener's interpretative mechanism (the traditional rock mode of treating songs as stories or statements), but rather through heightening perception through the sheer intricacy of the music: its rhythmic detail, otherworldly textures and spatial depth. Most of this music is devoid of lyrics, and when it does have them, they tend to be simple catchphrases or clichéd evocations of celebration, hope, intensity, mystical feelings. Ultimately, this music is not really about communication but about communion: a sensory unity experienced by everybody on the dancefloor. Hence the slogan 'house is a feeling', used in countless dance tracks. The word 'feeling' refers both to an emotional mood (elation tinged with a hint of blues, the sense of the club space as a blissful sanctuary circumscribed by a hostile, unstable outside world) and to a physical sensation: the waves of sound caressing your body, the collective feeling of being locked in a groove, every body in the house synchronized, entrained to the same rhythmic cycle, on the same track. Dance tracks are like vehicles, taking you on a journey, a pleasure-ride; there's a reason DJs use the term 'train wreck' to describe when they do a bad mix between records.

The vagueness of the saying 'house is a feeling' contains its own eloquence: this sensational sensation is hard to verbalize, almost impossible to explain to those who've never felt it. It bypasses 'meaning' in the rock sense but is intensely meaningful. Hence dance music's recurrent use of religious imagery, its references to a knowledge that is privy only to initiates: slogans like 'you know the score', 'this is for those who know'. Crucial distinction: this secret knowledge isn't elitist, but it is tribal, working through a powerful inclusion/exclusion effect.

5) Surface versus depth

People coming to this music from 'outside' – that's to say with no direct club experience – often complain about an 'emptiness' to the music: the sense that it is superficial, lacking in real-world referents, mere escapism. One of the most radical aspects of the music, though, is the way that electronica abolishes the depth model used by most criticism (in which some art is profound, some shallow) because all its pleasures are out there on the surface. The music is a flat plane of sensuous bliss.

You can see this in the way dance music uses the human voice. House divas have always been somewhat anonymous and depersonalized, rarely being the star focus of a song but more like a technically skilled artisan playing a role in a team effort. As the music evolved, producers increasingly used vocals in a non-expressive way, treating the singer as a source of raw material, a plastic substance to be folded, snipped, recombined, processed. From the simple voice-riffs in early house music (vocal samples distributed across a sampling keyboard and played, so that the voice becomes just an instrumental colour) this has evolved into the complicated 'vocal science' in today's 2-step garage. Here samples from R&B songs are chopped up, resequenced, and turned into percussive elements of the groove. 'Soul' is emptied out, and the human voice becomes two-dimensional, just one of an array of special effects and sonic pyrotechnics.

This depersonalizing of the voice connects to a general anxiety that many people feel about electronic music: because it is not 'saying' anything, its pleasures seem vicarious, indulgent, mere empty hedonism devoid of spiritual nourishment. Often detractors use metaphors like 'ear-candy' to convey this sense of something that isn't good for you but just offers an empty sugar-rush.

6) Drug me

Talking of getting a rush, electronic dance music is intimately bound up with drug culture. Even when it isn't designed explicitly to enhance drugs like Ecstasy, the way the music works on the listener is drug-like, and seems to demand drug metaphors. People use the music as a mood-modifier, something that swiftly transports them into a different emotional state with no necessary connection to their life-situation.

Drugs have played a crucial role in dance music's evolution. Specific music-technology innovations have synergized with particular drugs at different points: for instance, Ecstasy meshed with the trippy bass-patterns of the Roland 303 bass-synthesizer to catalyse the acid house revolution of the late eighties. Changing drug use patterns also propel the music's evolution: escalating Ecstasy and amphetamine use in the early nineties caused techno to get faster and faster, leading to hyper - kinetic styles like jungle and gabba. Ultimately, what has happened is that the drug-sensations get encoded into the music, abstracted. By itself, the music trips you out, stones you, gives you a speed-rush.

This drug-tech interface syndrome is not unique to dance music, of course. You can see it with psychedelic rock (LSD coincided with the arrival of 8-track studios), and even late seventies soft rock (the endlessly overdubbed guitar lines and overbright sonic sheen of The Eagles or Fleetwood Mac reflect superstar cocaine abuse – the cocaine ear likes glittering treble frequencies and tiny detailed sounds, while stimulant abuse makes people filigree-fussy and perfectionist). Electronic dance music is unique, however, in the way it has developed an entire musical language of sounds, riffs, and effects that are explicitly designed to trigger Ecstasy rushes or accompany the aural hallucinations induced by LSD, the coma-like disassociation caused by ketamine, etc. Moreover, because drug-states are essentially excursions outside normal consciousness, a lot of this music can be seen as involving temporary trips into insanity and schizophrenia: the paranoid rhythmic delirium of jungle, the catatonic trance of minimal techno DJs like Richie Hawtin, the psychotic fury of gabba.

7) This is journey into sound

Electronic dance music is all about being in lost in music, whether it's being engulfed by the sonic tsunami streaming out of a gigantic rave sound system, or being meditatively absorbed by the microscopic sonic events that pervade more experimental forms of electronica. These states of ego loss and oceanic connection, of being overwhelmed or entranced, are the reason why drug imagery is central to electronic imagination. And they also explain the recourse to religious language, whether taken from the Christian mystical tradition of surrender and Gnostic grace, or Eastern spiritual notions of nirvana and kundalini.

In some Eastern religions, the universe is sounded into being; hearing is the primary sense. Electronic dance culture likewise overthrows sight in the Western hierarchy of the senses, which privileges the eye. There's a good reason why clubs take place in the dark, why some warehouse raves are almost pitch black: diminishing the visual makes sound more vivid. Retinal perception is eclipsed by the audio-tactile, a vibrational continuum in which sound is so massively amplified it's visceral. This orientation towards sound can be seen in the way that ravers will literally hug speaker stacks, sometimes even climbing inside the bass-woofer's cavity and curling up like a foetus.

Beyond this worship of sound, electronic dance culture resists the tyranny of the visual in pop culture. The electronica revolution will not be televised (at least, not without being hugely compromised). Video channels like MTV are looking for stellar faces and heavenly bodies, but electronica promos tend not to feature either (indeed the video signature of some artists – The Chemical Brothers, Fatboy Slim – is only appearing in their own promos for a few seconds!). Success in pop depends on videogenic charisma, dance moves, even acting skill (with videos increasingly like mini-movies). All this is irrelevant to electronic dance music, which is simply not in the business of selling personalities. Moreover, electronic dance music simply sounds terrible through a television's mono speakers and non-existent bass: it is mixed for big club sound systems, with panoramic stereo and seismic sub-bass. A large proportion of this record's auditory content is inaudible on a television set.

Part of electronica's 'underground'-ness relates to precisely this refusal of our contemporary culture of the icon. Video is about specta-torship, whereas dance culture is about participation. And so the more underground a club is, the less there will be in terms of visual distrac-tions: the more hardcore the scene, the less there is to be seen. Clubs will always skimp on visuals and decor before cutting back on the sound system. Many rock fans who go to see a DJ spin or a dance outfit play 'live' find it dull because there's nothing to look at: no theatrics, no performance vocabulary of flamboyant gestures as there is with rock – just a few unglamorous-looking guys twiddling knobs on machines. But that misses the point, because you're not supposed to focus on the artist. The crowd is the star.

8) Faceless techno bollocks

When rave culture first took off in the UK, some diehard rock fans started to rail against 'faceless techno bollocks'. Soon the slogan started appearing on T-shirts, but worn by techno fans who'd flipped it around into a badge of pride. In its purest forms, electronic dance music is a revolt against celebrity culture and the cult of personality. Artists deliberately seek anonymity by adopting an array of alter-egos. Marc Acardipane, the German hardcore techno pioneer, may have the world record, having used over twenty different pseudonyms. Richard D. James illustrates how contact with the record business can conven-tionalize someone's career: early on, he used multiple aliases, but as he became an iconic figure with a long-term album deal, he started to release his output via only one identity, Aphex Twin.

Sometimes there are pragmatic reasons for having multiple names. The artist's primary identity may be signed to one label, but they allow him to release stuff on different labels using other names. Some artists actually have discernibly different sonic characters in their different names. But the main effect of all this is to create an effect of distancing, a break with the traditional pop impulse to connect the music to an actual human being. Along with the use of depersonalized, technical-sounding or numeric names, this intensifies the music's post-human aura, its abstract, disembodied quality. Unlike with rock or rap, you don't identify with the music-maker, you 'intensify' with the music's energy. Facelessness also has the effect of disrupting the mechanism of band or brand loyalty, the rock fan's habit of following artists through their careers. Some connoisseurs of electronic music do this, priding themselves on collecting every last item of their favourite artist's oeuvre, under all the different alter-egos. But for hardcore dance fans, producers are only as good as their latest track.

The group Underground Resistance use anonymity as part of their anti-corporate, we-are-guerrillas-of-techno aura: they are literally face-less, refusing to be photographed except wearing masks. This militant stance is all the more resonant given the rise of a dance music industry in which DJs are sold as pseudo-personalities and magazines conduct interviews that ignore the only things interesting about them (their taste in music and mixing skills) and instead talk about the DJs' career struggles, drug intake, sex lives and VIP lifestyles.

9) Death of the auteur

We look at rock music in terms of innovators: the individual artists who revolutionized music and influenced others (or, if they failed in the marketplace of their day, who were 'ahead of their time'). We look always to trace things back to the trailblazing originators, and deplore the swarm of copyists following in their wake. One of the worst insults that can be directed at a rock group is 'generic'. In electronic dance music, things work quite differently. It is often difficult, and pointless, to strive to identify who first came up with a breakthrough in rhythm or sound. Ideas mostly emerge through anonymous processes of collec-tive creativity. Look at the genesis of acid house in mid-eighties Chicago or the emergence of jungle in early nineties England, and you'll see the cultural equivalent of an ecosystem. Maybe one individ-ual happens to stumble upon an untapped potential in a piece of music-making technology, like the weird 'acid' noises inside the Roland 303 bass synthesizer. But almost immediately this idea was seized upon by other producers and instead of being diluted in the process (as usually happens with rock) the new sound was intensified. Over the course of a year, the acid tracks got weirder, fiercer, more deranging, thanks to the intense competition between producers to drive dancefloor crowds wilder, until the new effect was taken as far as it could go and became exhausted.

With jungle's chopped-up, sped-up breakbeats, it's impossible to work out who came up with the idea first, or when exactly the style crystallized. Dozens, maybe scores, of rave producers started to experiment with the idea of using sampled breakbeats instead of programmed rhythms. Through a collective musical conversation stretched across 1990–1993, 'breakbeat science' (digital techniques of micro-editing and resequencing beats) emerged in an incremental process: weekly instalments of small-scale innovation, a ping-pong match of ideas going back and forth between people who never met.

Brian Eno has dubbed this syndrome 'scenius', punning on the words 'scene' and 'genius'. He argues that our old Romantic notions of the auteur as an autonomous, endlessly fertile individual were precisely that: overly romanticized, out-of-date. And he called for a more depersonalized notion of creativity influenced by cybernetic theory, ideas of self-organizing systems and feedback loops. Another way of conceptualizing 'scenius' is in terms of biogenetics or virology, metaphors of mutation or cultural viruses (memes). Like a successful gene characteristic, electronic dance innovations achieve their highest success by becoming clichés: sounds so good that nobody can resist using them. (At least until they're all used up, at which point the underground abandons them to mainstream pop, and dismisses the sounds as 'corny' and 'cheesy'. Some sounds do enjoy an afterlife, though, coming back under the sign of camp ironic nostalgia.)

Ideas in dance music sometimes seem to evolve according to an immanent non-human logic of their own. It's tempting to talk mystically of machines like the 303 having their own agenda. In reality, the creativity is entirely human, it's just collective rather than auteur-driven. Because dance cultures have a very fast turnover, a track can come out and within a week another producer has picked up the baton. The life-cycles of sonic evolution are incredibly rapid. Unlike with rock music, even the rip-off artists, the clone merchants and copyists, play a role, because each replication of a sound unavoidably warps it. Indeed, in dance music, 'bastardization' is positive, productive, progressive.

Another reason 'generic' isn't an insult in electronic dance discourse is that tracks exist in a context. A 'generic' track is a functional track: it has the right elements to enable the DJ to mix the tune in with a bunch of similar tracks, thereby creating a flow. This play of sameness and difference is something that electronic dance music has in common with black music, where what initially seems homogenous reveals subtle inflections and shifts through concentrated immersion by the listener. From the Motown sound in the sixties through James Brown-style funk to the stop-start rhythms in modern R&B, black American music goes through different Beat-Geists. These innovations may originate with specific labels (Motown) or producers (like Timbaland with contemporary R&B), but they become the rhythmic template used by everybody. Jamaican music culture goes even further, being based not just on generic sounds but rhythms that are literally identical: different singers and MCs do new vocals over the same currently hot, endlessly reused riddim track.

One side effect of all this is that dance music has a different distribution of brilliance than other kinds of music. Rock's aesthetic hierarchy divides everything between the handful of visionary geniuses and a vast mass of mediocre non-originals. But in electronic dance music, there's a huge number of good (meaning useful-to-DJs) tracks, and a much smaller number of true landmark records. In a word, dance music is democratic.

10) We bring you the future

Another aspect to all this is that genres and scenes take the place of stars and artists – this is the level on which it's most productive to talk about the music. In dance culture, a huge amount of energy goes into cultural taxonomy: identifying genres and subgenres like species. This profusion of new sounds, scenes and genre names is also what is offputting to some newcomers to the music, who understandably find it confusing, and suspect that hype or wilful obscurantism is involved. Actually, the endless generic splintering is simply a result of dance culture's twenty years of existence, the huge number and diversity of people involved, and the global span of the culture. Anything that big is going to fracture, and many of the fractures are going to be worth talking about.

Mostly the names emerge for practical reasons. In the beginning (meaning the mid-eighties) people talked about 'house' and that was pretty much it. Later, different flavours of the music were distinguished, using prefix terms: deep house, hard house, tribal house. Why? More and more records were being made, and the stylistic parameters were starting to drift apart. Clubs found it useful to specify what their sound was, and people working in record stores started to get terminologically precise, to help customers find exactly what they wanted. Some of the terms achieved currency and became established throughout the culture. Eventually, stylistic dispersal increased to the point where the primacy of 'house' was overthrown, and brand new words – jungle, trance, gabba – came into use (often after an intermediary phase where people talked of jungle house or gabba house).

Confusing to the uninitiated and offensive to genrephobes this may be, but these definitions become urgent and crucial once you get involved in the culture. It becomes a way of talking about the music, arguing about where it should go next. It's an expression of enthusiasm and excitement, not hairsplitting or an attempt to baffle and exclude by talking in code. Above all, the hunger for the next big thing or new sound is an expression of electronic dance culture's neophilia, its impatience for the future to arrive.

11) Let's submerge

Along with 'living for the future', electronic dance culture is united by a vague, open-ended ideology of 'underground-ism', in which grass-roots scenes are positioned against the pop mainstream and the corporate record industry. 'Underground' as a concept doesn't have a huge amount of political content, though; it's not attached to any specific revolutionary aspirations, ideas about a utopian form of social organization, or even counter-cultural ideals (beyond a libertarian attitude towards drug-taking). Anti-corporate without being anti-capitalist, 'undergroundism' expresses the struggle of micro-capitalist units (independent record labels, small clubs) against macro-capitalism (the mainstream leisure-and-entertainment industry).

Electronic indie labels can be as small as a single individual making music in his bedroom and putting out the tracks himself. More often, it'll be a small gang or crew that is tightly loyal, almost communistic, and typically clustered around a central figure – an engineer/producer who owns the equipment and enables DJs to realize their ideas and become producers. Another common syndrome is independent labels that start off based around a record store. The people who work in the store, who are often aspiring DJs, develop a good sense of what is selling and what works in the clubs; they also get to know more established DJs and aspiring producers who come in to check the latest releases. The obvious next step is to take this developing A&R instinct and start releasing records by new talent. And so, to give just one example, the East London record store Boogie Times gave birth to the influential jungle label Suburban Base.

This sort of small independent tends to be unstable, though, and often doesn't survive the high turnover of dancefloor trends. Inevitably the indies that do endure are those who adopt sound business plans and managerial structures – in other words, start to behave like small corporations. Warp Records started from a record store in Sheffield, England, but watching other labels of the early rave era fall by the wayside, they developed long-term album-based deals with their artists (like Aphex Twin), and evolved into a successful company specializing in 'electronic listening music' (also know as IDM, short for 'intelligent dance music'). For many in the hardcore underground, Warp now represents the new establishment, catering to an audience of ex-clubbers and lapsed ravers with sounds that are basically dance music for the home environment.

Electronic dance music's antagonism towards the corporate music industry isn't based on political principles but aesthetic ones: the idea that the mainstream dilutes the underground's music, blunts the music's edge, tones down its harsh futurism, turns it into mere pop. In a crucial paradox, dance scenes are populist but opposed to pop culture in the 'weak', universal sense of the word. Their populism takes the form of tribal unity against what they perceive as a homogenous, blandly uninvolving mass culture. Subcultural initiates are felt to have a more committed, active, participatory relationship with the music than the desultory, passive pop consumer. Often people who believe in underground music use military rhetoric, and talk of being a 'soldier' or crusader, fighting for the cause, staying hardcore.

12) Site-specific

Part of the inclusive/exclusive aura of these subcultures is that the music is site-specific. You have to go to clubs to get the full experience. This doesn't apply to home-oriented IDM, obviously, but there is a vast swathe of this music that simply doesn't really make sense outside the club context. Often I'll buy a house or 2-step twelve-inch single and play it at home, and it'll sound weak, the beat monotonous and numbing. Hear the same song through a huge sound system, though, and the unrelenting pump and pound of the groove becomes the whole point. Massively amplified, the kickdrum becomes so thick and wide, it's a cocooning environmental pulse: you feel like you're actually inside the beat. Similarly, there are numerous genres of dance music based around floor-quaking sub-bass frequencies that are barely audible on a domestic hi-fi, let alone a boom box. And there's an entire vein of 'big room' dance tracks designed for superclubs, whose dancefloors hold a thousand plus people and are surrounded by towering speaker stacks. Often these 'big room' tracks contain hardly any music in the traditional sense – only the most rudimentary two-note bass-pulses, barely any melody lines. They don't sound good at home but they work in the superclub context because they're full of effects and whooshing noises that swoop and pan across the stereofield, sounds that are literally spectacular, designed to astonish your ears.

The more functionalist kinds of dance music can sound 'flat' at home because the tracks are essentially unfinished work. They are raw material for the DJs to transform into music by mixing very minimal tracks together: superimposing or cutting back and forth, creating dynamics by using EQ-ing effects to boost certain frequencies, and all manner of turntable tricks. These records are often described as 'DJ tools'. With other genres, particularly those – jungle, 2-step – that have a strong influence from dancehall reggae and hip hop – the tracks really come alive through the combination of the DJ's mixing and the MC chanting over the music: hyping the crowd, ordering the DJ to do a 'rewind' (i.e. stop the track mid-song and go back to the start).

Beyond this, there's a sense in which the music is like the screenplay to a movie, and is completed by 'the cast' – the crowd on the dance-floor. Styles like jungle and trance are full of behavioural cues encoded in the music – breakdowns, drum builds, bass drops, climaxes – all of which trigger certain mass responses: ritualized gestures of abandon, like hands shooting up in the air at the entrance of a certain kind of riff or noise. The music sounds diminished in the absence of such tableaux of crowd frenzy. Ultimately, most dance tracks are components in a subcultural engine – heard decontextualized and isolated, they can seem as perplexing and functionless as a carburettor outside the car. And while it might have a certain surreal appeal to keep an engine part in the middle of your living room, you'd definitely not be getting full use of that component.

'Context' can be really specific. There are some tracks that are associated with just one specific club, like the song 'Twilo Thunder', made in homage to the New York club Twilo. Its sound was tailored to the immense Twilo sound system and designed to fuel the special atmosphere generated by the crowd who religiously attended Sasha & Digweed's eight-hour DJ sets. For a culture that typically boasts of its global reach and its transcendence of geography, electronica can be disconcertingly fixated on a sense of place. What these privileged sites, these temples of sound, create is a form of postmodern tribalism: people from different backgrounds and locations gather together to experience the same 'tribe-vibe'.

Part of the conditions of existence for these transient communities, argues Michel Gaillot, is that people check their ideologies at the door with their coats. This isn't apolitical so much as anti-political, or perhaps pre-political: an attempt to cut through all the divisions and rediscover some primal basis of connection, even if that unity is as simple as sharing the same sonic (and often drug) sensations, occupying the same space ('Everybody in the Place', as the Prodigy titled one of their early rave anthems). Which helps explains electronic dance culture's suspicion of words, its urge to dispense with language.

Because words divide. And this music is about the urge to merge, about becoming part of something larger than yourself, whether it's the dancing crowd, a sublime vastness of sound or the cosmos.

13) Only connect

One of the key words in dance culture is 'mix', a term with multiple applications and resonances. Mixed crowds: most dance scenes at least pay lip service to the idea that all are welcome and that clubs with a good social/racial/gender mix are the ones with the best vibe. Mix-and-blend: the musical ethos shared by most genres of electronic dance is a belief in stylistic border-crossing – a notion of hybridity similar to *mesticagem*, the national ideology of Brazil, which takes pride in that that country's miscegenated culture and music. (Which may explain why a lot of house producers have an almost utopian vision of Brazil and are infatuated with samba and bossa nova rhythms.) Remixes: rather than a definitively complete and inviolate work of art, a dance track is treated as a provisional collection of sonic resources to be rearranged – hence the vogue for multiple remixes (sometimes as many as ten different versions), and for remix albums where the DJ/producers pay tribute to an admired artist by reworking, sometimes to the point of obliteration, their music. Mix: the art of DJ-ing involves taking disparate tracks and connecting them into a meta-track, a potentially interminable flow. Repetition and interconnection evoke a feeling of boundless pleasure. Time is abolished ('3-AM Eternal', as one track title put it). Lack, too. The music insists 'go with the flow' and 'be here now', lose yourself in a never-ending present of pure sensation.

* * *

So there you have it: the principles and parameters of electronic dance music. BUT, *but*, this culture is so vast, contains such multitudes, that for every one of these precepts outlined above, there are exceptions, things that contradict my claims. Let's take a few examples.

Death of the auteur: there are many producers working in electronica who do think of themselves as capital A artists in the old-fashioned sense, and who operate as mavericks who transcend genre limits. In a kind of culture-lag, new forms of art are often appraised using the old-fashioned terminology and values appropriate to earlier forms. This kind of thinking can affect creators as much as critics. So a figure like drum & bass pioneer Goldie conceives what he does using quaint categories like expression, catharsis, 'getting my demons out'. Every noise and beat in his records seem to have a biographical correlate, is telling the story of his turbulent life. Personally, I think the most exciting music he made was early in his career when he was more like a vital cog in the 'scenius' of the nascent jungle scene. But clearly his own sense of himself as a Towering Visionary Genius has crucially shaped both his aesthetic trajectory (all those concept albums like *Timeless* and *Saturnz Return*) and his public reception.

Form & Function > Content & Meaning. In fact, some dance producers are trying to 'say stuff', sometimes through song-form and actual lyrics, sometimes through using resonant samples, sometimes through the artist names they choose and the titles they give their tracks. Overtly politicized dance music is rare (Underground Resistance, Atari Teenage Riot) but there's an implicit politics and real-world resonance to much electronic music, whether it's the redemptive utopian vision of house culture, or the ghetto renegade street realism that pervades jungle (which comes through as much in the militant feel of the rhythms and the ominous menace of the basslines as through apocalyptic samples like the roots reggae derived cry 'alla da youth shall witness the day that Babylon shall fall').

Rhythm/Texture > Melody/Harmony. The former might be dance culture's true claim to cutting edge status, but electronica abounds with gorgeous tunes: from melodists supreme like Orbital and Boards of Canada, to the hook-laden work of drum & bass producers like Omni Trio and LTJ Bukem, to the songfulness of deep house producers like Chris Brann and Herbert. Many dance producers are trained in traditional music-making, have played in bands, know about key changes, etc. This may actually constrain them from making the breakthroughs achieved by those who don't know the rules, but the loveliness of their music is undeniable.

Machine music vs 'musicality'. There are substantial swathes of electronic dance culture that pay homage (often to an excessive degree) to traditional musical ideals – jazzy swing, pianistic dexterity, 'feel', subtlety. In particular, there is a fetish for the fusion jazz of the early seventies – the 'warmth' of instruments like the Rhodes electric piano. Paradoxically, many dance producers feel that 'progress' involves sounding less alien, futuristic and mechanistic, and instead bringing in acoustic instrumentation: double-bass, flute and saxophone solos, strings. Hence the veneration for soundtrack composers like John Barry, auteur arrangers like David Axelrod, and jazz-funk bandleaders like Roy Ayers – all of whom are imitated or sampled. Moreover, software has got so sophisticated that beats can be programmed with an infinitesimal complexity, full of accents, inflections, human-sounding discrepancies and irregularities. 'Swing' and 'feel' have returned. And some drum & bass rhythm programming is so detailed and constantly shifting that it sounds like a jazz drummer doing a solo.

Futurism. There are several strands of dance culture – the mellow, jazzy strains within drum & bass and trip hop, the Afro-Brazilian infatuated elements within house – that are actually rather conservative. Producers often seem to feel that the present is a less distinguished era than some idealized golden age, and that standards of musicality have dropped off. (Many blame drug culture for lowering standards, making people want banging beats and cheesy anthems.) For all its fascination for the futuristic, dance culture feels an equally potent tug towards the past – it is obsessed with roots and origins, and is surprisingly prey to nostalgia. Hence the vogue for all things 'old school', whether that term refers to seventies disco, eighties electro and synthpop or the golden age of hardcore rave. Back to 1992 raves, retro-oriented clubs, reissues, remakes, tribute albums – the culture has become more and more obsessed with its own history.

Mixing it Up. A lot of vital electronic music is made by purists, who have narrowed their focus to a single style of music, refined and distilled the form. Conversely, mixed-up music can often be a haplessly eclectic mess, or a bland blend with all the distinctiveness of the original sources smoothed out.

As you can see, my list of foundational principles is just a partial blueprint: culture is always messy, evading our attempts at definition. The aspects I've highlighted, though, represent this music's claims to radicalism. They are the 'emergent' elements, to use a concept from cultural studies referring to tendencies that point towards future aesthetic and social formations. Any cultural phenomenon that has real impact in the present, however, must inevitably be a mixture of 'emergent' and 'residual' (meaning traditional). Generally speaking, music that is totally avant-garde and ahead-of-its-time subsists in the academic ghetto, depending on state subsidies or institutional support. You can see this with the most advanced forms of 'sound art' or 'sound design': they can't survive in the rough-and-tumble of the pop marketplace, but inhabit the world of art galleries, museums, seminars and symposiums and festivals. Which is fine, but for me the most exciting thing about electronic dance music is that you get avant-garde ideas working in a popular context, carried by groove and catchy hooks, and enlivened by a context of fun and collective celebration. One example is jungle's vibrant blend of 'roots 'n' phuture' (as one early jungle track put it). The 'emergent', avant-garde elements in jungle wouldn't have worked without the 'residual' stuff: to have 'breakbeat science', you need to have breakbeats (sweaty, human musicians playing hot funky percussive breaks) in the first place, providing the raw material to be sampled and digitally recombined.

Ultimately, electronic dance music is at its most enjoyable when it's impure: rhythm/texture colliding with songcraft, soul-less machinery fighting it out with traditional ideas of sonic beauty, avant-garde auteur impulses checked by the crowd's demand for danceable grooves. These tensions are what keep the music vital.

Prologue (written 2001) to the electronic music book
Loops: Una historia de la musica electronica, Historia Electronica,
edited by Javier Blanquez and Omar Morera, 2002

Often your ideas about something reach their point of absolute starkest clarity long after the event, and so it was with this essay, which really ought to have been either the prologue or conclusion to *Energy Flash*, rather than a preface for a Spanish guide to electronic music. It also serves pretty much as my personal funeral oration for the movement, which of course is still alive but as far as I can see (from an admittedly non-involved vantage point) has ceased to actually move. Oh, it throws up good stuff to listen to quite regularly but it will never again be what it was between 1988 and 1998, just as rock never really recovered the combination of epochal centrality and aesthetic forward-surge that it possessed between 1964 and 1974.

B-BOYS ON E

Hip Hop Discovers Ecstasy

'World, get on one / If you not afraid to fly . . . Nothing but love / I'm feeling X-traordinary freaky / And I know you hoes wanna roll with me . . .' On the cold printed page, these lyrics look like they're from a song by The Beloved, back in the days when singer Jon Marsh was a blissed-out Shoom regular. Listen to the track, and the music sounds like a classic rave anthem, maybe a Todd Terry classic like CLS's 'Can You Feel it'. But the word 'hoes' – hip hop slang for women – is the giveaway. This isn't some old-school Balearic anthem but 'Ecstasy' by gangsta rapper Ja Rule, just one of a new breed of 'love thugs' rhyming about the thrills of pills. Prime examples from the last year include such subtly titled gems as 'Let's Get High' by Dr Dre, 'Hennessy & Ecstasy' by B.G. and 'Ecstasy' by Bone Thugs 'n' Harmony. And there are references to E (or X, as Americans call it) and 'rolling' (US raver slang for taking pills) in tracks by Jay-Z, DJ Quik, Nas, Three-6-Mafia, Saafir, Big Tymers and Xzibit.

It's not just the stars that are indulging, either. 'It's hitting the 'hoods, it's hitting the niggas,' Bizzy Bone of Bone Thugs told one US magazine. At a recent show in Philadelphia, Ja Rule asked the crowd, 'How 'bout that Ecstasy?', obviously confident that most of the audience knew the score.

What's striking about this is that Ja Rule is most famous for the menacingly drawled 'murdah' chants of his 1999 hit 'Holla Holla'. His record label is called Murder Inc., and Rule is also a member of the charmingly named rap collective The Murderers. So how has Rule managed to go from gangsta rap's gun talk and bloody sagas of paranoia and revenge to loved-up ditties about nights rolling on Mitsubishis?

330

Let's be honest, though. The E-influenced lyrics that have emerged so far haven't seen Ja Rule and Co. swapping their Glocks for glow-sticks. And the lyrics about dissing hoes, humiliating 'haters', flaunting wealth and eliminating rivals have not disappeared in favour of P.L.U.R. (peace/love/unity/respect, the motto of the US rave scene.) For instance, on *Lights Out*, the latest album by New Orleans rap superstar Lil Wayne, rhymes like 'Pop X and drink Cris' / My life is the shit' jostle next to grisly threats like 'I'll cock the Glock and spray ya'. Hip hop's macho codes of behaviour are too entrenched to be melted overnight, and so far the culture has adapted Ecstasy to its own needs: getting freaky between the sheets.

In 'Let's Get High', Dr Dre's lyric about dropping MDMA ('I just took some Ecstasy / Ain't no tellin' what the side effects could be') goes straight into 'All these fine bitches equal sex to me', while Bone Thugs 'n' Harmony's 'Ecstasy' has the choice verse 'Feelin' hot and exotic with an arced cock / I'm feelin' too sexy for my muthafuckin' self / Gotta find my bitch and I'm gonna fuck her ass to death'. There are stories floating around about major players in the rap industry throwing parties at their mansions in the Hamptons (an expensive summer home area favoured by Manhattan's wealthy and famous) where E is primarily used to get the ladies 'in the mood' for multiple-partner sex.

'Hip hop's always been a sexual culture,' says human conduit between house and hip hop, Armand Van Helden. 'Ecstasy is just amplifying the sexuality. I like going to rap clubs in New York at the moment, cos the girls are rolling on E and they're like, feeling you up and stuff!'

According to Van Helden, one of the major routes via which Ecstasy use filtered into the hip hop scene was the sex industry, specifically strip clubs. 'The club owners want the girls to do the job with a good attitude, to perform and project in this really full-on way. And it's a boring job, so to make sure the girls don't get into moping, they give them E. A lot of the girls live back in the ghettos and barrios, and it crossed over that way – the strippers bringing Ecstasy back to the 'hood, turning people on.'

Hip hop's getting loved up is a side effect of the astonishing surge in Ecstasy use among the general American population over the last two years. The *New York Times* reported a 450 per cent increase between 1998 and 1999 in Ecstasy seizures by police and customs. This was partly triggered by a return to reliable, high-dose MDMA thanks to Mitsubishis and other pills that followed in its wake. For the first time since the early eighties, when Ecstasy was still legal, the drug is popular outside the rave scene, with college students and yuppies throwing E parties. Finally, the drug has made significant inroads into the rap community. Van Helden says that black and Hispanic kids started attending raves, despite the fact that most hip hoppers have traditionally regarded raves as a scene for wealthy white kids or, in the case of house clubs, as a gay scene.

'They're looking for a good time at the weekend and they can't go to bars or clubs, cos the drink laws in America say you have to be twenty-one to get in. So they go to raves, where anyone can come in cos there's no alcohol served. Just for somewhere to hang out. Eventually, they got cats coming up and saying "wanna do some X?". They'd try it, bug out, and go back to the neighbourhood to spread the news.'

Another factor behind the rise of Ecstasy is that its price makes it competitive as a party-hard potion. Rap playas like to flash cash – hence the vogue for Cristal champagne and Hennessy – but at a certain point the economics get undeniable. 'Ecstasy's about twenty bucks,' says Van Helden. 'Compare that to buying a bottle of Moet, which is about 120 dollars in a club – for four glasses of champagne! E is cheaper and it lasts for hours.' In Ja Rule's 'Ecstasy', the rapper rhymes about how 'Nobody sippin' on Cristal? They all got an Evian or OJ,' and marvels at how weird he feels, as a 'big baller', to be 'ordering all that damn water'.

Whether as a result of Ecstasy use or just an eerily prophetic prelude, the last eighteen months have seen a flood of rap and R&B tracks that feature techno-like sounds and riffs. Ja Rule's 'Holla Holla' used a snaking, writhing riff that sounds uncannily like a Roland 303 acid bassline. There's staccato rave-stabs in R&B tunes by Destiny's Child and Ginuwine's 'What's So Different', and house vamps and techno pulses appear in countless tracks from the Cash Money roster of Juvenile, B.G. and Lil Wayne. On Lil Kim's *The Notorious K.I.M.*, two tracks were based on eighties house anthems 'French Kiss' by Lil Louis and 'Break 4 Love' by Raze, while her recent single 'How Many Licks' is full of Daft Punk-like noises. Ludacris's massive hit 'What's Your Fantasy?' sounds like an old rave tune played at 33 rpm instead of 45 rpm, all stabs and muffled fuzzy bass. His 'Get Me Off' could be LFO circa *Frequencies*, while 'Southern Hospitality' (produced by the Neptunes, of Kelis fame) features 'Mentasm'-style hoover-riffs seemingly AWOL from a Lisa Lashes hard house set.

Van Helden is sceptical about the idea that there's a direct link between all these techno textures and hip hop's infatuation with Ecstasy, though. 'House and hip hop have always had a relationship, they're using the same technology after all. The weird, techy sounds you get in rap and R&B now, that was mainly started by Timbaland. He invented that double-time beats thing that's almost like an Americanized form of drum & bass. After him, all the rap and R&B producers really started attacking new sounds, and shit started flying.'

Still, last year Timbaland did produce three tracks that positively dripped with the influence of European Ecstasy culture, if not E itself: Aaliyah's smash hit 'Try Again' with its burbling Roland 303, Jay-Z's 'Snoopy Track' with its Human Resource/'Dominator' style dirge-bass riff (plus Jay Z couplet 'I like my women friends feminine / I like my hoes on X like Eminem'), and Nas's 'You Owe Me', whose slinky pulsations and jerky flow sound uncannily close to 2-step garage.

Nevertheless, you've yet to hear top rap producers like Rockwilder, Swizz Beatz and The Neptunes bigging up Jeff Mills, Thomas Bangalter or Timo Maas. Nor has there been a big wave of hip hop fans leaving the Tunnel, where Funkmaster Flex deejays the hottest hardcore rap night in New York, to check out Twilo, just a few hundred yards down 27th Street. So far OutKast are the only rap group to talk openly about being directly influenced by rave music and Ecstasy culture. The duo, Big Boi and Andre 3000, have talked about going to raves in their home town Atlanta, Georgia, and even going on field research missions in London clubland. They gave their latest album, the hugely acclaimed *Stankonia*, faster bpms than its mellow predecessor *Aquemeni* because 'nowadays you got different drugs on the scene. X done hit the 'hood. It ain't chronic no more.' OutKast even dabbled in drum & bass on their single 'Bombs Over Baghdad', trying to connect with the faster metabolic rate of 'a whole new breed of kids ... You got little kids doing cocaine, doing Ecstasy and all kinda speed-'em-up drugs. That's the heartbeat of what's going on.'

For Van Helden, this particular moment in hip hop recalls a lost golden age that briefly occurred in the late eighties: hip-house. Then you had artists like Doug Lazy, Fast Eddie and Tyree rapping over house beats, and rap groups like The Jungle Brothers doing tracks like 'I'll House You' (which was produced by Todd Terry). 'Hip hop was uptempo back then anyway, and it was normal in New York clubs to mix it with house. Then in the nineties, the bpms in hip hop got slower and the clubs were moody – everybody just drinking and blazing trees [smoking spliffs] and it just kind of dragged. I really missed that kind of hands-up-in-the-air shit. I hate to say it, but E is responsible for making the rap clubs good again.'

The first rapper to talk openly about his Ecstasy use, of course, was Eminem – rhyming about his preference for E and mushrooms, brazenly gobbling handfuls of pills (or look-alikes) at concerts, pretending to spill the little white fellers out of his pockets onstage at the MTV music awards, and even reportedly throwing Es into the audience during his tour of Germany. In a kiss-and-tell memoir written by his former bodyguard Byron Williams, Eminem is described as a compulsive Ecstasy user who has to take the drug before shows or interviews to get vibed up, and who coined personal nicknames for pills such as 'helicopters' or 'little men'. Although Eminem's management denied the 'six pills a day' addiction slurs, Eminem's producer Dr Dre has talked about recording songs during two-day Ecstasy-fuelled sessions in the studio. 'We git in there, get bugged out, stay in the studio for two days,' Dre told one US magazine. 'Then you're dead for three days. Then you wake up, pop the tape in, like 'let me see what I've done'.

Eminem is a perfect example of the paradoxes of the 'B-Boys on E' phenomenon. MDMA softens one's emotional defences, promotes feelings of trust and tactile tenderness, melts the ego. In other words, it basically creates the exact opposite mindset to rap's paranoid aggression, its threats and boasts and delusions of grandeur. But Eminem hasn't noticeably become a more enlightened or peaceful person as a result.

Hip hop's embrace of Ecstasy is changing the music and culture of the scene, but it's also challenging many of our assumptions about the utopian, consciousness-changing powers of the drug. Hip hop's ethos of 'keeping it real' conflicts with rave's Ecstasy-fuelled positivity. Things are changing, but don't hold your breath for the smiley facey to replace the scowling sneer of the 'screwface' that characterizes hip hop photoshoots. Bizzy Bone of Bone Thugs told *Vibe* magazine that Ecstasy 'is for people who can't deal with the world'. And he expressed disgust for E's swoony, androgyny-fuelling effects: 'That's some feminine-ass shit, make a motherfucker act all sweet. Anything that makes a man want to drop to his knees and give another man fellatio, something ain't right . . .'

Then again, Ecstasy is such a powerful drug that it's certain to have some effects on hip hop, both as culture and as music. But what about attitudes? Ecstasy's 'loved up' vibe fits perfectly with hip hop's endless professions of loyalty for the crew, family, click, posse. E will only exaggerate this aspect of blood-brother solidarity and 'thug love'. But what about the hate side of rap's soul? Will E have the same calming effect on hip hop's tough guys as it did on the UK soccer casuals in the late eighties? Can Ecstasy lead to a truce in rap's symbolic warfare? Will 'call-that-a-worldview?!?' couplets like 'all I know is that bitches suck dick and niggas bleed' (The Lox) lose their appeal to hearts that no longer feel hard? After the massive influence it's had on the global dance scene, it seemed that E held no more surprises in terms of its cultural effects. But now that the drug has filtered through to one of the few groups it had left untouched – Black American youth – it could be that Ecstasy has new tricks up its sleeves, new stories to tell.

Director's cut of feature for *Muzik*, April 2001

I stumbled on my first clue about the B-Boys on E phenomenon in *The Wire* magazine of all places – in an Xmas list of personal highlights from 1999, El-P of underground rap outfit Company Flow listed trying Ecstasy 'for the first, second, third, fourth, fifth, sixth, seventh and eighth time'. That caught my eye! Then I came across Dre's 'Let's Get High', followed shortly by Bone Thugs 'n' Harmony's 'Ecstasy', and mindful of the old journalist's adage 'two's a coincidence, three's a trend', wrote up a piece for the webzine *Hyperdub*, which led to my drastically remixing and expanding it as a *Muzik* cover story. The B-boys on E syndrome didn't change rap culture in the end (the real-world pressures that shape the hip hop mindset are just too strong for that) but it did create some fantastic music along the way. And rave-inflected rap continued to emerge after this piece was published, from the Dirty South style called crunk (which often sounds like a fusion of gabba and gangsta) to the Bay Area's hyphy, which sonically resembles a slightly tripped out version of the electro that so much Southern rap is based on. Hyphy has its own colourful slang: thizz = E, thizz face = grimace caused by the yukky taste of a pill going down, thizzle dance = the scene's loony style of moving to the music, something like a mixture of rave-style 'liquid' and the clown-dancing of 'krumping'.

SO SOLID CREW

They Don't Know (Independiente/Relentless)

So I'm listening to the So Solid Crew album for the first time when this paramedic ambulance whizzes past my window, and its stuttering siren synchs exactly with the syncopated 2-step beat. Perfect: So Solid's music is nothing if not urban, in both the Souf-Lundun-innit and US-radio-euphemism-for-black senses. When it comes to the latter, it's hardly news that American R&B and rap have massively impacted Britain's own street culture. Just as the twitchy stop-start rhythm running through *They Don't Know* wouldn't exist without Timbaland, similarly So Solid's MC squadron are steeped in US rap – the songs teem with thugged-out slanguage like chasing 'paper', smoking 'trees', stealing another man's 'honey', 'spittin'' lyrics. The very concept of the So Solid collective with its thirty-plus associates is modelled on B-boy clans like Wu-Tang, Roc-A-Fella, and No Limit: entrepreneurial dynasties with street roots and shady pasts.

So Solid Crew and similar outfits like Pay As You Go Cartel are spearheading one of the most significant developments in recent British dance culture: UK garage's transformation into a mutant form of British rap, with MCs becoming as important as DJs and producers, and actually starting to say stuff rather than simply hyping the crowd. So while the hip hop stylings (the doo-rags on the Crew's heads, the ice and gold, the titles like 'Ride Wid Us') are America-inspired, this is just a fantasy patina overlaying UK inner-city realism.

You can hear this distinctive Englishness in the wiry voices (making me flash on 3 Wizemen and the endless false dawn for homegrown UK rap) and in the sheer speed of the MC-ing. In Black British sound system culture from reggae to jungle, the mic' chat has always been hyperkinetic. So instead of the slurred growl of a DMX, the So Solid

MCs are incredibly crisp, nimble, even dainty. On the title track, the line 'they don't know about my flow' is enunciated with a prissy precision that's almost fey. Elsewhere vocal tricks, like the 'human timestretch' bit on 'Deeper', where Romeo slows down and speeds up, testify to the legacy of a decade-plus of London pirate radio MC-ing. Indeed, So Solid run their own pirate station.

Sonically, So Solid are equally steeped in the hardcore continuum that runs from rave to jungle to UKG: you can hear it in the murky, viscous basslines, the icy plinking keyboard riffs. Alongside their satellite crew Oxide & Neutrino, So Solid pioneered the shift in UKG away from pop R&B crossover to a stripped-down electro-like sound. In the course of eighteen months, UKG has gone from boom-time music to a recession soundtrack, its ominous sub-bass and rigid-with-tension beats evoking the desperate struggle for a share of the shrinking economic pie. Which is why nearly every song on *They Don't Know* addresses 'haters' who resent So Solid's success. (Forgivably, perhaps, given that the Crew's lyrics relentlessly rub the group's prowess, prestige and prosperity in the faces of non-VIP losers.)

'Hater' is a concept that aims to discredit any egalitarian impulse, attributing it to envy. So Solid's pinched, paranoid outlook is the logical upshot of twenty-two years of post-socialist Britain and the emergence of a permanent underclass. 'Solid' carries a faint melancholy echo of the days when people talked of strikes staying solid. But that idea of class solidarity has long since contracted to the gang, the click, the crew: a sort of micro-socialist haven within dog-eat-dog capitalism. For all its don't-fuck-with-us collective swagger, though, and the lyrical emphasis on living large, the overwhelming impression left by *They Don't Know* is of constraint. This is actually inscribed into the structure of their Number 1 smash '21 Seconds', where each MC has just a few bars, lasting only twenty-one seconds, in which to shine. On that track, and the whole album, you hear the hectic sound of talent squeezing itself through a tiny aperture. And while it's amazing how the street realities of exclusion and disadvantage continue to simultaneously obstruct and catalyse underclass creativity, who would actually want to live the lives that produced this grimly thrilling music?

Uncut, January 2002

So Solid Crew are one of those bands that are Important but have not left much of a spoor of great recordings. '21 Seconds' is epochal but not very good (the grime equivalent to 'Rock Around the Clock', perhaps). They didn't call it grime at this point, of course, but if anyone deserves to be considered the founding fathers it's So Solid – them and Oxide & Neutrino.

One of the odd things about grime is that it started as pop crossover (Oxide & Neutrino's 'Bound 4 Da Reload' hit Number 1 in May 2000, '21 Seconds' topped the chart in August 2001) and then went downhill from there in terms of its mainstream profile. The hits got more infrequent, they placed lower in the chart and lingered for a shorter time, even as the genre achieved self-definition, the scene got stronger and more productive, and the media lavished press and attention. So Solid Crew's Number 1 success also gave what-would-be-grime a sense of just how far the music could go (unrealistic, as it happened). Their fame and infamy – the hits and TV appearances galore combined with the column inches of media panic about violence at their gigs and the banned shows – showed that a UK crew could have as big an impact as American rappers. So while their underground peers Pay As U Go Cartel and Roll Deep ultimately had a grander legacy in terms of the MCs that came through their ranks, a tip of the hat to So Solid – pioneers.

THE STREETS

Original Pirate Material (Locked On)

Just when you think pop's got no more surprises up its sleeve, along comes a record that proves there's always a new twist around the corner. *Original Pirate Material* is the first record in a long while I've wanted to play again *immediately* after it's finished; the sort where you have to ration the number of playings in order to pace your pleasure, to avoid using up all its joy too soon. It's a little eerie how the album keeps getting better (the first track, though stunning, is the weakest!), how it never flags.

The Streets is Mike Skinner, twenty-two years old, from Birmingham, a beat-maker and rhyme-spitter. On this debut album, Skinner's taken what is already the only truly exciting development in British dance culture – MCs rapping over UK garage – and single - handedly pushed it to the next level. So far UK garage MCs haven't gone much beyond their original function in hardcore and jungle: hyping the crowd, bigging up the DJ, extolling their own skills. By contrast, Skinner is really saying something, telling stories etched with such a richness of observation and reference and emotional nuance that So Solid Crew, tirelessly/tiresomely railing against playa-haters, suddenly look awfully mono-thematic. If So Solid are 2-step's NWA, The Streets is something like its Rakim, De La Soul, Nas.

Original Pirate Material is a massive gauntlet throwdown to Skinner's peers. 'This ain't a track, it's a movement,' he declares on 'Let's Push Things Forward' – a clarion call for aesthetic ambition and real content, with Skinner decrying formula (the nuff-catchy chorus goes 'You say that everything sounds the same / Then you go buy them / There's no excuses my friend') and mocking the forked-American-tongue of gangsta-wannabes ('Around here we say birds not bitches'). The Englishness comes through not just in his slanguage (all the 'geezers' and 'dodgy fucks') but sonically too. All mournful roots-reggae horns and skankin' B-line, 'Let's Push' echoes The Specials' 'Ghost Town' while the balalaika-laced 'Too Much Brandy' sounds like a homage to 'Stereotypes' from the muzak-influenced *More Specials*. A hilariously vivid tale of a bender to end all benders, 'Too Much Brandy' is suffused with a wry, bleak humour that recalls Terry Hall. It's a Midlands thing.

Outside London, Skinner points out, UK garage isn't a club phenomenon, it's music for driving or for stay-at-home smokers. 'Has it Come to This', his unlikely hit single about 'a day in the life of a geezer', captures this submerged reality of dance culture: the iceberg bulk of people who dig the music but don't go out often, cos they can't afford the bar prices or the brand-name gear required for larging-it. Instead, they save their hard-earned cash for drugs and get wasted at home, locked into the pirate signal, surrounded by PlayStation and similar pleasure-tech. 'All Got Our Runnins', a song about being broke, is even more radical in UK garage's flash-yer-cash context. All spend and no thrift, the protagonist is paying for last week's 'living for the moment', dodging the landlord, eking out 'one beer to last all evening', trying to smuggle brandy into clubs, and hanging around his mum's house cos his own larder's empty.

Skinner's persona mixes old-head-on-young-shoulders with there-but-for-the-grace-of-God-go-I. He's intimately acquainted with the working-class culture of consolation but, like Irvine Welsh, he's too smart not to see through it, to the desolation that fuels its desperate forms of release. 'Same Old Thing' evokes the treadmill grind of prole leisure, a mind-numbing miasma of booze, birds and bovver. 'Geezers Need Excitement' diagnoses ruckus as both a safety valve for boredom and as symptom of the hard-man culture of respect-maintenance. 'The Irony of it All' is a comic take on the same idea. Skinner brilliantly acts two characters across alternating verses: lairy lout Terry versus Tim, a student who home-makes bongs and knows all the statistics in favour of legalization. 'In the eyes of society I need to be in jail / For the choice of herbs I inhale . . . We pose no threat on my settee,' reasons Tim, but he's such an irritatingly smug know-it-all you're almost glad when his path crosses Terry's and he gets a battering.

It's breathtaking the way Skinner takes English idiom and cadence – even soft-spoken Tim's prissy speech patterns – then works it into a flow that's pure B-Boy. Rarely resorting to black British slang or patois, he creates an authentic poetic spark from the base materials of UK demotic language. There's that same electric sensation you got on first hearing 3D and Tricky rhyming on *Blue Lines*, when all of a sudden that stillborn child, 'Britrap', seemed like it might have life in it yet. Indeed, tracks like 'Turn the Page' and 'It's Too Late' actually recall the string-swept majesty of 'Unfinished Sympathy'. Elsewhere, you flash on John Cooper-Clarke, or imagine Jarvis Cocker if he'd grown up on nothing but street beats, MCs and Class A's.

Speaking of Pulp, 'Weak Become Heroes' shoves 'Sorted for E's and Whizz' off its throne as the definitive double-edged evocation of rave's dream-and-lie. A house classic playing in a café triggers a Proustian flash-back to Skinner's Ecstasy baptism five years earlier. Adrift on memory bliss, scrambled images unfurl in his mind's eye of that magical night when every stranger became a friend and 'all of life's problems I just shake off'. The chorus mashes together a soul singer crooning, 'Weak become heroes / And the stars align,' with Skinner's all-choked-up, 'We all smile / We all sing', over a soft-focus piano vamp looped for eternity. Outside on the street, 'memories smoulder' but the real world's unchanged ('new beats though'). The promised revolution never came, and Skinner's life's 'been up and down since I walked from that crowd'.

With its steadfast locked groove and inspirational chorus ('just try staying positive'), the gorgeous 'Stay Positive' conjures a mood of martial resilience in the face of all 'the dark shit'. Skinner counsels keeping away from pain-killing narcotics and instead proposes true love and follow-your-dreams individualism as sole rays of sunshine in the murk. 'I ain't helping you climb the ladder / I'm busy climbing mine / That's how it's been since the dawn of time.' A shortfall of vision, maybe, this rejection of solidarity and political solutions, this buying into the big lie of anyone-can-make-it. But then Skinner 'ain't no preaching fucker and I ain't no do-goody-goody either,' and he would-n't be half the poet if he was. 'Stay Positive' ends the album, like 'Feed Me' did *Maxinquaye,* with a necessary mirage of hope. Indeed, Tricky's debut – a dispatch from the front lines of the chemical degeneration, a street-level survey of Britain's stasis quo – is the best parallel for *Original Pirate Material.* It's that good.

Uncut, April 2002

Loads of comparisons thrown around here, but an obvious one I missed: Ian Dury, who half-jokingly claimed to have invented rap with 'Reasons to Be Cheerful (Part 3)' and who also was something of a Mockney, operating from slightly outside the 'bacon rind' realities he depicted with such seeming verisimilitude. Talking of grubby realism, the cash-flow crisis ditty 'All Got Our Runnins' was on the advance CD, but by the time *Original Pirate Material* hit the stores the tune (my favourite on the album) had been mysteriously shunted off in favour of 'Don't Mug Yourself' . . .

WHO SAYS THE BRITISH CAN'T RAP?

The UK's New Wave of MCs confront American Hip Hop Isolationism

The British have always had a flair for taking Black American music, giving it a twist, and then exporting it back stylishly repackaged. Blues, R&B, soul, funk, disco, house: each in turn has been the source music for a series of British Invasions of the American pop mainstream. Yet this native genius for appropriation has spectacularly failed in one area: hip hop.

From late eighties contenders like Ruthless Rap Assassins to nineties non-events like The Brotherhood, British rappers share two things: their nationality and their failure to make the slightest impression in hip hop's homeland. After nearly two decades of sustained non-achievement, most American rap aficionados find the very concept of UK hip hop absurd. Some baldly declare: 'British people just shouldn't rap.'

Yet the British obsession with hip hop – which goes back to the early eighties – is currently stronger than ever. So pervasive is its influence on urban street style that there is an entire UK mini-genre of rap satire that includes the TV comedy character Ali G and the cult rapper MC Pitman. The latter purports to be a Yorkshire coal miner and raps about dunking McVitie's digestive biscuits in his tea. As well as deflating gangsta machismo with a dose of English bathos, this sort of rap parody taps into British anxieties about Americanization. Gangsta rap, for instance, is often accused by British newspaper pundits of glamorizing incivility and lawlessness.

The more positive side of hip hop's influence in Britain is the resurgence of homegrown rap, as reflected in the nominations for the 2002 Mercury Prize, a prestigious UK music industry award. For the first time, a British MC, Ms Dynamite won the prize, seeing off competition from two other rappers, bookie's favourite The Streets, and Roots Manuva. Both The Streets's Mike Skinner and Ms Dynamite typify a generation of young English MCs who – careers blocked owing to the 'lost cause' status of Britrap – found an alternate route to success via dance music. Specifically, they have hijacked the genre known as UK garage, a hybrid of house, R&B and reggae. Over the last two years, MC-fronted UK garage outfits like So Solid Crew and Pay As U Go Cartel have gone from London's underground scene of pirate radio and raves, to the pop charts and mainstream media.

A thirty-strong collective comprising MCs, vocalists and producers, So Solid based themselves on the family-as-corporation model pioneered by American rappers like Wu-Tang Clan. Like Wu-Tang, So Solid established the collective brand-name first with the UK Number 1 hit '21 Seconds' and are currently shrewdly spinning off solo careers for individual members. Canny entrepreneurs with roots in the shadier side of the streets, So Solid have numerous business interests, including owning their own pirate radio station. Yet there's one major obstacle to their drive towards world conquest – the group's hugely successful 2001 debut album *They Don't Know* has yet to be picked up by an American label.

Because British rap's commercial track record is so pitiful, UK MCs face scepticism and indifference from American record companies. With such a rich supply of native talent, A&R scouts basically have no incentive to pay even cursory attention to the British scene. 'You have an overload of hip hop here in America,' says Black Shawn, Director of A&R at Rawkus Records. 'You can get mixtapes with hot new MCs on any street corner.' The risks of attempting to market a Britrap act – even one with the UK fame, bad-boy charisma and proven success of So Solid Crew – outweigh any potential gains.

* * *

Hip hop's influence pervades the globe from Sweden to Japan, but the transmissions are one-way. As far as American hip hop's concerned, the world comes to an end a few miles off the coast of Long Island. This isolationism is not based on racial prejudice so much as nativism. After all, white American MCs from Eminem to El-P get plenty of respect these days. Conversely, Black British MCs, even those with impeccable 'street' backgrounds, rate no higher than their pasty-faced compatriots. 'I think the Black English rappers sound just as bad as the white ones,' says Jeff Mao, a columnist for hip hop magazine *XXL*. Rap cognoscenti often diagnose Britrap's perennial failure with vague talk about an alleged British lack of an 'organic' relationship with hip

343

hop, or argue that English speech patterns simply don't lend themselves to hip hop 'flow' (that crucial blend of phrasing, swing and personality that is the MC's signature). 'When rappers try to project "hardness" in a British accent,' argues Mr Mao, 'it can sound forced and false.'

At the same time, British MCs don't get any respect when they develop an authentically British style. Most UK garage MCs, for instance, have a distinctive UK 'flow': sinuous, fastidiously enunciated, often featuring a syncopated stutter effect. To American ears attuned to the gruff growl of DMX or the relaxed swagger of Jay-Z, though, this English style can sound overly dainty, even 'prissy'. It's as if Britrap can't win: if it imitates America, it's treated as second-rate, but if it originates, then the results aren't accepted as 'real' hip hop.

* * *

Yet British hip hop culture has deep roots. Almost as soon as it existed, hip hop was embraced – not just the music, but the whole subcultural package of graffiti, breakdancing and scratching. But when another imported American music – Chicago house – hit Britain in the late eighties, the fledgling UK rap scene was eclipsed. The rap influence was largely absorbed into this electronic dance music, with British producers emphasizing hip hop traits like booming basslines, funky breakbeat rhythms and sampling. British MCs adapted to rave culture by taking on a new, subservient role onstage or on pirate radio – praising the DJ's skills and hyping up the crowd. During the nineties, these MCs developed a British style of fast chat, emphasizing tongue-twisting agility and gimmicky catchphrases, rather than the narrative skills and poetic imagery that are valued in American rap. Recently, though, with UK garage, the MCs have gradually eclipsed the DJs, emerging as stars in their own right.

Few are storytellers to anything like the degree that is valued in America. Instead, pirate radio MCs like Horra Squad use raw garage instrumentals as the springboard to fire off fusillades of boasts and threats. Both Ms Dynamite and Mike Skinner of The Streets have been hailed for bringing real content to 'garage rap'. But where Ms Dynamite's A Little Deeper album is heavy on consciousness-raising lyrics (she's been hyped as a UK Lauryn Hill), Mr Skinner manages to be socially acute without preaching. On The Streets' debut album Original Pirate Material, his songs are sharply observed, bleakly funny tales of everyday life situated in the nondescript areas – neither suburban nor inner-city – where most Britons live. Along with his wit and wordcraft, what is really unprecedented about Skinner is the way he's taken the idiom and halting cadences of colloquial English and given it an authentic hip hop flow. Although Skinner, like most of his multi-cultural generation, occasionally uses dancehall reggae patois and B-Boy lingo, mostly he sticks to British slang like 'geezer' and 'twat'. In one song on *Original Pirate Material*, he even mocks other British MCs for speaking in pseudo-American: 'around here we say birds not bitches'.

Ironically, Skinner is hard pressed to think of any British MCs he rates as inspirational. Most people in the UK who are into hip hop, he says, share the American view that British rap is simply inferior. Skinner says all his influences are American, citing Nas and Wu-Tang Clan MCs like GZA and Raekwon. Now aged twenty-three, he began rhyming as a member of a Wu-Tang-styled collective, but the group winnowed down to just Skinner as rapper/producer. Around this time, he made an almost overnight breakthrough and started rapping in conversational English. 'All the people I'd been working with had a bit of an American accent. But I just realized that to be like your idol, you shouldn't *sound* like them, you should be like them – original.' He points out that 'just standing up and saying this is me, with no tinges of an American accent' has got him further in the USA than pretending to be a gangsta ever would have done. His album has been picked up domestically by the new label Vice (which goes through major company Atlantic) and is already getting rave reviews here.

If the album succeeds as more than a critical favourite, though, it'll be because the very English mundanity that Skinner captures might seem exotic to Americans. 'It could almost work here like hip hop works for Brits – as a fantasy,' speculates Skinner. 'For Americans it could be like, "Who's he? He says 'geezer' all the time!" And that's what could make British rap more powerful ultimately, because American rap today is a TV show – really conservative.'

Director's cut of piece published in
New York Times, 20 October 2002

It's tough for non-black Americans whose primary musical identification is with hip hop. The contradictions gnaw at the guts and tie the mind in knots. Hence the overcompensation syndrome, from the extremes of wigga-ism to the way critics who operate from that mindset become over-vigilant custodians, warding off improper developments like jungle or The Streets. White rap musicians too: think of 3rd Bass's video for 'Pop Goes the Weasel', in which they give Vanilla Ice a baseball bat beat-down for disgracing their own attempt to be credible white rappers. In Britain, it's always been easier because hip hop came originally as an import and thus equally at-one-remove whether you're Black British or white. In Massive Attack, 3D and Tricky were both coming at the music from an equally 'inauthentic' position.

British receptivity to Black American music, British ability to refract and mutate that source, British flair for selling it back to white America in various exotic-but-appealing packages . . . would rock history as we know it be the same without this three-stage process? The breakdown of this mechanism began in earnest in the early nineties with the UK takes on house music and hip hop; there were still successful UK exports to America, but the success of things like EMF or Stereo MCs or The Prodigy had no real repercussions. The transmissions became one-way, creating a kind of cultural trade imbalance. The UK was inundated by hip hop and R&B, but its response was ignored. Craig David made it as proxy for an entire subculture, 2-step; The Streets won a US Anglophile cult sized mid-way between Pulp and Blur; Dizzee Rascal's debut sold about as many as the first albums by Roni Size/Reprazent or Tricky. In the age of urban radio and rap video channels like BET, Britain's intermediary role (introducing white suburbia to black American music) is most definitely surplus to requirements. But has our spin on the music become completely superfluous too?

RAVE-PUNK

The Genre Soon-to-be-Known-as Grime Emerges

Rave-Punk: Two Years Old Already? Like the original punk, any rave-punk contender worth its salt would have to work as both a return and a reversal; as simultaneously the resurrection/renewal/intensification of rave-as-musical-style, and the total jettisoning or inversion of all its values. Gabba-gangsta-garage [i.e. the genre soon-to-be-known-as grime] fits the bill. Sonically, it's full of hardcore echoes (the Belgian tekkno bombast, the caustic acid bass, the death-ray riffs that hark back to 'Dominator', Reinforced, even PCP). In every other respect, the subculture is anti-rave. Empathogen-enhanced tenderness is replaced by coke-numbed callousness; open minds and hearts give way to the barricaded self-as-fortress (there's actually an MC called Armor!). This music is 'fuckin' hostile', to borrow the title of a gabber classic – not loved-up but hated-up.

In terms of sexual politics, rave's angelic asexuality/androgyny has been swapped for a starkly gender-polarized universe of lechery mixed with misogyny (pirate anthem 'Swallow', about girls who do, gives the Hot Boys a run for their cash money when it comes to sheer horny malice), spiced with rampant homophobia (so much for garage's roots in gay disco culture). The 'feminine pressure' aspect that was so refreshing and striking in 2-step (its lover's rock sweet melodiousness, the ladies-first deference) has been totally reversed, with a drastic remasculinization of every aspect of the music and culture. The bump 'n' flex, the sexy swing, has stiffened into the phallomorphic rigor mortis of beats that are inspired by, or unwittingly resemble, electro and gabba. Treble frequencies are purged to revel in a bass-too-dark undertow as viscose and lethal as that oil slick off the coast of Portugal. Lyrically too, gabba-garage is alpha-male predatory to the most gloating and vindictive degree. Just check lyrics like these from a Horra Squad freestyle: 'Every weekend I got your girlfriend freaking . . . Creeps back to you later that evening / Kiss her on the lips and you're tasting my semen.' Not that there aren't girls who spar with the rude boys, like Horra's foul-mouthed and cruel-tongued Tough Chick. And the he-said/she-said verses in Dizzee Rascal's 'I Luv U' present an evenly matched war-of-the-sexes when it comes to sourness and derision.

Horra Squad are the resident MC collective on Horra FM, one of the most hip hop-aligned UKG pirate stations in London (they even have station idents from American rappers like Jadakiss). The Squad have this little catchphrase which seems acutely resonant. 'Horra FM: keepin' it *separate*', Tough Chick boasts at the end of one of the station's jingles. Or MCs will just declare 'Separate!' as a sort of freefloating praise-word or expression of triumph. 'Separate' suggests being both apart and above. This is rap's defining superiority complex, its fantasy of absolute distinction, utter uniqueness (my style identical to none) and total unapproachability. 'Separate' as ethos couldn't be further from rave's 'only connect' spirit. Instead of rave's 'communism of the emotions', the egalitarianism of its anonymous collectivity, what it proposes is a thugged-out aristocracy of the streets, lording it over the small-fry horde of haters and nonentities. Community and communion shrink to at best the feral solidarity of the gang.

None of that rave-era 'crowd-as-star' crap; everybody wants to shine in the spotlight, make it to the top. All those MCs nursing identical cookie-cutter fantasies of transmedia success, launching their own Jay-Z style dynasties, bringing up their crew behind 'em like Eminem and Nelly did (or tried to). Each proclaiming his uniqueness and distinction in that totally generic dibby-dibby first-syllable stutter-style of UKG rhyming.

Perhaps the truest mark of gabba-gangsta-garage's break with rave-as-was is the return of the MC to the forefront and focal position, and the new dominance of WORDS over SONIX. In rave, the MC – crawling from the wreckage of the acieeed-eclipsed Britrap scene of the late eighties – survived the nineties by taking on a subservient role, praising the DJ and hyping the crowd. Ever so slowly the MC shed this menial, accessory function and clawed his way back to the dominant position. (No wonder the old-school speed garage superstar DJs like Dreem Teem were so threatened by Oxide & Neutrino: they could see it was going to cut into their earnings one day.) Rave music has a tendency towards the wordless, favouring instrumentals over songs and using the human voice as an instrument (orgasmic texture-riffs of abstracted diva). If there are words, rave (and house) tends to go for inane chants and catchphrases. Compare and contrast with the rabid, foaming-at-the-mouth *wordiness* of 'garage rap'. On the pirate shows especially, there's a sort of virulent verbosity, the music almost drowned out by the prolix gabble of metaphor and simile. You really get a vivid sense of the expression 'spitting' – there's a compulsive expectorant quality to the freestyles, like the MCs are discharging truly toxic stuff, feelings from the sewer of the soul. The pinched meanness of the MC's flow is very English – mean both in its lyrical content, and in the delivery: a meagreness of grain, an inhibited tightness of delivery (so much less expansive and regal than American MC-ing), like their very throats have narrowed like slitted skrewface eyes.

Like punk and hip hop before it, gabba-gangsta-garage revels in linguistic inversions: its current lexicon of praise words and superlatives includes 'gutter', 'messy', 'horrible', 'disgusting', 'stinking'. When Wiley & Roll Deep boast about being 'terrible', they don't mean they're performing poorly but terrible as in Ivan. Just check the Vicious and Rotten-like names of the groups: Heartless Crew, Nasty Crew, Slew Dem. As if in a nod to DMX, the matey greeting 'bruv' has turned to 'blood' – as in 'it's messy, blood!' or 'ya get me, blood?' – the word spelling out the sanguinary fraternity of gangsta culture, the bonds of shedding others' and being prepared to shed your own.

Oh, there's lots of neat critic-pleasing historical parallels; So Solid Crew as Sex Pistols (complete with violence-riddled gigs and banned tours); droll yarn-spinning Mike Skinner as Ian Dury, loved by everyone outside the scene but not rated by the real punks; feisty-turned-worthy Ms Dynamite as Tom Robinson Band. And what could be more UK punk-like than this music's manifest destiny of abject commercial failure in America (despite being highly influenced by gangsta rap, as UK punk was by New York punk)? Except it's worse today: *Never Mind the Bollocks* dented the Billboard Top 200, but So Solid can't even get a fuckin' deal in the States. Another nifty parallel: where punk identified with roots reggae and dub, gabba-gangsta-garage has dancehall to draw on as a reliable reservoir of new rhythmic tricks and fresh slanguage for its homophobic tendency.

Of course, a crucial point to make is that this is *not* the Next Thing, it's the Right Now/Already Well Underway thing. I'd say we're already approaching the end of '1977', the year of both the explosion and the (temporary) bubble-burst. So Solid feel like they've dropped off a tiny bit (puff pieces for the solo stars in the colour supplements), just like the Pistols did. The hits aren't quite as big. There's a sense of the sound going back into the underground to an extent, and festering there . . .

. . . Key turning points for the new sound's emergence were Oxide & Neutrino's 'Bound for Da Reload' and So Solid's pre-fame pirate smash 'Dilemma': UK garage in only the most nominal sense, owing nothing to house 'n' garage either rhythmically or attitudinally. Steeped in electro, those tunes instantly erected a massive generation gap; most older UKG fans were baffled, affronted, massively turned off. Like punk, this is a kids sound. My spies tell me the sixteen-year-olds get well rowdy on the floor when Dizzee Rascal or Musical Mobb drop, damn near trashing the joint.

Seeing More Fire Crew on *Top of the Pops* earlier this year (hooray for BBC America!!!) doing their jump-up-junglizm-turned-into-Britrap-Y2K-style anthem 'Oi!' was as alien and uproarious as seeing The Angelic Upstarts play 'Teenage Warning' live on TOTP. And 'Oi!' as song title: how perfect is that? Big catchphrase on the 'ardkore scene too.

The next wave of groups, I wager, are going to make right-now-incredibly-exciting outfits like K2 Family, GK Allstars and Highly Inflammable seem as tame as Eddie & the Hot Rods and The Vibrators did by 1978.

Just like punk rock, gabba-gangsta-garage is telling us some very ugly things about life in the UK, and like punk (especially the Oi! strand) it defends itself using the time-honoured 'reality' clause: 'we're just showing what it's like out there on the streets. We're not glamoriz-ing it, honest.' Yeah, right. So 'big shout to the violent crew' and lyrics like 'talk back and get your face opened' (and that's Tough Chick!) are just social realism.

Perhaps I haven't made it sound very appealing. But then if I'd lived through the hippie era like I partook of the rave dream-and-lie, I'd probably have had some serious ambivalences about punk. And I recall that, however much the liberal media establishment (*Guardian*, *New Society*, BBC, etc.) eventually came around to punk as a legitimate expression of working-class frustration blah blah, at the time a huge part of punk's appeal (to suburban fifteen-year-olds like myself at any rate) was the idea of it as sheer wanton evil: the monstrousness of Sid Vicious; Rotten's 'I wanna destroy'; McLaren's amoral mischief-making and 'cash from chaos'. Punk as terrorism and tyranny.

The last two are what the 3 G Sound (gabba-gangsta-garage) are all about. So yes, this is the antithesis of rave. And yet the music *raves*, it's raving mad.

Blissblog, 21 November 2002

As with the 'junglist' column, this piece catches a genre at such a formative moment that it hasn't even named itself yet, hence my use of the ungainly hyphenate 'gabba-gangsta-garage' to denote the three principal constituents of the hybrid. (I should really have added a 'ragga' in there too.) This piece came after spending the summer of 2002 back in London, doing research for *Rip It Up*. When I wasn't poring over bound copies of ancient yellowed music papers in the British Library's National Sound Archive, or interviewing aging post-punk musicians, I had my ears glued to the pirates. There was a fitful quality to the transmissions; sometimes it seemed like UK garage culture was on the verge of sputtering out altogether. But every so often you'd hear flashes of the New Thing. The two brightest were Dizzee Rascal's 'I Luv U' and 'Pulse X' by Musical Mobb, a bare-bones slice of barely music designed purely for MCs to chat over. Fired up by 'Pulse' and 'I Luv U' (the only twelve-inches I got around to buying before returning to NYC) plus a handful of incredibly energized pirate sessions captured on tape, I came home to New York in the autumn of 2002 and started *Blissblog*, a primary motivation being to have somewhere to write about this latest paradigm shift from pirate radio culture a.k.a. the hardcore continuum.

RAP VIDEOS AND THE 'ONE WHITE DUDE'

Hip hop may not love you back, whitey, but it loves your *dollar*. There was something faintly scandalous about the revelation, last year, that 70 per cent of rap CDs are bought by white kids. It seemed like the sort of information that really ought to cause hip hop to implode through its own contradictions. It could be the statistics are skewed (presumably white suburban youth have more disposable income than black inner-city youth, probably buy more CDs per capita and make more casual purchases, while urban youth buy a lot more bootlegs and mixtapes and other stuff that's below the statistical radar). Still and all, it seems like a fucked-up disparity. What are the examples, historically, of a music where such a high proportion of its consumers feel discouraged from participating creatively in the culture they identify with? . . . Between Beasties and Eminem, who's there been, of any credibility or any significant success? What's striking about Eminem is his absolute isolation in the mainstream. I'm sure part of the massiveness of his success, beyond his ability, is that he's been embraced out of sheer relief: at last one of ours who's so good he's undeniable. (And there's *still* holdouts among hip hop performers and critics – Armond White for instance – who refuse to give him any props, see him as an Elvis-type appropriator/exploiter/con!). Don't bring undie rap, with its slightly larger complement of non-blacks, into this, because undie is irrelevant to the black pop mainstream. And that mainstream is organized around the concealment from one chunk of its audience of the existence of another larger chunk of its audience – the invisible majority of white rap fans.

Now there are lots of good reasons why it is important for hip hop to sustain itself as a cultural enclave where blacks are the overwhelming majority. It's also possible that white fans prefer it that way, too, that it's part of the fantasy of real-ness they're buying into, that double-whammy of exoticism and authenticity. Perhaps that's why studio audiences at BET or hip hop videos with in da club scenes are 99 per cent black. (If you see footage of live hip hop shows, though, 50 per cent or more of the audience are white, and I'd be interested to know the racial breakdown of BET's home viewership.) The pathos-shading-into-patheticness of a figure like Serch [the fat bespectacled MC in 3rd Bass] with his always-already-hopeless desire to be accepted as 'the baddest white MC out there' has a visual echo in the form of that peculiar rap video convention, the one white dude. The first OWD that caught my eye was way way back, in one of the Dr Dre videos, 'Nuthin' But a "G" Thang' I think. You know it, there's a house party, the fridge is stacked with malt liquor, some Gs take revenge on a snooty black chick with airs and graces by shaking up 40 oz bottles and drenching her in frothy symbolic semen. As the camera pans across the dancefloor, all of sudden, there he is: the white dude, lurking by a pillar. Looking hopelessly out of place and distinctly uncomfortable. It's like, what's he there for? Why did they even bother? (Or is he there precisely to be outnumbered?) Look for the OWD, he crops up more often than you'd think. Always on his own.

Blissblog, 28 April 2003

Classic OWD sighting – Notorious B.I.G., 'Juicy', on MTV2's Old Skool slot last night. There he is, grooving away. He's not the only white person in the video of course – there's the maid serving the bubbly and, even more symbolic, the accountants who take care of managing Biggie's money so he can enjoy spending it the more.

Blissblog, 29 April 2003

Lone White Guy Strikes Again. Never noticed it before but there is a classic one in the R. Kelly 'Ignition (remix)' video (one of the very few Kelly songs I've liked actually) and instead of being a subliminal thing they make it into a major feature of the promo. The Lone White Guy – looking exactly like the popular stereotype of a bespectacled rock critic actually (he resembles a cross between Michael Azerrad and Lou Barlow) – hits the floor and starts throwing these wack (if concerted and earnest) R&B type dance moves, surrounded by a circle of black folks staring in mingled amazement and amusement (among them a *second* white guy hovering in the background with an ambivalent expression on his face, as well he might). So here the LWG syndrome reaches a kind of self-consciousness. Seems like quite a rich text for a reading in terms of inclusion/exclusion effects, cultural ownership, the wigga, concepts of natural rhythm versus white dis-embodiment. Also the victory of Pop-ism and post-Timbaland R&B: even the guys who look like they grew up on (or are even members of) Sebadoh, like they write/read *Pitchfork*, can't resist getting down to our stuff!

Blissblog, 31 August 2003

Parallel syndrome to the OWD: the SBG, or Solitary Black Guy. You might have seen him at a Smiths or R.E.M. gig in the eighties, or in the crowd moshing to Nirvana in the nineties, or even at a psychedelic trance or gabba rave, dressed fully appropriate for the scene and totally into the vibe. There's an odd mixture of heroism and pathos to these guys who refuse to stick to their own kind and instead respond to the summons of a sound calling to them across the great divides.

DIZZEE RASCAL

Boy in Da Corner (Dirtee Stank/XL)

Dizzee Rascal is the best MC that Britain has ever produced, period. His words are as sharp as Tricky in his prime, but his delivery's sharper, more in-yer-face. Dizzee's got way more personality than anybody in the perennial underwhelming UK hip hop scene, and tougher beats too – which he makes himself, to boot. All these local comparisons add up to faint praise, though, so how about this? Eighteen years old, East London bred Dizzee Rascal is as good as any rapper currently active on Planet Earth.

Every UK garage MC brags about how his style's unique, and almost every MC does it using the same flow and timbre. But Dizzee really does sound 'identical to none', from his jagged, half-choked phrasing to his highly strung, edge-of-losing-it grain (like he's perpetually on the brink of lashing out, or bursting into tears, or both at the same time). Better still, he's got something to say as well as a unique way of saying it. Too much, maybe: listening to his verbal torrent, you feel like his head must be all set to EXPLODE.

Boy in Da Corner is bookended by two songs, 'Sittin' Here' and 'Do It', that open up whole new vistas of emotional terrain for 'garage rap'. Dizzee voices the fragility and doubt underneath the thug armour, the suppressed, caged tenderness and tentativeness behind the you-can't-touch-me postures of mannish boys trying to act hard and heartless. Draped in glinting synth-keys that could be Japan circa 'Ghosts', 'Sittin' Here' features Dizzee as the painfully acute observer: 'I watch all around / I watch every detail / I watch so hard I'm scared my eyes might fail.' Those eyes have seen too much in too few years: 'Only yesterday life was a touch more sweet / Only yesterday we were standing firmly on our feet / Only yesterday girls were innocent, they kept us calm.' When he spits that he's 'vexed at humanity / vexed at the earth', you can hear the ingrown cyst-like rage of a generation for whom social-political deadlock and corruption is just 'standard business', kids who've never seen in their own lifetime a glint or hint that things can be any other way. On 'Do It' – also bizarrely redolent of Sylvian-Sakomoto circa 'Bamboo Music' and 'Forbidden Colours' – Dizzee mourns how 'everyone's growing up too fast', contemplates non-existence ('sometimes I wake up wishing I could sleep forever'), and confesses 'it's almost like I've got the world on my shoulders sometimes'.

It's not So Solid Crew, in other words. Oh, Dizzee's got few peers when it comes to the boasts and threats. He slays haters, biters and rival MCs who wanna test him with a murderous exuberance that is alternately chilling and hilarious: 'flushing MCs down the loo / if you don't believe me bring your posse and your crew . . . Come to me with an attitude, come a cropper / I'm old school like Happy Shopper.' But it's not the gun talk that's the draw, it's the vulnerability that peeks out and exposes the invincibility complex as a desperate sham. And what can seem like mean-minded cynical sexism in songs like 'Jezebel' and 'I Luv U' is really just curdled romantic idealism.

I have to mention the music, which is self-produced (Dizzee is like Dre 'n' Eminem in one body) and stunning. The summer 2003 sound of London pirate radio, this is a totally post-garage genre – what some are already calling 'Grime' or 'Grimy Garage'. It's a mindboggling and bodyfreaking hybrid that draws on beat-science and bass-knowledge from dancehall, hardcore techno, electro, jungle and gangsta rap. (And, on the hilarious 'Jus' a Rascal', opera and Sepultura-style thrash-metal!) The result is as angular and futuristic as any weirdtronica coming out of Germany, as shake-your-ass compulsive as any Dirty South bounce, as aggressive as punk rock. On which subject, it turns out Dizzee's a massive Nirvana fan (especially the ultra-gnarly *In Utero*). It may only have creased the outer edge of the UK Top 30 instead of rampaging to Number 1 like it should have, but his savage war-of-the-sexes single 'I Luv U' is a 'Smells Like Teen Spirit' for the new millennium.

In summation: *Boy in Da Corner* is a front-runner for this year's Mercury (yeah, right – big deal). Mike Skinner should be shitting his pants. So should everyone else. Because next to Dizzee Rascal every-body looks pale, uninteresting, and irrelevant.

Uncut, September 2003

There's people who seemed to find it strange, even unseemly, that a person like myself (forty-something white middle class, raised in the picturesque Chilterns-y end of Hertfordshire, Oxford-educated and now in the meeja) could identify so strongly with someone like Dizzee (black teenager from East London). But that's the miracle of music, isn't it? What we're all in this for, surely: the leap across the gulf, music as a means of healing the 'wounds of class and race', as someone once put it. Besides which, it's not like we have *nothing* in common; the noise that was my heart's passion through the nineties (MCs spitting freestyle over junglistic breakbeats on pirate radio) was what these grime kids grew up on, it's just that they were *kids* and I was, erm, turning thirty. Still, it seems to unsettle people, a little – they start going on about social workers, about liberal guilt (but what's wrong with that? Liberals *should* feel guilty, it's the least they can do!), as if paying attention to the culture of the urban underclass was an unpleasant duty done out of piety, rather than a deliriously addictive pleasure. But it's true, there is another element to it beyond enjoyment. I would invoke an old-fashioned word (here I'm ripping a riff off John Berger) and that word is 'solidarity'. It's partly political (along with sheer empathy, you can't help but admire people who do something creative when the social odds are stacked against them), but mostly it's an *aesthetic* solidarity. I thrill to the hunger-to-make-it-big that pulses inside grime, but I wouldn't be nearly so involved by the artists' struggle if they weren't trying to do something that was so in line with my ideas about music. The compelling paradox of grime (and other populist vanguards and hardcore underground sounds) is the way they want to achieve success but do it through making challenging, uncompromising music. If they just want to generate cash, there's all manner of non-strenuous options in dance music. But they make music that's relatively dark and difficult and non-commercial. There's something inspiring about the way the grime kids, like the junglists before them, take the path of most resistance.

357

KANYE WEST

Kanye West, *The College Drop Out*

Obviously he's got a lot more strings to his bow than this, and real musicality, but I think the most interesting thing about KW is the tracks where he uses such large chunks of old soul records that it's really blurring the line between a sample and the whole fucking song. Which re-raises all sorts of questions about sampling as artistry/sampler as auteur, where the creativity *is* in this thing? Also the question of the continued parasitism (not just hip hop here but d&b/downtempo/broken beat etc., etc.) on what LTJ Bukem called 'the golden age of music' (i.e. the seventies where most sampled funk 'n' soul 'n' fusion lickage still comes from) and whether it'll just get utterly depleted at some point, mined to exhaustion. So like for instance when in 'Last Call', the interminable yet sheer genius rambling and un-rapped account of his career tribulations that closes the record . . . he quotes Jay-Z saying on their first encounter after he's heard some of KW's beats, 'oh you're a real soulful dude', but of course the 'soul' in question is entirely Harold Melvin's or Bobby Bland's or whoever else in whatever song where it's the entire basis bar the drum programming for that particular beat ('beat' in hip hop meaning 'all the music'). So 'real soulful dude' means you've got good taste in soul music, you can rework someone else's soul . . .

Blissblog, 18 March 2004

Being a bit slow on the uptake, just realized that it's Kanye who 'did the music' for 'Takeover', my absolute favourite track on Jay-Z's *The Blueprint* (well 'All I Need' and 'Song Cry' come damn close) but – and this is why I put the scare quotes around 'did the music' – that track is

358

another 'Thru the Wire' in so far as it pushes sampling to the edge of noncreativity/plain theft. Cos 'Takeover' basically IS 'Five to One' by the Doors. Slightly rearranged, but musically there's almost nothing else to the track – apart from a Boogie Down Productions soundbite and an interpolation from ANOTHER classic rock song, 'Fame' by David Bowie.

Now 'Takeover' is an amazing feat of pop intertextuality but what I've always wondered is whether the games it plays with rock history and the sixties are in fact completely inadvertent and unintended. See, the original song is about collective emancipation: Jim Morrison's hoarsely hollered 'gonna win, yeah / we *takin' over*', that's youth/the counterculture versus the gerontocracy/AmeriKKKa. But in Jay-Z's hands this undergoes a brutal privatization: the sixties 'we' shrivels to the 'wego'-mania of thug rap; a sixties anthem of unity and hope becomes a noughties battle-cry of disunity and cynicism: all against all, dogg pack eats dogg pack. It's even more of a contrast cos 'Takeover' is such an incredibly (brilliantly!) spiteful song, just an incomparably vicious takedown of two rival rappers – Nas and the little feller from Mobb Deep – pure lyrical OVERKILL, stomping on their symbolically dismembered credibility. Now you could map all that on to the parallel deterioration of the black sixties – the civil rights movement and its collective thrust for full citizenhood and racial sovereignty, shrinking down to the gangsta rap era's individualized putsch for prestige. Or at best the drastically contracted collectivity of your clan/crew/dynasty/quasi-mafia ... linguistically paralleled by reduction in hope-scope from 'brother' to 'nigga' ...

I'm reasonably confident though none of this was on Jay-Z's mind when he wrote the lyrics. Mind you there's that weird echo of Morrison's 'they got the guns, but we got the numbers' in J's 'you need more people' – addressed to the Mobb Deep crew being foolish enough to spar with the mighty Roc-A-Fella. Well it's almost *pointed*. Jim Morrison's 'five to one' and 'no one here gets out alive' take on a totally different meaning in the new context! Sort of ROC got the guns *and* the numbers. As for Kanye, smart guy and 'soulful dude' that he is, he could hardly have been aware of all these resonances because when he made the beat he can't have known what J was going to rap over it ...

Blissblog, 9 April 2004

...With Kanye, I just think it's intriguing how he's praised for doing something that Puff Daddy was *reviled* for. In fact, given KW's recent declaration that Ma$e is his favourite rapper EVER ... it seems that

Bad Boy circa 1997 really IS the biggest influence and precursor to what Kanye W does. . . . 'Through The Wire' and 'Takeover' almost approach the mash-up sensibility where there's this pride is seeing *how little* new material you can add to the source elements. In 'Through the Wire' the creative act of musicianship (ignoring the lyrics for now) is loving the Chaka Khan song, making the through the fire/through the wire pun, speeding up the vocal and selecting the bits you want to loop. And that's IT – apart from the drums – that's the entire musical content of the track

With the comparison to Puff and Bad Boy, I'm not implying KW doesn't deserve his praise . . . it's just interesting the way it verges on that kind of conceptual art practice where the citation is the act of authorship, the extreme being that 'painter' (help me out here somebody) who just appends his signature to reproductions of famous artworks.

It also relates to that curious syndrome familiar to anyone who's ever deejayed, or in a slightly paler form, ever made a mixtape, whereby just the *selection* of a track somehow accrues a tiny portion of the credit properly due solely to the person or persons who made the track. I say 'tiny' but the whole cult of DJ in housetechnoclub etc. is based around the near-wholesale migration of applause and worship from those who made the tracks to those who re-present the tracks . . .

Blissblog, 13 April 2004

. . . My favourite track on *College Dropout* is the oft-maligned finale, 'Last Call'. KW took real risks with this one, I think, not just through doing such a protracted and self-reflexive track but through his demystifying the hip hop industry, both through detailing the career moves and games you have to play (like the cringy-but-hilarious bit where he's sycophantic to Jay-Z) to get anywhere, and through letting in the humdrum (the oft-cited references to shopping at IKEA). What's really touching is the sense of precariousness. At certain points in the long, long track (which always induces in me the feeling 'when's it going to stop?' then 'actually, I don't want it to stop'), you really feel like he's *not* going to make it – that Kanye's ascent wasn't at all inevitable, he could easily have failed. Then from that, you get a painful glimpse of how contingent everything is in life, how much the breaks you get or don't get play in determining outcomes, all the different places you could be in your own life if something had gone just a little bit different. There's one bit where he's discouraged by some setback, by how long it's taking to get anywhere, and the music gets really tentative and crestfallen-sounding, almost idyllictronica-wistful. Always brings a tear to my eye.

Blissblog, 29 December 2004

I read somewhere that *The College Dropout* is the first instalment of a quintology (is that the right word?). I'm not sure I can make it to album number five. The refreshingly 'honest confusion' (neither 'conscious' nor a bad-boy chasing bling and bitches, but a hungry soul trapped in a body prey to venality, etc., etc.) is starting to look more like 'having your cake and eating it'. The best things on *Late Registration* (which I had to review off the publicist's i-Pod, based on less than half the album, and most of the tracks still lacking for guest raps or final remixing) still do wonderful things with sampling ('Addicted', a gorgeously hang-dog account of male shame and weakness pivoting around a 'My Funny Valentine' sample) but others cross the line into the wacker side of Puff Daddy, e.g. 'Touch the Sky', with its lifts from Curtis Mayfield's 'Move On Up'.

LIL JON & THE EASTSIDE BOYZ

Crunk Juice (TVT)

'Crunk' is one of those words that sounds like what it is. The word is probably a contraction of 'crazy drunk', but even if you don't care about etymology, you can instantly understand it as a call to unleash your inner beast. Crunk evokes the instinctive or involuntary things in life that make you go *unngh*. No songs about shitting yet (surely it's just a matter of time), but plenty of sex and violence, with the borders between the two blurred: in crunk, the nookie is rough and TLC-free, and the violence is almost voluptuous.

Although he didn't coin the term 'crunk', Atlanta crunk mogul Lil Jon has trademarked it and turned it into a transmedia empire encompassing everything from CRUNK!!! energy drinks to porno movies to pimp cups sold online. And it's his productions for Petey Pablo and Usher that have propelled this regional underground sound into the mainstream. One couplet in 'Throw it Up' from Lil Jon's previous album, 2002's double-platinum *Kings of Crunk*, distils the genre's rapacious worldview into four words: 'fuck him/fuck her.' But 'Get Low', that album's monstersingle, was the true Crunk manifesto. Linking base desires and bass frequencies, it featured the immortal couplet "til the sweat drips down my balls / 'til all these bitches crawl'. We're talking caveman-dragging-the-wife-by-her-hair stuff here, reptile-brain bizniz, life reduced to appetite and aggression, testosterone and adrenalin.

In 'Get Lower', a skit on Lil Jon's new album, comedian Chris Rock offers a hysterical parody of crunk's abasement shtick: 'get *under* under, get lower than a pregnant ant's belly'. Which does introduce the question: how can music with such bass-ic premises as crunk actually progress?

362

Crunk Juice doesn't break much with Lil Jon's winning formula. Rather, staying true to the genre's binge approach to pleasures, it offers an intensified version of the same old same old. So the beats hit harder, the bass is gnarlier, the lyrics surpass previous peaks of lewdicrousness, and the rowdy choruses are even more blearily belligerent. Along with synth riffs modelled on house and techno (music Lil Jon first encountered at strip clubs, not raves!), these growly baritone chants are the producer's hallmark. Layering a single voice to sound like a mob, the effect is in-your-face like a barking blast of bad breath.

'In This Club' is the best example of the standard Lil Jon sound, featuring one of those signature whistling synth refrains as heard on Usher's 'Yeah'. *Crunk Juice*'s two other killers are less typical. On 'Aww Skeet Skeet', girlish voices chant the X-rated chorus ('skeet' is crunk-speak for ejaculate) over rumbling go-go percussion, like some porno version of the Tom Tom Club. Slow and stealthy, 'Da Blow' is a stoner's anthem: the icy sharpness of the synth melody and the heart-palpitating drum rolls evoke the paranoia zone you enter after one toke too many.

The most strikingly novel aspect is Lil Jon's newfound Superproducer clout, manifested by the multitude of famous guests: Snoop Dogg, Nas, Ice Cube, Pharrell Williams, Ludacris and Usher (on the inevitable cloying ballad 'Lovers & Friends', a transparent and – in this context – somewhat incongruous attempt to make nice to the ladeez). There are even guest producers on a couple of tracks. The Neptunes offer the nothing-special 'Stick That Thang Out', while Rick Rubin builds on his recent Jay-Z/'99 Problems' comeback with 'Don't Fuck Wit Me', pivoting around a thrillingly jagged metal riff in classic Def Jam circa 1986 style.

Crunk seems to favour brawn over brains. But it's not so much stupid music (there's smarts and even a kind of refinement involved in constructing these brawling rampages) as music whose purpose is to stupefy. The bass, for instance, is a rolling cloud of concussive low-end, a doom-boom sound that's literally stunning.

What's slightly eerie about Lil Jon's music is how, for all the party-up intent, the actual feel of the tracks is dirge-like. It's a vibe we've encountered in rap before, with 50 Cent's oddly joyless 'In Da Club' and the bleak nightlife treadmill grind depicted on Jay-Z's 'Do it Again'. Tilt your ears just a little, and the voices on this album can start to sound like agony, rather than people in the throes of pleasure. For just a moment, *Crunk Juice* summons to mind a Dirty South update of Dante's Inferno: sinners tormented according to their vices, gorging on chicken and beer, lap dancers and weed, until gluttony becomes its own kind of punishment. Even though the hallucination passes quickly, and the record becomes 'fun' again, this much is clear: Crunkonia might be a great place to visit, but it's not somewhere you'd really want to live.

Blender, January/February 2005

The conditions in which critics review Big Name artists have gotten increasingly constrained. And that's particularly so with rap albums (see aforementioned *Late Registration* circumstances), because the CDs are generally being tweaked right up to the week of release, with guest raps added at the last minute. There are also big concerns about security, the loss of revenue owing to bootleg copies sold cheap on the street. So it came to pass that I reviewed Lil Jon's album at a sort of launch party/playback session at Electric Lady, the studio built by Jimi Hendrix. After what seemed like an eternity, Lil Jon sauntered in with a huge entourage, including several barely dressed strippers, and wended his way through the throng handing out clumps from a big freezer bag full of what looked like sticky green. Finally the CD was pumped out through the deafeningly loud sound system and I started scribbling in my notepad. After a while I noticed the scanty-clad girls were giving the guests free lap-dances. Already somewhat jittery having necked one can too many of Lil Jon's energy drink, I started to get apprehensive that I was next to be favoured – part professionalism (this was my one chance to hear the record), part feminism (I don't really believe in that sort of thing, quaint as that may seem), and part simple awkwardness about whether I should go along with the crunky 'vibe' out of good manners. I kept my head down, but of course, the kindly (or perhaps not so kindly?) publicist sent a lap-dancer my way. This was perhaps the longest ten minutes of my life: absolutely excruciating, but also eye-opening (yet not the least bit erotic). There was a good three-track segment of the album there where I was barely conscious of the music, but in another sense it was an edifying experience that informed the review indirectly and coloured my response. I should also mention that at one point in the night's melee Lil Jon – truly a tiny fellow – ended up right behind me, and his body kept bumping up against mine, making it the first time I've been in physical contact with an artist during the process of reviewing their music. Returning home, frazzled and ragged with *CRUNK!!! drink*, nervous tension and bass fatigue, I felt like I'd done the rock critical equivalent of a double shift in a coal mine.

MOTHER NATURE'S SONS

Animal Collective and Ariel Pink

Animals, anthropomorphism and animism are common preoccupations in psychedelic music. Think of Syd Barrett with his *Wind in the Willows* obsession, his worship of trees and his ditties about effervescing elephants and a mouse called Gerald; or Incredible String Band's songs about hedgehogs, puppies, snakes and minotaurs. The four members of American group Animal Collective revere the natural world: their record label is named Paw Tracks, their song titles include 'Penguin Penguin', 'Bat You'll Fly', 'Who Could Win a Rabbit' and 'We Tigers'. David Portner thinks the obsession relates to 'the wild aspect of when we play live – it's kinda animalistic', while Josh Dibb reckons it relates to the kind of stripped-down, bullshit-free communion you can experience with cats and dogs. When Dibb talks about his mother, a holistic healer, her outlook sounds precisely how you'd imagine Animal Collective's worldview: a pantheism in which the cosmic and the mundane intermingle. 'She was very supportive of the idea that I could find beauty and wonder – or, if you wanna call it that, God – in everything,' he says. 'She experiences God in anything from the deities that any given religion across the world has, to our pets. She totally worships our animals.'

If it's a truism that bad experience – hardship, heartbreak, neurosis – makes for great music, Animal Collective is one of the rare exceptions that proves the rule. Their music is rooted in happiness. David Portner, Noah Lennox, Brian Weitz and Josh Dibb grew up together in an environment verging on paradise. For the bulk of their pre-college years they attended 'progressive' schools that emphasized creativity, imagination and artistic self-expression as part of 'a complete kind of education', as Lennox puts it. The kernel of the group formed when the teenage Portner, Dibb and Weitz bonded at a small private school in Baltimore County, Maryland, near the US's East Coast. Noah Lennox would join the gang at weekends, having already formed a close friendship with Dibb at an even more hippyish elementary school. Much of Baltimore County consists of woods and farmland, and Portner recalls idyllic times spent at his cousin's twenty-acre farm and nights listening to music under the stars on friends' back porches. Even the high school was situated in fields, allowing the gang to go on nature walks during lunch breaks.

Far from rebelling against their upbringing, then, Animal Collective have essentially tried to live up to its values. You sense that they carry the blessed beatitude of their pretty unusual adolescence within them; it's what nourishes their music and informs the whole sensibility of their label, Paw Tracks. Like a spinney full of rare wildflowers circumscribed on all sides by housing developments and road building, this inner resource is both precious and precarious. Because the way of the world will wear it away. 'I feel very much like the space I've created with these guys as friends came out of high school,' confirms Dibb. 'It's also trying to figure out a way to continue the total playful imagination you had when you were five years old. Comparing it to how you feel as an adult, I equate it to almost like being high all the time. Music is the most powerful means I have to find that again.'

Music-making began for the four friends during their high school idyll. Early attempts at forming a group ran in parallel with each of them making recordings individually on tape. Pavement introduced them to the buzz of esoterrorism – the encrypted song-titles, the opaquely evocative artwork. From lo-fi indie rock, the friends quickly progressed to the noise cassette micro-scene of the Pacific North West, centred on outfits like Climax Golden Twins and Noggin. Then, via their love of horror soundtracks such as Tobe Hooper and Wayne Bell's incidental music for *The Texas Chainsaw Massacre*, they discovered twentieth-century classical music. 'Ligeti and Penderecki are on *The Shining* soundtrack,' recalls Portner. 'We had never heard so-called experimental music at the time, we didn't know that people made music with textures and pure sound. So we started doing that ourselves in high school, walls of drones with guitars and delay pedals and us screaming into mics.'

Real life gave this teenage cocoon a hard knock in the late nineties when the future members of Animal Collective dispersed to college. For Portner, especially, his three years at NYU felt like pure misery. But although the group was scattered between New York and Boston, they kept the music alive, discussing what they wanted to do sonically and investigating all kinds of arcana. In parallel with his environmental policy and marine biology studies, Brian Weitz hosted a noise show at WKCR, Columbia's college radio station. 'We'd borrow all the avant-garde records and take them to Brian's dorm room and listen to them all night,' recalls Portner. 'It wasn't academic stuff to us. In fact it was more lighthearted music than rock 'n' roll, in a way, because you could imagine a sound as a weird animated character.' Adds Weitz, 'It was never, "listen to those microtones", it was, "that sounds like a bird!".' In Boston, meanwhile, Lennox was exploring electronic music, a passion ignited back at boarding school when he moved into a room whose previous occupant had left behind a bunch of records, including The Orb's *UFOrb*.

The friends found each other again in the summer of 2000, convening at Portner's apartment on Prince Street in downtown New York for several months of exploratory jamming using antiquated synths, acoustic guitars and household objects. 'If you got tired of playing an instrument you could go and get a fork and a plate!' laughs Weitz. The nascent Animal Collective sought a sound that would organically mesh their diverse interests, from Portner's and Weitz's love of horror movie scores to Lennox's techno penchant, and their shared passion for vocal harmonies. 'We'd try to approach playing an acoustic guitar like you were making techno,' recalls Portner. 'It wasn't a very big apartment, but we'd work with space a lot, setting up this stereo microphone and an amp on the other side of the room. So it became less about delivering a song than occupying a space.'

Sadly, the copious tape documentation of this summer-long 'drunken haze and hash haze' was stolen when Portner moved apartments. Unwisely, the friends packed up the car the night before to make it less stressful on the day, in the process learning a traumatic lesson about leaving belongings in a parked vehicle. Still, as Lennox puts it, 'everything since then has been a variation of what we explored that summer. Dave and I had already made the *Spirit They're Gone* record, but during the summer we really cracked the egg open. It seemed like we could go anywhere we wanted after that.'

Although it's now regarded as the first Animal Collective release, *Spirit They're Gone, Spirit They've Vanished* was originally credited to just Avey Tare & Panda Bear – the 'character' names taken by Portner and Lennox respectively. (Weitz goes by the moniker Geologist, and Dibb is known as Deaken.) As its title hints, *Spirit* is ethereal psych-folk that finds a gorgeous diagonal between transcendental and twee. Songs like 'April and the Phantom' and 'Everyone Whistling' bring to mind Tyrannosaurus Rex tweaking out on nitrous oxide. The album explores the disorientation potential of high frequencies, its sound palette largely consisting of acoustic guitar ('jangled to create this fluttering feeling', says Portner), Lennox's skittering drums, chirruping and twittering keyboards, and the duo's high-pitched harmonies. 'We started singing in this way where we'd end every phrase with clicks and it was like we were creating these almost-electronic sounds with our voices,' says Portner. 'And we could record it in a way where you wouldn't know what were the voices and what were the other instruments. We like sounds to come into the room and play with your ears. Confusion is always a good thing in music!' *Spirit* certainly confused the first distributor they sent it to. 'Southern Records called us back immediately and said "Is there something wrong with this? This music makes our dogs run out of the room"!'

The next emanation from the Collective camp – Avey Tare, Panda Bear & Geologist's 2001 album *Danse Manatee* – was the first swerve in an aesthetic journey that typically involves the group reacting against its previous release. 'This Heat meets Incredible String Band' is the description one record shop assistant gave me of the record. Amazingly, *Danse Manatee* fully lives up to this intrigue-piquing sales pitch, melding these seeming incompatibles into a delicious delirium of songfulness and abstraction. In 2001, the group also made (but didn't release until later) the stripped-down *Campfire Songs*. Recorded on a back porch in the open air, the album's strumming troubadour vibe is the only time Animal Collective have truly intersected with the neo-folk scene.

Animal Collective's real aesthetic kinsmen at this point were New York-based abstract sound outfits Black Dice and Gang Gang Dance. 'We started to find a bit of a community,' says Portner. The three groups still share a Brooklyn rehearsal space and play gigs together regularly. Although they are very different entities, all have a commitment to – and reputation for – turning gigs into events, with a vibe that's electric, verging on shamanistic. 'Our way of doing that was wearing masks, to portray the names we had,' explains Portner. According to Dibb, the masks and make-up weren't theatrical (a la Caroliner Rainbow, an outfit AC are often compared to), but something they did for themselves more than the audience, a way of signalling they were crossing into a 'special space'. More recently, though, AC have dropped the dressing-up, except for Geologist, who still sports a headlamp of the type worn by miners and spelunkers. Usually decorated, the lamp has a practical as well as ritual function. When it comes to stage lighting, AC prefer their shows to be as dark possible, and Geologist needs the headlamp so he can see the minidiscs and mixer controls he uses to warp and addle the other members' playing.

The unique vibration between the four friends was only seriously tested for the first time when Black Dice invited Animal Collective to accompany them on tour in early 2002. 'It was our first big tour, going through the South of the US, and pretty brutal,' recalls Portner. 'Lots of sleeping on floors. We all lost our minds on that tour.' Lennox, the most sensitive of the foursome, suffered particularly. 'Noah's always had this love/hate thing about playing music with us. He's the most tour-shy and homebodied. After every tour, he always has this break-down period, where he's like, "I don't wanna play any more, guys, I need to do my own thing".'

Fortuitously, this fraught period resulted in what many regard as the group's masterpiece, *Here Comes the Indian*. Returning exhausted from the deep South tour, Animal Collective immediately started writing the material in their cramped and cluttered Brooklyn practice space. 'The darkness of that period, it all related to space, in a literal and a metaphorical way,' explains Weitz. 'We were in this cramped room, equipment everywhere, not soundproofed, so noise from other bands came through the walls.' It was also the first time all four members had worked on a record together, Weitz elaborates, 'so there were issues of trying to find your space in the music'. Poverty and the fact that Lennox and Portner shared an apartment and had the same day job (working at the hip Manhattan record store Other Music) exacerbated the sensation of claustrophobia. Then the group embarked on another cabin-fever tour before returning to record *HCTI* in the summer of 2002, 'the absolute heart of that darkness', as Weitz puts it. 'That's why the album's so hectic and chaotic. It was trying to shove all this weird energy into one recording.'

Vocal extremism is an Animal Collective hallmark, and *Here Comes the Indian* teems with unhinged incantations, animalistic throat noise, heavily processed voices and grotesque lattices of harmony. The stand-out track 'Panic', made almost entirely out of vocal sounds, seems like an attempt to capture the vertigo and paralysis of an anxiety attack. But it also transmits something of the original ancient Greek meaning of 'panic': a transport of ecstasy-through-terror. It's a bit like Tim Buckley's blissed voicescape 'Starsailor' turned inside out. '"Panic" is based off a vocal thing Dave and I did in my old bedroom in Brooklyn,' says Lennox. 'I'm following Dave's voice in a kind of Indian style.' Portner stumbled across the eerie ululation on a minidisc and persuaded the group to take it to the next level, adding a swarm of vocal overdubs and feeding them through effects.

During this troubled time for the four friends, the collective pressure cooker was further stoked by Lennox's having to deal with his father's terminal illness. He began working on what would become the 2004 Panda Bear album *Young Prayer*, a tribute and elegy to his dad. 'It was a gift for him. And he did get to hear the roughs of the album's songs, if not the finished version. That was recorded in the room he actually died in, so it was especially intense. With *Young Prayer*, I wanted to tell him that he had taught me really well. I wanted to be like, "It's been really good hanging out and learning from you, you've been a really good man and set a good example."' Apart from fitting the record's sentiment, the liturgical title suits the psalm-like purity of Lennox's singing, influenced by his high school stint in a chamber choir. 'It was an extracurricular thing, but I would stay after school to do it because I loved it so much.'

After finishing *Here Comes the Indian*, the frayed Collective dispersed for a while (Geologist even moved to Arizona for a whole year). Their next record, *Sung Tongs*, was another Avey Tare & Panda Bear project (although it was credited to Animal Collective, the group having reluctantly submitted to the market logic of having a consistent brand identity). *Tongs* veered away from the studio-laboured intensity of *HCTI* to a more song-focused and lighter-hearted approach. Portner's and Lennox's acoustic guitars occupied the centre of the sound. 'Every song or group of songs we did has its own tuning, and they're usually open tunings,' says Portner. 'With acoustic guitars especially, the strings resonate really well, and when the tones are similar, you almost get more tones than are actually there. It makes it really warm.' Yet the inspiration for this approach wasn't the new acoustica of minstrels like Devendra Banhart, but electronic music. Standout track 'Visiting Friends', says Portner, was influenced by Kompakt's Pop Ambient compilations and Mike Ink's project Gas. 'Just like a wall of hums. We wanted that feeling, but with acoustic guitars.'

Sung Tongs received flak in certain quarters for being a bit blithe and fey. Yet the essence of Animal Collective, what makes them so remarkable, is the way they collapse polarities: they can be sacred and whimsical, cosmic and cute, noisy and pretty, all at the same time. In this sense, they are true inheritors of psychedelia's imperative towards con-fusion: the bringing together of things usually kept separate.

At the heart of psychedelia lies the ideal of being 'lost' – lost in sound, lost for words. Portner claims that the group don't assign words like 'sacred', 'pagan' and 'mystical' to their music. 'People often say to us, "You guys have a shamanistic, ritualistic thing going on at your shows," as if we had all got together one time and said, "let's all be shamans!".' Yet Animal Collective have talked candidly and eloquently about their spiritual leanings in the past. When I press them on the subject, it turns out that it's another facet of their beatific Baltimore County upbringing. As previously stated, Josh Dibb's mother Jessica is a syncretist of many forms of spiritual practice and alternative medicine. She has influenced not just her son's worldview, but the whole Collective's vision. 'In college, Noah and I went through really tough times,' recalls Portner. 'So Josh said, "My mom might be able to help you clear your mind and get back on track." And she was, like, "Well, you know, what you need to do, you need to just breathe. Most people on earth don't take in enough of the oxygen that their mind and body needs." I started doing these breathing exercises with her, and it makes your body feel crazy, it just goes through your whole body. She started doing it with Noah, too. It totally cleared everything up, gave everything this calm.'

Perhaps Animal Collective should consider putting Dibb's mom on a retainer and have her accompany them on tour and into the recording studio, judging by the way the stresses of success seem to affect them. Time compression has interfered with their free 'n' easy approach to creativity, a problem exacerbated by the fact that Lennox has married a Portuguese girl and now lives in that country. But they've set aside a whole month to do nothing but record *Feels*, the much anticipated follow-up to *Sung Tongs*, relocating to Seattle and working with producer Scott Colburn of Climax Golden Twins.

It's a bitter irony for musicians: the thing you chose as an alternative to having a career prospers to the point where it turns into a career, bringing with it all kinds of sapping ancillary obligations (like doing press). 'College', a seemingly throwaway ditty on *Tongs*, has assumed unexpected resonance as an anthem for slackers looking to step off the career track. 'You don't have to go to college,' the lyric counsels, which translates as 'message to you, bourgie: don't worry about your future, be here now'. Says Weitz, 'The response to that song has been amazing. People at gigs scream for us to play it, and we get emails from kids asking for advice.' Mind you, there was one guy who got pissed off with AC for playing college gigs where only students get entrance, acidly quipping, 'So now I can't see you *unless* I go to college?'

The members of Animal Collective are too hard-working to be considered dropouts, but there is something hippy-like about the foursome, from their love of Mother Nature to the way they'll talk about a song as 'a sweet jam'. Their increasingly devout following has something of this quality (lots of early-twenties men with beards), which may be why some unkind folks diss them as a Deadhead-style jam band, a hipster Phish. Portner, in particular, was a huge fan of The Grateful Dead as a youth, and talks about aspiring to create the same

371

sense of electric communion between group and audience. At the same time, AC are at pains to distance themselves from the new beardy folk, stressing the role of electronics and effects in their music. Odd, then, that their latest release, the *Prospect Hummer* EP, sees them hooking up with the nu-folk icon nonpareil, Vashti Bunyan, who's become a touchstone icon for your Devendra Banharts and Joanna Newsoms – as much for her free-spirited life as for her music.

A huge fan of The Incredible String Band, Portner checked out Bunyan's 1970 LP *Just Another Diamond Day* after learning that Robin Williamson played on it. 'Immediately I was like, "Wow, I can listen to this record when I have a hangover, or when I want to go to bed." It's such a soothing, pretty record.' Through the auspices of Four Tet's Kieran Hebden, who has also been working with Bunyan, Animal Collective met her in Edinburgh. Soon the idea of a collaboration was mooted. Bunyan says she fell in love with the group's music 'instantly', captivated by its 'inventiveness and humour'. *Hummer* isn't a fully fledged collaboration, though: it's billed as an Animal Collective release and Bunyan is singing songs written by Portner and Lennox. Nonetheless, it feels like the EP's beatific radiance emanates from the singer as much as the songs.

'My daughter says she can hear me smiling on the title track,' says the singer, 'and I was. I loved having the freedom to sing as I wanted. I was still finding my voice after burying it for years.' The experience has encouraged Bunyan to embark on her first album in more than thirty years, due on Fat Cat before the end of 2005.

The other current AC release is situated at the further end of the group's sound spectrum. *Jane* is Lennox's techno project with his DJ friend Scott Mou, and *Berserker*, a four-track album, features his gaseous vocals wafting over warmly pulsating electronica. There's a twist, though: most of the music is Mou spinning records made by other people. 'It's like a mix CD with toasting over the top,' says Lennox, who is confident that despite the music consisting mostly of 'other people's backing tracks and rhythms, we make the songs our own because the way we move from track to track is unique.' When I tell him his cloud-drift vocals remind me of Robert Wyatt's scattier excursions such as Matching Mole's 'Instant Pussy', Lennox says he's honoured by the comparison, then pre-empts the next flattering reference point I had lined up. 'Do you know Arthur Russell? I first heard that guy's records a year or so ago, after we did the *Jane* stuff, but I was like, "wooah, I sound like this dude". I felt sort of bad!'

* * *

One of Animal Collective's many tours took them to the West Coast, and in the aftermath of a show, a young man approached Portner and handed him a tape. 'It sat on the floor of the van for a week or so,' recalls Dibb. 'Finally we played it and we were just like "Wooah!" Brian was, like, "I'm making it my goal in *life* to put this kid's record out on our label."' Most band-based labels go wrong immediately by signing groups that sound just like them (but aren't as good). Ariel Pink doesn't sound anything like Animal Collective, but by tapping into a similar magical, transcendental feeling he totally fits the Paw Tracks 'vibe'. 'Ariel's created his own world for himself,' says Portner. 'That was the first thing we picked up on.'

Ariel Rosenberg, the one-man band that is Ariel Pink, echoes this idea when he talks of his desire to 'make new worlds'. *The Doldrums/Vital Pink*, his first release for Paw Tracks, certainly sounded like a transmission from another realm. Upsettingly, if you scan the uniformly adulatory reviews for *Doldrums*, you'll notice that the same metaphor has occurred to virtually every writer: the Ariel Pink sound as some variation on a broken or badly tuned radio. Listening to the album on its release last year, an almost identical image entered my brain: a wireless heard from the bottom of a swimming pool, diffracted and reverb-shimmery.

The unanimity of this response suggests that maybe this is what Rosenberg was actually trying to do. But he insists it's just a side effect of his technical limitations, the antiquated eight-track tape recorder he uses. 'If you chop off the frequencies at the top and bottom that's what you get – a compressed signal like from a cheap radio.' He claims he's 'just trying to shine through' the lo-fi smog. 'Shining through' certainly captures the way his gorgeous melodies peek like watercolour sun-shafts through the mist of hiss.

'Radio' probably recurs as a description because Ariel Pink's sound conjures the bygone wondrousness of pop music when you first encounter it as a child – most likely through a tinny transistor. The term that springs to mind is 'indiscriminate listening'. As I recall it, there's a threshold beyond which you learn to listen 'properly'. Prior to this, the young ear doesn't really differentiate between strands of sounds. I can distinctly recall acquiring the perceptual acuity to isolate the bassline in songs. On one level, this is obviously an enrichment; on another, you lose that rapturous swirliness of pop hitting the virgin ear as a blur of exciting sound. Perhaps psychedelia, with its effects and saturated timbres, is partly an attempt to recover that blissed indistinction.

Ariel Pink's music suggests a different kind of indiscriminate hearing, too: the child's capacity to listen without prejudice, before it has any inkling of 'cool' and 'uncool'. Rosenberg's melodies, keyboard lines and guitar riffs hark back to long-lost styles of music made primarily for the radio – soft rock, blue-eyed soul, and pop-rock; performers like Steve Miller Band, ELO, the latterday Blue Oyster Cult. In other songs, he'll have you flashing on forgotten new wave one-hit wonders like It's Immaterial or Men Without Hats. But rather than AM radio (in America, poppier in content and poorer in signal than FM), Rosenberg says it's MTV that shaped his pop sensibility. An addict from the age of five, he watched the channel almost from its inception. 'MTV was my babysitter!'

Like his tape music hero R Stevie Moore, Rosenberg has made so much music, he could keep an entire classic rock radio station (or oldies-oriented video channel) going for at least a month. Recorded from the late nineties onwards, some of the backlog has seen limited release via tiny labels. Rosenberg would like to put all of it out, but the sequence is already jumbled: there are five whole albums between *Doldrums* (number two in the original sequence) and his glorious 'new' album on Paw Tracks, *Worn Copy* (number eight). Beneath the glittering fog of Echoplex and corroded wooziness caused by dumping tracks and overdubbing, Rosenberg's playing seems disconcertingly high calibre. He insists it's all 'smoke and mirrors, an illusion I create through editing. I do edits with my toe while playing the instruments, and can build up impressive musical lines in tiny increments.' His most remarkable trompe l'oreille feat is the drum sounds, which are all created using his mouth. 'It's like tongue-clicking; I've got certain places I hit in my mouth,' he explains, before demonstrating his kickdrum, snare, hi-hat and tom-tom sounds. 'The vocals and the drums are actually the easiest part of the recording process. But I'm probably flexing muscles I was never meant to use!'

If gorgeous tunes like 'Among Dreams', 'For Kate I Wait' (a love song to Kate Bush) and 'The Ballad of Bobby Pyn' had been recorded 'correctly', with proper drums, you can easily imagine them as huge Billboard hits – perhaps not in the pop market of 2005, but in whichever radio era each song's stylization refers to. Rosenberg's versatility is astonishing, and especially noticeable with his vocals, which run the gamut from Roy Orbison-like falsetto to Hall & Oates-style rock 'n' soul. 'I'll do different vocal affectations to see what kind of song I'll get. It's all pretend, it's all trying to find something. The style is almost unintentional. Because nothing is "dry", because the instruments all go through crappy effects boxes, I'll put a chorus sound on the guitar and suddenly it begs to be played like Christopher Cross!' Pink can occasionally come over like a pop formalist, a pasticheur a la

Chris Isaak or Marshall Crenshaw. But most of the time, the stylization of any given song is flooded by a passion that feels not just real, but ecstatic and transcendent.

Take 'Trepanated Earth', the eleven-minute song-suite that starts *Worn Copy*. It's simply one of this decade's most shatteringly emotional pieces of music. Veering from melodic Rick Springfield-like passages to noisy blowouts (including a middle eight that features a half-buried 'Eight Miles High' citation), the song is dramatic too, in the classic rock radio tradition of 'Don't Fear the Reaper': the kind of drama that doesn't wear out with reiteration. Great pop songs have a mysterious capacity for repetition unequalled by any other artform. They're closer to drugs than culture, Rosenberg reckons. 'You can "take" them every time and experience that high.'

This neo-psychedelic notion of music is the point of convergence between Ariel Pink's 'radio mysticism' and Animal Collective's pantheistic awe. Seeing with the enchanted eyes of a child (or hearing with the bliss-delirious ears of a child, in Ariel's case) is one aspect of the psychedelic quest. (Disorientation, ego-death and eclipse of reason being the darker side: Syd Barrett, Roky Erikson, et al.) 'As you get older, you start to lose the child's ability to create visions and have hallucinations and imagine you're somewhere else than you really are,' argues Portner. Music, for Animal Collective and Ariel Pink alike, isn't 'this dry, "sound" thing', he says. It's all about dreams and flight. 'Maybe our music *is* escapist – a different world that people can go into.'

The Wire, July 2005

'You don't have to go to college': that's when I realized that AC and the 'freak folk' scene they're loosely aligned with came from the same place as the slacker rock of the late eighties, groups like Butthole Surfers and Dinosaur Jr. That same bourgeois-bohemian impulse to *un*make the most of yourself, tune in/turn on/drop out, dissipate and radiate, get lost in the trippy untethered soundswirl. Middle-class youth stepping off the career track, laying waste to their own potential. This often involves leaving the city, home of ambition and competitiveness, just like sixties bands such as Traffic 'getting it together in the country'. Freak folk's sonic *mise en scène* often makes you picture a raggle-taggle commune on the periphery of society, banging instruments in some Finnish wildland or Vermont grove; the photographs of groups like Wooden Wand and the Vanishing Voice or Espers actually look like the album cover images of Incredible String Band nestling in the foot of a tree. Another crucial aspect of the scene is its craft economy vibe: the lathe-cut vinyl, the small-run pressings, the antiquated formats (cassette has made a comeback) and customized packaging (hand-painted and decorated tapes, singles, LPs), all constitute an attempt to transcend commerce and re-enchant the commodity that echoes the original folk movement's rejection of pop culture commercialism. What's intriguing, but also slightly dispiriting, is the element of recurrence: the beards, the syncretic religiosity, the freeform jamming, the hunger to reinvent ritual and trance, the bias towards acoustic instruments, the abandonment of worldly things in favour of the otherworldly. You get a sense that this is almost a structural fixture of Western societies: the children of affluence who see through their parents' values, reject the spiritual void of a life based around ambition/acquisition, and look to find or build a space 'outside' society.

AGAINST ALL ODDS

2005, Grime's Make-Or-Break Year

The first thing that hits you is the clashing reek of twelve different brands of cheap perfume. The second is how weird it is to stand in a crowd of teenage girls waving gun-fingers and yelling 'BRRAP BRRAP BRRAP'. The trigger for their frenzy is Crazy Titch, an East London MC who's the closest thing the UK grime scene has to a heart-throb. He's hoarsely hollering his anthem 'Sing Along' over a bizarre rhythm made from a chopped-up classical symphony. One thirteen-year-old black girl stands stock still, staring at Titch with awe and adoration, intently biting her fingernail. Everybody else in the auditorium is going mad. When it gets too rowdy – some heavy-set ruffnecks are crushing girls up against the stage – an organizer halts the music and grabs the mic': 'Settle, boys. There's girls down there. They want hugs and kisses.'

Grime is usually seen as bad-boy music, its blaring bombast and mosh-activating aggression making it the UK's counterpart to crunk. Yet the huge number of young females at this show proves that grime isn't necessarily synonymous with testosterone. The high proportion of teenagers present is partly due to the fact that the venue, Stratford Circus, is an art centre, meaning that the entertainment ends at midnight – when most raves are just getting started. Tonight's all-star grime bonanza offers a rare opportunity for under-eighteens to see in the flesh the MC idols they've watched only on Channel U, a digital/satellite TV station that airs UK urban music on an equal footing with American rap and R&B. It juxtaposes the latest glitzy videos from 50 Cent with shakily choreographed, low-budget promos from local heroes like Bruza.

Grime events have a reputation for trouble. The music builds up tension, but offers little scope for release – a recipe for fights on the dancefloor. And people often bring outside-world antagonisms into the club. Police are always 'locking off' grime parties, which makes promoters increasingly reluctant to hold them in the first place. At one point in the night, the host Peaches comes on to report the disappearance of a cell phone, then delivers an impromptu lecture. 'Stop thiefin'! Stop the armshouse!' she berates, 'armshouse' being grime slang for bloodshed. 'They're locking off grime raves, dancehall bashments – where you gonna go? Country & western nights?!' Later, she reports that the young lady's phone has been found and returned. 'Honest black people!' she notes with mock incredulity. 'This will be a newspaper story: BLACK PEOPLE FIND PHONE.' She's taking the piss out of stereotypes about ethnic youth, forgetting how quickly she'd jumped to the assumption that the phone had been stolen.

The specific worry tonight is that the beef between two rival crews, Roll Deep and Fire Camp – will lead to mayhem. Although either group could claim the headlining spot, Fire Camp perform much earlier in the night, so there's no frictional hand-over of the stage. Later I learn that Roll Deep were only let onstage once Fire Camp and their vast entourage had left the building. A couple of days later I ask Lethal Bizzle, leader of Fire Camp, about his feud with Wiley, the Roll Deep don. 'Wiley is into lyrical battles, he's done records dissing everyone from Durrty Goodz to Crazy Titch,' says Bizzle. When Wiley put out a record attacking him, Lethal took it as a backhanded compliment – a sign that he was an adversary to be reckoned with. 'I was happy, my name was hot. And retaliation was gonna build up my name even more. Everyone calls him "Kylie" so I got "Can't Get You Out of My Head" and dissed Wiley over it. That just put the curtains on him. Cos the streets said I won.'

Wiley and Lethal are duking it out on the underground and overground simultaneously. While stoking their hardcore fanbase with the battle tracks, both hope to seduce the mainstream with crossover grime albums this summer – Roll Deep's *In at the Deep End* and Lethal Bizzle's solo album *Against All Oddz*. Bizzle's ahead at the moment, having scored grime's biggest UK hit with 'Pow', a massive jolt of sonic adrenalin that even turned some heads in America, getting airplay from Funkmaster Flex on Hot 97 and talk of Lil Jon protégé Pitbull versioning the track's frantic 'Forward' riddim for his debut album. But Roll Deep is more densely stacked with talent, their fifteen-strong ranks boasting some of the scene's finest producers (Wiley, Target, Danny Weed) and MCs (Trim, Flow Dan, Riko, Wiley again).

Still, for all the big noise that grime has made in the UK mainstream media – Ms Dynamite and Dizzee Rascal won the Mercury Prize in successive years and Dizzee appeared on the remake of Band Aid's 'Do They Know It's Christmas' – it remains a small scene. Only a few people within grime can make a living out of it. 'There's not a lot of MCs that are just MC-ing and not doing something else,' says Kano, one of the most touted performers on the scene. The doing 'something else', he hints, could be a day job or it could be something nefarious – 'shottin' weed', in some cases. Selling 500 copies of a twelve-inch is considered a good result these days, and after production costs, that would generate less than a thousand pounds profit. When they perform at raves, most MCs 'get paid about 150 pounds, which is not good money', says Kano. 'And there's less raves than there was. Clubs don't want to deal with it. People get banned from playing certain areas, certain clubs – blacklisted. Cos of what promoters *think* is going to happen.'

* * *

The day after the Stratford Circus festival, Roll Deep divide their energies. One half plays a gig at a trendy hip hop club in Hoxton, a recently gentrified area of East London. The other faction stays underground with their regular Sunday night show on pirate radio station Rinse FM. Although Channel U is increasingly important, grime's primary medium remains illegal radio stations. Rinse is literally an underground operation, its HQ being a former travel agent's office in the basement of a nondescript building. Pass through an unremarkable-looking anteroom (pine floors, shabby sofas serving as a makeshift hospitality lounge) and you enter the spartan studio. In addition to turntables and audio equipment, there's a brightly flashing fruit machine and a TV tuned to a spycam monitoring people in the street outside (in case of a raid by OFCOM, the government organization dedicated to stamping out the pirates). The walls are bare (Rinse FM prides itself on its professionalism, and graffiti is forbidden) and apart from a few empty soft-drink containers, the room is incongruously tidy.

Before Roll Deep turn up, legendary grime MC D Double E does his weekly show. Nearly six feet tall, but weighing only 130 pounds, he has elegant, cut-glass features that border on emaciated. You wonder if the sheer rapidity and intricacy of his flow burns up all his calories. 'I'm gonna start zonin' out in a minute,' he warns, and there's something faintly redolent of Joy Division's Ian Curtis in the way he stares sightlessly into the middle distance, one hand darting in dainty, air-carving gestures. Double's imagery is relentlessly violent – 'I'm on the way to stardom / Anyone test me I will scar dem' – but the vibe he transmits is entranced reverie rather than menace. Every so often he emits an eerie ululation, what he calls 'the D Double signal' – 'Mwui! Mwui!'

After some ads – revenue from these, plus subscription fees from each crew that has a regular show, keep Rinse FM afloat – Roll Deep take over. The night before, at Stratford Circus, they made a Roots-like manoeuvre and performed a set with a live band, leaving the teenage girls long-faced with boredom, chins in hands like school kids sitting through morning assembly. Tonight, yelling into microphones to an invisible audience, Roll Deep are in their true element. Wiley, dressed in a blue Nike coat, rhymes over a new riddim built by Target out of an accordion riff, describing himself as 'the black 007'. Two new recruits to the sprawling Roll Deep family dominate the mic'. Skepta, a lean black youth, pulls his jacket over his head and spits from inside this murky cocoon. 'Draw for the 'chete,' he warns some nameless adversary. 'Bullets fall down like confetti / Make you look like spaghetti' (presumably served with marinara in this scenario). Syer, a stocky white kid, launches into a rant about 'dutty girls' who 'give brains' (head, geddit) 'to every breh in the 'hood.' There's a constant nerve-jangling bleeping of cell phones – 'missed calls' that assure Roll Deep the faithful are out there (without the listeners having to pay a phone charge) or texted requests for a shout-out. 'Big up the HMP massive,' intones Trim, a reference to those listeners detained at one of Her Majesty's Prisons. 'Hang tight the E3 crew.'

E3 is a zip code, or as they call it in England, a post code. Grime is intensely territorial. The major divisions used to be between East London, South London and so forth, but the imperative to represent your 'hood has devolved into a Balkanized welter of mailing districts. 'E3's the big one,' says Bruza, one of the scene's most charismatic MCs. 'That's where Roll Deep are mostly from. E3 is like the Queensbridge of grime, bare talent comes from there. But it's the same with my area, E17.' According to Roll Deep's Target, 'If you're from E3 and I'm from E15, it's not like we have to fight or anything. It started with just biggin' up East London, and then you want to big up your exact *bit* of East London!'

What most of the postal zones have in common is that they correspond to a large swathe of the East End that's not served by the subway system. You can only get there by car, bus, or the overland railway system that traverses much of London on decrepit, redbrick Victorian viaducts. This slight diminishment of ease of access to the area has contributed to its peculiar insularity. It's also delayed the tide of gentrification, meaning that the East has remained a largely working-class area. East London (the heartland of musical innovation in Britain since at least the early nineties emergence of jungle) has a sort of unpretentious, street-level cosmopolitanism, the result of the area having absorbed wave after wave of immigration over the last century. First came the Jews, many of them from Russia. Then, after the Second World War, migrants arrived from all over the former British Empire – from the Caribbean, from South Asia (Indians, Pakistanis, Bangladeshis), and from Africa. Most recently, the alien tongues of East European asylum seekers have been audible on the streets. From drum & bass to grime, the influence of Jamaica dominates (most grime MCs cite dancehall and jungle chatters as their primary influence, rather than American rappers). But the actual variety of ethnic origins on the grime scene is staggering. At Stratford Circus, Peaches called out to the audience, asking 'Anybody here from Nigeria? Ghana? How about Antigua? Trinidad & Tobago?' Each country triggered a flurry of hands in the air.

Possibly even more crucial than its multicultural mix, though, may be East London's dreariness, the bleak featurelessness of its landscape. The architecture mixes shabby old buildings that hark back to the area's industrial and warehousing past, with the kind of Brutalist architecture that was fashionable in the 1960s and 1970s. In some areas, the sky is punctured by ugly slabs of high-rise tower blocks of the kind that formed such a crucial part of punk's imagery. More common, though, are smaller, undistinguished three-storey blocks of flats, interspersed with melancholy recreational areas. On a sunny day, East London can look reasonably pleasant. But most of the year English skies are grey, which means most of the time East London looks grim. Grim, and yes, grimy.

In between jungle and grime came a late nineties sound called UK garage. You could see garage as an attempt by London youth to manufacture their own sunshine. One of the scene's biggest anthems was called 'Spirit of the Sun'. All shiny treble frequencies (high-pitched divas, skittering snares and fizzy hi-hats), garage streamed out of the pirate airwaves like aural champagne. The sun-drenched Greek island Ayia Napa became the garage scene's very own equivalent to Ibiza, that raver's paradise at the other end of the Mediterranean. Every summer, grime fans still flock out to Napa, but the idea seems wrong somehow. Because grime is winter music. Cold, brutal, and desolate, it doesn't seek to escape or soften its environment. It amplifies the punitive bleakness.

Wiley caught the sunless spirit of grime with a series of brilliant minimal instrumentals, designed for MCs to spit over, and themed around ice and snow: 'Eskimo', 'Ice Rink', ad infinitum. He says the idea came to him during a period when he felt 'cold inside as a person. I might make a warm tune now, cos I might not be angry any more.' Yet from its shivery synths to its real-world inspiration, his most recent tune 'Morgue' is as chilling as its title. The track is literally the mausoleum of a dead friendship. 'I used to hang around with this boy, Wonder,' Wiley explains, alluding to one of the scene's most talented producers. 'Me and him fell out 'cause of bunglings' [serious arguments]. 'Bunglings' – this time with a girlfriend – inspired the even more desolate 'Ground Zero', which was actually recorded on *that* September 11th. 'I realized that was the day when I'd never see that girl again. I felt like my world came down as well then, just like those buildings.'

But private discord or woe can't explain why a whole genre of music takes a sharp turn to the dark and doomy. Target says that 'as things went bad, away from music' – meaning in the outside world – 'the music's just got darker and darker'. Wiley agrees: 'The music reflects what's going on in society. Everyone's so angry at the world, and each other. And they don't know why.' Tony Blair's New Labour government, elected in 1997 after almost two decades of Conservatism, promised a fresh start for Britain. The economy was booming. It's still strong, but in 2005 the rewards are mostly going to the already well-off young professionals in media, marketing and management. As a post-socialist party, Labour no longer even pays lip service to ideas of wealth redistribution, but instead talks in the bland neo-conservative language of enabling people to help themselves. The UK has become much closer to America than Europe, in the sense that people do believe 'anyone can make it', despite the fact that the social odds are stacked unfairly. If you don't make it, it's your own fault, the result of a deficit of get-up-and-go.

Grime kids constantly spout this kind of talk. Target has put out a series of CD/DVD compilations called *Aim High*, while Bruza's new single is called 'What You Waiting For' – 'a get up off your arse song', as he puts it. As well as the culture of enterprise built by Thatcher and maintained by Blair, these attitudes have been assimilated from American rap. Although virtually every grime artist stresses that they grew up on the fast-chatting style of jungle MCs like Shabba and Skibadee, they have been profoundly influenced by US hip hop: not so much stylistically but in terms of ambition, a sense of the scope of what can be achieved. Bad Boy, in particular, was the role model. One of Roll Deep's earliest tunes, 'Terrible', starts with a soundbite from Puff Daddy: 'Sometimes I don't think you motherfuckers understand where I'm coming from, where I'm trying to *get* to.' Explains Wiley,

'Puff was a big person at the time I made that tune. He had a set-up that everyone wants to have – own label, clothing line. That's what I'm doing it for.' The Bad Boy leitmotif crops up elsewhere in grime. Guesting on a track last year called 'One Wish', Bruza offered a hilarious rejoinder to Notorious B.I.G. – 'more money more problems, though? / Forget the problems, GIMME THE MONEY!!!!'. Bruza also appears on a new tune that remakes the Ma$e smash 'Can't Nobody Hold Me Down', vowing to 'hold me head up and keep on movin' and bruzin".

Grime lyrics teem with expressions of hunger and ambition, drive and dedication. Eight years of New Labour have not improved options and opportunities significantly for inner-city youth. If they haven't applied themselves in school, they typically face the prospect of working in a service sector job, selling things. 'I think that's why most people in our area have got on it,' says Target, referring to grime and the dream of making it as an MC or producer. 'When they get to eighteen, they don't know where they're going. They've got no money, they didn't care about school. Where we are from, most people's lives are *not good*. If we didn't have music to express our lives, I don't know what we'd do.'

* * *

As grime's profile surges to its highest level yet – major-label albums for Roll Deep, Lethal Bizzle, Kano and Lady Sovereign – 2005 is turning into a weirdly conflicted moment for grime. For every motivational tune like Bruza's 'What You Waiting For', there's a lyric advising wannabe MCs to not give up the day job. On the surface, the scene is bursting with confidence. But UK pirate culture has been here before – a host of jungle artists got signed to album deals, but only Goldie and Roni Size got anywhere near crossover. 2-step garage crossed into the pop mainstream hugely, but didn't endure (where's Artful Dodger now?). Grime too has already had its fair share of failure – More Fire, Lethal Bizzle's first group, released a flop album in 2003, as did Wiley.

On the track 'Sometimes' from his debut *Home Sweet Home*, Kano documents a rare (or rarely acknowledged) moment of self-doubt: 'When I see the fans go mad I think, "Why do they like me?" / There's about a thousand other boys just like me . . . I know I've got far / Is it too far to turn back? . . . Sometimes you'll see me in a daydream / Thinking, "Can the underground go mainstream?"'

A soft-spoken, sombre fellow, Kano is realistic about grime's prospects, especially in America. Recently, he got to support Nas on his UK tour – a big deal for the grime MC, but not for the rap superstar.

'Met Nas once, got a handshake,' Kano notes wryly. 'That was it.' The respect will come, he reckons, when grime acts start selling records. 'Not even over there, but over here, in the UK. We can't just fly into America and think we can bang with 50 Cent and all them lot! But if they come over here and see, "Oh, you've got a little thing going on," and it's selling, they'll notice.'

Of all grime's major stylists, Kano's flow seems like the one most likely to appeal to American hip hop ears. An admirer of Jay-Z's conversational delivery and the laidback West Coast style of Snoop Dogg, Kano sounds smooth and poised even rapping in quick time. Playing to this slick panache, *Home Sweet Home* is front-loaded with mid-tempo joints. Roll Deep's debut likewise skimps on uncut grime in favour of conventional hip hop and novelty tunes. Lethal Bizzle even promises some grime/rock fusions on his solo debut *Against All Oddz*, saying he's a big fan of Green Day ('I love that "American Idiot"') and Nirvana. Terror Danjah, the innovative beatmaker behind Bruza and the Aftershock label, dreams of one day recording tunes 'with Robbie Williams or Franz Ferdinand'. The gamble with all these tentative moves to court the mainstream is that grime will lose what it has now. The strategy doesn't even seem that sensible: difference sells, and grime is more likely to succeed by amplifying what's unique and exotic about it. Lethal B should take heed of the success of 'Pow' – his grimiest, rowdiest tune is the one that's grabbed the ears of the world beyond London.

If grime does go pop, the most likely perpetrator is Lady Sovereign, a nineteen-year-old white MC. Some scowling scene purists refuse to take her seriously, partly because she's from North-West London as opposed to East, but mainly because she bypassed pirate radio and instead made a name for herself through the Internet forums where young fans chit-chat in cell-phone text-speak (e.g. 'sov ur buf'). Yet Sovereign has guested on numerous grime tracks, while her 'Cha Ching' is one of the highlights of the scene-defining *Run the Road* compilation. Her mic' skills are undeniable.

Sovereign's also a star, something that's apparent the minute you clap eyes on her. She keeps me waiting for ninety minutes, staring morosely out of the windows of the fourth-floor Bethnal Green studio where she and her producer Medasyn work, taking in the lugubrious vistas of East London, the only splash of colour coming from a car dealers called RUDE MERCS. But when Sov arrives – a tiny ball of colour and rude energy herself – any irritation is charmed away in an instant. Five-foot-one but only eighty-two pounds, with hazel eyes and hair pulled back tightly into a long ponytail, she weirdly reminds me

384

of Audrey Hepburn – if she'd grown up in a North London estate listening to ragga and UK garage, that is.

Lady Sovereign has signed to Island for a four-album deal reputedly worth £3 million (a figure Sov denies, while admitting the true amount was 'nice, really nice'). It's easy to imagine record-company execs with dollar signs reeling in their eyes, imagining the spin-offs (video games, a cartoon series, Lady Sov dolls, a Spice Girls-style movie). When she discusses how her forthcoming debut album – working title *Straight Up Cheeky* – has veered off into 'alternative grime', with influences from ska and punk, you wonder if her backers are steering her in some kind of Gwen Stefani meets The Streets direction. But it turns out her dad used to be a punk rocker and she grew up listening to X-Ray Spex and the Selecter, so the direction is somewhat organic. And when she plays a couple of tracks from the album, it's clear the grime-goes-new-wave notion is inspired. 'Tango' and 'Public Warning' fizz with cartoony humour, from Sov's killer inflections and irreverent lyrics to Medasyn's romping beats and arrangements dense with quirky detail.

The 2-Tone echoes aren't just cute, they're appropriate, given how grime echoes the multiracial ethos and urban-realist approach of bands like The Specials. Bizarrely, that group has inspired two new grime tracks, Kode 9's eerie remake of 'Ghost Town' and Alias's 'Ska', which samples 'Gangsters' then literalizes the title with gruesome lyrics like 'You don't want fluids leaking out yer body / No you don't.' But Lady Sov's thing is altogether more lighthearted. 'Tango', for instance, is a put-down of a former friend who's overdone the fake tan. 'She was once really pale but now she's orange,' says Sovereign. 'It's actually scary.' The title, she explains, comes from a tangerine-coloured soda popular in the UK.

It was hearing Ms Dynamite's early tracks like 'Booo!' on the pirates that really inspired Sovereign to take MC-ing seriously. But instead of sparring with the bad boys (like other female MCs on the scene such as Lady Fury) or moving into socially conscious lyrics (like Dynamite did on her crossover album), Sovereign carved out her own identity. 'I'm not a mean MC, I'm cheeky,' she twinkles, puffing on a cheap brand of cigarette called Sovereign. Although her first record was called 'The Battle' and she's just done a limited-circulation EP called *Bitchin'*, Sovereign's rhymes are closer to playground taunts than the ego-maiming verbal drive-bys other MCs traffic in. Perhaps that's what galls some grime gatekeepers, the sense that it is just fun 'n' games for 'the multi-talented munchkin' (as Sov dubbed herself on 'Cha Ching'), rather than deadly earnest struggle.

385

The London scene is overflowing with talent. 'You see kids in the street just spitting to themselves,' says Bruza. 'One kid'll be human beatboxing, and another'll be spraying his lyrics or clashing another MC. You see it everywhere, every day.' What's poignant is that only a few will ever have a chance of making it. 'Everyone is rushing for that one small gap and there's that many people trying to get through,' says Terror Danjah. 'Everyone can't get through that gap, cos everyone's pushing and shoving. That's life though, innit?'

Spin, August 2005

I was struck from early on by the frequency in grime of expressions of uncontainability: 'we're coming through, whether you like it or not', 'this style be original / we can't be stopped'. There'd be this rich sense of destiny and determination that would have seemed pie-in-the-sky if not for the scrawny ardour behind lines like 'always believing / follow my heart, keep up the dreaming / behind the cloud, there is a shining . . . I know my time is coming' (GK Allstars). Talk of dedication, hard work, discipline, focus . . . this almost-American insistence, not that anyone can make it, but *I'm* gonna make it (I've *got* to make it; there is no alternative). Flying in the face of statistical realities. Peter York wrote about the beneficial side-effects, in terms of the vibrancy of this nation's pop music and street fashion, that stem from Britain being a class-stratified country with a poor rate of social mobility. 'If you have a whole lot of people who are blocked, then the steam is much more intense. And where it finds a crack it rises more violently.' A hydraulic theory of creativity and social pressure echoed in Kanye West's couplet 'Now I can let these dream-killers kill my self esteem / Or use my arrogance as steam to power my dreams!' Grime's libidinal economy, if you'll pardon my French, required some kind of explosive entry into the mainstream. It never came, though, and by mid 2005 it was starting to feel like an endless, blue-balled fuck whose climax was receding into the never-never. You could sense the momentum stalling, the energy imploding. The crossover compromises weren't really paying off, scoring only middling hits; unsigned big boy MCs who felt they deserved major deals weren't getting the offers. One alternative future for grime would involve a collective reality-check cum ego adjustment: a scaling back of expectations, and the slow-and-steady building of a solid infrastructure to sustain its long-term survival as just another semi-popular micro-culture. But what would the music be *like* in this 'perpetual underground' scenario? So much of its actual quality and vibe is bound up with its expansionist drive, its extroversion, its sheer hunger. Grime needs *lebensraum*.

2005

The Year Black Pop and White Pop Stopped Talking

The most striking thing about Pop in 2005 is how little conversation there is between black music and white music. Mainstream UK rock, from Coldplay to whoever's on the cover of *NME* this week has never sounded so bleached. The main effect of this (apparently, hopefully) unconscious drive towards sonic segregation is a grievous lack of rhythmic spark and invention. Catch some highly touted Brit hopeful on the TV programme *Later With Jools*, and it's instantly audible how the drummer contributes nothing to the music in the way of feel, tension or dynamism, but instead just dully marks the tempo. He's seemingly there simply because that's what proper rock bands have – a live drummer.

Things aren't much different on the rock underground, where the coolest thing around is freak-folk (a.k.a. free-folk, psych-folk ...). Ranging from beardy minstrels like Devendra Banhart to trippy jam bands like Animal Collective and Wooden Wand & the Vanishing Voice, freak-folk is a recombinant sound that draws on a whole range of historical sources beyond the obvious traditional music and Folk-Rock ancestors. It just so happens that none of them (apart from a trace of utmostly 'out' free jazz) are black. Freak-folk's accompanying ideology – a mish-mash of mystical pantheism, paganism and sundry shamanic/tribalistic impulses – places it in the same continuum as the hippies and the beats but, significantly, it has broken with Beat's 'white negro' syndrome. Elsewhere in the leftfield, there's the neo-post-punk fad, fading somewhat after a good three-year run. These groups engage in white-on-black, punk-to-funk action, but only by replaying genre collisions from twenty-five years ago. Whereas the true post-punk spirit manifested today would involve miscegenating indie-rock with grime or crunk.

Because its internal socio-cultural dynamics force it to keep on generating freshness, black music has never really needed to borrow from white music. Hip hop has two advantages over rock. It can draw on a deeply rooted set of black music traditions, characterized by a strong sense of regional identity (hence the plethora of new city-based sounds), and this ensures that it retains, even in this allegedly post-geographical era, qualities of a folk culture. Its other advantage is disadvantage. There's an urgency to rap music, fuelled by inequalities of opportunity, that results in ferocious competition between produ-cers and between MCs and stokes the furnace of creativity. That said, the half-decade from 1999 onwards did see hip hop giving itself an extra boost by ransacking the best licks and noises from techno-rave and Euro electronica. That pattern began to fade last year, with black pop reverting to its usual awesome self-sufficiency. Which would be just fine, if the genre hadn't also start to sputter. For most of the past decade, street rap and R&B has been the engine of pop culture, both in its pure form and various teenybop dilutions. Give or take a gem – Amerie's '1 Thing', Three Six Mafia's 'Stay Fly'– its remorseless rate of innovation stalled this year. And formal advance was always the compensation for its counter-revolutionary content of bling and booty-worship.

Grime would love to be the UK's hip hop, enjoying the sort of pop culture hegemony that African American street music holds in its home-land. But you can sense the London scene's self-belief is flagging. 2005 produced one immaculate scene-reflexive anthem, Kano's 'Reload It', a celebration of grime's dog-eat-dog competitiveness; the MC hierarchy where rank is measured by how many rewinds your tune gets. Grime also produced two more low-key but equally inspired tunes about the out-of-reachness ('Sometimes', also by Kano) or hollowness (Lethal Bizzle's 'Against All Oddz') of the prize that everyone on the scene is striving so strenuously for. Reporting a grime story for an American magazine last spring, I was struck by how little presence it had on the streets of London in this, the year of its expected crossover, compared with the way jungle streamed out of passing cars and Oxford Street boutiques in 1994 (the equivalent breakthrough year). As a critic cham-pioning grime, one of my angles – beyond the sheer excitement of the music, the brilliance of the wordplay, the charisma of the MCs – has been 'you really ought to check this, it's the voice of the UK streets'. But I suspect that not many people actually want to hear what the voice of the streets has to say: partly, because it ain't pretty, and partly, because most people honestly don't give much of a fuck. Twenty years ago, the likes of Kano or Bizzle would be *NME* front cover stars, no questions asked, purely as a matter of basic journalistic responsibility.

388

White and black music, then, seem to agree on just one thing at the moment: 'you can go your own way', in the immortal words of Lindsay Buckingham. But it's not clear what conclusions could, or should, be drawn from this. After all, earlier phases of musical miscegenation didn't, in the end, augur some multicultural Utopia of the future; the last major upheaval of mixing-it-up (Rave culture) was heavily dependent on chemicals. Nevertheless, if there's any credence left in the notion that the times manifest themselves in music, then this increasing separate development within pop culture isn't a promising portent.

Frieze, January 2006

Perhaps the idea that white music 'ought' to engage with black music (pay attention to it, try to keep up with it, borrow its ideas and rework them) is outmoded. Perhaps 'all that' was just a distinct and bounded period of pop time that's now over; a historical aberration or unusually blessed era rather than the natural state of things. Still, relinquishing the idea feels like a loss to me. Actually, it's the third part of the white-on-black mechanism (borrow/rework, appropriate/mutate) that's really faded away. There's no shortage of white hipsters who zealously follow black music of different kinds; what seems to have eroded significantly is the confidence, or gall, that they could *add* anything to the music themselves. Since the decline of rave (the last upsurge of genuinely mixed-up musical multiculture in this country?) there's a sense in which a segment of white bohemia has outsourced the burden of building a vibrant counterculture on to black youth. Some of us have maybe lived vicariously through black resistance and black futurism. Partly that's been a response to how lame and Luddite rock music has been in the age of retro, but it's also been a kind of shirking. White music culture needs to get its shit together!

ARCTIC MONKEYS

Whatever People Say I Am, That's What I'm Not (Domino)

[Adapted from an inter-blog debate with Mark Fisher of K-punk about the merits of Arctic Monkeys.]

. . . I must admit when I wrote that bit in the *Frieze* piece about rhythmically inert Britbands and referenced 'whoever's on the cover of *NME* this week' I had Arctic Monkeys in mind. I just assumed from what I'd read that they'd be just another nowt-going-on-in-t'-rhythm-section indie-rock combo, fronted by an excessively cocky Northern lad singer, drawing on an ever-more insular set of quintessentially English sources. On this occasion, though, the inbreeding has paid off: the family tree is narrow (Jam, Smiths, Oasis, Libertines, etc.), but for once the result isn't an enfeebled poodle, it's a mighty attack dog spliced out of the most potent and poignant genes of their ancestors. The drummer and bassist are uncommonly dynamic and flexible, several cuts above the Brit norm – just listen to the way they switch, on 'Perhaps Vampires is a Bit Strong But . . .' from Sabbath-style 'heavy' dynamics to punk-funk that casually out-grooves Franz Ferdinand. Unlike Oasis, who were really like Joe Carducci's 'electric busking', singalong-plus-riffalong but dead-below-the-waist, Arctic Monkeys make physically involving music.

Also unlike Oasis, their lyrics aren't gibberish, they are actually about something. People compare Alex Turner's words to The Streets and Pulp (actually Alex himself has made that comparison, saying he walks 'the lyrical tightrope between Jarvis Cocker and Mike Skinner'), but in some ways he reminds me as much of Dizzee Rascal: the combination of cockiness and sensitivity; the way the melodies curl around the natural cadence and flow of his regional speech patterns; the *jouissance* of the moments when his accent, always present, asserts itself with a word or syllable that rings out completely and jarringly askew;

the combination of proximity to the experiences he's writing about and being ever so slightly above/beyond/outside them (old head on young shoulders); the sense of locality and rich verisimilitude in the details; the hunger that shakes through the voice and whips out of the speakers . . . I once fantasized about Dizzee becoming a Morrissey-like figure, his account of a very particular and relatively unusual troubled youth and his alienation from everything, coming to represent a much larger unity of alienation. Well, of course, Britain being how it is, the black artist doesn't get to be the *NME*-readership-beloved Everykid spokesperson. Instead it's another white Northerner who gets to be the Morrissey-like figure.

One thing that's oddly engaging about the Arctic Monkeys is how they actually subvert Sheffield's own pop myth as the city of electr(on)ic dreams. I wonder if that's a subconscious impulse lurking behind the line in 'I Bet You Look Good on the Dancefloor' about the girl 'dancing to electropop / like a robot / from 1984' . . . sort of, 'that was *then* [synth Sheffield], this is *now*'?

Their use of guitars alone is probably enough to condemn the Monkeys in some people's eyes, including Mark's. But you know, *synthesizers* have been around a long while now, twenty or thirty years, haven't they? Long enough to signify their own kind of retro, even if it's a retro-futurism. So have samplers. This brings me to a larger point about the 'chorus of disapproval and disquiet' that Mark feels ought to have greeted the Arctic Monkeys but is dismayingly absent. It's not just that the group are great enough to be an exception to the rule, it's that the rule itself is ailing. The trouble with all the arguments that can be mustered against Arctic Monkeys is partly that these charges (Luddite, Anglo-inbred, parochial, etc.) have become as stale and predictable as their music itself is purported to be. It's a critique that goes back at least as far as Oasis (although I remember people also making it about The Smiths in the mid-eighties, come to think of it). What's different now from Oasis days, though, is not simply the relative freshness of the critique; it's the fact that there is much less of a sense of there being an aesthetico-moral high ground from which to make it. Circa Britpop, you could argue 'this stuff is *retro*gressive, if people want the *true* modern British pop they should listen to jungle/Tricky/UK post-rockers like Disco Inferno/et al.'. Nowadays it's harder to see where are the vanguardist bastions on behalf of which one could launch one's volleys of indignation and disgust. Not dance music, which, give or take a handful of peripheral innovators like Villalobos, has for the last half-decade or so been recycling its own history as assiduously as rock has. Hip hop and R&B are puttering along at a snail's pace; there is a

391

definite 'same old shit in shiny new cans' syndrome at play, except the cans aren't that startlingly novel either – e.g. I love Lil Wayne's 'Fireman' but lyrically it's the same bleeding metaphor that Cash Money were caning seven years back (Hot Boys, 'we on fire', etc.) . . .

Sure there are innovators and extremists way out on the fringes of music, but most people can't live on fringe fare, that's not the kind of action that Mark is pining for, that's never going to be war-inside-pop. Like the poor, the remote-periphery experimentalists are always with us.

I don't really buy this notion of the nu-Pop (Girls Aloud, Rachel Stevens, Sugababes, et al.) as a nouveau New Pop. What it is, it's like New Pop if New Pop had only been in the mould of Dollar; if there'd been Trevor Horn, but no ABC, no McLaren, no Frankie, no Art of Noise/Morley. The characterless vocals, the choreographed routines, the quirk-less personalities . . . it couldn't be further from the New Pop menagerie of Adam Ant, Kevin Rowland, or even the spark of a Clare Grogan . . .

Grime worked as the high ground for much of this decade, but . . . well, that banner is looking a bit dog-eared right now. As for dubstep: jolly good stuff, I'm chuffed on the scene's behalf that its morale is so high, that the buzz is building and spreading . . . But the idea that it is stepping fearlessly into the future is, well, an over-estimation; it strikes me as very much a consolidation sound, it moves forward slowly and steadily, but it works from a tradition and a set of historical sources that are just as narrow as that which nourishes Arctic Monkeys. You'll hear elements from techstep 96, from bleep 'n' bass, from digi-dub, from On U Sound . . . It's roots 'n' future music, like all hardcore continuum sounds, but to these ears it feels like the ratio of rootical to futuroid is weighted to the former . . .

None of these points diminishes the overall thrust of *K-punk*'s critique – he's against Arctic Monkeys-type music on principle (a jihad I might have signed up for even a few months ago). But I do think there is a sense in which, at the moment, it's much harder to single out Brit-rock as especially culpable on the retro front. There's probably a sense in which the Arctic Monkeys are a disaster in the grander sense, their very excellence will inevitably lead to the Oasis → Northern Uproar syndrome – droves of dismal soundalikes given a warm welcome by hapless A&R executives. In that sense I'm 'against it' – but not to the actual point of denying myself the delights of the album.

Blissblog, 6 February 2006

It's weird, when I read Mark's riposte, I can still feel the pull of this ultra-futurist rhetoric, the allure of this severity stance . . . A number of points to be made . . .

Record Collection Rock

See, Arctic Monkeys' music doesn't strike me as that really . . . 'record collection rock' in my usage has a much more specific application than just 'the group has precedents' or 'they work within a tradition' or 'sounds familiar'. Record Collection Rock is music where the listener's knowledge of prior rock music is integral to the full aesthetic appreciation of the record ('full' because the creator put the allusions there for you to spot with a smile). Prime exponents include Jesus & Mary Chain, Spacemen 3, Primal Scream, and – to a lesser degree but still part of the sensibility, I think – Stereolab . . .

Oasis are the paradigm case: you get Beatles deja vu flashbacks from the melodies, the title 'Wonderwall' is sampled from a George Harrison album and 'What's the Story Morning Glory', slightly more esoteric, comes from 'Tomorrow Time' on John and Beverley Martyn's *Stormbringer* . . . But AMs strike me as more along the lines of The Smiths: precedented, for sure, but not a pastiche, you don't listen and spot specific steals and quotes. The hints of Mozz and Gallagher in Turner's voice here and there are fully integrated into a vocal identity that's totally sure of itself; the guy is very much his own man. Is it even 'retro'? Not in the sense of intentionally flashing us back to a specific era or lost golden age (e.g. The Cult circa 'Love Removal Machine', any number of nouveau garage punk bands you care to list . . .), or being taggable to a single illustrious ancestor band.

Indie

And you know, there's moments when I don't even feel that word applies, except as a vague and derogatory social designation based on their assumed audience. See 'indie' to me always implied a certain lameness, what Carducci calls a 'feeb' aesthetic, you think either of twee C86 tunesmithery or Wedding Present-type scruffiness; deficiency is part of the music's point and appeal, its *rhetoric of sound*. Musically Arctic Monkeys strike me as simply a British rock band; the key difference is the way they're plugged into the rhythmic power and fluency of British beat music of the sixties, i.e. the side of the sixties that indie bands always used to ignore in favour of melody/guitar-jangle, or were simply too inept to duplicate. In that sense AMs are very much a post-White Stripes band, which won't placate the futurists one bit, but at

393

least they're reactivating some of what's actually *worth* keeping in rock and something that most British bands since Madchester and baggy have been grievously lacking in (Stone Roses being one of the last UK bands with a really moving rhythm section, although it should be noted that the Libertines are relatively dynamic on that front).

'Be reasonable, capitulate to the available'

The angle I pursued last time – nothing really futuristic around at the moment, so non-innovation is more forgivable – is of course way too negative. I actually think this would be a splendid album in any year, that it would stand up to the competition like Pulp's *Different Class* did in 1995, a futurism-crammed year by any measure. *Whatever People Say I Am, That's What I'm Not* is in fact the strongest record of its sort since *Different Class*, and if Turner isn't yet the match for Jarvis Cocker lyrically, he's real close. Plus he's, like, sixteen years younger than Cocker was when he wrote those songs. What does 'of its sort' mean though? I think Mark hits the nail on the head in the various places he's brought up 'New Wave'. If musically the sheer potency of *Whatever People Say* shakes off the limp designation 'indie', lyric-wise the content is New Wavey – songs of love and lust with bite and a hint of bitter; social realism, observational lyrics. In 1979 it would have been filed alongside Costello, Specials, Dury, The Jam.

The Specials seem worth picking out from that list, because the title *Whatever People Say I Am, That's What I'm Not* is something Arthur Seaton, the bloodyminded young wage-slave in *Saturday Night and Sunday Morning,* says, and the best songs on the AMs album remind me a bit of 'Friday Night Saturday Morning', the last great Specials song, track three on the *Ghost Town* EP. Turner's songs give much more sense of the lust-for-life boiling inside the teenprole leisure tread-mill than Terry Hall on that tune (or 'Nite Klub' on The Specials debut), but he's just as aware that the short-term-buzzy bad things are long-term bad for you, dissipating energy and life-force as well as money. That's why the CD front cover of the lad smoking a cigarette down to its nub opens up to display a CD picture of an ash-tray crammed with fag-ends. It seems significant that two tunes on the album – probably the two most subtle and evocative and no-one's-written-about-this-before – involve young people being locked inside a vehicle by authority figures. 'Red Light Indicates Doors Are Secure' must surely be the first song ever about getting a cab home after a drunken night out. Turner sketches it all with keen-eyed economy: the driver refusing to let six in the taxi ('especially with the food'), eyeing the meter anxiously and considering doing a runner, reliving the night's highlights, from the fight that erupted in the taxi queue to the 'beyond belief' babe in the pub that another lad nabbed first. In 'Riot Van', Turner observes bored local youth expertly baiting the police to within an inch of getting arrested but no further – well, most of the time. Twenty years old, Turner is near enough to these lads in age to remember feeling that same mix of restlessness and cheek, high spirits and insubordination; he also knows they're gonna get burned sooner rather than later.

To me, what the Arctics are doing is analogous to someone working with the conventional novel form and coming up with something fresh, if not precisely innovative. Like Jonathan Coe's *The Rotters' Club* . . . now, that guy is very interested in avant-garde literary forms – he wrote a biography of B.S. Johnson (*Like a Fiery Elephant*). But Coe's own novels are fairly conventional (in fact his big cited influence is Henry Fielding). But that doesn't stop *Rotters* being an amazing book. Actually, a better comparison for the Arctics, given the youth landscape it depicts, is Alan Warner's *The Sopranos:* young people grabbing for fun and sparkle in the face of all the forces that would crush their spirit, whether its psycho bouncers, limited finances, or simply the sapping dreariness of the weather. And then in a clever touch, seemingly to circumvent the romanticization of working-class teen life that invariably wraps itself around or permeates from the inside out such depictions (Warner being a case in point), the album ends with a song set off on its own in the credits, as a coda or afterword: 'A Certain Romance', which says, no, actually, there's no romance in this life, this place – nothing glamorous about it at all.

Daft comparisons and the impulse to make them

Whether it's Kingmaker/Cud/Wonderstuff, or The Ruts/The Members, to me it's no different to someone saying 'Dizzee Rascal, Kano, that's just Derek B and Rebel MC all over again – more black blokes, boasting over beats, heard it all before.' Indeed I think there is a sense in which, for a certain 'informed sector', hating indie-rock saddos and *NME* readers is an OK form of bigotry, almost an inverted racism.

Turn to face the strange change-lessness

Correspondent Matt Wright wonders whether 'advocating for a return to a past aesthetic ideal', namely 'the modernist principle of pushing forward and advocating the Truly New' as espoused by *K-punk* and (most of the time) myself, whether that was in some senses nostalgic itself, in so far as one of the salient features of modernity as it's been for some while now is the fading away of the idea of the vanguard, its retreat from the centre of cultural life.

This is an idea I'm presently trying out, like a new pair of shoes that are slightly uncomfortable, that you have to wear in a bit: the idea that we are now in different times, or more profoundly, living with a different sense of temporality. Indeed, have been for some while.

I do think the uncanny persistence of indie-rock, the fact that it has outlasted all the obituaries written for it, is something to reckon with. Explaining it by positing an inherent lameness or laziness to its audience seems . . . inadequate. Perhaps it's a format that does a certain thing particularly well, and the mystery is not the survival of the format, but the survival of the *need* for it (society's to blame?). Maybe it's that indie-rock is actually like metal, a fixture on the music-culture menu now, serving a certain population that keeps reforming itself and renewing itself, again because of a certain stasis in society. Most of the time, metal's internal fluctuations are of no interest to those not immersed in it, but every so often it'll throw up something that grabs the wider world's ear. And yet, metal *does* change, almost imperceptibly; you put a metal track from 2006 next to one from 1984 and they're not the same. And so it goes with 'indie', that increasingly inadequate term; if you tele-transported an Arctic Monkeys song back to 1985, it wouldn't, actually, fit right in.

Talking of a sense of temporality changing radically, the fading or disruption of a former sense of forward propulsion through time . . . Alex Turner is twenty, which means he was born in 1985, the *annus disappointingus* at which *Rip It Up* ends; the year when retro-oriented, sixties-pillaging 'indie' displaced the early innovation-seeking ideals of 'independent' music; his is a generation perhaps that was *born* under the sign of 'anachronesis' (my term for that uncanny sense of living in a time with a diminished feeling of now-ness).

Except perhaps not . . . because in the nineties there *was* a sense of future-tilted motion, largely due to E-lectronic music (do all the hurtling-into-the-future periods – sixties, punk/post-punk, rave – have in common the quickening of culture caused by amphetamines?).

Then again, it's bizarre how 'indie' has outlasted the irruption of 'faceless techno bollocks', the culture of DJs, beats, and E's; how it's outlived the future-surge of the nineties. This struck me really forcefully with the unexpected appearance, near the end of 'I Bet You Look Good on the Dancefloor', of the phrase 'banging tunes in DJ sets'. It suddenly made me wonder what dance music *meant* to this generation. The last convulsion of dance culture in Sheffield presumably would have been Gatecrasher and the second explosion of trance, and that would have been 1999–2000 – *six years ago,* an eternity when you're young. It would be something that the Arctics' older brothers and sisters would have been involved in, *maybe;* music for their generation begins with the Strokes' debut album most likely. Jesus, for some young kids getting into Arctics-type music now, the ones aged twelve, raving might even be something their parents did! Or maybe – and this is almost worse in a way – perhaps clubbing-and-drugging is something that's around still but relegated to a leisure *option*, something they'll dabble in a bit for a while (a teen rite of passage, doing your first pills), or even something to keep on dipping into, now and then . . . but not a cause or a creed, no longer based on the military/religious models that underpinned rave in the nineties, not even a vibe-tribe or A Way of Life.

Blissblog, 13 February 2006

While writing the second instalment of this inter-blog debate, I listened to a special dubstep-oriented edition of radio DJ Mary Anne Hobbs's *Breezeblock* show, which I'd never checked out before (having lived in New York since the end of 1994) but now, thanks to the wonders of the Net, I could 'tune in to', no trouble. An enjoyable melange of the darker end of dance music – grime, drum & bass, weirdtronica, and so forth – Hobbs's show was pretty much my cuppa, except that midway through I suddenly got this uncanny sensation: a feeling that 'the future' itself had somehow become a minority interest, a niche market to be catered to; an enclosure where the nineties *never stopped happening.* The people who keep faith with that nineties idea of what music should be about – generally folk who've been through the rave adventure – are definitely my usual crowd; normally I'd share their anti-indie virulence, their phuturist disdain for the latest hot new *NME* Brit-rock saviour. But this apparent turnabout with Arctic Monkeys wasn't as dramatic a break as it seemed, more like a culmination. Time and again with new touted guitar outfits – first the Strokes, then the White Stripes, and then again with the Libertines – I'd had the knee-jerk instant reaction ('what is this retro shit?!?!?') and then, with further exposure, the gradual and grudging admission that there was something there, the excitement wasn't entirely baseless. Finally, with Arctic Monkeys, the barrier of prejudice, severely eroded, collapsed almost instantly into unequivocal love. That said, in this piece there's definitely an element of enjoying the perversity of going against type, even of 'thinking against oneself'. For Mark Fisher's side of the debate, visit first http://k-punk.abstractdynamics.org/archives/007289.html; then 007321.html; finallly 007364.html.

The comparison between Alex Turner and Dizzee Rascal was a bit of a stretch, I thought, but then I read later that the Arctics were huge fans of hip hop, especially Britrappers like Roots Manuva, and that moreover Turner and drummer Matt Helders were involved in a funk band called Judan Suki concurrent with the early days of the Monkeys. So maybe there's something there after all . . .

GREEN-EYED SOUL

Hot Chip and Scritti Politti

The British have always had a *thing* for the music of Black America. An almost-random example: Paul Weller. In the mid-eighties, shortly after ending the rock-y Jam and launching the soul-oriented outfit Style Council, Weller opined that black people were 'the only people making any good music, like they've always been'. This attitude is surprisingly common among UK music hipsters. What makes it different from black music devotees in other countries is the combination of pious reverence with a *lack* of humility. From The Rolling Stones onwards, British artists have always been totally confident that they can not only master these foreign forms, but contribute to their development; they're not content with being curators, they want to be creators. So Weller, for instance, immediately ignored the implication of his remark (hands off, whitey) and churned out his own faux-soul and faux-jazz, even (shudder) making a few stabs at ersatz rap and the more gospel-tinged side of Chicago house.

Embedded in the British response to blues, soul, funk, hip hop, deep house, et al. is a paradox: the strenuous effort to be authentic to the source *immediately* creates inauthenticity. The fiercer you identify with the original, the more you erase your own identity and end up producing something not only lacking originality but deeply redundant. A cruel dilemma – fidelity versus mutation – has convulsed British music repeatedly over the decades: from the schisms of trad jazz versus free jazz and blues purists versus progressives right through to more recent debates over whether British rappers should ape American MCs or try to inject stilted Anglo cadences into their flow and parochial references (Tennent's lager, salt-and-vinegar crisps) into their lyrics. Two new albums from London offer the latest twists to this long-running saga:

the peculiar susceptibility of the British to Black American music and their struggles to express something true to themselves through it. *White Bread Black Beer* is the highly acclaimed comeback of Scritti Politti's Green Gartside, whose shift from post-punk to soul pre-dated and quite possibly influenced Paul Weller's. Equally warmly received, *The Warning* is the latest from Hot Chip, indie-rockers a couple of decades younger than Gartside but similarly besotted with the blingy sounds of today's R&B and rap.

One of the instant stumbling blocks to the UK embrace of soul is that a deficiency of fiery passion is precisely what's authentic to the English – not necessarily soul-lessness, but a certain detachment and diffidence. This isn't just about the clichés of English reserve (although the reason that they are clichés is . . .) but also to do with the contrast between the blood-and-fire fervour of so many American churches and the wishy-washy torpor of Anglicanism (whose services hardly any Britons bother to attend anyway). Soul wouldn't exist without gospel, but in the UK a much smaller fraction of the population believes in God than in America.

Green Gartside once described Scritti's songs as 'hymns for agnostics, for the disillusioned like myself'. Circa 1980 the band abruptly swerved from fractured post-punk with Marxist lyrics to seductive blue-eyed soul whose words addressed the quandaries left when you've lost confidence in politics altogether. 'Faithless now, just got soul,' he crooned sweetly on the gospel-flavoured single 'Faithless'. Like many left-wing theory fiends at that time, Gartside had had his world radically unsettled by deconstruction, causing him to lose his belief in Marxism as a 'science of history' that mapped the righteous course to utopia. The result was doubt and existential drift, but also a liberating giddiness and joy, captured on a jaunty Scritti tune entitled 'Jacques Derrida'. The latter also featured early evidence of the singer's enduring passion for hip hop in the form of a section where Gartside 'raps' about the voraciousness of Desire – Sugarhill Gang meets *Semiotexte*. Twenty-five years on, the new Scritti album *White Bread Black Beer* starts with a paean to rap music, 'The Boom Boom Bap'. The title evokes hip hop's looped breakbeats and 808 bass – 'the beat of my life', croons Gartside – while the final verse is composed entirely of song titles from the first Run DMC album ('hard times, sucker MCs, jays game . . .' et al.). 'Boom Boom Bap' is confessional, Green has said, all about the thin line 'between being in love with something and being unhealthily addicted to it'.

A self-conscious pop version of what the French crit crew called 'intertextuality' has long been a hallmark of Gartside's songwriting.

'Getting', Havin' and Holdin'" (on 1982's *Songs to Remember*) inter- polated a lyric from Percy Sledge's 'When a Man Loves a Woman' . . . *Cupid & Psyche 85*, Scritti's breakthrough album on both sides of the Atlantic, contained the UK hit single 'Wood Beez', whose chorus goes 'each time I go to sleep / I pray like Aretha Franklin'. It would be cloy- ingly cute if Green didn't really *mean* it: soul for him served as a salve for the anomie of an existence without the comforting fictions of truth, progress, justice and identity. Hence his 'unhealthy addiction' to black music's pain-killing power. If Gartside could no longer believe in any 'Absolute' (the title of his second UK hit – no, really!), if he knew even the Sweetest Girl hymned in his songs was a myth, then at least he could believe in the mystery of melody. On *White Bread,* the singer reaffirms his faithlessness ('After Six' beseeches 'oh Jesus, keep your love away from me') but has found a secular surrogate for salvation in the form of his wife Alys, whom he married early in 2006. The Lacan fan who once sang 'now I know to love you / is not to know you' now lives a life of marital bliss in East London.

Hailing from the West side of the city, Hot Chip have their own equivalents to Gartside's 'pray like Aretha'. 'Look After Me', one of the highlights of *The Warning,* nods to Dionne Warwick with the couplet 'every time I see your face I breakdown and cry / I see it in your family as they walk on by' while last year's *Coming On Strong* was even more blatant with songs like 'Down with Prince' and the cheeky lyric 'I'm like Stevie Wonder, but I can see things'. You can certainly hear seven- ties and eighties funk 'n' soul – Wonder, Prince, Jam & Lewis – in the group's sound. But Hot Chip's primary passion is contemporary rap and R&B. Where post-structuralist Green gets around the faux-black problem by worrying away at the very concept of authenticity, Hot Chip use their lack of street credibility to make their music simultane- ously touching and comic, injecting an element of bathos that rings true while also exposing the exaggerated 'realness' of rap.

The approach is easily mistaken for smirky irony; sometimes (as with the Stevie Wonder wisecrack) you might think they're simply taking the piss out of black music. And Hot Chip *have* triggered some bizarrely over-the-top hostility: one reviewer described the group as 'kids with urine on their fingers, laughing five-deep in the stalls and sniffing each other's cold stink'. As an instant fan of Hot Chip's gorgeous melodies, delectably wan vocals and quirky arrangements, I thought this reaction ridiculous until I saw the video for 'Playboy', which sabotages the poignancy of the song with its goofy, Devo-meets-Ween geekitude.

What really seems to confuse some people, though, is the way Hot Chip deal in mixed emotions. Soul is about strong feelings, rap is about force of personality ... but what do you do if your inner core is passive-aggressive, listless, a little lukewarm? The group's two singer/songwriters, Alexis Taylor and Joe Goddard, aren't parodying rap and R&B, then, they just keenly feel the gulf that separates black pop's high-gloss fantasy world and the scuffed 'n' shabby reality that nearly all of us inhabit – especially those who live in the rain-spattered, narrow terraced streets of West London. So in 'Playboy', the sadsack protagonist soothes his heart-ache by cruising Putney in his Peugeot and imagining he's a gangsta: '20-inch rims with the chrome now / Blazin' out Yo La Tengo'. The title track of *The Warning* reads thuggish – 'Hot Chip will break your legs, snap off your head / Hot Chip will put you down, under the ground' – but is delivered in voices that sound more Modest Mouse than Mobb Deep.

On *Coming On Strong*, tracks like 'You Ride, We Ride, In My Ride' and 'Shining Escalade' had a translucent faintness, as if they're diagrams of Timbaland or Dr Dre productions that have yet to be coloured in. *The Warning* retains the R&B and G-funk influences but adds some rave energy. 'Over and Over' is a double-edged celebration of trance-dance monotony. The music – mindless boogie at the exact intersection of Daft Punk and Foghat – enacts its theme perfectly, but the lyric seems to almost-mock the listener for responding to the dance-floor summons: 'Like a monkey with a miniature cymbal / the joy of repetition really is in you.' At the opposite sonic extreme, the slow-soul ballad 'Look After Me' is a crestfallen tune about the breakdown of a relationship ('look after me and I'll look after you / that's something we both forgot to do') gently propelled by tender-hearted clicks of rhythm guitar straight out of a classic-era Stax session.

Talking about his own first encounter with the Memphis soul sound, Green Gartside once declared: 'There was something about when I found Stax, that beat, that snare drum ... all its voids required me to fill them, and sometimes that was very violent, a theatrical excess.' But it's more the case that Black American music fills the holes in the British soul; the healing pain of soul music offers a mirage of wholeness. The sharpest UK operators feel both the pull of this fantasy passion and its out-of-reachness. Or as Hot Chip sing it in 'The Warning', an oblique paean to machine soul and synthetic funk: 'Excuse me sir, I'm lost / I'm looking for a place where I can get lost / I'm looking for a hope for my malfunctioning being / I'm looking for the mechanical music museum.'

Director's cut of piece published in
Slate Magazine (www.slate.com), July 2006

At the close of *The Death of Rhythm & Blues*, Nelson George argues that 'whites no longer have to imitate R&B, but have, to a degree unprecedented in the post-war era, matched their black contemporaries. How? Through a deeper understanding and (dare I say) love for the currents in black music history.' Significantly, nearly everyone in his list of soulful white dudes was British: Peter Gabriel, Steve Winwood, George Michael, PhilfuckingCollins wouldya-believeit ('There's a lot of love for Phil Collins in the black community,' George claimed else-where), and he might easily have added Mick Hucknall, Paul Weller, and countless others, to the list. It *is* a peculiarly British thing, this projection towards Black America, and needless to say I prefer this syndrome when it's not a straight replication of the source but comes with either a form-mutating twist, or the insertion of new content, or even better, both. In recent years, though, it seems like the white-on-black mechanism has pretty much broken down. Perhaps the experiential gulf between the UK middle class and the world depicted in US hip hop is just too vast (mind you, that didn't deter the sixties Brit blues boys from having a go). Then again, it seems significant somehow that my three favourite albums of 2006 are by white Britons who have an intense and complex relationship with black music: Scritti, Hot Chip, and dubstep producer Burial. I can't quite say what the significance *is* exactly, but perhaps it's one clue to 'what's missing?'. Which takes us back to where we started . . .

BONUS MATERIAL

M.I.A

Piracy Funds What?

Sass, Radical Chic, and the Inevitable Emanation of Shanty House Theory, but Is That Enough?

M.I.A.'s *Arular*, for me, falls into that gap between 'what's not to like?' and actual outright love. The record sounds great. The voice, with its expertly slack enunciation and insistent insolence, is addictive. And yet, trust me here, it's not simply knee-jerk recalcitrance in the face of hype that makes me feel there's something ever so slightly off-putting about the whole phenomenon.

The music's canny composite of street beats makes all the right connections, organizing a pan-global conference call between Kingston's concrete jungles, Dalston's grimy council estates, Rio's funky favelas, and, er, whatever the name is for the bad areas reggaeton hails from. Brit blogger Woebot coined the witty term 'shanty house' as a catchall for all these world-is-a-ghetto musics: impurist genres (see also: kwaito, Desi) that typically suture bastardized vestiges of indigenous folk forms to pirated elements of rap, rave, and bass 'n' booty. Locally rooted but plugged into the global mediasphere, these scenes don't bother overmuch with sample clearances, and vibe-wise they typically project ruffneck raucousness leavened with party-up calls to shake dat ass. They also speak, vividly if obliquely, of a new world disorder where Tupac Shakur vies with Bin Laden as a T-shirt icon and terrorists keep in touch via text messaging.

Seemingly the inevitable emanation of the shanty house theory, M.I.A. isn't just a perfect pushes-all-the-right-now-buttons package for media and marketers to build a buzz around. She's a veritable vortex of discourse, catalyzing fevered debate around most likely irresolvable questions concerning authenticity, postcolonialism, cultural tourism, appropriation, and dilettantism. She's a dissertation (*Riddims of*

Resistance: Sub-Bass and Sub-altern Pressure) given *fine* fleshly form.

Pulp's Steve Mackey has some production involvement in *Arular*, which is sorta funny given that M.I.A., a former St. Martin's College art student, has a tiny bit in common with 'Common People' 's downwardly mobile posh girl, also enrolled at St. Martin's. Neneh Cherry often comes up as a reference point, but I'd say Neneh's former flatmate, the white Rasta Ari Up, is more apt: the outsider who's worked hard to master the walk and the talk. Don't let M.I.A.'s brown skin throw you off: She's got no more real connection with the favela funksters than Prince Harry. There's also some sleight of hand involved in her refugee/'freedom fighter father' credentials. (*Arular* gets its name from her dad's guerrilla alias.) Sourced in the insubordinate energy of street soljas across the globe, her music vaguely evokes Third-World-versus-First-World struggle, but the actual independence movement M.I.A.'s dad was involved in (Tamil Tigers versus the Sinhalese majority government of Sri Lanka) doesn't fit that model. Like Rwanda, it's an ethnic war within a Third-World nation.

Seeing M.I.A. onstage at the Knitting Factory a couple weeks back didn't really help dislodge me from the proverbial fence in either direction: Swayed by her chutzpah and ability to deliver live, I was also turned off by the stencil-sprayed projection imagery of grenades, tanks, and so forth (redolent of the Clash with their strife-torn Belfast stage backdrops and Sandinista cred by association). And what was up with having four genuwine black girls from the 'hood troop onstage to dance for a bit, before M.I.A. herself materialized? They danced, not very well as it happens, to her DJ Diplo's expert meshing of the Cure's 'The Lovecats' with Snoop's 'Drop It Like It's Hot' (cats and dogs, geddit?), while the 99 percent white audience punched the air.

Perhaps they simply don't care (and fair enough) about the rockist trinity of categories by which music is usually judged valid: (1) context, (2) content, (3) intent. For (1), as we've seen, the modus operandi on *Arular* essentially is decontextualization (placing her in the tradition of Malcolm McLaren's *Duck Rock* as much as, say, Ms Dynamite). Content-wise, we're talking a blend of undeniable sass and radical chic, the latter ranging from the already infamous no-surrender line about the PLO in 'Sunshowers' to the distinctly incoherent politicking of 'Pop' (hidden track thirteen) to the way the drum machine beats often sound like gunfire. As for 'intent', I'm inclined to give M.I.A. the benefit of the doubt and take her desire to be down with the most exciting sounds around as both pure-hearted and totally understandable. Nor is it likely, as some accuse, that her success will impinge on the sales of grime, baile funk, etc. (If anything there'll be a slight trickle-down effect.) In the end, what keeps me teetering on that fence is that for all M.I.A.'s evident intelligence, feistiness, great taste in Other People's Music, and terrific backstory, what's missing from *Arular* is character: not quirkiness (although she's no Bruza or Elephant Man) so much as local character – those telling details that transmit the true flava of a scene. *Arular*, strictly speaking, comes from nowhere.

Village Voice, 15 February 2005

NOTES ON THE NOUGHTIES: IS M.I.A ARTIST OF THE DECADE?

Surveying the best-of-the-decade lists, I was surprised to see M.I.A. not featuring as high as one might have expected. When 'Paper Planes' was at its peak of crossover success last year – #4 in *Billboard*, sampled in T.I. and Jay-Z's 'Swagga Like Us', included in *Slumdog Millionaire* – there was a smatter of chatter to the effect that she was Artist of the Decade. That appears to have ebbed, leading to the just respectable showings for *Arular* and *Kala* on the various lists. Which surprised me not only because of the massive fervour for those albums on their release in 2005 and 2007 but also because, while not a fan myself, I can't actually think of too many other contenders for Artist of the Decade. Entirely a creature of the noughties, M.I.A. arrived mid-decade to dramatize some of the central issues of the era. If preeminence was measured purely in terms of talk – the ability to generate acres of newsprint and blogospheric comment, to turn oneself into a fulcrum of fevered pro- and anti- debate – you'd have to say that M.I.A. beat all-comers.

As the decade draws to a close, it seems timely to consider once more the M.I.A. phenomenon. But as these Notes are 'oblique angles', the route will be roundabout, starting in an unlikely place: the *Wall Street Journal*'s review of a book by veteran rock writer Robert Hilburn, formerly pop critic of the *Los Angeles Times*. *Corn Flakes with John Lennon* is a memoir of a life spent writing about, meeting, and in some cases befriending such music-with-a-message icons as Bob Dylan, U2, Bruce Springsteen, Stevie Wonder, Chuck D, and, obviously, John and Yoko. *Wall Street Journal* reviewer Jim Fusilli observes that 'Mr. Hilburn's model post-Presley rock star is a larger-than-life idealist who writes passionate songs about personal and social issues.' And he points out that this approach, common among the baby-boomer generation of rock critics and shared by many boomer fans too, has a weakness: a tendency to skim past purely musical value (instrumental virtuosity, innovation, production, etc.) 'in a search for heroes.' In his review of *Corn Flakes with John Lennon*, Fusilli quotes an elegiac passage: 'I wondered again about whether rock's golden age was ending,' muses Hilburn. 'Rock and roll was never just about a sound; it was about an ideal.'

Reading this, I started wondering myself: How many candidates for Hilburn-style hero treatment had the noughties produced, artists who made socially-conscious music lent authenticity by its being rooted in personal biography and lived experience? Really, there was only M.I.A., maybe Dizzee Rascal, and perhaps Kanye West (early on, before his subject matter became his own fame/torment). Part of critics' attraction to *Arular* and *Kala* related to the back story, the way it substantiated the 'pull up the people' sentiments (which are easy to express but certainly carry more weight if you're from the people yourself). Although the looking-for-a-populist-spokesperson syndrome is very babyboomer, there are certainly critics from the postpunk and post-rap generation who prize this kind of commitment and conscious-ness in their musical heroes – writers like Jeff Chang, author of *Can't Stop Won't Stop*, a superb history of hip hop that focuses largely on its political impact. (Chang's also a big supporter of M.I.A., writing about *Kala* for American left-wing magazine *The Nation*.) Much of the posi-tive critical reception for M.I.A. was framed in Hilburn-esque terms: *Billboard*, of all places, described M.I.A. as 'a revolutionary leading a class war' while *NME* said that The Clash sample in 'Paper Planes' gave the 'clearest indication of where she sees herself, as the inheritor of true rebel music in an era of corporate punks'. Hilburn himself picked *Arular* as his #8 album of 2005.

Clearly there is a substantial reservoir of sentiment out there (espe-cially in America) that hungers for some kind of redemptive populist voice within popular music, for contemporary figures to carry on the tradition that runs from Lennon via Bob Marley, Joe Strummer and Chuck D to Pearl Jam, Nirvana and Rage Against the Machine. But overall, you'd have to say that in the noughties, this way of thinking about and relating to music faded significantly. The realities of how music is made, distributed, consumed, experienced, seem to agitate against investing belief in artists as spokespersons/saviours. Fewer people are looking for that, and fewer artists are coming forward to take on that role. There is widespread incredulity towards the notion that a musician making a statement actually achieves anything. These days, a performer who wanted to have any kind of political effect would most likely not bother writing a song about an issue but get involved in activism or use their fame for high-profile lobbying (as Thom Yorke and Bono do for Third World debt relief). But even this will tend to get mocked as superstar grandstanding or noblesse oblige.

M.I.A adroitly straddled the residual demand for a Clash/Public Enemy-type hero and the new twenty-first-century pop reality organized around the virtual and the viral, where a pop brand is built through blog buzz, mixtapes circulating on the web (Piracy Funds Terrorism, in M.I.A. and Diplo's case), remixes and mash-ups. (Musically too, she merged rebel-rock slogans with the post-rap/post-rave culture of beats, basslines and MC catchphrases.) Something inherent in these webby modes of discovering and consuming music tend to erode the rockist mindset, with its emphasis on intent, integrity, context. Attachment to artists becomes more fleeting; the emphasis is much more on the listener's pleasure, on the endless chase for the next thrill and the new cool. In the old days, a band built up a community of fans through live performance, becoming a grass-roots phenomenon that the media and the industry noticed and moved in on. Today, buzz comes first; live performances and tours come later, they're the seal of a success made through other means.

With M.I.A., two mighty machineries of hype – the quaint, lumbering rock critical process of nominating candidates for the hero role versus the lateral networks of online buzz – meshed perfectly. A speck of grit caused the gears to grind to a halt momentarily, when M.I.A. allowed 'Galang' to be used in a Honda Civic commercial: a dissonantly corporate move for a champion of the Third World, made worse by the justification offered that the Honda was a poor person's car. But in a sign of the fading of the rockist mindset, this inconsistency – the kind of contradiction that might have badly damaged the credibility of a rebel-rock band in the seventies or eighties – was brushed aside by most fans. Nobody really believes in concepts like 'selling out' anymore; the feeling seems to be that if you've established a successful brand, you're entitled to milk it. Besides, in the new pop reality of the noughties, a TV commercial is just another way of getting across. Everybody nowadays uses this sort of means to their various ends. Sixties icons like Bob Dylan and Paul McCartney teamed up with Starbucks to sell their records because, with traditional retail outlets withering away, this was the best way to reach their ageing audience. U2 partnered with Apple, synergizing their respective brand power to double-promote *How to Dismantle an Atomic Bomb* and a special U2 iPod.

From its Clash/'Bankrobber'-style lyric about wealth redistribution to the actual sample from 'Straight to Hell', 'Paper Planes' almost seems like a sop to that segment of M.I.A.'s constituency who still believe in the old 'roots rock rebel' ideals. But the song's route to success was totally noughties, via the film trailer and TV commercial for *Pineapple Express*. I've always found 'Paper Planes' mildly irritating. Partly because of the 'sample-stain' (opposite of the sample epiphany) it's now indelibly left on 'Straight to Hell' (I'm not really a Clash fan as such, but that's one of the half-dozen songs by them I love). And partly because, both as performed lyric and printed words, the song doesn't deliver anything to me I can recognize as resonance. M.I.A.'s own explanation of what 'Paper Planes' is about doesn't really help: The song's apparently about immigrants 'driving taxicabs all day and living in a shitty apartment and "appearing" really threatening to society. But not being so. Because, by the time you've finished working a twenty-hour shift, you're so tired you [just] want to get home to the family.' Still, I must admit the track worked brilliantly in *Slumdog Millionaire*, blasting out of the movie theater speakers in Dolby Digital Sound. Here M.I.A.'s music found its perfect context: the bright, flashy excitement of a movie that offers a vicarious thrill-ride through a harder, real-er world than its Western audience are ever likely to experience first-hand, complete with a feel-good, million-to-one happy ending where the hero beats the system and takes the money.

The Guardian, 16 December 2009

THE PEOPLE VS. VAMPIRE WEEKEND

In an enervated year for music, when pop was rightfully eclipsed by Far More Important Matters, Vampire Weekend were as close as our little community got to a polarizing controversy. Why, this very newspaper felt obliged to run two opposed reviews of the New York City quartet's self-titled debut upon its January 2008 release: Mike Powell's tempered praise facing off against Julianne Shepherd's *a priori* indignation.

Variations on these memes rippled across the criticscape and blogosphere all year long. Yet even the accolades were oddly defensive, hedged with disclaimers. British hipster mag *FACT*, for instance, prefaced its endorsement of 'I Stand Corrected' as #11 in their Top 100 Tracks of 2008 with 'There are a million reasons to hate Vampire Weekend', while only the other day I stumbled on a LiveJournal entry that began: 'I have about a million reasons to reject Vampire Weekend, but . . .' (*One million*? Clearly these are some pretty loathsome fellows!) I'd like to get to the other side of that 'but' myself, to talk about rapture and shining eyes and that rare aesthetic sensation of miraculousness that happens when you encounter, against the stacked historical odds, Something New Under the Sun. But the reasons-to-be-sneerful are interesting, deserve dissection, might even be revealing.

Already I hear the naysayers bleating, 'Something New?! But they're so derivative!' (This, from Deerhunter fans.) No new instruments have been invented, it's true, and here and there on *Vampire Weekend* you'll pick up a faint scent of things you might have heard before: a bounce of Beat in 'A-Punk', Orange Juice's just-brushed sheen, Monochrome Set's suave wit. The most common reference point (apart from *Graceland*, which seemingly crops up because it's the sole example of African-influenced rock most people know) is early Talking Heads. And that's a telling comparison, not because VW sound like them – they don't – but because of the crisp, clutterless clarity of the sound, a transparency of structure that allows you to see both the perfection and the unorthodoxy of the way the songs move and build. Unfugged by nu-shoegaze haze, the equality between the instruments shines through – the bass, the keyboards, the guitar, the drums, all take turns to be the star.

But where the Talking Heads comparison really fits is the identical set of accusations hurled at both bands: politeness, calculation, detachment, neatness. (In its charticle survey of 2008, *New York* magazine placed Vampire under 'Despicable' for 'further digging rock and roll's grave' by appearing on *SNL* in sweaters!) These insults are predicated on the positing of a subversive power to rudeness, spontaneity, wildness, mess – a too-easy equation, shaky even in Byrne & Co.'s day, and now fully crumbled (although you can find its pantomime enacted still at any number of Wolf Eyes or Monotonix shows). Given the nature of modern media and our crazed archival culture, it's obvious that no halfway sentient band can come into being without premeditation, the meticulous marshalling and coordination of influences and reference points. Knowingness irretrievably entered the water table long ago, and Vampire Weekend simply take this foundation of modern music – the impossibility of *not* overthinking things, of *not* riddling your work with footnotes and hyperlinks – and push through to full-blown conceptualism. They began with a handful of ideas (including the occasional convergence of Johnny Marr's playing in the Smiths with African guitarpop, along with an impulse to investigate the preppy aesthetic) and proceeded to assemble a tour de force amalgam of form and content.

Pressed to distil that merger's essence to a phrase, I'd offer 'form and formality.' The latter is obviously a thread through those odious-to-some lyrics, like the archly phrased dandy disdain of 'Your collegiate grief has left you/Dowdy in sweatshirts/Absolute horror!' But it equally pervades the music, whose symmetry and serenity recalls the gardens of English stately homes, all terraced geometric flower beds, manicured topiary, and exquisitely landscaped slopes. The most audacious and delightful aspect of Vampire's sound is the seeming incongruity between the African guitar parts and the quasi-classical flourishes, supplied equally by a genuine palm-court string section and Roslam Batmanglij's keyboard ersatz. This sound-clash works like a charm because the European and African elements share an emotional tone (uplifting, rhapsodic), but also stem from hierarchical societies. The kind of African ensembles from which Vampire Weekend have borrowed licks set a high premium on slickness, tightness and regimentation; early King Sunny Adé albums often feature songs titled after local dignitaries – a doctor or chieftain or, in one case, 'The Late General Murtala Mohammed', a Nigerian military dictator.

Vampire Weekend's (alleged, assumed) membership of the upper class often garners Strokes comparisons, with the underlying implication that 'people like that simply shouldn't be in popular music, because they're not of The People'. The affinity between the two bands runs deeper: As Regina Spektor noted, 'The thing that blew my mind first hearing the Strokes was that they were the closest I had heard rock come to classical. Their music is extraordinarily orderly and composed.' As Mike Powell further noted, Vampire Weekend are as much Anglophiles as Afrophiles, with most of their musical touchstones and lyrical allusions relating to Old England or New England. Vampire have merely outed the truth of indie, which was never really 'The People's Music' for all its affected sloppiness and 'beautiful loser' tropes, instead always much more of an upper-middle-class milieu, the kids recoiling from the commercial and mass-produced just like their parents did via artisanal foodstuffs and antiques. In his *Spin* profile, Andy Greenwald observed Ezra Koenig's 'encyclopaedic knowledge' of pop history and his 'clinical, removed' way of speaking about it – 'as if it were all a glorious steam table that had been laid out specifically for him to feast upon'. Ouch! Except that for better or worse, we're all of us aristocratic listeners these days, able to sample 'vibes' from anywhere and everywhere.

Vampire Weekend make more amusing and thought-provoking play from the signifiers of wealth and exclusivity than any rapper I've heard these past several years. (But then, they have more interesting rhythms than any hip hop record I've heard these past several years). Vampire Weekend's shit is tight, like their asses, because flawlessness is part of their aesthetic game plan – it's what the record had to be and is. (The only defect I can find on the album is that the lyric doesn't actually read as 'Peter Gabriel II.') How righteous that 2008 should have started with some literally African-American music to herald a literally African-American president. Funny, too, how all the attributes that describe (and, in some eyes, condemn) the band – cultivated and cosmopolitan, calm and collected, cautious and clean-cut – apply so amply to Obama. It's as if history had twisted its way around to arrive at a place where the virtues in our polity are also the virtues in our pop music. Unlike sax addict Bill C. or faux-populist George W., our prez doesn't have a rock 'n' roll bone in his body, and neither do Vampire Weekend. This year's very best, their album is not *Gossip Girl* set to music, but a soundtrack for the liberal elite taking over.

Village Voice (Pazz & Jop special issue) January 21 2009

NOTES ON THE NOUGHTIES #2:
WHEN WILL HIP HOP HURRY UP AND DIE?

A month or so ago *New Yorker* pop critic Sasha Frere-Jones wrote a column about the state of rap, starting with the proposition ('procla-mation' would be too bombastic a word) that 2009 was in fact the year of hip hop's death. I read it and couldn't find a thing to disagree with. My only quibble was that he might have called it earlier. Perhaps in 2006, when Nas released *Hip Hop Is Dead*. Or even in 2004, when Timbaland 'repeatedly voiced . . . a frustration with pop music, partic-ularly the hip-hop end of it' (according to his *New York Times* inter-viewer, one Sasha Frere-Jones) and further declared, 'It's time for me to retire, because it ain't the same . . . I'm tired of stuff now, even stuff that I do.' (He also, said, mind-blowingly, that 'Coldplay and Radiohead are the illest groups to me. That's music.') That same year, 2004, Jay-Z also confessed – on the eve of his (ha ha) retirement and moving on to bigger, more challenging fields of endeavour – that he too was 'bored' with hip hop. Rap had become 'corny,' he said, and accordingly he no longer felt peer pressure to raise his game (something underlined by the steady decline of his output after 2001's magisterial *The Blueprint*).

As I read Frere-Jones's piece, I also knew there'd be complaints and counter-arguments galore. And sure enough they came – droves of pissed-off fanboys brandishing obscure mix-tapes and overlooked albums as proof of the genre's continued vitality. Some whined that the sample on which his genre survey was based was too small (Jay-Z's new slab of going-through-the-motions, efforts by Kid Cudi and Wu-Tang clansman Raekwon, unsigned rapper Freddie Gibbs), while others questioned the entitlement of a white forty-something to pronounce on the vital signs of a black pop genre in the first place.

Dunno, I'd have thought twenty-five years of attentive fandom would at least justify having an *opinion*. Plus it's not as though this kind of gloom-and-doomy assessment of hip hop hasn't been voiced repeatedly by black critics and black fans, not to mention the performers themselves.

Pundits who deem something to be in decline are invariably accused of nostalgia, so another angle of retort was that Frere-Jones was pining for the Lost Golden Age: the late eighties/early nineties, rap in its first flush of artistic maturity, but still a genre primarily oriented around samples and breakbeats. The era of DJ/producers like the Bomb Squad and Eric B, Marley Marl and Prince Paul, Premier and Pete Rock. But you don't need to go back that far to locate a peak now passed. You just have to think of the first four years of this decade, which were the continuation in full force of a late-nineties resurgence of mainstream rap that effortlessly managed to be commercial and street at the same time, combining pop hooks and jagged rhythmic innovation, glitzy entertainment and edge. This seven-year-long surge was largely but not exclusively driven by the Dirty South: cities like Atlanta, New Orleans, Memphis and Houston; producers like Timbaland, Neptunes, Mannie Fresh, Lil Jon, and Mr. Collipark; MCs like Ludacris, Missy Elliott, Three 6 Mafia, Clipse, Ying Yang Twins, and those Cash Money hot boys Juvenile, B.G. and Lil Wayne. But the rest of the U.S. played its part, from the Ruff Ryders family (DMX, The Lox, Eve, plus producer Swizz Beatz) through Ja Rule and Nelly, to the Dre/Eminem/50 Cent axis.

Underground rap fans sniffed at this brash, bolshy sound, based not on the breaks-and-samples template of classic hip hop (partly because licensing samples had become too costly) but favouring instead synthesizer riffs and refrains modeled on techno-rave and eighties pulp movie soundtracks. The drum machine rhythms had an eighties vibe too, the double-time hi-hats and 808 bass-booms reactivating that whole other side of early hip hop based around electro not looped breaks, Bambaataa not JB. Backpackers also complained about all these crossover rap hits with R&B choruses, which they saw as selling out the ideal of hip hop as a showcase for MC virtuosity. But even as the ascendant street rap sound borrowed R&B's hook power and gloss, the nu-skool rap influenced R&B. In truth, by the turn of the millennium, the genres were less separate than Siamese twins (something symbolized by the union of Beyoncé and Jay-Z). Together, street rap and nu-R&B flooded global pop music with rhythmic pizzazz and in-yer-face attitude. The fall-out in the U.K. alone includes the 'chav-pop' swarm of girl groups and boy bands, M.I.A., and grime (not so much in the MC-ing, which owes more to jungle and dancehall, but in terms of beats and production, plus what would prove to be false expectations for mega-fame and Puffy/Jay-Z-style transmedia empire building).

415

It's the vigour and invention of the first third of the noughties that makes the last five years of rap look stalled and sapped, not old-skool days so remote only grey-hairs remember them. By any sensible metric, rap has slipped hugely from where it was when this decade began. It's not dominating the pop charts anymore, and neither is it irrigating the mainstream with new beats, styles, and slanguage. It's not producing major album-length statements, give or take an *808s & Heartbreak* (revealingly, not rapped but sung). It's not even coming up with compelling new personalities. The last, by my reckoning, were Lil Wayne (whose debut was released in 1999) and Kanye West (who debuted in early 2004). West has turned out to be a mixed blessing, while Wayne spread his brilliance thin across innumerable mix-tapes, plus 2008's uneven *Tha Carter III*. Some swear by T.I. and Young Jeezy as charismatic artists, but neither came up with an MC persona we've not seen before. And for the most part, rap these past three or four years has been a desperately unmemorable procession of cookie-cutter ballers – Jim Jones, Gucci Mane, Yung Doc, Soulja Boy, Lil Boosie, Gummi Bares – whose lyrics trudge a hedonic treadmill of bling and booty, punctuated by the occasional inane dance craze. Even the sound of rap – always its saving grace in the absence of political engagement or MC-as-poet depth – deteriorated in the second half of this decade. The odd angles and eerie spaces in productions by Mannie Fresh or Mr. Collipark were flattened out, replaced by portentous digi-synth fanfares and lumbering beats, a brittle bass-less blare that seemed pre-degraded to 128kbps to cut through better via YouTube and mobile phone ('ringtone rap', some called it), rendered all the more cheapo-sounding and plastic non-fantastic by the endless Auto-Tune fad.

One of the most interesting observations in Frere-Jones's piece is that rap producers are abandoning swing and syncopation for more pulse-based club rhythms (house/trance/electropop), resulting in a shift to a European rather than African-American feel. Flo Rida's 'Right Round', based on Dead or Alive's eighties Hi-NRG hit, is a good example, and new nadir. Actually, I still hear quite a lot of bump and skitter in street rap, but there's a pedestrian familiarity to the beats: They do the job solidly enough but they're the rhythmic equivalent of comfort food, reflexively tugging at your hips and shoulders but never approaching the stark strangeness of early noughties productions like Ludacris's 'What's Your Fantasy' or J-Kwon's 'Tipsy.'

I quizzed Josiah Schirmacher, a young DJ friend who disagreed vehemently with the *New Yorker* piece, and he replied that there was plenty of life in hip hop but it was all 'on the local level', pointing to styles like jerk, as favored by teenagers in Los Angeles. This was another story of the hip hop noughties: the succession of city-based sounds, starting with New Orleans bounce and continuing with crunk, hyphy, snap, juke, etc., which hatch as regional styles but thanks to the marvels of the net (and especially YouTube) are chased avidly by an international cadre largely comprised of white, middle-class beat nerds. I was one for a while but then started to feel that underneath the cool local quirks (for instance, in the Bay Area, hyphy MCs shout out to freeway exits, which is how the different neighbourhoods know themselves, as opposed to, say, wards in New Orleans), all these sounds were, at base, the same: electro variant + goofy dance + bawdy lyrics + (optional) drug-of-choice (E, with hyphy; purple drank a/k/a cough syrup in other places; and so on). In a funny way, the pasty-faced, steroid-popping North West England scene donk is a distant cousin of all these black American sounds: same anonymous rapping, same humorously boastful/sexist lyrics, same chav/bling videos, same utterly local orientation offset by the occasional break-out nationwide hit. The Blackout Crew basically are Cold Flamez.

Haven't talked about underground rap yet, but it doesn't exactly impose itself on your consciousness, does it? Like the lo-fi indie it resembles, this sector puttered on much like it did through the nineties, odd flashes of genius (Cannibal Ox, Dilla, Quasimoto/Madlib, etc.) amid the crate-digging antiquarianism. Barely creating a ripple in the larger pop culture, undie rap is probably pretty content with its niche, a haven of 'quality' in a mercenary world. This stuff bears the same relationship to Dirty South-type rap that someone like Elvis Costello did to rock after 1984 (and what d'ya know, Costello recently teamed up with The Roots to perform some of his classics on a US chat-show). But as with the late-eighties golden age, the late-nineties/early-noughties surge showed that during rap's heyday phases, the most innovative music rises to the top; it's not something you have to seek out, because it dominates the radio and the music-video channels, booms from passing cars.

The 'Death of . . .' piece is a genre of criticism that's fallen into disrepute (there was a period when you'd be constantly tripping over essays announcing the end of something: art, theory, rock, rave . . .). Nowadays people seem to feel that 'no genre ever really dies' (to adapt the Neptunes/N.E.R.D. motto). Was this in fact one of the problems with the noughties? No genre went gently into that good night: They all clung on, cluttering up the musical landscape. This not only made it harder for new things to emerge, it's meant that we've all come to forget that, in fact, totally new things have emerged in the past. There was, for instance, a time when hip hop didn't exist. The refusal to

417

admit that a genre can die (which doesn't mean literally disappear – it may even generate good stuff now and then – but refers to stagnation, irrelevance, becoming uncoupled from the zeitgeist) is a denial of the possibility of change, renewal, the unexpected. The very vitality of a form of music implies the possibility of its eventual death.

I sympathize with the Frere-Jones dissenters; it must be galling, having built up all that expertise and knowledge, to have your subcultural capital voided by some old git in a bow-tie (compulsory at the *New Yorker*, don't you know) airily declaring the area obsolete. One of the cunning rhetorical ruses used in these critical turf wars between enthusiasts and curmudgeons is the suggestion that the latter are projecting their physical decrepitude onto the state of music. But you could just as easily reverse that and argue that the young are projecting their physical vitality onto the senescent body of pop (every fibre of their hormonally flushed being shouts, 'It still LIVES!'). I won't say that hip hop is dead. But it does seem to be doing a good impersonation of being at death's door. More to the point, judging by its output in recent years, it's become a deadening force: as a listening experience, but also as something that maintains a deadlock on the musical imagination (and personal ambitions) of Black American youth. I doubt very much that this demographic has no more surprises up its sleeve in terms of sound and style, judging by past form(s) (jazz, rhythm & blues, funk, house, et al.). But that New Thing won't come until they tire of hip hop themselves and turn against it.

The Guardian 26 November 2009

BRING THE NOISE: A LISTENING LIST

The Jesus and Mary Chain – 'Upside Down' (Creation, 1984)
—— 'Never Understand' (Blanco Y Negro, 1985)
—— *Psychocandy* (Blanco Y Negro, 1985)

Nick Cave – *From Her to Eternity* (Mute, 1984)

The Redskins – *Neither Washington Nor Moscow . . .* (Decca, 1986)

Zapp – *Zapp* (Warner, 1980)
—— *The New Zapp IV U* (Warner, 1985)

Shambling/C86

The Bodines – 'Therese' (Creation, 1986)
Felt – 'Primitive Painters' (Cherry Red, 1985)
James – 'Hymn From a Village' (Factory, 1985)
Jesse Garon and the Desperadoes – 'Splashing Along' (Narodnik, 1986)
The June Brides – *There Are Eight Million Stories . . .* (Pink, 1985)
—— 'No Place Called Home' (In Tape, 1985)
The Pastels – 'Truck Train Tractor' (Glass, 1986)
—— *Up For a Bit With The Pastels* (Glass Records, 1987)
Primal Scream – 'Velocity Girl' (Creation, 1986)
The Shop Assistants – 'Safety Net/Somewhere in China' (53rd & 3rd Records, 1986)
Talulah Gosh – 'Beatnik Boy' (53rd & 3rd Records, 1986)
The Woodentops – 'Move Me' (Rough Trade, 1985)
—— 'Well Well Well' (Rough Trade, 1985)
Various – *C86* (NME/Rough Trade, 1986)

Rap: late eighties #1

Boogie Down Productions – *Criminal Minded* (B-Boy Records, 1987)

Mixmaster Gee and the Turntable Orchestra – 'The Manipulator' (MCA)
Schoolly D – *Schoolly D* (Schoolly D, 1986)
Skinny Boys – *Weightless* (Warlock, 1986)

Beat Happening – *Beat Happening* (K, 1985)

Band of Holy Joy – *The Big Ship Sails* (Flim Flam, 1986)
—— *More Tales From The City* (Flim Flam, 1987)
The Mekons – *Crime And Punishment* (Sin, 1986)
—— *Fear and Whiskey* (Sin, 1985)
—— *The Edge of the World* (Sin, 1986)

Rap: late eighties #2

Eric B and Rakim – *Paid in Full* (Island, 1987)
—— *Follow the Leader* (Island, 1988)
DJ Jazzy Jeff and Fresh Prince – *Rock the House* (Jive, 1987)
Salt N' Pepa – *Hot, Cool And Vicious* (Next Plateau, 1986)
Ultramagnetic MCs – 'Travelling at the Speed of Thought' (Next Plateau, 1987) (12-inch)
—— *Critical Beatdown* (Next Plateau, 1988)

Husker Du – *Zen Arcade* (SST, 1984)
—— *Flip Your Wig* (SST, 1985)
—— *Warehouse: Songs and Stories* (WEA, 1987)

Mantronix – *The Album* (Ten, 1985)
—— *Music Madness* (Ten, 1986)
  Related: Mantronik productions
  T. La Rock – 'Back to Burn' (Ten, 1987)
  T. La Rock – 'Breakin' Bells' (Ten, 1986)

The Smiths – *The Smiths* (Rough Trade, 1984)
—— *Hatful of Hollow* (Rough Trade, 1984)
—— *The Queen is Dead* (Rough Trade, 1986)
—— *Singles* (WEA, 1995)

Public Enemy – *Yo! Bum Rush the Show* (Def Jam, 1987)
—— *It Takes a Nation of Millions to Hold Us Back* (Def Jam, 1988)
—— *Fear of a Black Planet* (Def Jam, 1990)

LL Cool J – 'Rock the Bells' (Def Jam, 1986)
—— *Radio* (Def Jam, 1986)
—— *Bigger and Deffer* (Def Jam, 1987)

—— *Mama Said Knock You Out* (Def Jam, 1990)
Dinosaur Jr –*Your Living All Over Me* (SST, 1987)
—— *Bug* (SST, 1988)
Various – *The Wailing Ultimate* (Homestead, 1987)

Red Hot Chili Peppers – *Freaky Styley* (EMI, 1985)
—— *The Uplift Mofo Party Plan* (EMI, 1987)
The Pixies – *Come On Pilgrim* (4AD, 1987)
—— *Surfer Rosa* (4AD, 1988)
—— *Doolittle* (4AD, 1989)
  Related: The Breeders – 'Cannonball' (4AD, 1997)

Morrissey – *Viva Hate* (HMV, 1988)
—— *Your Arsenal* (HMV, 1992)
—— *Vauxhall and I* (Parlophone, 1994)

Living Colour – *Vivid* (Epic, 1988)
  Related: A.R. Kane – *69* (Rough Trade, 1988)
  Bad Brain – *Banned in D.C. Bad Brains Greatest Riffs* (Astralwerks, 2003)

Various – *Sub Pop 200* (Sub Pop, 1988)
  Related: Mudhoney – 'Touch Me I'm Sick' (Subpop, 1988)
  Tad – *God's Balls* (Subpop, 1989)

The Stone Roses – *The Stone Roses* (Silvertone, 1989)
—— *Turns Into Stone* [singles compilation] (Silvertone, 1992)
—— *The Complete Stone Roses* [singles/B-sides compilation] (Silvertone, 1995)

Positivity 1990

The Beloved – *Happiness* (East West, 1990)
Deee-lite – *World Clique* (Elektra, 1990)
De La Soul – *3 Feet High and Rising* (Tommy Boy, 1989)
A Tribe Called Quest – *People's Instinctive Travels and the Paths of Rhythm* (Jive, 1990)
Soul II Soul – *Vol 1 Club Classics* (Virgin, 1989)
—— *Vol II A New Decade* (Virgin, 1990)

Gangsta rap vs righteous rap
Boogie Down Productions – *Edutainment* (Jive, 1990)
Brand Nubian – *One For All* (Elektra, 1990)
The Geto Boys – *The Geto Boys* (Rap-A-Lot, 1990)
—— *We Can't Be Stopped* (Rap-A-Lot, 1991)

NWA – *Straight Outta Compton* (Ruthless/Priority, 1989)
—— *Efil4zaggin* (Priority, 1991)
Poor Righteous Teachers – *Holy Intellect* (Profile, 1990)
X-Clan – *To the East, Blackwards* (4th and Broadway, 1990)

Happy Mondays – *Squirrel and G-Man Twenty Four Hour Party People Plastic Face Carnt Smile (White Out)* (Factory, 1987)
—— *Bummed* (Factory, 1988)
—— *Madchester Rave On* EP (Factory, 1989)
—— *Pills 'n' Thrills and Bellyaches* (Factory, 1990)
Ride – *Nowhere* (Creation, 1990)
—— *Going Blank Again* (Creation, 1992)
  Related: My Bloody Valentine – *Isn't Anything* (Creation, 1988)
  —— *Loveless* (Creation, 1991)
  Slowdive – *Slowdive* EP (Creation, 1990)
  —— *Morningrise* EP (Creation, 1991)
  —— *Holding Our Breath* EP (Creation, 1991)
  Moose – *XYZ* (Hut, 1992)
  Swervedriver – *Mezcal Head* (Creation,1993)

Manic Street Preachers – *Generation Terrorists* (Columbia, 1992)
—— *The Holy Bible* (Epic, 1994)

Pavement – *Slanted and Enchanted* (Matador, 1992)
—— *Westing (By Musket & Sextant)* [compilation of early singles] (Drag City, 1993)

Nirvana – *Nevermind* (Geffen, 1991)
—— *In Utero* (Geffen, 1993)

N-Joi – 'Anthem'(Deconstruction, 1991)
K-Klass – 'Rhythm is a Mystery' (Deconstruction, 1991)
Bassheads – 'Is Anybody Out There?' (Deconstruction, 1991)
Various – *Deconstruction Classics – A History of Dance Music* (Deconstruction, 1995)

Hardcore rave

Various – *A History of Our World Part 1* (Sm:)e, 1994)
Various – *Psychotic Reactions: Give Peace a Dance Volume 3* (CND Communications, 1992)

Alice In Chains – 'Man in the Box' from *Facelift* (Epic, 1990)
—— *Dirt* (Epic, 1992)
Soundgarden – *Badmotorfinger* (A&M, 1991)

Jungle 1993

Various – *The Dark Side* and *The Dark Side II* (React, 1993)

Onyx – *Bacdafucup* (Def Jam, 1993)
   Related: Cypress Hill – *Cypress Hill* (Ruffhouse/Columbia Records, 1991)
   —— *Black Sunday* (Ruffhouse/Columbia Records, 1993)
   Wu-Tang Clan – *Enter the Wu-Tang (36 Chambers)* (Loud/Columbia, 1993)

Suede – *Suede* (Nude, 1993)

PJ Harvey – *Dry* (Too Pure, 1992)
—— *Rid of Me* (Island, 1993)

Dr Dre – *The Chronic* (Death Row/Interscope, 1992)
Snoop Doggy Dogg – *Doggystyle* (Death Row, 1993)
   Related: Eazy-E – *It's On (Dr. Dre) 187um Killa* (Ruthless, 1993)
   Ice Cube – *The Predator* (Priority, 1992)

Pearl Jam – *Ten* (Epic, 1991)
—— *VS* (Epic, 1993)

Beastie Boys – *Cooky Puss* EP (Ratcage, 1983)
—— *Licensed to Ill* (Def Jam, 1986)
—— *Paul's Boutique* (Capitol, 1989)
—— *Check Your Head* (Grand Royal, 1992)
—— *Ill Communication* (Grand Royal, 1994)
Luscious Jackson – *In Search of Manny* (Grand Royal, 1992)

Post-rock

Disco Inferno – *D.I. Go Pop* (Rough Trade, 1994)
Insides – *Euphoria* (Guernica/4AD, 1993)
Main – *Hydra-Calm* (Beggar's Banquet, 1992)
—— *Motion Pool* (Beggars, 1994)
Seefeel – *More Like Space* EP (Too Pure, 1993)
—— *Pure, Impure* (Too Pure, 1993)
—— *Quique* (Too Pure, 1994)
Techno Animal – *Ghosts* (Pathological, 1991)
—— *Re-Entry* (Virgin, 1995)
   Related: Bark Psychosis – *Hex* (Circa, 1994)
   Laika – *Silver Apples of the Moon* (Too Pure, 1994)
   Pram – *The Stars Are So Big, The Earth is So Small* (Too Pure, 1993)
   Scorn – *Evanescence* (Earache, 1994)

Stereolab – *Mars Audiac Quintet* (Duophonic, 1994)
—— *Emperor Tomato Ketchup* (Duophonic, 1996)
Tortoise – 'Gamera/Cliff Dweller Society (Duophonic, 1995)
—— *Millions Now Living Will Never Die* (Thrill Jockey, 1996)

Swingbeat/R&B #1

SWV – *It's About Time* (RCA/BMG, 1992)
Blackstreet – *Blackstreet* (Interscope, 1994)
Warren G – *Regulate . . . The G Funk Era* (Island, 1994)

Various – *Ragga Ragga Ragga 2* (Greensleeves, 1994)

Jon Spencer Blues Explosion – *Orange* (Matador, 1994)
—— *Experimental Remixes* (Matador, 1995)
    Related: Royal Trux – *Cats and Dogs* (Drag City, 1994)
    —— *Thank You* (Virgin, 1995)
    Urge Overkill – *The Supersonic Storybook* (Touch and Go, 1991)

Blur – *Modern Life is Rubbish* (Food, 1993)
—— *Parklife* (Food, 1994)
—— *The Great Escape* (Food, 1995)

Oasis – *Definitely Maybe* (Creation, 1994)
—— *(What's the Story) Morning Glory?* (Creation, 1995)

Pulp – *Separations* (Fire, 1992)
—— *Intro* (Island, 1993)
—— *His 'n' Hers* (Island, 1994)
—— *Different Class* (Island, 1995)
—— *We Love Life* (Island, 2001)

R&B #2

Aaliyah – 'One in a Million' (Blackground, 1996)
Blackstreet – 'No Diggity' (Interscope, 1997)
Missy Elliott – *Supa Dupa Fly* (Elektra, 1997)
Timbaland and Magoo – *Welcome to Our World* (Blackground, 1997)
    Related: TLC – 'Waterfalls' (LaFace, 1995)

Roni Size & Reprazent – *New Forms* (Talkin' Loud/Mercury, 1997)

2-step garage

Amira – 'My Desire (Dreem Teem Remix) (VC/Virgin/Slip 'n' Slide, 1998)

Architechs – 'B&M Remix/The Boy is Mine' (White Label, 1999)
Dem 2 – 'Destiny (Sleepless)' (Locked On, 1998)
Lenny Fontana – 'Spirit of the Sun (Steve Gurley Remix) (Public Demand, 1998)
Groove Chronicles – 'Stone Cold' (Groove Chronicles, 1998)
KMA – 'Cape Fear' (Urban Beat, 1996)
——— 'Kaotic Madness' on *Breakin Out* EP (KMA Productions, 1997)
Various – *Locked On, Vol 3: Mixed by Ramsey and Fen* (Locked On/Virgin, 1998)
Various – *Pure Garage: Mixed Live by E-Z* (Warner ESP import)
Various – *Locked On . . . The Best of* (Locked On, 2000)
Various – *Pure Silk: The Album* (Pure Silk, 1999)

Aaliyah – 'Are You That Somebody?' (Blackground, 1998)
Ginuwine – *100 % Ginuwine* (Epic, 1999)
Missy Elliott – *Da Real World* (Goldmind/Elektra, 1999)
——— *Miss E . . . So Addictive* (Goldmind/Elektra, 2001)
  Related: Eve – *Ruff Ryders' First Lady* (Ruff Ryders/Interscope, 1999)
  The Clipse [Neptunes-produced] – *Lord Willin'* (Star Trak/Arista, 1992)

The Notorious B.I.G. – *Ready to Die* (Bad Boy, 1994)
——— *Life After Death* (Bad Boy, 1997)
Ma$e – *Harlem World* (Bad Boy, 1997)
Puff Daddy and the Bad Boy Family – *No Way Out* (Bad Boy, 1997)
Puff Daddy – *Forever* (Bad Boy, 1999)

B.G. – *Chopper City in the Ghetto* (Cash Money 1999)
Hot Boys – *Guerrilla Warfare* (Cash Money, 1999)
Juvenile – *400 Degreez* (Cash Money, 1998)
Lil Wayne – *Tha Block is Hot* (Cash Money/Universal, 1999)

Rap: late nineties

DMX – *It's Dark and Hell is Hot* (Def Jam, 1998)
——— *Flesh of My Flesh, Blood of My Blood* (Def Jam, 1998)
——— *And Then There Was X* (Def Jam, 1999)
Ja Rule – 'Holla Holla' (Def Jam, 1999)
The Lox – *We are the Streets* (Ruff Ryders/ Interscope, 2000)
Various – *Ruff Ryders Ryde or Die Vol. 1* (Ruff Ryders/Interscope, 1999)

Roots reggae/dub/the UK DJ talkover continuum

Linval Thompson – 'Straight to Babylon Boy's Head' on *King Tubby's Special 1973–1976* (Trojan anthology, 1989)

Lee Perry – *Blackboard Jungle Dub* (Upsetter, 1973)

—— *Revolution Dub* (Upsetter, 1975)

—— *Arkology* (Island, 1997)

Various – *Macro Dub Infection* (Virgin, 1995)

Smiley Culture – 'Cockney Translation' (Fashion, 1984)

The Ragga Twins – *Reggae Owes Me Money* (Shut Up and Dance, 1991)

Oxide & Neutrino – 'Bound 4 Da Reload (Casualty)' (EastWest, 1999)

Various MCs – *The Warm Up* EP (Middle Row, 1999)

    Related: DJ Luck and MC Neat – 'A Little Bit of Luck' (Red Rose, 1999)

    M-Dubs featuring the Emperor Richie Dan – 'Over Here' (Babyshack Recordings, 1998)

    Corrupted Crew – 'G.A.R.A.G.E.' (Kronik Records, 1999)

    Teebone featuring Sparks and Kie – 'Fly Bi' (Rhythm Records, 1999)

    Genius Cru – 'Boom Selection' and 'Course Bruv' (Kronik, 2001)

Radiohead – *OK Computer* (EMI/Parlophone, 1997)

—— *Kid A* (EMI/Parlophone, 2000)

—— *Amnesiac* (EMI/Parlophone, 2001)

Destiny's Child – *The Writing's on the Wall* (Columbia, 1999)

Dancehall

Beenie Man – 'Who Am I? (Greensleeves, 1998)

Elephant Man – *Comin' 4 You!* (Greensleeves, 2000)

—— *Log On* (Greensleeves, 2001)

Capleton – *More Fire* (VP, 2000)

Various – *The Biggest Ragga Dancehall Anthems 2000* (Greensleeves, 2000)

B-boys on E

Bone Thugs 'n' Harmony – 'Ecstasy' on *Greatest Hits* (Ruthless, 2004)

Eminem – *The Slim Shady LP* (Aftermath, 1999)

—— *The Marshall Mathers LP* (Aftermath, 2000)

Ja Rule – *Rule 3:36* (Def Jam, 2000)

Jay-Z – 'Snoopy Track' on *Vol. 3: Life and Times of S. Carter* (Roc-A-Fella, 1999)

Ludacris – *Back for the First Time* (Def Jam, 2000)
OutKast – *Stankonia* (LaFace, 2000)

So Solid Crew – 'Dilemma' (So Solid, 2000)
—— *They Don't Know* (Independiente/Relentless, 2001)
  Related: Oxide & Neutrino – 'Up Middle Finger' (East/West, 2000)
  Pay as U Go Cartel – 'Know We' (Solid City, 2001)
  Wiley and Roll Deep – 'Terrible' (Solid City, 2001)

The Streets – *Original Pirate Material* (Locked On, 2002)
—— 'Let's Push Things Forward/All Got Our Runnins' (Locked On)
—— *A Grand Don't Come For Free* (679, 2004)

Ms Dynamite – *A Little Deeper* (Polydor, 2002)
Sticky Featuring Ms Dynamite – 'Booo!' (ffrr/London, 2001)
  Related: Pitman – 'Phone Pitman/Pitman Sez' (Pitman, 2002)
  Goldie Lookin Chain – *Greatest Hits* (Atlantic, 2004)

Garage rap/grime #1

Dizzee Rascal – 'I Luv U/Vexed' (XL, 2003)
Musical Mob – 'Pulse X' (Inspired Sounds, 2002)
Platinum 45 featuring More Fire Crew – 'Oi!' (Go Beat, 2002)
  Related: Wiley – 'Eskimo' (Wiley Kat, 2002)
  —— 'Ice Rink' (Wiley Kat, 2003)
  Various – *Garage Rap, Vol. 1* (Eastside)

Dizzee Rascal – *Boy in Da Corner* (Dirtee Stank/XL, 2003)
—— *Showtime* (Dirtee Stank/XL, 2004)

Kanye West – *The College Drop Out* (Roc-A-Fella, 2004)
—— *Late Registration* (Roc-A-Fella, 2005)
  Related: Jay-Z – *The Blueprint* (Roc-A-Fella, 2001)

Lil Jon and the Eastside Boyz – *Kings of Crunk* (TVT, 2002)
—— *Crunk Juice* (TVT, 2004)
  Related: Ying Yang Twins – 'Salt Shaker' (TVT, 2003)
  —— 'Wait (The Whisper Song)' (TVT, 2005)
  —— *U.S.A. (United State of Atlanta)* (TVT, 2005)
  Various – *Crunk Hits Vol 1* and *Vol 2* (TVT, 2005/2006)

Animal Collective/Paw Tracks

Animal Collective – *Here Comes the Indian* (Paw Tracks, 2003)
—— *Sung Tongs* (Fat Cat, 2004)

—— *Feels* (Fat Cat, 2005)
Ariel Pink's Haunted Graffiti – *The Doldrums* (Paw Tracks, 2004)
—— *Worn Copy* (Paw Tracks, 2005)
—— *House Arrest* (Paw Tracks, 2006)
Avey Tare and Panda Bear – *Spirit They're Gone, Spirit They've Vanished* (Animal, 2000)
Avey Tare, Panda Bear and Geologist – *Danse Manatee* (Catsup Plate, 2001)
Panda Bear – *Young Prayer* (Paw Tracks, 2004)
   Related: Wooden Wand and the Vanishing Voice – *XIAO* (Troubleman Unlimited, 2005)
   —— *Buck Dharma* (5RC, 2005)

Grime #2

Bruza – 'Not Convinced' (Aftershock, 2005)
Crazy Titch – 'Sing Along' (In the Hood, 2005)
Jammer featuring D Double E – 'Birds in the Sky' (Hot Sound, 2003)
Jammer featuring Kano – 'Boys Love Girls' (Hot Sound, 2003)
Kano – *Home Sweet Home* (697, 2005)
Lady Sovereign – *Vertically Challenged* [mini-LP compilation of early singles] (Chocolate Industries, 2005)
—— *Public Warning* (Def Jam, 2006, Island, 2007)
Lethal B featuring Fumin, D Double E, Nappa, Jamakabi, Neeko, Flow Dan, Ozzi B, Forcer, Demon, and Hot Shot – 'Pow (Forward)' (Relentless, 2004)
Lethal B – *Against All Oddz* (V2, 2005)
Terror Danjah – *Industry Standard* EP (Aftershock, 2003)
Terror Danjah featuring Hyper, Bruza, D Double E and Riko – 'Cock Back' (Aftershock, 2003)
Various – *Pay Back* EP *(the Remix)* (Aftershock, 2003)
Various – *Run the Road* (679)

Arctic Monkeys, *Whatever People Say I Am, That's What I'm Not* (Domino, 2006)

Hot Chip – *Coming On Strong* (Moshi Moshi, 2004)
—— *The Warning* (EMI, 2006)
Scritti Politti – *White Bread Black Beer* (Rough Trade, 2006)

M.I.A.

Arular (Interscope, 2005)
Kala (Interscope, 2007)
Maya (Interscope, 2010)

Vampire Weekend

Vampire Weekend (XL, 2008)
Contra (XL, 2010)

Hip Hop in the Late 2000s

The Blackout Crew, "Put A Donk On It" (All Around the World, 2008)
J Dilla, Donuts (Stone's Throw, 2006)
—— The Shining (BBE, 2006)
Gucci Mane, The State vs. Radric Davis (1017 Brick Squad/Warners/ Asylum, 2009)
—— The Appeal: Georgia's Most Wanted (1017 Brick Squad/Warners/ Asylum, 2010)
Lil Wayne, Tha Carter II (Cash Money, 2005)
—— Tha Carter III (Cash Money, 2008)
T.I., King (Grand Hustle/Atlantic, 2006)
—— T.I. vs. T.I.P (Grand Hustle, Atlantic, 2007)
Young Jeezy, The Inspiration: Thug Motivation (Corporate Thugz/ Def Jam, 2006)
—— The Recession (Corporate Thugz/Def Jam, 2008)

ACKNOWLEDGEMENTS

Love and gratitude to my wife Joy Press, for her customary but never taken for granted guidance and patience; to my kids Kieran and Tasmin; and to my parents Sydney Reynolds and Jenny Reynolds for sparking in me a passion for reading and writing.

Thanks to my editor Denise Oswald and all at Soft Skull; to my American agent Ira Silverberg; and to cover designer Jason Snyder. Thanks also to those at Faber & Faber who worked on the original UK edition of *Bring the Noise*, including my editor Lee Brackstone, and to my UK agent Tony Peake.

My first editor was actually my soon-to-be-best-friend Paul Oldfield, who took something appallingly affected and *NME*-damaged I'd contributed to a university arts mag he ran and transformed it into something clean and clear – a crucial, lasting lesson in the power of lucidity and ever-so-slightly-severe starkness. Well, the lesson slipped my mind more than a few times over the years, but Paul showed me the righteous path back then and for that I'm hugely grateful. Big thanks to Steve Sutherland, who in 1985 plucked me from obscurity when he was reviews editor at *Melody Maker*. Equally large thanks to him and editor-in-chief Allan Jones for not long after this giving me a job as a staff writer – the happiest period of salaried employment I've ever had (an indication: in 1987 I simply *forgot to take* the five weeks' holiday to which I was entitled). On the freelance front, I'd like to thank Malcolm Imrie (*New Statesman*); Jon Savage and Neil Spencer (*The Observer*); Dylan Jones and later Matthew Collin and Avril Mair (*i-D*); a long line of people at *Spin*, including Frank Owen, Steven Daly, Craig Marks, Charles Aaron, Will Hermes, Sia Michel; *Village Voice* music editors Joe Levy, Ann Powers, Eric Weisbard, Chuck Eddy, Robert Christgau; David Frankel at *Artforum*; Fletcher Roberts at the *New York Times*'s Arts & Leisure section; a series of helmsmen at *The Wire* – Mark Sinker, Tony Herrington, Rob Young, Chris Bohn – and one helmswoman, Anne Hilde Neset; Matthew Slotover and Dan Fox at

Frieze; Christian Holler at *Springerin; Groove's* Heiko Hoffman; Paul Lester, David Peschek and John Mulvey at *Uncut;* Rob Tannenbaum at *Blender; Slate's* Michael Agger and Meghan O'Rourke; Caspar Llewellyn-Smith at *Observer Music Monthly,* and many more besides.

Finally a BIG shout to all the people who have been comrades/catalysts and friends/foils these past twenty-plus years, their passion, erudition and pugnacity serving as a constant source of inspiration. First up, the *Monitor* team: Paul Oldfield, David Stubbs, Chris Scott, Hilary Little. Oldfield and Stubbs went on to be my crew at *Melody Maker* along with the Stud Brothers (Ben Mothersole and Dominic Wills). Although we only coincided at the *Maker* for a year, Frank Owen was a great co-conspirator and influence. Across the ensuing years, there's really too many folk to list with whom I've had entertaining and educational dialogues about music, both in person and via email, but I must mention here Paul Kennedy, Pat Blashill, 'Bat' Bhattacharyya, Bethan Cole, Mike Rubin, Susan Masters and Nick Terry and the rest of the *Lizard* crew, Kodwo Eshun, Sasha Frere-Jones, Rupert Howe, Keith Riches, Kevin Martin, Simon Biddell . . . In recent years, it's been the bloggers who have sparked the tinder of my thought, so big up ya chest to Matthew Ingram (Woebot), Mark Fisher (*K-punk*), Jon Dale (Worlds of Possibility), Luke Davis (Heronbone), Simon Hampson (Silverdollarcircle), Geeta Dayal (the Original Soundtrack), Tim Finney (Skykicking), Carl Neville (the Impostume) and many others.

And last, as she was first, Joy. Always.

INDEX